Religious

LYRICS

Religious

LYRICS

of the

XIVth CENTURY

Edited by

Carleton Brown

Second Edition

Revised by G. V. Smithers

OXFORD
At the Clarendon Press

Oxford University Press, Amen House, London E.C.4

GLASGOW NEW YORK TORONTO MELBOURNE WELLINGTON
BOMBAY CALCUTTA MADRAS KARACHI LAHORE DACCA
CAPE TOWN SALISBURY NAIROBI IBADAN ACCRA
KUALA LUMPUR HONG KONG

FIRST EDITION 1924
SECOND EDITION REPRINTED LITHOGRAPHICALLY
IN GREAT BRITAIN AT THE
UNIVERSITY PRESS, OXFORD
FROM CORRECTED SHEETS OF THE FIRST EDITION
1952, 1957 (CORRECTED), 1965

PREFACE

THE original edition of this book convincingly displayed the distinction of its author as a collector of MS. materials. The most valuable part of the apparatus contained in it was the notes, which have therefore been reproduced with only a limited number of essential changes (chiefly arising out of the interpretation of the texts). Most of the readily accessible MSS. have been collated; for information about MSS. that have become available since the first edition was published, reference may be made to Brown and Robbins, *The Index of Middle English Verse* (Columbia University Press, 1943). Special attention has been given to textual problems, and a number of new readings and emendations by the reviser are made available. The glossary has been extensively revised, and it is hoped that most of the more serious errors and inaccuracies and many of the minor ones have been corrected. For a few difficult problems, the original entry has been retained in default of a better interpretation. It has unfortunately not been possible to eliminate certain slight inconsistencies of arrangement in the original form of the glossary. G. V. S.

1956.

TABLE OF CONTENTS

PAGE

INTRODUCTION xi

LYRICS OF THE BEGINNING OF THE CENTURY.

1. Candet Nudatum Pectus: A, Durham Cathedral
A. iii. 12; B, Bodley 42 1
2. Respice in Faciem Christi : Shorter version, Bodley
42 ; Longer version, St. John's Coll. Camb. 15 . 1
3. Think, Man, of my Hard Stundes, Royal 12 E. i . 2
4. Look to Me on the Cross, New Coll. Oxf. 88 . . 3
5. Thole a Little ! New Coll. Oxf. 88 3

LYRICS FROM MS. HARLEY 2253 (ca. 1310).

6. An Old Man's Prayer 3
7. 'Suete Iesu King of blysse' 7
8. 'Iesu Crist Heouene Kyng' 9
9. A Winter Song 10
'Iesu suete is þe loue of þe.' See No. 89.
10. An Autumn Song 11
11. A Song of the Five Joys 13

HYMNS BY FRIAR WILLIAM HEREBERT (†1333), FROM
PHILLIPPS MS. 8336.

12. Hostis Herodes impie 15
13. Vexilla Regis prodeunt 15
14. Gloria, Laus et Honor 16
15. Popule meus quid feci tibi ? 17
16. An Orison to the Blessed Virgin . . . 18
17. Aue Maris Stella 20
18. Veni creator spiritus 21
19. Alma redemptoris mater 22
20. Conditor alme siderum 22
21. Christe redemptor omnium 23
22. Tu Rex glorie Christe 24
23. Make Ready for the Long Journey . . . 25
24. Iesu Nostra Redempcio 27
25. Quis est iste qui uenit de Edom ? . . . 28

PAGE

MISCELLANEOUS LYRICS BEFORE 1350.

26. An Orison of the Five Joys, St. John's Coll. Camb. 256   29
27. The Four Foes of Mankind, Advocates 19, 2. 1
    ('Auchinleck MS.') 32
28. Lollai litil child whi wepistow so sore? Harley 913 . 35
29. An Orison to the Trinity, Cotton Vespas. A. iii . 37
30. The Matins of the Cross, Cotton Vespas. A. iii . 39
31. A Song of the Five Joys, Göttingen Univ. theol. 107 44
32. William of Shoreham: Marye, mayde mylde and
    fre, B.M. Addit. 17376 46
33. An Orison to the Blessed Virgin from the *Aȝenbite
    of Inwit*, Arundel 57 49
34. The Hours of the Cross, Bodl. MS. Liturg. 104 . 50

A GROUP OF LYRICS COLLECTED BY BISHOP SHEPPEY
(†1360), IN MERTON COLL. OXF. 248.

35. Jesus Have Mercy on Me. 51
36. How Christ shall Come 52
37. Aurora lucis rutilat 53
38. O gloriosa domina excelsa 53
39. The Evils of the Time 54
40. Crux fidelis 55
41. Ave Maris Stella 55

MISCELLANEOUS LYRICS OF THE MID-CENTURY.

42. Lady Fortune and her Wheel, Camb. Univ. Oo. 7. 32 56
43. All is Phantom, Camb. Univ. Ee. 1. 5 . . 56
44. Veni Creator Spiritus, Bodley 425 . . . 57
45. Ave Maris Stella, Bodley 425 58
46. Abide, Ye Who Pass By, Rawlinson poet. 175 . . 59
47. 'How Crist Spekes tyll Synfull Man of His Gret
    Mercy,' Rawlinson poet. 175 60
48. The Sweetness of Jesus, Rawlinson poet. 175 . 61
49. All Other Love is like the Moon, Eton Coll. 36,
    Part II 65
50. The Tower of Heaven, Advocates 18. 8. 1 . . 66
51. Christ's Appeal to Man, Harley 2316 . . . 67
52. A Prayer of the Five Wounds, Harley 2316 . . 68
53. The Vanity of Life, Harley 2316 68
54. The Sinner's Lament, Harley 2316 68

PAGE

LYRICS FROM THE COMMONPLACE BOOK OF JOHN GRIMESTONE (1372).

55. The Hours of the Cross 69
56. Dialogue between the Blessed Virgin and her Child 70
57. A Song of the Nativity 75
58. A Song of the Blessed Virgin and Joseph . . 78
59. Christ weeps in the Cradle for Man's Sin . . 80
60. The Blessed Virgin's Appeal to the Jews . . 81
61. A Song of Mercy 81
62. Christ's Prayer in Gethsemane 82
63. Jesus, Man's Champion 82
64. Lamentacio dolorosa 82
65. A Lullaby to Christ in the Cradle 83
66. Christ's Love-song to Man 84
67. Dialogue between Jesus and the Blessed Virgin at the Cross 85
68. Ecce sto ad hostium et pulso 86
69. Lovely Tear from Lovely Eye 87
70. Homo vide quid pro te patior 88
71. I would be Clad in Christis Skin 88
72. Popule meus quid feci tibi ? 88
73. Christ's 'Love-Aunter' 90
74. O vos omnes qui transitis per viam . . . 90
75. The Christ Child shivering with Cold . . . 91
76. Christ's Three Songs to Man 92

LYRICS OF THE SCHOOL OF RICHARD ROLLE, FROM CAMB. UNIV. Dd. 5. 64.

77. Homo Vide quid pro Te Patior 93
78. Christ pleads with His Sweet Leman . . . 94
79. A Lament over the Passion 94
80. A prayer to Jesus 95
81. A Song of Mortality 96
82. A Song of Mercy 98
83. A Song of Love-longing to Jesus 99
84. A Song of the Love of Jesus 102
85. A Salutation to Jesus 106
86. Thy Joy be in the Love of Jesus 107

MISCELLANEOUS LYRICS FROM ABOUT 1375.

87. A General Confession, Burton MS. 109
88. Hand by Hand We Shall us Take, MS. Bodley 26. 110
89. Iesu Dulcis Memoria, Hunterian Mus. V. 8. 15 . 111

Contents

PAGE

90. Christ's Gift to Man, Hunterian Mus. V. 8. 15 . 113
91. Ihesu that hast me dere I-boght, Longleat, MS. 29 114
92. Oracio de sancta Maria, Camb. Univ. Ii. 6. 43 . 119
93. An Orison to the Trinity, B.M. Addit. 37787. . 121
94. A Prayer to Jesus, Stonyhurst Coll. MS. XLIII . 124

THE 'VERNON SERIES' OF REFRAIN POEMS.

95. Mercy Passes All Things 125
96. Deo Gracias. I 131
97. Against my Will I take my Leave 134
98. Deus Caritas Est 136
99. Deo Gracias. II 138
100. Each Man ought Himself to Know . . . 139
101. Think on Yesterday 143
102. Keep well Christ's Commandments . . . 148
103. Who says the Sooth, He shall be Shent . . 152
104. Fy on a faint Friend! 155
105. Ever more Thank God of All, MS. Ashmole 343 . 157
106. This World fares as a Fantasy 160
107. Merci God and graunt Merci. 164
108. Truth is Best 168
109. Charity is no longer Cheer 170
110. Of Women cometh this Worldes Weal . . . 174
111. A song of Love to the Blessed Virgin . . . 178
112. Maiden Mary and her Fleur-de-Lys . . . 181
113. Verses on the Earthquake of 1382 . . . 186
114. Love Holy Church and its Priests 189
115. Always try to Say the Best 191
116. Tarry not till To-morrow 194
117. Make Amends! 196
118. Suffer in Time and that is Best 200
119. Marie nobiscum Domine 202
120. But thou say Sooth thou shalt be Shent, B.M. Addit. 22283 205

MISCELLANEOUS LYRICS OF THE END OF THE CENTURY.

121. The Bird with Four Feathers, MS. Bodley 596 . 208
122. A Prayer by the Five Joys, Rawl. liturg. g. 2 . 216
123. A Prayer to be delivered from the Deadly Sins, Rawl. liturg. g. 2 218
124. A Prayer for Three Boons, Rawl. liturg. g. 2 . . 219
125. The Knight of Christ, Bodley 416 . . . 223
126. Jesus Pleads with the Worldling, Bodley 416 . 225

		PAGE
127.	Jesus appeals to Man by the Wounds, Harley 2339	227
128.	The Blessed Virgin to her Son on the Cross, Balliol Coll. Oxf. 149	228
129.	I have Set my Heart so High, Douce 381 . .	229
130.	The Spring under a Thorn, Magdalen Coll. Oxf. 60	229
131.	An Acrostic of the Angelic Salutation, Camb. Univ. Gg. 4. 32	230
132.	Quia Amore Langueo, Douce 322	234
133.	Wretched Man, why art thou Proud? MS. Laud. Miscell. 111	237
134.	Cur Mundus Militat, Trinity Coll. Camb. 181 .	237
135.	Esto Memor Mortis, Camb. Univ. Ee. 6. 29 . .	239

NOTES 241

GLOSSARY 289

INTRODUCTION

THE present collection of lyrics is to be followed—within a short time, it is hoped—by similar collections from the thirteenth century and the fifteenth. Accordingly, I have thought it better to postpone a full Introduction to the fourteenth-century material here presented until it can be discussed in connexion with the lyrics which preceded and followed. Meantime these texts are offered as documents useful in themselves as illustrating the important contribution of this century to the development of the English lyric.

The collection makes no pretension to completeness. Of the conventional types of devotional verse only representative examples are given, for to have included the whole body of those poems would have greatly expanded the volume without increasing appreciably its value. My objects have been to publish hitherto unprinted material; to offer better texts of poems already printed from inferior MSS.; to give trustworthy texts of poems that have been printed inaccurately; to bring together texts that are found in scattered and often inaccessible publications; above all, to represent the lyrical development of the century.

It is, of course, difficult, indeed impossible, to mark off exact boundary lines at the years 1300 and 1400 so as to include only poems composed within those limits. In an age when literary production was for the most part anonymous the evidence on which we must rely is, in most cases, the date of the manuscript. In choosing the pieces for this collection I have therefore, with few exceptions, excluded all that are not found in fourteenth-century MSS. But even this method is not altogether satisfactory. On the one hand, poems which have come down to us in MSS. of the early fourteenth century may actually have been composed before 1300 ; and I am inclined to suspect that the whole group of lyrics printed as of 'the beginning of the century' have been carried over from the closing decades of the thirteenth. On the other hand, it is equally possible that poems which survive only in fifteenth-century MSS. may have been composed before 1400. It was this possibility which led me to include *Quia Amore Langueo* (no. 132) and *Cur Mundus Militat* (no. 134), though neither of these exists in a MS. which palæographers are willing to date before 1400. The fact that there are, respectively, seven and ten MSS. of these poems, some of them of the very early fifteenth century, shows that they circulated widely, and suggests that the original texts may have been written before the end of the fourteenth century.

Within the limits of the century there are troublesome problems in arranging the poems in a chronological series, and these I have sought to evade by grouping the poems under more or less definite heads. Even this classification is attended by uncertainties. No. 88, a particularly interesting, as the earliest, example in English of the carol type, occurs in a MS. which, a more careful examination convinces me, can hardly have been written later than 1350. It would have been better included among the 'Miscellaneous Lyrics before 1350'. A similar instance is no. 133, which, since it is included in

the *Fasciculus Morum,* may have been composed
as early as the reign of Edward II, the period to
which the *Fasciculus* is tentatively assigned by
Mr. A. G. Little,[1] the eminent authority on the
history of the English Franciscans.

Some surprise may be felt that more space has not
been devoted to pieces from Harley 2253, the most
notable fourteenth-century collection of lyrics. The
date of this MS., however, falls within the first decade
of the century; and of its religious pieces many
occur also in MSS. of the thirteenth century.
Evidence is steadily accumulating to show that the
monk of Leominster Priory by whose hand this MS.
was written was the compiler rather than the author
of this material; and I have come to believe that
virtually all the religious songs which this MS. con-
tains are an inheritance from the thirteenth century.

We are unquestionably within the limits of the four-
teenth century when we pass on to the verses by
Herebert—the earliest known author represented in
this collection. William Herebert was a Franciscan
who died, Bale states, in 1333, and was buried in
the Convent of his Order at Hereford.[2] The series
of seventeen pieces of translation by Herebert (of
which all but three are here printed) is found in the
last quire of Phillipps MS. 8336. In the margin,
opposite the beginning of each, appears the name
'Herebert'. At the foot of the first page (fol. 203ᵃ)
is written in the same hand:

---

[1] *Studies in English Franciscan History,* Manchester, 1917, p. 143.

[2] For a biographical notice of Herebert see Tanner, *Bibl. Britannica,*
p. 398; see also notes by Brewer, *Mun. Francisc.,* Rolls Ser., i. 553,
and by A. G. Little, *Grey Friars in Oxford,* Oxf. Hist. Soc., p. 167.
For notes of several books owned by Herebert see Little, *Collectanea
Franciscana I* (Brit. Soc. of Francisc. Studies, v), pp. 114, 117, and
120.

Istos hympnos & Antiphonas quasi omnes & cetera transtulit
in Anglicum non semper de uerbo ad uerbum sed frequenter
sensum aut non multum declinando & in manu sua scripsit
frater Willelmus Herebert. Qui usum huius quaterni habuerit:
oret pro anima dicti fratris.

The natural presumption that these pieces were
written in the MS. by Herebert himself is confirmed
by the presence in an earlier section of the MS. of a
trial draft of a portion of one of them written in the
same hand (see note on no. 23).

The value of Herebert's translations is greater, it
may be conceded, from the linguistic than from the
literary point of view. This is probably due in large
part to the obligation which Herebert felt to render
the Latin hymns in literal translation. In his para-
phrase of the Anglo-French verses, where he used
greater freedom, it is noticeable that the English
version compares favourably with the original. But
perhaps the chief claim of Herebert's verses to con-
sideration is their historical importance as an early
attempt on the part of the friars to introduce
vernacular versions of the hymns into their preaching.
There can be little question, I think, that these
pieces were designed primarily for pulpit use.

From the *Cursor Mundi* I have taken three lyrics
(nos. 29, 30, 31) which are incorporated in that
cyclopaedic poem, but which, as the difference in
metre is in itself sufficient to show, did not originally
belong to it. The fact that they do not occur in all
the MSS. of the *Cursor* suggests that they are later
embellishments rather than insertions by the original
author.

The only known authors who contribute to the
group of ' Miscellaneous Lyrics before 1350 ' are the
two Kentishmen, William of Shoreham and Dan
Michel. From the poems of the former I have in-

cluded an Orison to the Blessed Virgin (no. 32), in which she is saluted, as in a host of the Latin Marian hymns, by a long series of allegorical types, all of them (except the unicorn) found in the Scriptures. From Dan Michel I have taken the very simple and direct prayer of six lines with which he concluded the *Aʒenbite*.

The curious set of lyrics associated with Bishop Sheppey's name exhibits marked differences of dialect: nos. 35–8 show the Southern forms which we should expect from a Bishop of Rochester; nos. 39–41, on the other hand, are consistently Northern. Clearly, then, they are not the work of the same person. Whether any of these pieces can be ascribed to Bishop Sheppey himself is not certain. They are scattered through a series of Latin sermons, or more properly notes and outlines of sermons, collected in the Merton College MS. by Bishop Sheppey, very likely during the period of his connexion with Oxford University as Doctor of Theology. Opposite a number of these sermons is entered what appears to be the name of its author, though I have not succeeded in identifying the persons whose names are thus recorded. The interest of these lyrics is increased by the testimony which they afford to the habit of some preachers of embellishing their sermons by introducing English verses.

The material in the group of 'Lyrics of the Mid-century' presents a wide variety both in theme and poetic merit. We again find translations from the Latin hymns; and nos. 44 and 45, compared with Herebert's versions of the *Veni Creator Spiritus* and *Ave Maris Stella*, show no improvement in freedom or flexibility. On the other hand, in a number of the shorter pieces, like 'Lady Fortune', 'All is Phantom', and 'The Tower of Heaven', the thought

is expressed easily in idiomatic English. We still
find Appeals to Man from the Cross (nos. 46 and
47) which follow essentially the tradition of similar
pieces from the beginning of the century. But there
are, again, such lyrics as no. 48, in which there is a
heightened emotion and warmth of feeling surpassing
anything met with earlier; in no. 49 we meet with
verses which impress us with their sincere, even
personal, note. Indeed, within the limits of this
group we find poems which measure the extremes of
formalism and spontaneity.

One of the most important collections of religious
lyrics is that preserved in John Grimestone's Common-
place Book (Advocates MS. 18. 7. 21). At the end of
the Table of Contents (fol. 9ᵇ) the compiler has
recorded his name and the date of the compilation:

> Orate pro anima fratris Iohannis de Grimistone qui scripsit
> istum librum cum magna solicitudine Anno domini 1372. Aue
> maria pro anima sua pro amore dei.

And on the same page, immediately above, is re-
corded in a bold hand, in lines which have been well-
nigh scraped away, the name of the person to whom
Friar Grimestone—no doubt at the time of his death
—left the book:

> Iste liber est Fratris Nic. de Roma de dono Fratris Ioh. de
> Grimestone. Ave Maria pro anima sua.

A later entry (fol. 108ᵇ) discloses the name of a
subsequent owner: 'Iste liber constat Willᵐᵒ broin
quem deus amat et deabolus odit.'

The compiler states that he was a friar, and the
contents of the book show that he belonged to the
Franciscan order. Section 119, for example, is
headed: 'De Regula beati Francisci'; and at fols.
95ᵇ and 110ᵇ we find narrated in detail the adventures
of Ægidius Assisias and Bernardus a Quintavalle,

two of the earliest disciples of St. Francis. Diligent search, however, has failed thus far to identify John Grimestone. We cannot even be certain whether Grimestone was his family name or a place name,[1] though the former seems the more likely. The Grimston family, of Grimston Garth, south-east Yorkshire, is well known to the genealogist.[2] But we search the records of this family in vain for any one who could with any probability be identified as our John Grimestone. More likely our Franciscan was of humbler lineage, for in the local records of Yorkshire in particular this name occurs with great frequency among the craft-gilds and small householders.[3]

A further clue is supplied by the name of the person to whom John Grimestone gave his book, ' Nicholas de Roma '. Here we are assuredly dealing with a family name and not with a place name. The

---

[1] There was a Grimston in the East Riding of Yorkshire, another in the Hundred of Freebridge, Norfolk (see Blomefield, viii. 441–52), and a third in the parish of Wellow, co. Notts. (see *Hist. MSS. Com.*, Report VII, App., p. 364).

[2] The most recent and most authentic genealogy of this family is that by the Rev. C. Moor, D.D., *Erminois: A Book of Family Records*, Kendall, 1918, pp. 117–28.

[3] John Grymston is mentioned under dates 1330 and 1342 in the *Feet of Fines for the Co. of York* (Yorksh. Archæol. Soc., Record Series, xlii. 32, 158): ' Johannes de Grimston, nailler' and ' Johannes de Grymeston, tailliour ', were freemen of York in 135$\frac{6}{7}$ and 137$\frac{6}{7}$ respectively (*Register of Freemen of the City of York*, i, Surtees Soc., 1896, pp. 52 and 75). ' Johannes Grymston, walker' and ' Johannes Grymston, capellanus, fil. Simonis Grymston, boucher' are entered in the same Register for 143$\frac{0}{1}$ and 144$\frac{4}{5}$ (*ibid.*, pp. 145 and 164). Again, the name ' John Grymston ' appears as one of the inquisitors in an inquisition at Cromwellbottom (Yorkshire), March 4, 139$\frac{7}{8}$ (*Yorkshire Deeds*, Yorksh. Arch. Soc., xxxix. 57). To be sure, Yorkshire held no monopoly of Grimestones—there was, for example, ' John de Grimston ' instituted rector of the Church of Hackford, Norfolk, in 1383 (Blomefield, viii. 225)—but it is notable that the name occurs much more frequently in this county than elsewhere in England.

surname repeatedly appears in Yorkshire records but is very rarely met with elsewhere.[1] Too much reliance, of course, should not be placed on evidence of this kind: friars migrated from convent to convent, so that even if we could establish the Yorkshire origin of Brothers John and Nicholas it would not fix the home of the book. Nevertheless, the district toward which these family names point agrees fairly well with the dialect of the Grimestone lyrics, which is that of the northern border of the East Midlands. On the

---

[1] Adam de Roma 'tunc Ianitore S̄c̄e̅ Marie' (i. e. Benedictine Abbey at York) witnessed a thirteenth-century charter (Dodsworth MS. VII, fol. 2ᵃ), and granted lands at Acaster to Selby Abbey (*Coucher Book of Selby*, Yorksh. Arch. Soc., Record Ser., 1891, pp. 323–5). 'John de Rome' is mentioned in an inquisition in 1299 in regard to the manor of Seton (near Whitby) (*Yorkshire Inquisitions*, iii, Yorksh. Arch. Soc., Record Ser., p. 100); an entry 'de Johanne de Roma' is entered under Clifton (near York) in the Subsidy Roll for 130½ (*Yorksh. Lay Subsidies*, Yorksh. Arch. Soc., Record Ser., 1897, p. 112); at an ecclesiastical trial at Durham in 1370 testimony was given by 'Johannes de Rome' (*Depositions and Eccl. Proceedings*, Surtees Soc., 1845, p. 14). The name occurs repeatedly in the lists of Freemen of York—e. g. 'Iohannes de Rome camber' 135½, 'Elias de Rome bakster' 13⁶⁵⁄₇₀, 'Henricus de Rome sawer' 137⅘ (*Register of Freemen of City of York*, Surtees Soc., pp. 45, 67, 71). Among the wills in the York Registry are those of 'John de Rome', buried at Northwell, 1391, 'John de Rome' of Leeds, 1403, Peter Rome of Catebeston (parish of Leeds), 1434, and Peter Rome of Catbeston, 1490 (*Wills in York Registry*, Yorksh. Arch. Soc., Record Ser., 1889, p. 140). 'Peter de Rome' is also mentioned in an inquisition taken at Leeds, 1413 (*Yorkshire Inquisitions* v, Yorksh. Arch. Soc., p. 98); mention of the younger Peter Rome is found in the will of Henry Dyneley of Leeds (1480) (*Test. Ebor.* iv, Surt. Soc., p. 247). The only mention of a person of this name outside of Yorkshire which I have noted occurs in a bequest to 'dominum Iohannem de Rome, rectorem de Overe' (Cambridgeshire) dated 1405 (*Test. Ebor.* iii, Surt. Soc., p. 30). And this bequest, it is to be noted, is found in the will of a Yorkshireman! [After this note was in type, however, I stumbled upon an instance of Romes quite unconnected with Yorkshire: in the 'Poll Tax and Civil Population of Oxford, 1380', occurs the entry, 'De Roberto Rome sissore et Isabelle vxore eius' (J. E. Thorold Rogers, *Oxf. City Documents*, Oxf. Hist. Soc., 1891, p. 34).]

basis of the linguistic forms we may take the Humber as the northern and Norfolk as the southern limit for these poems.

John Grimestone compiled his book, evidently, as a storehouse of pulpit material. The contents are arranged under 143 topics in alphabetical order, beginning with 'De Abstinencia' and concluding with 'De Veste'. The great bulk of the book is in Latin, but English verses and phrases are scattered throughout. To what extent these verses were composed by Grimestone and to what extent they were merely copied by him we cannot say. ·The fact that the book contains in many places riming Latin lines with an English paraphrase subjoined strongly suggests that the compiler had a turn for versifying in English. On the other hand, a number of the lyrics in this book exist in other (mostly later) manuscripts, and these, it is easy to suppose, Grimestone found and appropriated for his purpose.

The lyrics of the Richard Rolle School are taken from the series in the Cambridge University MS., where they are headed, 'Cantus compassionis Christi et consolacionis eterni'. At the end is written : 'Expliciunt cantica diuini amoris secundum Ricardum Hampole'. Whether they were composed by Rolle himself is open to question. All of them (except nos. 77 and 81) exhibit the fervid (at times even erotic) mysticism which characterizes his attested writings. If any of the songs in this series is to be ascribed to him, it would certainly be the 'Song of the Love of Jesus' (no. 84), in which this fervour reaches its climax, and the greater part of which, as Miss Hope Allen has recently shown, is directly translated from the *Incendium Amoris*. Whether by Rolle or not this group of lyrics at least reflects his influence.

The mystics are also well represented among the
'Miscellaneous Lyrics from about 1375'. It would
be difficult to find an example of ecstatic religious
feeling which surpasses 'Christ's Gift to Man' (no.
90). And although in no. 91 we have the familiar
type of meditation on the pains of the Passion, these
verses are infused with a human sympathy which dis-
tinguishes them from most devotional pieces of this
type. 'For a more devout prayer', the scribe wrote
above these verses, 'found I never of the Passion,
whoso would devoutly say it.'

The series of twenty-six refrain poems, usually
known as the 'Vernon lyrics', exhibits at first sight a
uniformity which disappears on closer examination.
Not only do they differ widely among themselves in
literary merit, but they reflect the most diverse and
contradictory points of view. No. 103, as the fifth
stanza indicates, was written by a friar; no. 114 was
certainly written by a secular priest; and so also, with
little doubt, was no. 117, in which the parishioner is
warned not to leave his parish priest and confess to a
friar. No. 119 is an expression of fervent, simple
devotion, whereas no. 106—one of the most remark-
able in the series—voices an intellectual dissatisfaction,
even cynicism, which recalls the 'Vanitas vanitatum'
of the Preacher.

The scribe of the Vernon MS., then, unless I am
mistaken, was not the author, but the collector of
these pieces. But he was not merely their collector,
for he took the liberty (which he used elsewhere in
the MS.) of editing his material. Nine of these
twenty-six poems are preserved in other MSS. as well
as in the Vernon and its echo, the 'Simeon' MS.
(B.M. Addit. 22283), and from a comparison with these
independent texts we discover that in most cases the
Vernon text has been 'edited', sometimes by trans-

posing stanzas, sometimes by adding new ones, most frequently by altering lines and phrases.

For nos. 105 and 115 I have used other MSS., but with these two exceptions I have printed the Vernon text, for the reason that it is the oldest extant MS. and is usually freer from purely scribal errors (as distinguished from editorial changes).

The concluding section, 'Lyrics of the End of the Century', may not, perhaps, be said to cast a sunset splendour on the collection. No. 121 is more in the nature of allegory than of lyric. But its refrain and its moral observations relate it so closely to many of the Vernon poems that I decided to include it, especially as, in spite of its length, it is not wanting in pithy phrase and vigorous description. The three prayers which follow come from a liturgical manuscript, and were written for a liturgical purpose. They are significant as illustrating the way in which vernacular verse was invading even manuals of devotion. No. 126 is interesting as a distinctly fresh treatment of the old theme of Christ's appeal to man; the contrast between the fashionable worldling and the pains of the Passion is effectively drawn. So, too, is the brief dialogue (no. 128) between the Virgin and her Son on the Cross. On the other hand, the Acrostic of the Angelic Salutation (no. 131) is included merely as representative of a large class of verse, Latin, French, and English.

In striking contrast to the forced phrasing in this devotional exercise is the mystical beauty of the *Quia Amore Langueo* (no. 132), which follows. It is a satisfaction to make this lyric accessible for the first time in a text which fairly represents its original form. Nothing is more characteristic of mediaeval mysticism than the note, 'Take me for thy wife', with which this poem concludes. At the same time we are not surprised that later copyists emended this stanza or omitted it entirely. The two sombre reminders of mortality with which the lyrical record of the century ends are not without literary interest. The former preserves to a notable degree the dignity and vigour of its Latin original; the latter offers a conspicuous example of the ingenuity which often characterized macaronic verse. The English and Latin phrases, arranged antiphonally, produce a pleasing contrast of directness and sonorousness.

I should like to suggest that the reader who has worked through the volume should turn back and compare the early pieces with the latest. Only in this way can he measure justly the lyrical progress of the century.

I cannot conclude without expressing my grateful appreciation of the hearty co-operation which has been accorded by the staff of the Oxford University Press in the labour of putting this book through the press. The liberal patience which they have shown in the matter of corrections and alterations has exceeded the measure which an editor might reasonably expect ; and the pains which they have taken to ensure the accuracy of the texts have been in themselves a stimulus to scholarly endeavour. C. B.

OXFORD, *July* 1923.

THE TEXTS

THE texts here printed have been collated with the manuscript originals except no. 31 (Göttingen MS.) which is reprinted from the EETS. ed. of . *Cursor Mundi*. All variations from the readings of the MSS. have been indicated either in the text itself or in the foot-notes. Words or letters which have been supplied are placed within caret brackets 〈 〉, and words in the MS. which should be ignored are placed within square brackets [ ]. The usual MS. contractions have been expanded without italics. In the matter of capitalization the manuscripts have been followed, but the punctuation is editorial. Hyphens also have been introduced by the editor, chiefly in compounds and after prefixes which are separated in the MSS. In a few of the poems the MSS. show accent marks over the vowels in certain words. These have been scrupulously retained.

Sometimes the MS. reading, though unmistakable, presents difficulties which are not readily resolved by emendation. In such cases the reading has been retained in the text, and the crux discussed in the notes.

1. *Candet Nudatum Pectus.*

A. Durham Cathedral MS. A. III. 12.

WYth was hys nakede brest and red of blod hys
   syde,   f. 49ᵃ
Bleyc was his fair handled, his wnde dop ant wide,
And hys armes ystreith hey up-hon þe rode;
On fif studes on his body þe stremes ran o blode. 4

B. MS. Bodley 42.

WIt was his nakede brest and red of blod his
   side,   f. 250ᵃ
Blod was his faire neb, his wnden depe an uide,
starke waren his armes hi-spred op-on þe rode;
In fif steden an his bodi stremes hurne of blode. 4

2. *Respice in Faciem Christi.*

A. Shorter version : MS. Bodley 42.

Loke man to iesu crist   f. 250ᵃ
  hi-neiled an þo rode,
and hi-þitz his nakede bodi
red hi-maked mid blode;   4
his reg mid scurge i-suunge,
his heued þornes prikede,
þo nailes in him stikede.
þuend and trend þi lordes bodi,   8
þurch wam þu art i-boruhe,
þer þu mit hi-uinde blode an sorue.

---

2. 3 hi-þitz: MS. hi-þicȝ.   2. 8 þuend: MS. þuend.

B.   Longer version: St. John's Coll. Camb. MS. 15.

Loke to þi louerd, man, þar hanget he a rode,   f. 72ᵃ
   and wep hyf þo mist terres al of blode.
Vor loke hu his heued biis mid þornes bi-wnde,
and to his neb so bispet and to þe spere-wnde.   4
Faluet his feyre luer, and desewet his sicte,
drowepet his hendi bodi þat on rode biis itiht.
Blickied his brest nacked and bledet hiis side,
stiuiet hiis arms þat istreid beð so wide.   8
Loke to þe nailes on honde and on fote,
hu þe stremes hurned of þat suete blod.
Bigin at his molde and loke to his to,
ne saltu no wit vinde bute anguisse and wo.   12

3.   *Think, Man, of my Hard Stundes.*

MS. Royal 12. E. i.

þenc man of min harde stundes ;
þenc of mine harde wndes.

Man, þu haue þine þout one me,   f. 194ᵇ
   þenc hou dere i bouthe þe ;
I let me nailen to þe tre—
hardere deth ne mai non ben—   4
þenc, man, al hit was for þe.

I gaf mi fles, i gaf mi blod,
for þe me let i-don on rod,
Vt of mi side ern þe flod ;   8
I þoled hit al wid milde mod—
Man, hit ⟨was⟩ al for þi god.

Mine peines weren harde and stronge,
Mi moder þouth es swiþe longe :   12
þenc, man, er þu do þi sinne,
Wath i þolede for man-kinne ;
Min harde deth þe shal don blinne.

2. 6 MS. droweyet.   *3.* 14 Wath : only *w* now legible.

4. *Look to Me on the Cross.*

New Coll. Oxford MS. 88.

Man and wyman, loket to me,   f. 179ᵃ
u michel pine ich þolede for þe ;
loke up-one mi rig, u sore ich was i-biten ;
loke to mi side, wat Blode ich haue i-leten.   4
mine uet an mine honden nailed beth to þe rode ;
of þe þornes prikung min hiued urnth a blode.
fram side to side, fro hiued to þe fot,
turn mi bodi abuten, oueral þu findest blod.   8
man, þin hurte, þin hurte þu turne to me,
for þe vif wndes þe ich tholede for þe.

5. *Thole a Little!*

New Coll. Oxford MS. 88.

Louerd, þu clepedest me   f. 179ᵇ
an ich nagt ne ansuarede þe
Bute wordes scloe and sclepie :
'þole yet ! þole a litel !'   4
Bute 'yiet' and 'yiet' was endelis,
and 'þole a litel' a long wey is.

6. *An Old Man's Prayer.*

MS. Harley 2253.

Heȝe louerd, þou here my bone,   f. 72ᵃ
þat madest middelert & mone
ant mon of murþes munne.
trusti kyng ant trewe in trone,   4
þat þou be wiþ me sahte sone,
asoyle me of sunne.

5. 4 MS. þet.   5. 5 MS. þiet.

Fol ich wes in folies fayn,
In luthere lastes y am layn,   8
    þat makeþ myn þryftes þunne,
þat semly sawes wes woned to seyn,
Nou is marred al my meyn,
    away is al my wunne.   12

vnwunne haueþ myn wonges wet,
    þat makeþ me rouþes rede ;
Ne semy nout þer y am set,
þer me calleþ me fulle-flet,   16
    ant waynoun wayteglede.

Whil ich wes in wille wolde,
In vch a bour among þe bolde
    yholde wiþ þe heste ;   20
Nou y may no fynger folde,
Lutel loued ant lasse ytolde,
    y-leued wiþ þe leste.
A goute me haþ ygreyþed so,   24
ant oþer eueles monyc mo,
    y not whet bote is beste.
þat er wes wilde ase þe ro,
nou y swyke, y mei nout so,   28
    hit siweþ me so faste.

Faste y wes on horse heh
    ant werede worly wede.
Nou is faren al my feh,   32
Wiþ serewe þat ich hit euer seh;
    a staf ys nou my stede.

when y se steden styþe in stalle   f. 72ᵃ
ant y go haltinde in þe halle,   (col. 2)
    Myn huerte gynneþ to helde.   36
þat er wes wildest inwiþ walle

27 MS. þar.   28. MS. yswyke.

nou is vnder fote yfalle
    ant mey no fynger felde ;   40
þer ich wes luef icham ful loht,
ant alle myn godes me at-goht,
    myn gomenes waxeþ gelde ;
þat feyre founden me mete & cloht,   44
hue wrieþ awey as hue were wroht—
    such is euel ant elde.

Euel ant elde ant oþer wo
    foleweþ me so faste   48
Me þunkeþ myn herte brekeþ a-tuo !
suete god, whi shal hit swo ?
    hou mai hit lengore laste ?

whil mi lif wes luþer & lees.   52
glotonie mi glemon wes,
    wiþ me he wonede a while ;
prude wes my plowe-fere,
lecherie my lauendere—   56
    wiþ hem is gabbe & gyle—
Coueytise myn keyes bere,
Niþe ant onde were mi fere,
    þat bueþ folkes fyle,   60
Lyare wes mi latymer,
sleuthe & slep mi bedyuer,
    þat weneþ me vnbe while.

vmbe while y am to wene,   64
    when y shal murþes meten.
Monne mest y am to mene,
lord, þat hast me lyf to lene—
    such lotes lef me leten.   68

64 MS. whene.

such lyf ich haue lad fol ʒore—
merci, louerd, y nul namore,
    bowen ichulle to bete;
Syker hit siweþ me ful sore.   72
gabbes, les, & luþere lore,
    sunnes bueþ vn-sete.
godes heste ne huld y noht,
bote euer aʒeyn is wille y wroht—   76
    Mon lereþ me to lete.
such serewe haþ myn sides þurhsoht
þat al y weolewe a-way to noht
    when y shal murþes mete.   80

To mete murþes ich wes wel fous   f. 72^b
    ant comely mon ta calle
(y sugge by oþer ase bi ous)
alse ys hirmon halt in hous,   84
    ase heued-hount in halle.

Dredful deþ, why wolt þou dare
bryng þis body þat is so bare
    ant yn bale ybounde?   88
Careful mon ycast in care,
y falewe as flour y-let forþfare,
    ychabbe myn deþes wounde.
Murþes helpeþ me no more;   92
Help me, lord, er þen ich hore,
    ant stunt my lyf a stounde.
þat ʒokkyn haþ yʒyrned ʒore,
Nou hit sereweþ him ful sore   96
    ant bringeþ him to grounde

to grounde hit haueþ him ybroht—
    whet ys þe beste bote
bote heryen him þat haht vs boht,   100
vre lord þat al þis world haþ wroht,
    ant fallen him to fote?

Nou icham to deþe ydyht,
    y-don is al my dede,   104
god vs lene of ys lyht,
þat we of sontes habben syht
    ant heuene to mede !   amen.

7.   *Suete Iesu King of blysse.*

MS. Harley 2253.

SUete ihesu, king of blysse,   f. 75ᵃ
  myn huerte loue, min huerte lisse, (col. 2)
þou art suete myd ywisse—
Wo is him þat þe shal misse !   4

Suete ihesu, min huerte lyht,
þou art day wiþ-oute nyht,
þou ȝeue me streinþe & eke myht
forte louien þe aryht.   8

Suete ihesu, min huerte bote,
in myn huerte þou sete a rote
of þi loue þat is so swote,
ant leue þat hit springe mote.   12

Suete ihesu, myn huerte gléém,
bryhtore þen þe sonne béém,
ybore þou were in Bedlehéém —
þou make me here þi suete dréém !   16

Suete ihesu, þi loue is suete—
wo is him þat þe shal lete !
þarefore me shulden ofte þe grete
wiþ salte teres & eȝe wete.   20

20 MS. wepe.

Suete ihesu, kyng of londe,
þou make me fer vnderstonde
þat min herte mote fonde
hou suete bueþ þi loue bonde.   24

Swete ihesu, louerd myn,   f. 75ᵇ
my lyf, myn huerte, al is þin ;
vndo myn herte & liht þer-yn,
ant wite me from fendes engyn.   28

Suete ihesu, my soule fode,
þin werkes bueþ bo suete & gode ;
þou bohtest me vpon þe rode,
for me þou sheddest þi blode.   32

Suete ihesu, me reoweþ sore
gultes þat y ha wroht ȝore ;
þare-fore y bidde þin mylse & ore.
Merci, lord! y nul na more.   36

Suete ihesu, louerd god,
þou me bohtest wiþ þi blod ;
out of þin huerte orn þe flod—
þi moder hit seh þat þe by stod.   40

Suete ihesu, bryht & shene,
y preye þe þou here my bene,
þourh erndyng of þe heuene quene,
þat my bone be nou sene.   44

Suete ihesu, berne best,
wiþ ⟨þe⟩ ich hope habbe rest ;
wheþer y be souþ oþer west,
þe help of þe be me nest !   48

34 MS. wroþt.

Suete ihesu, wel may him be
þat þe may in blisse se!
after mi soule let aungles te;
for me ne gladieþ gome ne gle.   52

Suete ihesu, heuene kyng,
feir & best of alle þyng,
þou bring me of þis longing
& come to þe at myn endyng.   56

Suete ihesu, al folkes rééd,
graunte ous er we buen ded
þe vnderfonge in fourme of bred,
ant seþþe to heouene þou vs led!   60

8.   *Iesu Crist Heouene Kyng.*

MS. Harley 2253.

I Esu crist, heouene kyng,   f. 75^b
    ȝef vs alle god endyng   (col. 1)
        þat bone biddeþ þe.
at þe biginnyng of mi song,   4
ihesu, y þe preye among
        In stude al wher y be.
For þou art kyng of alle,   (col. 2)
to þe y clepie ant calle,   8
        þou haue merci of me!

þis enderday in o morewenyng
wiþ dreri herte ant gret mournyng
        on mi folie y þohte: 12
one þat is so suete a þing
þat ber iesse þe heuene kyng,
        merci y besohte.

ihesu, for þi muchele myht,   16
þou graunte vs alle heuene lyht
      þat vs so duere bohtes.
for þi merci, ihesu suete,
þin hondy-werk nult þou lete,   20
      þat þou wel ȝerne sohtest.

Wel ichot ant soþ hit ys
þat in þis world nys no blys
      bote care, serewe, & pyne ;   24
þare-fore ich rede we wurchen so
þat we mowe come to
      þe ioye wiþ-oute fyne.

9.   *A Winter Song.*

MS. Harley 2253.

WYnter wakeneþ al my care,   f. 75ᵇ
   nou þis leues waxeþ bare ;   (col. 2)
ofte y sike & mourne sare
      when hit comeþ in my þoht   4
      of þis worldes ioie hou hit geþ al to noht.

Nou hit is & nou hit nys,
also hit ner nere ywys.
þat moni mon seiþ soþ hit ys :   8
   ' al goþ bote godes wille,
   alle we shule deye þah vs like ylle.'

al þat gre⟨i⟩n me graueþ grene
nou hit faleweþ al by-dene—   12
ihesu, help þat hit be sene
      ant shild vs from helle,
      for y not whider y shal ne hou longe her duelle.

['Iesu suete is þe loue of þe'—see No. 89: *Iesu Dulcis Memoria.*]

10 MS. þaþ.

10.   *An Autumn Song.*

MS. Harley 2253.

NOu skr⟨y⟩nkeþ rose & lylie flour   f. 80ᵃ
   þat whilen ber þat suete sauour   (col. 2)
    in somer þat suete tyde;
ne is no quene so stark ne stour,   4
ne no leuedy so bryht in bour
    þat ded ne shal by-glyde.
whose wol fleysh lust forgon
    & heuene blis abyde,   8
on ihesu be is þoht anon,
    þat þerled was ys side.

from petres-bourh in o morewenyng,
as y me wende o my pley3yng,   12
    on mi folie y þohte;
menen y gon my mournyng
to hire þat ber þe heuene kyng,
    of merci hire bysohte.   16
Ledy, preye þi sone for ous,
    þat vs duere bohte,
ant shild vs from þe loþe hous
    þat to þe fend is wrohte.   20

myn herte of dedes wes for-dred,
of synne þat y haue my fleish fed
    ant folewed al my tyme,
þat y not whider i shal be led   24
when y lygge on deþes bed,
    In ioie ore in-to pyne.
on a ledy myn hope is,
    moder ant virgyne;   28
we shulen in-to heuene blis
    þurh hire medicine.

29 MS. whe.

betere is hire medycyn
þen eny mede or eny wyn—
    hire erbes smulleþ suete — 32
from catenas in-to dyuelyn
nis þer no leche so fyn
    oure serewes to bete. 36
Mon þat feleþ eni sor
    & his folie wol lete,
wiþ-oute gold oþer eny tresor
    he mai be sound ant sete. 40

of penaunce is his plastre al,
ant euer seruen hire y shal
    nou & al my lyue;
nou is fre þat er wes þral
al þourh þat leuedy gent & smal— 44
    heried be hyr ioies fyue!
wher-so eny sek ys
    þider hye blyue; 48
þurh hire beoþ ybroht tó blis
    bo maiden ant wyue.

for he þat dude is body on tre
of oure sunnes haue piete
    þat weldes heouene boures! 52
wymmon, wiþ þi iolyfte,
þah þou be whyt & bryth on ble,
    þou þench on godes shoures; 56
    .   .   .   .
    falewen shule þy floures.
Iesu, haue merci of vs,
    þat al þis world honoures.   AmeN. 60

55 and 56 transposed in MS.

II.   *A Song of the Five Joys*

MS. Harley 2253.

A Se y me rod þis ender day   f. 81ᵇ
   by grene wode to seche play,
mid herte y þohte al on a may,
    Suetest of alle þinge.   4
Lyþe & ich ou telle may
   al of þat suete þinge.

þis maiden is suete ant fre of blod,
briht & feyr, of milde mod,   8
alle heo mai don vs god
    þurh hire bysechynge;
of hire he tok fleysh & blod,
    ihesus, heuene kynge.   12

wiþ al mi lif y loue þat may,
he⟨o⟩ is mi solas nyht & day,
my ioie & eke my beste play
    ant eke my louelongynge;   16
al þe betere me is þat day
   þat ich of hire synge.

of alle þinge y loue hire mest,
My dayes blis, my nyhtes rest;   20
heo counseileþ & helpeþ best
    boþe elde & ȝynge—
nou y may ȝef y wole
   þe fif ioyes mynge.   24

þe furst ioie of þat wymman,
when gabriel from heuene cam
ant seide god shulde bicome man
    ant of hire be bore,   28
& bringe vp of helle pyn
   monkyn þat wes forlore.

25 MS. wynman.

þat oþer ioie of þat may
wes o cristesmasse day,   32
when god wes bore on þoro lay
    ant brohte vs lyhtnesse :
þe ster wes seie by-fore day—
    þis hirdes bereþ wytnesse.   36

þe þridde ioie of þat leuedy,   (col. 2)
þat men clepeþ þe epyphany,
when þe kynges come wery
    to presente hyre sone   40
wiþ myrre, gold, & encenȝ,
    þat wes mon bicome.

þe furþe ioie we telle mawen :·
on estermorewe wen hit gon dawen   44
hyre sone þat wes slawen
    aros in fleysh & bon—
more ioie ne mai me hauen
    wyf ne mayden non.   48

þe fifte ioie of þat wymman,
when hire body to heuene cam:
þe soule to þe body nam
    ase hit wes woned to bene.   52
crist leue vs alle wiþ þat wymman
    þat ioie al forte sene !

preye we alle to oure leuedy,
ant to þe sontes þat woneþ hire by,   56
þat heo of vs hauen merci,
    ant þat we ne misse
In þis world to ben holy
    ant wynne heuene blysse.   amen.   60

12.   *Hostis Herodes impie.*

Phillipps 8336.

HErodes, þou wykked fo, whar-of ys þy dred-
    inge?   f. 203ᵃ
And why art þou so sore agast of cristes to-cominge?
Ne reueth he nouth erthlich god þat maketh ous
    heuene kynges.

Þe kynges wenden here way and foleweden þe sterre, 4
And sothfast lyзth wyth sterre-lyth souhten vrom so
    verre,
And sheuden wel þat he ys god in gold and stor and
    mirre.

Crist y-cleped heuene lomb so com to seynt Ion
And of hym was y-wasзe þat sunne nadde non,   8
To halewen our vollouth water þat sunne hauet uor-
    don.

A newe myhte he cudde þer he was at a feste:
He made vulle wyth shyr water six cannes by þe leste,
Bote þe water turnde in-to wyn þorou crystes oune
    heste.   12

Wele, Louerd, boe myd þe, þat shewedest þe to-day
Wyth þe uader and þe holy gost wythouten ende-day.

13.   *Vexilla Regis prodeunt.*

Phillipps 8336.

ÞE kynges baneres beth forth y-lad,   f. 203ᵃ
    þe rode tokne is nou to-sprad,
Whar he þat wrouth hauet al monkunne,
An-honged was uor oure sunne.   4

Þer he was wounded and vurst y-swonge,
Wyth sharpe spere to herte y-stonge,
To wassȝen ous of sunne clene,
Water and blod þer ronne at ene.   8

Y-voluuld ys Davidþes sawe,
Þat soth was prophete of þe olde lawe,
Þat sayde: ' men ȝe mowen y-se
Hou godes trone ys rode tre.'   12

HA, troe! þat art so vayr y-kud,   f. 203ᵇ
And wyth kynges pourpre y-shrud,
Of wourþy stok y-kore þou were,
Þat so holy limes op-bere.   16

Blessed be þou þat hauest y-bore
Þe wordles raunsoun þat was uor-lore;
Þou art y-maked crystes weye,
Þorou þe he tok of helle preye.   20

Ha, croyz! myn hope, onliche my trust,
Þe nouþe ich grete wyth al my lust!
Þe mylde sped in rithfolnesse,
To sunfole men sheu milsfolnesse.   24

A god, þe heyȝe trinite,
Alle gostes heryȝe þe!
Hoem þat þou bouhtest on rode troe,
Hoere wyssere euermore þou boe.   Amen.   28

14. *Gloria Laus et Honor.*

Phillipps 8336.

WEle, heriȝyng, and worshype boe to crist þat
doere ous bouhte,   f. 203ᵇ
To wham gradden ' osanna!' chyldren clene of þoute.

Þou art kyng of israel and of Davidþes kunne,
Blessed kyng, þat comest tyl ous wyþoute wem of
    sunne.   4

Al þat ys in heuene þe heryȝeth under on,
And al þyn ouwe hondewerk and euch dedlych mon.

Þe volk of gywes wyth bowes comen aȝeynest þe,
And woe wyht boedes and wyth song Moeketh ous
    to þe.   8

Hoe kepten þe wyth worsȝyping aȝeynst þou shuldest
    deyȝe,
And woe syngeth to þy worshipe in trone þat sittest
    heyȝe.

Hoere wyl and here moekynge þou nome þo to þonk ;
Queme þe þoenne, mylsful Kyng, oure ofringe of þys
    song.   12

Wele, heriing and worshipe boe, &c.

15.   *Popule meus quid feci tibi ?*

Phillipps 8336.

MY volk, what habbe y do þe   f. 204ᵃ
  Oþer in what þyng toened þe ?
  Gyn nouþe and onswere þou me :

Vor vrom egypte ich ladde þe,   4
Þou me ledest to rode troe.
    My volk, what habbe y do þe? &c.

Þorou wyldernesse ich ladde þe,
And uourty ȝer bihedde þe,   8
And aungeles bred ich ȝaf to þe,
And in-to reste ich brouhte þe.
    My volk, what habbe y do þe? &c.

What more shulde ich hauen y-don   12
Þat þou ne hauest nouth under-uon?
 My volk, what habbe y do þe?

Ich þe vedde and shrudde þe;
And þou wyth eysyl drinkest to me,   16
And wyth spere styngest me.   My volk, what &c.

Ich egypte boeth uor þe,
And hoere tem y shlou uor þe.   My volk, &c.

Ich delede þe see uor þe,   20
And pharaon dreynte uor þe;
And þou to princes sullest me.   My volk, &c.

In bem of cloude ich ladde þe;
And to pylate þou ledest me.   My volk, &c.   24

Wyth aungeles mete ich uedde þe;
And þou bufetest and scourgest me.   My volk, &c.

Of þe ston ich dronk to þe;
And þou wyth galle drincst to me. My volk, &c. 28

Kynges of chanaan ich uor þe boet;
And þou betest myn heved wyþ roed. My volk, &c.

Ich ȝaf the croune of kynedom;
And þou me ȝyfst a croune of þorn. My volk, &c. 32

Ich muchel worshype doede to þe;
And þou me hongest on rode troe.   My volk, &c.

16. *An Orison to the Blessed Virgin.*

Phillipps 8336.

Þou wommon boute uere   f. 204^b
 Þyn oune uader bere.
Gret wonder þys was
Þat on wommon was moder   4
To uader and hyre broþer—
So neuer oþer nas.

Þou my suster and moder
And þy sone my broþer— 8
    Who shulde þoenne drede ?
Who-so hauet þe kyng to broder
And ek þe quene to moder
    Wel auhte uor to spede. 12

Dame, suster and moder,
Say þy sone my broþer,
    Þat ys domes-mon,
Þat uor þe þat hym bere, 16
To me boe debonere—
    My robe he haueth opon.

Soethþe he my robe tok
Also ich finde in bok 20
    He ys to me y-bounde ;
And helpe he wole ich wot,
Vor loue þe chartre wrot,
    Þe enke orn of hys wounde. 24

Ich take to wytnessinge
Þe spere and þe crounynge,
    Þe nayles and þe rode,
Þat he þat ys so cunde, 28
Þys euer haueth in munde,
    Þat bouhte ous wyth hys blode.

When þou ȝeue hym my wede,   f. 205^a
Dame, help at þe noede 32
    Ich wot þou myth uol wel,
Þat uor no wreched gult
Ich boe to helle y-pult—
    To þe ich make apel. 36

Nou, dame, ich þe byseche
At þylke day of wreche
    Boe by þy sones trone,
When sunne shal boen souht   40
In werk, in word, in þouht,
    And spek uor me þou one.

When ich mot nede apere
Vor mine gultes here   44
    To-uore þe domes-mon,
Suster, boe þer my uere
And make hym debonere,
    Þat mi robe haueth opon.   48

Vor habbe ich þe and hym
Þat markes berþ wyþ hym
    Þat charite him tok—
Þe woundes al blody,   52
Þe toknes of mercy
    Ase techeþ holy bok—
Þarf me noþing drede,
Sathan shal nout spede   56
    Wyþ wrenches ne wyþ crok.   Amen.

17.   *Aue Maris Stella.*

Phillipps 8336.

HEyl, leuedy, se-stoerre bryht,   f. 205ᵃ
  Godes moder, edy wyht,
Mayden euer vurst and late
Of heueneriche sely ȝate,   4
Þylk aue þat þou vonge in spel
Of þe aungeles mouhþ kald Gabriel.
In gryht ous sette and shyld vrom shome,
Þat turnst abakward eues nome,   8

Gulty monnes bond vnbynd,
Bryng lyht tyl hoem þat boeth blynd,
Put vrom ous oure sunne
And ern ous alle wynne.   12
Shou· þat þou art moder one,
And he vor þe take oure bone
Þat vor ous þy chyld by-com
And of þe oure kunde nom.   16
Mayde one þou were myd chylde
Among alle so mylde.
Of sinne ous quite oñ haste
And make ous meoke and chaste,   20
Lyf þou ȝyf ous clene,   f. 205^b
Wey syker ous ȝarke and lene
Þat we iesus y-soe
And euer blyþe boe.   24
To uader, cryst and holy gost beo þonk and heryinge ;
To þreo persones and o god, o menske and worshyp-
    inge.

18.   *Veni creator spiritus.*

Phillipps 8336.

COm, shuppere holy gost, of-sech oure þouhtes ; f. 205^b
    Vul wyth grace of heuene heortes þat þu wrouht-
        est,
Þou þat art cleped uor-spekere and ȝyft vrom god
    y-send,
Welle of lyf, vur, charite and gostlych oynement.   4
Þou ȝyfst þe seuene ȝyftes, þou vinger of godes honde,
Þou makest tonge of vlesȝe speke leodene of uche
        londe.
Tend lyht in oure wyttes, in our heortes loue,
Þer oure body is leoþe-wok ȝyf strengþe vrom aboue. 8

1. of-sech: MS. of seth.

Shyld ous from þe veonde and ȝyf ous gryth anon,
Þat woe wyten ous vrom sunne þorou þe lodes-mon.
Of þe uader and þe sone þou ȝyf ous knoulechinge,
To leue þat uul of boþe þou euer boe louinge.   12
Woele to þe uader and to þe sone þat vrom deth aros,
And also to þe holy gost ay boe worshipe and los.

19.   *Alma redemptoris mater.*

Phillipps 8336.

HOly moder, þat bere cryst   f. 205^b
     buggere of monkunde,
Þou art ȝat of heuene blisse
Þat prest wey ȝyfst and bunde.   4
Þou sterre of se, rer op þe uolk
Þat rysing haueht in munde.
In þe þou bere þyn holy uader,
Þat mayden were after and raþer,   8
Whar-of so wondreth kunde.
Of gabrieles mouþe / þou uonge þylke 'Aue' ;
Lesne ous of sunne nouþè, / so woe bisecheth þe.
                                               Amen.

20.   *Conditor alme siderum.*

Phillipps 8336.

HOly wrouhte of sterres brryht,   f. 206^a
     Of ryht byleue ay lastyng lyht,
Crist, þat bouhtest mon wyth fyht,
Her þe bone of moeke wyht !   4

Þou hédest ruþe of wordl vorlore
Þorou deth of sunfol rote ;
Þou sauuedest monkun, þeruore,
to gulty ȝeue bote.   8

Toward þe wordles ende
Þy wylle was t'alende
   In on maydenes bour ;
Ase spouse of chaumbre al-one   12
Out of þat clene wone
   Þou come t'oure honour.

To whas stronge myhte(s)
Knoen of alle wyhtes   16
   Bendeth hoem ymone,
Of heuene and ek of eorþe,
And knoulecheth hym wourþe
   Vor bouwen to hym one.   20

Holy god, woe byddeth þe
Þat shalt þys wordle deme,
Vrom oure fykel fohes spere,
Þou þylke tyme ous ȝeme.   24

Herying, worshype, myhte, and weole
to uader and þe sone !
And also to þe holy gost,
and euer myd heom wone !   28

21.   *Christe redemptor omnium.*

Phillipps 8336.

CRyst, buggere of alle ycoren,   f. 206ª
   þe uadres olpy sone,
On to-uoren ey gynnyng boren
ouer alle speche and wone,   4

þou lyht, þou uaderes bryhtnesse,
þou trust and hope of alle,
Lust what þy volk þorou-out þe wordl
to þe byddeth and kalle.   8

Wrouhte of oure hele,
nou haue in þyne munde
þat of o mayde wemles
þou toke oure kunde.   12

Þys day berth wytnesse
þat noeweth uche ӡer,
þat-ou alyhtest vrom þe uader—
of sunne make ous sker.   16

Hym hoeuene and oerþe and wylde se
and al þat ys þer-on,
Wrouhte, of þy comynge
hereth wyth blisfol ron.   20

And woe nomliche þat boeth bouht   f. 206ᵇ
wyth þyn holy blod
Vor þys day singeth a neowe song
and makeþ blisfol mod :   24

Weole louerd beo wyth þe,
y-boren of o may,
Wyth uader and þe holy gost
Wyþouten ende-day.   Amen.   28

22.   *Tu Rex glorie Christe.*

Phillipps 8336.

Þou kyng of woele and blisse,   f. 206ᵇ
   louerd iesu crist,
Þou uaderes sone of heuene,
þat neuer ende bist,   4

Þou, uor to sauue monkunne
þat þou haddest whrout,
A Moeke maydes wombe
þou ne shonedest nouht ;   8

Þou þat ouercóme
þe bitter dethes stunchg,
Þou openedest hoeuene-ryche
to ryth byleues þrunchg ;　　　　　　　12

Þou sist in godes ryth hond
in þy uaderes blisse ;
Þou shalt comen to demen ous,
woe leueth al to wysse ;　　　　　　　16

Þe þoenne woe byddeth help ous
wham þou hauest y-wrouth,
Whóm wyþ þy doerewourþe blod
on rode hauest y-bouth.　　　　　　　20

Þe þoenne woe bysecheth,
help ous þyn oune hyne,
Whom wyth þy derewourþe blod
hast bouth vrom helle pyne.　　Amen.　　24

23. *Make Ready for the Long Journey.*

Phillipps 8336.

Bysoeth ȝou in þys ylke lyf
Of lyflode in þat oþer lyf.

SOethþe mon shal hoenne wende　　f. 206^b
　And nede déȝen at þen ende,
　　And wonyen he not whare,
God ys þat he trusse hys pak　　　　　4
And tymliche pute hys stor in sak
　　Þat not when hoenne váre.

　　Oeuch mon þenche uor to spede
　Þat he ne loese þe grete mede　　　　8
　　Þat god ous dythte ȝáre.

Þys lyf nys bote sorewe away,
Ounneþe ys mon glad-uol o day,
    vor sorewe and toene and káre ;   12
Mon wyth sorewe is uurst ybore,
And eft wyth sorewe rend and tore,
    ȝyf he ryth þencþ of hys wáre,
              Oeuch mon, etc.

What ys lordshype and heynesse,   16
What helpth katel and rychesse ?
    Gold and soeluer awey shal uáre,
Þy gost shal wonye þou ne wost nout where,
Þy body worth wounde in grete oþer here,   20
    Of oþer þyng þou worst al báre.
              Oeuch mon, etc.

By-þench, mon, ȝoerne on oeuche wyse
Er þou boe brouht to þylke asyse,
    On what þou shalt truste þáre.   24
What god þou hauest, mon, here ydon
Prest þer þou shalt ounder-uon,
    Elles euer þou worst in káre.
              Oeuch mon, etc.

Boe mon ȝong oþer boe he old,   28
Non so strong ne wel y-told
    Þat hoennes ne mot fare.
Deth is hud, mon, in þy gloue,
Wyth derne dunt þat shal he proue   32
    and smyte þou nost wháre.
              Oeuch mon, etc.

To-uore þe deth ys betere o dede
Þen after téne, and more of mede,
    and more quencheth kare :   36

Boe monnes wyttes hym byreued,
Hys eyen blynd, hys eren deued,
    þe cofres bóeth al bare.

Oeuch mon, etc.

Boe þe gost urom body reued,   40
þe bernes sone shulle boen sheued,
    Ne shal me noþyng spáre,
Boe þe body wyth groeth byweued,
þe soule sone shal boe leued,   44
    Alas! of froendes báre.

Oeuch mon, etc.

24.   *Iesu Nostra Redempcio.*

Phillipps 8336.

Esu our raunsoun,   f. 207ᵇ
    Loue and longynge,
Louerd god almyhti,
Whrouhte of alle þinge,   4
Vlesh þou nóme
and mon bicome
in times endinge.

What mil⟨s⟩folnesse awalde þe   8
þat oure sunnes bere,
So bitter deth to þolien,
urom sunne ous uor t'arere?

Helle clos þou þorledest   12
and bouhtest þine of bonde;
Wyht gret nobleye
þou op-steye
To þy uader ryht honde.   16

13 MS. bondes.

þylke mylse nede þe
t'awelde oure wyckenesse
Wyth þy mercy,
and vul ous ay   20
wyth þy nebshaftes blisse.

Þou boe nou oure ioie,
þat shalt boen oure mede,
And oure woele ay boe in þe   24
þat shalt ous wyth þe nede.

25.   *Quis est iste qui uenit de Edom?*

Phillipps 8336.

WHat ys he, þys lordling þat cometh vrom þe
       vyht   f. 208ᵃ
Wyth blod-réde wede so grysliche ydyht,
So vayre y-coyntised, so semlich in syht,
So styflyche ʒongeþ, so douhti a knyht?   4

Ich hyt am, Ich hyt am, þat ne speke bote ryht,
Chaunpyoun to helen monkunde in vyht.

Why þoenne ys þy schroud red wyth blod al y-meind,
Ase troddares in wrynge wyth most al by-spreynd?   8

Þe wrynge ich habbe y-trodded al mysulf on,
And of al monkunde ne was non oþer won.
Ich hoem habbe y-trodded in wreþe and in grome,
And al my wede ys by-spreynd wyth hoere blod
       ysome,   12
And al my robe y-uuled to hoere grete shome.
Þe day of þylke wreche leueth in my þouht,
Þe ʒer of medes ʒeldyng ne uorʒet ich nouht.
Ich loked al aboute som helpynge mon,   16
Ich souhte al þe route bote help nas þer non.

24. 18 t'awelde: MS. ta welde.

Hyt was myn oune strengþe þat þys bóte wrouhte,
Myn owe Douhtynesse þat help þer me brouhte.
On Godes mylsfolnesse ich wole by-þenche me,   20
And heryen hym in alle þyng þat he ȝeldeth me.

In epistola que legitur feria 4ᵃ maioris ebdomade non est plus.

Ich habbe y-trodded þe uolk in wrethe and in
    grome,
Adreynt al wyth shennesse, y-drawe doun wyth
    shome.

Istud est de integro textu libri [cf. Isa. 63. 6] sed non est de Epistola.

26.   *An Orison of the Five Joys.*

St. John's Coll. Camb. MS. 256.

HEyl be þou, marie, milde quene of heuene! p. 269
    Blessed be þi name & god it is to neuene.
To þe i mene mi mone, i preie þou her mi steuene,
Ne let me neuere deie in none of þe sennes seuene.   4
    Aue maria gracia plena dominus tecum.

Heil, seinte marie, quene cortas & hende!
For þe ioye þat þou haddest wan crist þe aungel sende;
& seide þat þe holi gost scholde in þi bodi wende,
Þou bring me out of sinne & schuld me fram þe fende. 8
    Aue maria gracia plena dominus tecum.

Ioyful was þin herte with-outen eni drede
Wan ihesu crist was of þe boren fayrest of alle þede,
& þou mayde bi-fore & after as we in bok rede;
Lefdi for þat ioie þou helpe me at nede.   12
    Aue maria gracia plena dominus tecum.

Ladi, ful of grace, gladful was þi chere
Wan ihesu crist fram deþ aros þat was þe lef & dere;
Ladi, for þe loue of him þat lay þin herte nere,
Help me out of senne þer wile þat i am here.   16

   Aue maria gracia plena dominus tecum.

Ladi, ful of myȝte, mek & milde of mode,
For þe loue of swe⟨te⟩ ihesu þat don was on þe rode,
& for his woundes fiue þat runnen alle a-blode,
Þou help me out of senne, ladi fayr & gode.   20

   Aue maria gracia plena dominus tecum.

Ladi, seinte marie, fair & goud & swete,
For þe loue of þe teres þat þi-se⟨l⟩f lete
Wan þou seye ihesu crist nayled hond & fete,
Þou ȝeue me grace in herte my sennes for to bete.   24

   Aue maria gracia plena dominus tecum.

In counsayl þou art best, & trewe in alle nede,
to sinful men wel prest & redi in goud dede.
Ladi, for þe loue of him þou seye on rode blede,
Þou help me now & euere & saue me at þe nede.   28

   Aue maria gracia plena dominus tecum.   p. 270

Ladi, flour of alle, so rose in erber red,
To þe i crie & calle, to þe i make my bed;
Þou be in stude & stalle þer i draue to ded;
Let me neuere falle in hondes of þe qued.   32

   Aue maria gracia plena dominus tecum.

Marie, for þat swete ioie þat þou were þan inne
Wan þou seie ihesu crist, flour of al mankinne,
Steye vp to heuene þer ioye is euere inne,
Of bale be þou mi bote & bring me out of sinne.   36

   Aue maria gracia plena dominus tecum.

Marie, for þat swe⟨te⟩ ioye wan þou fram erþe was tan,
In-to þe blisse of heuene with aungeles mani an,
& i-set bi swete ihesu in fel & flecsch & ban,
Þou bringe me to ioyes þat neuere schal be gon.   40

Aue maria gracia plena dominus tecum.

Marie, ful in grace, þat sittest in trone,
now i þe biseche þou graunte me mi bone :
Ihesu to loue & drede, my lif t'amende sone,
& bringe me to þat heye kyng þat weldeþ sune &
mone.   44

Aue maria gracia plena dominus tecum.

For þi ioies fiue, ladi fair & bryȝt,
& for þi mayden-hede & þi moche myȝt,
þou helpe me to come in-to þa iche lyȝt
Þer ioye is with-oute ende & day viþote nyȝt.   48

Aue maria gracia plena dominus tecum.

Ladi, seynte marie, ȝif þat þi wille were,
As þou art ful of ioye & i am ful of care,
þou help me out of sinne & lat me falle namare,
& ȝeue me grace in erþe my sinnes to reue sare.   52

Aue maria gracia plena dominus tecum.

Ladi, quene of heuene, þou here me wit wille ;
Y praye þov her mi steuene & let my soule neuere
spille
In non of þe sinnes seuene þorw no fendes wille :
Nou bri⟨n⟩g my saule to heuene, þer-in a place to
fille.   56

Aue maria gracia plena dominus tecum.

27.   *The Four Foes of Mankind.*

Advocates Lib. 19. 2. 1 ('Auchinleck MS.')

ÞE siker soþe who-so seys,   f. 303ᵃ
    Wiþ diol dreye we our days
& walk mani wil ways
    As wandrand wiȝtes.
Al our games ous agas,   4
So mani tenes ou⟨s⟩ tas
Þurch fonding of fele fas,
    Þat fast wiþ ous fiȝtes.   8
Our flesche is fouled wiþ þe fende—
Þer we finde a fals frende—
Þei þai heuen vp her hende
    Þai no hold nouȝt her hiȝtes.   12
Þis er þre þat er þra,
ȝete þe ferþ is our fa,
Deþ þat derieþ ous swa
    & diolely ous diȝtes   16

Þis world wileþ þus, y wat,
Þurch falsschip of fair hat;
Where we go bi ani gat
    Wiþ bale he ous bites.   20
Now kirt, now care,
Now min, now mare,
Now sounde, now sare,
    Now song, now sites,   24
Now nouȝt, now y-nouȝ,
Now wele, now wouȝ,
Now is in longing þat louȝ,
    Þat o þis liif lites;   28
Now geten, now gan—
Y tel it bot a lent lan,
When al þe welþ of our wan
    Þus oway wites.   32

29 MS. gente.

Now vnder, now ouer,
Now cast, now couer,
Now plente, now pouer,
    Now pine, now plawe,   36
Now heþen, now here,
Now feble, now fere,
Now swift, now swere,
    Now snelle, now slawe,   40
Now nouȝt, now y-nouȝ,
Now fals, now frouȝ—
Þe warld tirneþ ous touȝ
    Fram wawe to wawe,   44
Til we be broyden in a brayd,   f. 303ᵇ
Þat our lickham is layd
In a graue, þat is grayd
    Vnder lame lawe.   48

When derne deþ ous haþ ydiȝt,
Is non so war no so wiȝt
Þat he no felles him in fiȝt,
    As fire dos in tunder.   52
Þer nis no letting at lite
Þat he no tittes til him tite,
Þat he haþ sammned in site
    Sone wil he sunder.   56
Noiþer he stintes no stokes,
Bot ay prickes & prokes
Til he vnclustri al þe lokes
    Þat liif ligges vnder.   60
When y tent til him take
How schuld ich ani mirþe make
Or wele in þis warld wake?—
    Ywis it were wonder.   64

Deþ þat deries ous ȝete
& makes mani wonges wete—
Þer nis no liif þat he wil lete
    To lache when him list.   68
When he is lopen out of les,
No pray noman after pes,
For non giftes þat ges
    Mai no man til him trist.   72
Our gode frendes has he fot,
& put þe pouer to þe pot,
& ouer him y-knett his knott,
    Vnder his clay kist.   76
Derne deþ, o-pon þe ȝong
Wiþ þe to striue it is strong!
Y wold be wreken of mi wrong,
    ȝif y way wist.   80

When þou has gaderd & y-glened,
Long lyowen & lened,
Sparely þi gode spened
    & loþ for to lete,   84
Þe war leuer swelt vnder sword
Þan parti of þi peni hord;
Þou wringest mani wrang word
    Wiþ wanges ful wete.   88
& deþ dinges o þi dore
Þat nedes schal be þi neiȝebore,
& fett þe to fen-fore
    Foule vnder fete.   92
For al þe craft þat þou can,
& al þe wele þatow wan,
Þe mock & þe mad man
    No schul þai neuer mete.   96

82 lyowen: MS. lyopon.

Seþþen font ous fra filþ wesche,
Our fa haue founde we our flesche,
Wiþ mani fondinges & fresche
      & four-sum of fendes.   100
Is nan so þra of hem þre
Þat ma merres þan me,
Bisier mai nan be
      To bring ous on bendes.   104
Man, mene þou þi mis,
Trowe trustly on þis,
Þou no wat neuer y-wis
      In world whare þou wendes   108
No wat gat þatow gas.
Þis four er redi on þi pas—
Now haue y founden þi fas,
      Finde tow þi frendes!   112

28. *Lollai litel child whi wepistow so sore?*

MS. Harley 913.

Lollai, (Lollai), litil child, whi wepistou so sore? f. 32ᵃ
  nedis mostou wepe, hit was iȝarkid þe ȝore
euer to lib in sorow, and sich and mourne euer,
as þin eldren did er þis, whil hi aliues were.   4
    Lollai, (lollai), litil child, child lolai, lullow,
    In-to vncuþ world icommen so ertow!

bestis and þos foules, þe fisses in þe flode,
and euch schef aliues, imakid of bone and blode,   8
whan hi commiþ to þe world hi doþ ham silf sum
    gode—
Al bot þe wrech brol þat is of adam-is blode.
    Lollai, (Lollai), litil child, to kar ertou bemette,
    Þou nost noȝt þis world-is wild bifor þe is isette. 12

D 2

104 on bendes: MS. ouᵗbendes.

Child, if be-tidiþ þat þou ssalt þriue and þe,
Þench þou wer ifostred vp þi moder kne ;
euer hab mund in þi hert of þos þinges bre.
Whan þou commist, whan þou art, and what ssal com
        of þe.   16
      Lollai, l⟨ollai⟩, litil child, child lollai, lollai ;
       Wiþ sorow þou com into þis world, wiþ sorow
       ssalt wend awai.

Ne tristou to þis world, hit is þi ful vo,   f. 32ᵇ
Þe rich he makiþ pouer, þe pore rich al so ;   20
Hit turneþ wo to wel and ek wel to wo—
Ne trist no man to þis world, whil hit turniþ so.
      Lollai, l⟨ollai⟩, litil child, þe fote is in þe whele ;
       Þou nost whoder turne to wo oþer wele.   24

Child, þou ert a pilgrim in wikidnis ibor,
Þou wandrest in þis fals world, þou loke þe bi-for ;
deth ssal com wiþ a blast vte of a wel dim horre,
adam-is kin dun to cast, him silf haþ ido be-for.   28
      Lollai, l⟨ollai⟩, litil child, so wo þe worp adam,
       in þe lond of paradis þroʒ wikidnes of satan.

Child, þou nert a pilgrim bot an vncuþe gist,
Þi dawes beþ itold, þi iurneis beþ icast,   32
whoder þou salt wend norþ oþer est,
deþ þe sal be-tide wiþ bitter bale in brest.
      Lolla⟨i⟩, l⟨ollai⟩, litil chil⟨d⟩, þis wo adam þe
       wroʒt,
       Whan he of þe appil ete, and eue hit him be-
       tacht.   36

29. *An Orison to the Trinity.*

Cotton MS. Vespas. A. iii.

FAder and sun and haligast,　　　f. 142^b
　To þe i cri and call mast,　　　(col. 1)
　　þat treuest es in tron ;
An-fald godd i cal in thre,　　　　　4
Lauerd, loued in trinite,
　　To þe mak I mi bon.

þou sceild me bath fra sinn and scam,
Lauerd, for þin hali nam　　　　　8
　　þat helpes þine sa son ;
And wiss me þat right wai,
þar euermar es ioi and plai—
　　For hard es her to hon.　　　12

Hali fader, heuen king,
Lauerd, loued of al thing,
　　On þe i tru and call,
And on ihesu, þi suete sun ;　　　16
Arli and late i wil yow mon,
　　In bure and eke in hall.

Haligast, i call alsua,
In þe i tru and in nama,　　　　20
　　þou sceild me to fall.
And if i fall in ani skath,
þou do me for to rise all rath,
　　And mine frendes all.　　　24

þou þat has þis werld all wroght,
And has it sett al wit þi thoght,
　　And stabuld it in skill,
Of all þin sandes wild and tam,　　28
Man þou scop and gaf him nam,
　　And gaf him wijf to will.

Þof adam rap him in a res,
Thoru an apul þat eue him ches,   32
 Vs all for to spill ;
Þou, þat es crist and godd an-fald,
Lauerd be vr hope and hald—
 Þou do his flod to fill.   (col. 2) 36

Rape þe, lauerd, for to reu,
For ilk dai vr nede es neu,
 For fast i fund to fare ;
O mi sinnes me reues sare,   40
I wat þi merci es wel mare ;
 In hope i durk and dare.

Þou þat has þis werld to weld,
Reu me, lauerd, in mine eld,   44
 And wiss me waies þare,
Þare santes has þair seli sete ;
On domes-dai þar we sal mete,
 Þou sceild me fra care.   48

Ful derf i was to bidd vndo,
Þat luued i neuer rest na ro,
 Bot wildnes and wa ;
Ful leuef me was to cum in cri   52
Wit magote and wit mariori,
 Wit ma⟨r⟩iot, mald, and ma.

O mans-slaghter had i na mak,
Ne nan sa wild in wa to wrak,   56
 To riue þe grene and gra ;
Nu þan dos me held ta grith,
Lauerd, þi merci ta me wit,
 Fott was þe fallen fra.   60

60 MS. falsen.

Nu ask i noþer gra ne grene,
Ne stede, scrud, ne lorein scene,
 Ne purperpall, ne pride o pane,
Ne riche robe wit veir and grise;   64
O werlds aght ask i na pris,
 Ne castel mad o lime and stane.

Bot stedfast hope and trout right,
And ert clene and eien sight,   68
 Oþir gersum ask i nan.
Do me, lauerd, to wijt þi will,
And siþen heuen-rike to fill,
 For son er þir gammes gan.   72

O me es noght bot sin and sake,
Lauerd, bot þi merci it mak.
 Vnworthi am i, wel þou wast,
And al vnredi for to rise   76
On domesdai be-for iustise,
 Þar all es casten on a cast.

Þar santes sal þe dute and drede,
And all sal se þin wondes bled,   80
 Mi hope es in þi merci mast;
Als euer was and ai sal be,   f. 141ᵃ
Lauerd, loued in trinite,
 Fader and sune and haligast.   84

30.   *The Matins of the Cross.*

Cotton MS. Vespas. A. iii.

IEsus, þat wald efter mid-night   f. 141ᵇ
 Þi suete face, þat was sa bright,   (col. 2)
  With Iuus spitting file;
And suffer siþen, for vr sin,   4
Boffetes on þi soft chin,
 In þat ilk quile;

62 MS. me lorem.

þat ilk tim þou fra ded ras,
Lauerd godd, als þi will was,   8
   Mildli and still ;
Ken us, lauerd, for þi nam
Forsak bat sin and scam
   And vr werckes ill ;   12

Of vr sinnes son to rise,
And wis us euer wit þe wise,
   And leue vr gamens grill,
þat wit þin apostels hei,   16
Mai þow all se in galilei,
   If it be þi will.

[Lauds.]

Suet lauerd, wit-vten lese,
Mikel was þi tholmodnes   20
   In þat ilk time ;
þa felun Iuus dai and night,
Vild þe wit al þair might,
   Wald þai neuer fine.   24

þou giue vs, lauerd, might and mode
To luue ai þat es sa god,
   And thinc apon þi pine ;
Wit hand and werck, hert and will,   28
⟨Ay þe to luue bath lude and still,⟩
   To þe wit hert encline.   f. 142ᵃ
If we fall intil il fanding,
Defend us fra þe fule thing—   32
   þou wat þat we aı þin.

22 þa: MS. þai.   29 Missing line supplied from Göttingen MS.

[Prime.]

Iesus, þat was broght in present
Befor pilate to Iugement,
    At prime o dai i wen ;   36
Þat ilk time þou mistred þe,
Suet iesu, wit hert sa fre
    To maria magdalene.

Þou sceu þe, lauerd, al vntil us,   40
Þat al to mikel has ben vnbuxs
    Vnto þe suet trace ;
And giue us clene scrift at hald,
Of vr sinnes neu and ald,   44
    For þi suet grace ;

Þat na sinn be sene us on,
At þe mikel dai o dome,
    Þan we er broght in place ;   48
Þat we efter þat ilk dai,
Mai liue wit ioi for euer and ai,
    Be-for þi suete face.

[Undern.]

Suet iesu, at vndrin time,   52
For vr sin and noght for þin,
    Sufferd a-bute þi hert
O Iuus þat war fell and strang,
Wit knotted skurges hard and lang,   56
    Dintes sare and smert.

Þat ilk time al þat i neuen,
Þou sent þe haligast fra heuen
    To þine apostels suete ;   60
Þou send vs, lauerd, wijt and will
To mend us of vr dedis ill,
    And fall þe to fete.

If sinnes in vr hert be sene,　　　　　　64
Wit tere of ei mai was þam clene,
　　And wit wanges wete,
Þat ai mai be vr conforth mast,
Þe suetnes o þe haligast　　　　　　68
　　Wit þi merci to mete.

[Mid-day.]

At middai, ihesu, wit mild mode,
Þou spred þi bodi on þe rode,
　　To drau us all to heuen ;　　　　72
Þat ilk time, lauerd, þou wild
Tak flexs o þat maiden mild,
　　Thoru an angel steuen.

Receiue, lauerd, me and ma　　(col. 2)　76
In-to þi suet armes tua,
　　Þat er bright and scene.
Lauerd, þou hele wondes mine
Wit þi suet medicine.　　　　　　80
　　Grant þat it sua bene !

Mak vr bodijs fair and chast,
For to receiue þe haligast,
　　Wit hert god and clene ;　　　　84
Þat we mai clene all cum to þc,
Þar þou sittes in trinite,
　　And ioi es euer sene.

[None.]

Suete iesu, at time o none,　　　　　88
Þan þou was on rode done,
　　And had sufferd pine,

Þou þat was o mightes mast,
Vte of þi bodi þou gaf þe gast,   92
    In þat ilk time.

Þat ilk time til heuen stei þou,
And quicked vr hertes, suete iesu.
    Al luuelili þou vs lere   96
Þe to luue wit sothfast rede,
To haf mining o þi dede
    Þat þou boght sua dere.

Þi pines in vr hertes write,   100
Þar we gang and þar we sete,
    To-quils we be here ;
Þat we omang þat ilk trun
Þat serues ihesu, godd sun,   104
    Mai be felau and fere.

    [Even-song.]
Suete iesu, þat lauerd es,
Þou gaf sight o þi blod and flexs
    At euen-sanges time ;   108
In þat ilk time was tan
Dun o þe cros in flexs and ban,
    Als it me mai mene.

Do wickednes vte of vr thoght,   112
And feluni þat gains noght,
    And envie and tene ;
Þat we mai tak þat ilk flexs,
Lauerd, if þi wil it es,   116
    Wit bodi and hert clene ;
And þat it be vr warantise,
On domesdai quen þou sal rise,
    Al þis werld to deme.   120

91 MS. wat.

[Compline.]

Suet iesu, al þar þou stode,
Þi suete bodi in flexs and blod,   f. 142^b
   At time o compli;
For dred o þat bitter ded,   124
Þat þou sufferd for al man-hed,
   Þi hert was wel sari.

Þat ilk time þar was þou wonden,
Laid in sepulcre and noght funden,   128
   Wit maris þat þe soght;
Þou clens vr hert o soru and care,
And giue us ioi for euer-mare,
   Þat þou us vnto boght.   Amen.   132

31.   *A Song of the Five Joys.*

Göttingen Univ. MS. theol. 107.

HAile be þu, mari maiden bright!   f. 169^a
  Þu teche me þe wais right;   (col. 1)
I am a sorful dreri wight,
   als þu mai se
Quer i sal in þe hard pine of hel be.   4

(M)i sinful saule sighes sare;
Liued i haue in sin and care,
Leue i wil and do na mare.   8
   mi leued⟨i⟩ fre,
Saul and bodi, lijf and dede, bi-teche i þe.

Þar þu lay in þi bright boure,
Leuedi, quite als leli floure,   12
An angel com fra heue⟨ne toure⟩,
   sant gabriel,
And said, 'leuedi, ful of blis, ai worth þe wel!'

129 MS. martirs.

Stil þu stod, ne stint þu noght,   16
þu said til him þe boдword brogh⟨t⟩,
' Al his wil it sal be wroght,
    in his ancele '
Leuedi, bi-for þi suete sun mak vs lele.   20

(Þ)e toþer ioy i wate it was
Als sun schines thoru þe glas
Sua ert þu, leued⟨i⟩, wemles
    and ai sal be.   24
Leued⟨i⟩, for þat suete ioy, þu reu on me.

(Þ)e thrid ioy i vnderstand,
Thre kinges com of thrin land,
To fal þi suete sun til hand,   28
    and gaf him gift,
Mir, reclis and gold red, als it was right.

Þe king was riche, þe gold was rede,
Þe reclis fel til his goddhed,   32
Mir to man þat sal be dede
    for vr sake.
Leuedi, to þi suete sun at ane vs make.

Þe feird, it es al thoru his grace,   36
Quen he fra dede to lijf ras,
Quen he sua hard suongen was
    on rode tre.
Leuedi, of vr sinnes al þu make vs fre.   40

(Þ)e fijft, þu was til heuen broght,
Þe iuus þe soght and fand þe noght,
Als þi suete sun it wroght,
    almighti king.   44
Leuedi mari, be vr helpe at vr ending.

Leuedi, for þi ioies fiue,
Þu kid þi might and help vs suith,
Leuedi mari, moder o liue,   48
    wid flur and fruit,
Rose and leli þu sprede ay wide, and helpe þi suite.

Leuedi mari, wele þu wast,
Þe feindes fraistes me ful fast,   52
wele i hope i sal þaim cast
    thoru might of þe ;
Quen i neuen þi suete nam i ger þaim fle.

Þir iois er said als i can sai,   56
Mi site, mi soru, i cast away,
Nu help me leuedi, wele þu may,
    and be mi spere.
Fra þe har pain of hell þu me were.   60

All þat singes þis sang
And all þat ligges in paines strang,
Þu lede þaim right þar þai ga wrang,
    and haue merci   64
On all þat trous þat godd was born of þe, fair leuedi.

32.   'Marye, mayde mylde and fre.'

B.M. Additional MS. 17376.

MArye, mayde mylde and fre,   f. 204^b
    Chambre of þe trynyte,
One wyle lest to me,
    Ase ich þe grete wyþ songe :   4
Þaჳ my fet on-clene be,
    My mes þou onder-fonge.

Þou art quene of paradys,
Of heuene, of erthe, of al þat hys;   8
Þou bere þane kynge of blys
    Wyþ-oute senne and sore;
Þou hast y-ryȝt þat was amys,
    Y-wonne þat was ylore.   12

Þou ert þe coluere of noe
Þat broute þe braunche of olyue tre,
In tokne þat pays scholde be
    By-tuexte god and manne.   16
Suete leuedy, help þou me,
    Wanne ich schal wende hanne.

Þou art þe bosche of synay,
Þou art þe rytte sarray,   20
Þou hast ybrouȝt ous out of cry
    Of calenge of þe fende.
Þou art crystes oȝene drury,
    And of dauyes kende   24

Þou ert þe slinge, þy sone þe ston,
Þat dauy slange golye op-on;
Þou ert þe ȝerd al of aaron
    Me dreye iseȝ spryngynde.   28
Wyt-nesse at ham euerechon
    Þat wyste of þyne chyldynge.

Þou ert þe temple salomon,   f. 205[a]
In þe wondrede gedeon,   32
Þou hest ygladed symeon
    Wyþ þyne swete offrynge;
In þe temple atte auter-ston
    Wyþ ihesus heuene kynge.   36

Þou ert Iudith, þat fayre wyf,
Þou hast abated al þat stryf ;
Olofernes wyþ hys knyf
    Hys heuede þou hym by-nome.   40
Þou hest ysaued here lef
    Þat to þe wylle come.

Þou ert hester, þat swete þynge,
And asseuer þe ryche kynge   44
Þe heþ ychose to hys weddynge
    And quene he heþ a-uonge ;
For mardocheus, þy derlynge,
    Syre aman was y-honge.   48

Þe prophete ezechyel
In hys boke hyt wytnesseþ wel,
Þou ert þe gate so stronge so stel
    Ac euere y-schet fram manne ;   52
Þou erte þe ryȝte uayre rachel,
    Fayrest of alle wymman.

By ryȝte toknynge þou ert þe hei
Of wan spellede danyel ;   56
Þou ert emaus, þe ryche castel
    Þar resteþ alle werye ;
Ine þe restede emanuel
    Of wan y-spekeþ ysaye.   60

Ine þe hys god by-come a chyld,   f. 205[b]
Ine þe hys wreche by-come myld ;
Þat vnicorn þat was so wyld
    Aleyd hys of a cheaste :   64
Þou hast y-tamed and i-styld
    Wyþ melke of þy breste.

45 þe : MS. þey.   60 MS. wany spekeþ.

Ine þe apocalyps sent Iohn
Iseȝ ane wymman wyþ sonne by-gon,   68
Þane mone al onder hyre ton,
    I-crouned wyþ tuel sterre :
Swyl a leuedy nas neuere non
    Wyþ þane fend to werre.   72

Ase þe sonne takeþ hyre pas
Wyþ-oute breche þorȝ-out þat glas,
Þy maydenhod on-wemmed hyt was
    For bere of þyne chylde.   76
Nou, swete leuedy of solas,
    To ous senfolle be þou mylde !

Haue, leuedy, þys lytel songe
Þat out of senfol herte spronge ;   80
Aȝens þe feend þou make me stronge,
    And ȝyf me þy wyssynge ;
And þaȝ ich habbe y-do þe wrange,
    Þou graunte me amendynge !   84

33.   *An Orison to the Blessed Virgin.*

MS. Arundel 57.

MAyde and moder mylde,   f. 96^b
    uor loue of þine childe
    þet is god an man,
Me þet am zuo wylde   4
uram zenne þou me ssylde
    ase ich þe bydde can.   Amen.

69 MS. mowe.

34.   *The Hours of the Cross.*

Bodl. MS. Miscell. Liturg. 104.

SWete ihesu cryst, goddis sone of lyue,   f. 49ᵃ
   Þin passion, þin croys, þin ded, þin wondes five
Beelde us houre sinful soules in þin iugement,   f. 49ᵇ
Nou and in tyme of ded þat we ne be y-schent.   4
(D)eyne to ȝeue myt an grace to hem þat moten lyuen,
And to dare reste, here sinnes þou for-yyue.
To holi chirche and kyndom, loue and pes þou
    sende,   f. 50ᵃ
And to vs wreche sinful, lif wyt-outen ende,   8
Þat leuest kyng, god and man wyt-outin endingge,
Fader and sone and holy gost to þulke blisse us bringge.

At prime ihesus was y-lad pilatus by-fore,   f. 59ᵃ
Many false witnesse on hym were i-bore,   12
Hiis schines were y-beten, hiis honden weren y-bonden,
Hiis face hy gonne on spete, lyt of heuene þey fonde.

At hondren, ' day on rode!' þe giwes gonne grede: f. 64ᵇ
In schorn he was i-wonden in purpil-palle wede,   16
  .   .   .   .
On his schulder he bar þe crois to þe piningge.

At midday was ihesus crist y-nailed to þe rode,   f. 69ᵃ
Bi-twixe tweye þeues he hongid for houre gode,   20
For y-þurst of stronge pine y-fuld he was wy⟨t⟩
    galle,   f. 69ᵇ
Þe holi louird, so god y-wrout, þer buiȝt houre sinnes
    alle.

At none houre louerd crist of þysse lif he wende: f. 75ᵃ
He gradde, 'hely': þe holi gost to his fader he
    sende.   24

A knyt wit a kene spere þerlede his syde
Þe herþe quakede, þe sonne bi-com swart þat erer schon
    wel wide. **f. 75**[b]

At euensong he was i-nome adoun þat dere us hadde
    ibouȝt, **f. 80**[a]
His mytte, hys stre⟨n⟩gþe, lotede in heiȝe holi þout. 28
    f. 80[b]

Swech deþ he under-feng, hele of alle wo.
Alas! þe croune of worschepe to lowe hy leide þo.

He was y-ȝeue to beryyng ate laste tyde, **f. 88**[a]
Cristes body noble, hope of liue to byde; 32
In-oynt he was wyt aromat, holi writ to fulle;
ȝornful meynde of his deþ bee in myne wille. Amen.

35. *Jesus Have Mercy on Me.*

Merton Coll. Oxford MS. 248.

I Hesu, þat al þis world haþ wroȝt, **f. 66**[b]
    haue merci on me! (col. 1)
ihesu, þat wiþ þi blod vs bouȝt,
ihesu, þat ȝaf vs whanne we adde noȝt, 4
    ihesu, dauid sone! &c.

dauid sone, ful of miȝt
    haue ⟨merci on me⟩!
dauid sone, fair to siȝt, 8
dauid sone, þat mengeþ merci wiþ riȝt,
haue merci on me, & mak me mek to þe,
& mak me þenche on þe, & bring me to þe,
þat longeþ to þe, þat wolde ben at þe, 12
    ihesu ⟨dauid sone⟩! *prosequatur sermo sic.*

28 MS. hys his.

ihesu, þat al þis world ad wroȝt,
dauid sone, ful of myȝt,
haue merci on me!   16
& mak me meke to þe, & *isto modo concludendo prose-*
        quitur sermo.

.   .   .   .

louerd, þou þat foluest me   (col. 2)
wider-ward so i fle,   20
        dauid sone, fair to siȝt,
haue merci on me!
þat ich may habbe meknesse an sorwe of my sinne.
lord, þou þat faȝt for me   24
wan myn enemy folewed me,
        dauid sone, ful of myȝt,
haue merci on me!
þat i may helde my penaunce & stomble naȝt þer-
        inne.   28

Lord, þou þat ȝiuest me
al þat langeþ to me
        dauid sone, þat mengest merci wiþ riȝt,
haue merci on me!   32
& bring me to þe,
þat wolde ben at te,
þat langeþ to þe,
in þi muchel blis þat neuere more shal blinne.   36

36.   *How Christ shall Come.*

Merton Coll. Oxford MS. 248.

I sayh hym wiþ ffless al bi-sprad   He cam vram
                                                Est.   f. 139^b
I sayh hym wiþ blod al by-ssad   He cam vram
                                                West.

I sayh þet manye he wiþ hym brouȝte He cam vram
                                       souȝ.
I sayh þet þe world of hym ne rouȝte He cam vram
                                    north.   4

I come vram þe wedlok as a svete spouse, þet habbe
   my wif wiþ me in-nome.
I come vram viȝt a staleworþe knyȝt, þet myne vo
   habbe ouercome.
I come vram þe chepyng as a Riche chapman, þet
   mankynde habbe ibouȝt.
I Come vram an vncouþe londe as a sely pylegrym, þet
   ferr habbe ·i-souȝt.   8

37.   *Aurora lucis rutilat.*

Merton Coll. Oxford MS. 248.

AN Ernemorwe þe day-liȝt spryngeþ, f. 141ᵇ
  Þe angles in heuene Murye syngeþ,
Þe world is bliþe & ek glad,
Þe uendus of helle beþ sorwuel & mad,   4
Whanne þe kyng godus sone
Þe strengþe of þe deþ hadde ouercome :
Helle dore he brak wiþ his fot,
& out of pyne vs wreches he tok.   8

38.   *O gloriosa domina excelsa.*

Merton Coll. Oxford MS. 248.

LEfdy blisful, of muchel miȝt,   f. 148ᵇ
  Heyere þanne þe sterres liȝt,
Hym þe þe made wumman best
Þou ȝoue hym souken of þi brest.   4

36. 5 MS. habbbe.   37. 1 MS. de.

Þet þet Eue vs hadde by-nome
Þow hast i-ȝolde þorw þy sone.
Þow art in heuene an hole i-mad
Þorw which þe senful þorw-geþ glad ;   8
Þow art þe kynges ȝate idyȝt,
briȝtore þow art þan eny liȝt.
lif þorw Marye vs is i-wrouȝt,
alle ben glade þet crist haþ i-bouȝt.   12

39.   *The Evils of the Time.*

Merton Coll. Oxford MS. 248.

De falsitate

FAlsenesse and couetys er feris,   f. 166ᵇ
  wil neþer oþer be-sweke ;
lewte and pouert ar peris,
Haue þai no rithte in ys rike.   4
ilke man in lande no⟨u⟩ leris
wyt falsedam to pinchyn and pike ;
es þer no man þat þem sterys
bot heuer are vnlawis illyke.   8
falsenes, I vnderstande,
haues dreuen trwvte of lande,
and tort and fort as sworen þar owth
þat law sal lose is ouer-cloþe.   12

De cupiditate

I þinge al day, I þinge of nowth,
of nowth I-set al my thowth ;
nowth of owth brynkis me tyl nowth,
me wor bettyr I thowth yt nowth.   16

De Mundo

hallas ! men planys of litel trwthe ;
hit ys dede and tat is rwthe ;
falsedam regnis and es abowe,
and byrid es trwloue.   20

11 MS. shoren.   16 MS. be wor bertyr.

40. ### *Crux fidelis.*

Merton Coll. Oxford MS. 248.

STeddefast crosse, inmong alle oþer   f. 167ᵃ
  þow art a tre mykel of prise,
in braw⟨n⟩che and flore swyl⟨k⟩ a-noþer
I ne wot non in wode no rys.   4
swete be þe nalys,
and swete be þe tre,
and sweter be þe birdyn þat hangis vppon the!

41. ### *Ave Maris Stella.*

Merton Coll. Oxford MS. 248.

AYl be þow, ster of se!   f. 167ᵃ
  godis moder, blessed þow be
and euer maden haldan⟨d⟩ state,
of hewen þow art þe sely yate.   4
taket an þat ilke gretyn vncowþe
þat þe was sayd of Gabriel mowthe,
settan⟨d⟩ man in pes ful fane,
tornand þe name of heue a-gayne.   8
onely maden þorw godis gast,
of alle wemen meked mast,
vs of syn þow lees in aste,
and make vs boþe mylde and chast.   12
Sew tyl vs þi moder⟨hede⟩;
þow help vs euer at alle ower nede,
þat he þorw þe owre pray⟨er⟩ be-take,
þat [wat] was borne of þe for vrre sake.   16

13 MS. þu.   14 MS. oþer.   15 MS. be-tale.

Gladsum lewedy, mykel of myth,
Raysed a-bowen þe sternys bryth,
he þat þe mad dorw gode for-syth,
he soked ⟨þ⟩yn pappis þat wor ful rith.   20
þat sorwful eue bare away
þow yeldus vs þor⟨w⟩ þi haly birth.
Lat In þe wepan⟨d⟩ as ster of day,
als tow art wyndow of hewen mirth.   24
haly moder, fair and gode,
of ym þat bowth vs wyt is blod,
yate of hewen, ster of se,
þat we ne fall howre help þow be !   28
leche of folke, mary myld,
wyt ferly kynd þow bare þi chyld,
maden was and euer sal be,
has þe angel tald to þe   32
wen he gret the wyþe aue mari.
of synful man þow haue mercy !

42.   *Lady Fortune and her Wheel.*

Camb. Univ. MS. Oo. 7. 32.

P E leuedi fortune is boþe frend and fo,
  Of pore che makit riche, of riche pore also,
Che turneȝ wo al into wele, and wele al into wo,
No triste no man to þis wele, þe whel it turnet so.   4

43.   *All is Phantom.*

Camb. Univ. MS. Ee. 1. 5.

A L it is fantam þat we mid fare,   f. 2*b
  Naked and poure henne we shul fare,
Al shal ben oþer mannes þat we fore care,
But þat we don for godes loue haue we no mare. 4

20 MS. patpis.   22 MS. brith.
25 MS. maden.   30 MS. chyle.

44.   *Veni Creator Spiritus.*

MS. Bodley 425.   f. 93ᵃ

CVm, maker of gaste þou ert,   *ueni creator*
Þouhtes of þine þou seke and hert,
Of heiest hape fulfill in quert,
Þe brestes þat þou make gert.   4

Whilk þou art saide maker of gle,   *Qui paraclitus*
Gaste of god heiest is he,
Welle quic, fire, and charite
And gosteli seruise þe best mai be.   8

Þou seuen fold of gifte þat isse,   *Tu septifor.*
Of god righthand þou finger is,
Þou righwis hote of fadir blis,
richand þrotes with worde þou wisse.   12

Kynde⟨l⟩ liht in wittes for to wende,   *Accende*
In-yiet loue in hertes hende,
Þe vnmigh of oure bodi [oure] þou mende
. . . . festenand   16

a-wai þou fleme oure fo,   *Hostem*
and pais þou gif vs sone als so ;
þe leder so be-fore to go,
þar dering alle we fle þer-fro.   20

þe fadir gif we with þorou þe,   *Per te sciamus*
and knowe þe sone als so þe se,
þe hali gaste of lyþe wil be—
In al time we trowe þise tre.   ⎰   24

3 MS. fulfild.   12 MS. righthand.   13 MS. lik ; MS. wittenes.

Whilum ful mani a haleghed brest   *Dudum sacra.*
With þi hape þou fild and fest ;
for-giue þi sinnes, þat is best,
And times giue of ro and rest.   f. 93^b   28

To þe fadir an te sonne be louyng maste,   *Sit laus*
and to þe holi ronere with chaste ;
Til vs þe sune he sende on haste
Giftes of þe holi gaste.   32

45.   *Ave Maris Stella.*

MS. Bodley 425.

Ave Maris stella dei mater alma.

HEile ! sterne on þe se so bright,   f. 93^b
   To godes holi modir dight,
and euer maiden made of miht,
þat seli yate of heuen is bright.   4

Takand and hailsand was þou faine,   *Sumens illud*
Thurght gabrols mough and maine ;
In pais þou put vs out of paine,
Turnand þe name of eue againe.   8

Vnles bandes of sinful kinde,   *Solue vincula*
Þou bring forth liht vn-to þe blind,
Oure iuels put þou alle bi-hinde,
Alkine gode þat ve mowe finde.   12

Show þe for modir als tou is,   *Monstra te*
Oure preiere take þe þorou þi blis ;
He þat for vs and for oure mis
be-come þi sone, þou moder his.   16

Onely maiden and no mo,   *Virgo singularis*
A-mang vs all so meke to go,
Vs of sake lese of wo,
Meke þou make and chaste als so.   20

Clene lif in land vs lene,   *Vitam presta*
and seker gate vs graȝe be-dene,
Þat we Ihesu seand so shene,
Euer faine we vs be-twene.   24

To god fadir be louyng,   *Sit laus*
til holi crist wurschipe als kyng,
Þe holi gost wold of hem spring—
Þise þre haue oure wurcheping.   Amen.   28

46.   *Abide, Ye Who Pass By.*

MS. Rawlinson poet. 175.

Abyde, gud men, & hald yhour pays   f. 80ᵃ
  And here what god him-seluen says,
   Hyngand on þe rode.
Man & woman þat bi me gase,   4
Luke vp to me & stynt þi pase,
   For þe I sched my blode.

Be-hald my body or þou gang,
And think opon my payns strang,   8
   And styll als stane þou stand.
Bihald þi self þe soth, & se
How I am hynged here on þis tre
   And nayled fute & hand.   12

20 MS. made.

Behald my heued, bi-hald my fete,
And of m⟨a⟩ mysdedes luke þou lete;
   Behald my grysely face
And of þi syns ask aleggance,
And in my mercy haue affyance   16
   And þou sall gett my grace.
      Explicit.

47. '*How Crist Spekes tyll Synfull Man of His Gret Mercy.*'

MS. Rawlinson poet. 175.

M An, þus on rode I hyng for þe,   f. 93ᵇ
   For-sake þi syn for luf of me,
   Sen I swilk luf þe bede;
Man, I luf þe ouer all thing,   4
And for þi luf þus wald I hyng,
   My blyssed blode to blede.

Man, full dere I haue þe boght;
How es it so þou lufes me noght?   8
   Vnkyndely dose þou þare;
If þou will luf vnto me schaw
For my brother I will þe knaw.
   What may I do þe mare?   12

If þou be mast synfull man
Þat euer in world on erth ran,
   And þou will knaw þi state
And sadly seke to my mercy,   16
Þe to resayue I am redy
   Euer arely & late.

Of all þi mysdedes luke þou blyn,
Mare es my mercy þan þi syn ;   20
    þou call mercy with hert.
Ask mercy & þou sall haue,
And fra þe fende I sall þe saue,
    And fra his payns smert.   24

In my mercy dispaire þou noght,
Sen I þe so dere haue boght,
    And ensaumple þou take
Of synfull Mary maudelayne,   28
þat with syn was gastly slayne
    And sythen gan it for-sake.

All-so ensaumple may þou luke
Of saint Peter þat me for-soke   32
    And sythen rewed it sare.
Mercy had þai sone of me ;
Man þe same I will do þe
    þarfor lete at my lare.   36

48.   *The Sweetness of Jesus.*

MS. Rawlinson poet. **175.**

A Ihesu, þi swetnes wha may it se   f. 93[b]
    And þarof haue a clere langyng,
All erthly lust bytter sall be
Bot þine allane withouten lesyng.   4
I pray þe, lord, þat lare lere me
After þi luf to haue langyng,
And sadly sett my hert on þe
And of þi luf to haue lykyng.   8

Swa lykand luf in hert nane is,
In saule wha couth him sadly se,
Him to luf war mykell blys,
For kyng of luf cald es he ;   12
With trew luf I wald I-wys
So fast to him bonden be,
Þat my hert war halely hys,
Þat other luf nane lyked me.   16

If I for kyndnes suld luf my kyn,
Þan me think in my thoght
Be kyndely skyll I suld be-gyn
At him þat has me made of noght.   20
His sembland he sett my saule within
And þis world for me he wroght,
Als fader of fude my luf to wyn
Herytage in heuen he has me boght.   24

As moder of him I may mak mynde
Þat be-for my byrth to me ⟨toke⟩ hyed,
And sithen with baptym wesched þe strynd
Þat fyled was wyth Adam dede.   28
With noble mete he norysched my kynde,
For with his flessch he dyd me fede ;
A better fode may na man fynde,
For to lastand lyf it will vs lede.   32

Brother & syster he es by skyll,
For he sayd & lered þare lare,
Þat who-so wroght his fader will
Brother & syster to him þai ware.   36
My kynd all swa he toke þare tyll ;
Full trewly in him I trayst þarfore
Þat he will neuer lat me spyll,
Bot with his mercy salue my sare.   40

Bot oft þis passes I-wys
All erthly luf þat may be here ;
God & man my spouse is—
Wele aght me, wryche, to luf him dere— 44
Both heuen & erth halely es hys, f. 94ᵃ
He es a prynce of gret powere, (col. 1)
And cald he es þe kyng of blys ;
His luf me langes full sare to lere. 48

After his luf me bihoues lang,
For he has me full dere boght ;
When I was went fra him with wrang,
Fro heuen to erth here he me soght ; 52
My wrecched kynde for me he fang,
And all his noblelay he sett at noght ;
Pouert he sufferd and payns strang,
To blys ogayne or he me broght. 56

When I was thrall to mak me fre,
My luf fra heuen tyll erth him led ;
Mi luf all-ane haue wald he,
Þarfore he layd his luf in wed ; 60
With my fa he faght for me,
Wounded he was & bitterly bled ;
His precyouse blode full gret plente,
Full petefully for me was sched. 64

His sydes full bla & blody were,
Þat som tyme war full bryght of ble ;
His hert was perched with a spere,
His rewfull woundes was rewth to se ; 68
My raunsoune I-wys he payd þare,
And gaf his lyf for gylt of me ;
His ded burd to me be dere,
And perche my hert for pore pete. 72

For pete my hert burd brek in twa,
Till his kyndenes if I toke hede ;
Enchesoun I was of his wa,
He sufferd full hard for my mysdede ;   76
Till lastand lyf for I suld ga,
Þe ded he tholed in his manhede ;
When his will was, to lyf all-sa
He rayse ogayne thurgh his godhede.   80

To heuen he went with mykell blys,
When he had ouercomen his batail ;
His baner full brade dysplaid is,
When so my fa will me assail ;   84
Wele aght my hert to be hys,
For he es þat frende þat neuer will fail ;
And no thing will he haue I-wys,
Bot trewluf for his trauail.   88

Þus wald my spouse for me fyght,   (col. 2)
And wounded for me he was full sare ;
For my luf his ded was dyght,
What kyndenes myght he do me mare ?   92
To yheld him his luf haue I no myght,
Bot luf him lely I suld þarfore,
And wirk his will with wordes ryght,
Þat he lered with lufly lare.   96

His lufly lare with hert full fyll
Wele aght me wirk if I war kynde,
Night & day to do his will
And euermare haue him in mynde ;   100
Bot gastly faes greues me yll,
And my frele flesch makes me blynd ;
Þarfor his mercy I tak me tyll,
For better bote I kan none fynd.   104

102 frele : MS. frely

Better bote es nane to me
Bot to his mercy trewly me take
Þat with his blode boght me fre,
And me, wryche, his (spouse) wald make.　108
I pray þat lord for his pete
For my syn noght me forsake,
Bot gyf me grace my syn to fle,
And in his luf lat me neuer slake.　112

A Ihesu, for þe swetnes þat in þe is,
Haue mercy o me whare I wende,
Þat stedfast trowth my wittes wys
And defend me fra þe fende.　116
For þi mercy forgyf me my mys
Þat wicked werkes my saule noght schende,
Bot bryng me lord vnto þi blys,
With þe to won withouten ende.　120

　　A – M – E – N.

49.　*All Other Love is like the Moon.*

Eton College MS. 36, Part II.

AL oþer loue is lych þe mone　　f. 103ᵃ
　　þat wext and wanet as flour in plein,
as flour þat fayret and fawyt sone,
as day þat scwret and endt in rein.　4

Al oþer loue bigint bi blisse,
in wep and wo mak is hendyng:
no loue þer nis þat oure halle lysse,
(bot) wat areste in evene kyng,　8

Wos loue ys . . . & eure grene,
and eure ful wyth-oute wanyyng;
is loue suetyth wyth-oute tene,
is loue is hendles and a-ring.　12

　　9 A word missing; no gap in MS.

Al oþer loue y flo for þe ;
tel me, tel me, wer þou lyst ?
' In marie mylde an fre
i schal be founde, ak mor in crist.'   16

Crist me founde, nouht y þe, hast :
hald me to þe wiht al þi meyn ;
help geld þat mi loue be ste⟨d⟩fast,
lest þus sone it turne ageyn.   20

Wan nov hy⟨e⟩t myn hert is sor,
y-wys hie spilt myn herte blod :
god canne mi lef, y care na mor—
hyet y hoppe hys wil be god.   24

Allas! what wole y a Rome?
seye y may in lore of loue,
' vndo y am by manne dome
bot he me help þat syt a-boue.'   28

50.   *The Tower of Heaven.*

Advocates Lib. 18. 8. 1.

EUen, it es a richȝ ture—   f. 199^b
    wele bies im þat itte may win—
of Mirthes ma þan ert may think
and þa ioís sal neuer blin.   4
Sinful man, bot þu þe mend
and for-sak þin wikkid sin,
þu mon singge hay, ' wailaway ! '
for comes þu neuer mare þar-I⟨nne⟩.   8

Christ's Appeal to Man.

MS. Harley 2316.

M En rent me on rode f. 25^a
wiht wndes woliche wode,
al blet mi blode—
thenk, man, al it is ȝe to gode. 4

Thenk who ȝe first wroȝhte
for what werk helle ȝow sowhte ;
Thenk who ȝe ageyn bowhte—
werk warli, fayle me nowhte. 8

Biheld mi side,
mi wndes sprede so wide,
Rest-les i ride.
lok up on me ! put fro ȝe pride. 12

Mi palefrey is of tre,
wiht nayles naylede ȝwrh me.
Ne is more sorwe to se—
certes noon more no may be. 16

vnder mi gore
ben wndes selcowȝe sore.
Ler, man, mi lore ;
for mi loue sinne no more. 20

Fal nowht for fonding,
ȝat schal ȝe most turne to goode ;
Mak stif wiht-stonding—
thenk wel who me rente on ȝe rode. 24

19 MS. Der.

52.   *A Prayer of the Five Wounds.*

MS. Harley 2316.

IHesu cryst, myn leman swete,   f. 25[a]
  ȝat for me deye-des on rode tre,
Wiht al myn herte i ȝe bi-seke
for ȝi wndes to and thre,   4
ȝat al so faste in myn herte
ȝi loue roted mute be,
as was ȝe spere in-to ȝi side,
whan ȝow suffredis ded for me.   8

53.   *The Vanity of Life.*

MS. Harley 2316.

KYndeli is now mi coming   f. 25[a]
  in to ȝis ⟨werld⟩ wiht teres and cry ;
Litel and pouere is myn hauing,
briȝel and sone i-falle from hi ;   4
Scharp and strong is mi deying,
i ne woth whider schal i ;
Fowl and stinkande is mi roting—
on me, ihesu, ȝow haue mercy !   8

54.   *The Sinner's Lament.*

MS. Harley 2316.

GOd wiht hise aungeles i haue for-loren,   f. 25[b]
  Allas ! ȝe while ȝat i was boren.

To sorwe and pine i bringe at eende
Man ȝat me louet, i schal him schende.   4

To ȝe fend i owe fewte,
Truage, homage, and gret lewte.

55.   *The Hours of the Cross.*

Advocates Lib. 18. 7. 21.

Hora matutinalis

A T þe time of matines, lord, þu were i-take,   f. 2^b
& of þine disciples sone were for-sake ;
Þe felle Iewes þe token in þat iche stounde,
& ledden þe to Cayphas, þin handis harde i-
    bounde   4

  We onuren þe crist & blissen þe with voys,
  For þu boutest þis werd with þin holi
    croys.

Hora prima

At prime, lord, þu were i-lad Pilat be-forn,
& þere wol fals witnesse on þe was i-born ;   8
He smiten þe vnder þe ere & seiden, ' wo was
    tat ? '
Of hem þi faire face foule was be-spat

Hora tercia

At vnderne, lord, þei gunnen þe to crucifiȝe,
& cloþeden þe in pourpre in skoren & in
    enuyȝe ;   12
With wol kene þornes i-corouned þu were,
& on þi sulder to þi peines þin holi croys þu
    bere.

Meridies

At middai, lord, þu were nailed to þe rode,
Be-twixen tweyȝe theues i-hanged al on
    blode ;   16
For þi pine þu wexe a-þrist & seidest, ' *sicio* '.
Galle & Eysil þei ȝeuen þe to drinken þo

Hora
nona

At þe heyȝe non, lord, þu toke þi leue,
& into þi fader hond þe holigost þu ȝeue ;   20
Longis þe knith a sarp spere al to þin herte
        pithte ;
Þe herde quakede & tremlede, þe sunne les
        hire lithte.

Hora
vesper-
tina

Of þe rode he was i-don at þe time of euesong,
Mildeliche & stille he suffrede al here wrong; 24
Suich a detȝ he vnderfeng þat vs helpen may.
Allas ! þe crune of ioyȝe vnder þornes lay.

[Comple-
torium]

At cumplin time he was i-biriȝed, & in a ston
        i-pith
Ihesu cristes swete bodi, & so seit holi
        writh,   28
Enoint with an oniment ; & þan was cum-
        pliȝed
Þat be-forn of ihesu crist was i-propheciȝed.

Þis iche holi orisoun of þi passioun
I þenke to þe, ihesu crist, with deuocioun ; 32
Þat þu, þat suffredest for me harde piningge,
Be my solas & my confort at my last end-
        ingge.   Amen.

56. *Dialogue between the B. V. and her Child.*

Advocates Lib. 18. 7. 21.

Lullay, lullay, la lullay, Mi dere moder, lullay.   f. 3ᵇ

Als i lay vp-on a nith
    Alone in my longging,
Me þouthe i sau a wonder sith,
A maiden child rokking.   4

þe maiden wolde with-outen song
Hire child o slepe bringge ;
þe child þouthte sche de⟨de⟩ him wrong,
& bad his moder sengge.   8

' Sing nov, moder,' seide þat child,
' Wat me sal be-falle
Here after wan i cum to eld—
So don modres alle.   12

Ich a moder treuly
þat kan hire credel kepe
Is wone to lullen louely
& singgen hire child o slepe.   16

Suete moder, fair & fre,
Siþen þat it is so,
I preye þe þat þu lulle me
& sing sum-wat þer-to.'   20

' Suete sone,' seyde sche,
' Wer-offe suld i singge ?
Wist i neuere ȝet more of þe
But gabrieles gretingge.   24

He grette me godli on is kne
& seide, " heil ! marie.
Ful of grace, god is with þe ;
Beren þu salt Messye."   28

I wondrede michil in my þouth,
for man wold i rith none.
" Marie," he seide, " drede þe nouth ;
Lat god of heuene alone.   32

þe holi gost sal don al þis."
He seyde with-outen wone
þat i sulde beren mannis blis,
þe my suete sone.   36

He seide, " þu salt beren a king
In king dauit-is see,
In al Iacobs woniing
þer king suld he be."   40

He seyde þat elizabetȝ,
þat baraine was be-fore,
A child conceyued hatȝ—
" To me leue þu þe more."   44

I ansuerede bleþely,
For his word me paiȝede :
" Lo ! godis seruant her am i !
Be et as þu me seyde."   48

þer, als he seide, i þe bare
On midwenter nith,
In maydened with-outen kare,
Be grace of god almith.   52

þe sepperdis þat wakkeden in þe wolde
Herden a wonder mirthe
Of angles þer, as þei tolde,
In time of þi birthe.   56

Suete sone, sikirly
no more kan i say ;
& if i koude fawen wold i,
To don al at þi pay.'   60

' Moder,' seide þat suete þing,   (col. 2)
' To singen I sal þe lere
Wat me fallet to suffring,
& don wil i am here.   64

Wanne þe seuene daiȝes ben don,
Rith as habraham wasce,
Kot sal i ben with a ston
In a wol tendre place.   68

55 MS. þᵗ as.

Wanne þe tuelue dayȝes ben do,
Be leding of a stere
Þre kingges me sul seke þo
With gold, ensens, & mirre.   72

Þe fourti day, to fille þe lawe,
We solen to temple i-fere ;
Þer simeon sal þe sey a sawe
Þat changen sal þi chere.   76

Wan i am tuelue ȝer of elde,
Ioseph & þu, murningge,
Solen me finden, moder milde,
In þe temple techingge.   80

Til i be þretti at þe leste
I sal neuere fro þe suerue,
But ay, moder, ben at þin heste,
Ioseph & þe to serue.   84

Wan þe þretti ȝer ben spent,
I mot be-ginne to fille
Wer-fore i am hidre sent,
Þoru my fadres wille.   88

Ion baptist of merite most
Sal baptize me be name ;
Þan my fader & þe holi gost
Solen witnessen wat i ame.   92

I sal ben tempted of satan,   f. 4^b
Þat fawen is to fonde,
Þe same wise þat was Adam,
but i sal betre with-stonde.   96

Disciples i sal gadere
& senden hem for to preche,
Þe lawes of my fader,
In al þis werld to teche.   100

82 MS. sterue.

I sal ben so simple
& to men so conning
Þat most partiȝe of þe puple
Sal wiln maken me king.'   104

'Suete sone,' þan seyde sche,
'No sorwe sulde me dere,
Miht i ȝet þat day se
A king þat þu were.'   108

'Do wey, moder,' seide þat suete,
'Þerfor kam i nouth,
But for to ben pore & bales bete,
Þat man was inne brouth.   112

Þerfore wan to & þretti ȝer ben do⟨n⟩
& a litel more,
Moder, þu salt maken michil mon
& seen me deyȝe sore.   116

Þe sarpe swerde of simeon
Perse sal þin herte,
For my care of michil won
Sore þe sal smerte.   120

Samfuly for i sal deyȝe,
Hangende on þe rode,
For mannis ransoun sal i payȝe
Myn owen herte blode.'   124

'Allas! sone,' seyde þat may,   (col. 2)
'Siþen þat it is so,
Worto sal i biden þat day
To beren þe to þis wo?'   128

'Moder,' he seide, 'tak et lithte,
For liuen i sal a-ȝeyne,
& in þi kinde þoru my mith,
for elles i wrouthte in weyne.   132

To my fader I sal wende
In myn manhed to heuene ;
Þe holigost i sal þe sende
With hise sondes seuene.   136

I sal þe taken wan time is
to me at þe laste,
to ben with me moder in blis—
Al þis þan haue i caste.   140

Al þis werld demen i sal,
at þe dom risingge,
Suete moder, here is al
Þat i wile nou singge.'   144

Serteynly, þis sithte i say,
Þis song i herde singge,
Als i lay þis ȝolis-day
Alone in my longingge.   148

57.   A Song of the Nativity.

Advocates Lib. 18. 7. 21.

IN bedlem is a child i-born   f. 4^b
   sal comen a-mongus vs,
He's comun to sauen þat was lorn—
His name is ihesus.   4

For we were put in pine strong,
God hadde on vs pite,
His sone vs hat sent among,
Oure broþer for to be.   8

Wan gabriel hire grete gan   f. 5^a
& seyde sche was with childe,
Þe mayden wondrede of þat þan
As sche was meke & milde.   12

' *Ecce ancilla domini*,'
þat was hire ansuere,
' Wolde god i were worþi
His blisful sone to bere.'   16

He lithtede in þat loueli þing
for lounesse of hire lif;
þe prophetis spekin of is coming,
þat reson was wol rif.   20

Wol loweliche þat lord gan lithte
þou he were comen of kenne;
In pouerte þat prince him pitthe
to ben born in a bynne.   24

þis ensample he hat vs brouth
to liuen in lounesse,
& pride to putten out of oure þouth,
þat brout vs in bitternesse.   28

þe angel⟨s⟩ songin a mirie song,
þat sepperdis mithten it here:
' Crist is comen vs among
Of loue vs for to lere.'   32

' *Gloria in excelsis deo*,'
For þei songen þus,
' *& in terra*,' þei songen al so,
' With *pax hominibus*.'   36

Ioyȝe to god þat is abouen,
þat is to vnderstonde,
& pes to men þat pes louen
þoru-out eueri londe.   40

þei stoden & stareden after þe sterre   (col. 2)
þat lemede ful lithte;
þre kingges comen with gold & mirre,
þider þei riden ful rithte.   44

Þei riden þoru heroudis rengne
To maken here offringge ;
Heroudis bad hem comen ageyne,
& tellen him newe tidingge.   48

An angel on hey to hem was sent
to techen hem a-noþer weyȝe ;
for hadden þei be heroudis went,
Þei ,hadden al ben damnith to deyȝe.   52

Heroudis with hem hadde enuyȝe
Þat suich on sulde ben born ;
Alle Innocens he dede distruyȝe,
for cristis ded he hadde suorn.   56

An angel on hey to hem was sent
to wenden out of is weyȝe ;
& to egipte sche þider went,
Hire sone to sauen, i seyȝe.   60

Þus he fulfillede hem among
Þretti & þrid half ȝer ;
Siþen, loueliche as a lomb,
He put himself in here puwer.   64

Þe Iewes spoken of ihesus
& dampned him for to deyȝe ;
Þat sorwe suffrede he for vs
Oure blisse for to byȝe.   68

Þe wrechis him wroutten michil wo—
Al suffred he for oure sake—
To caluari þei kechin him þo,
His detȝ he bar on is bake.   72

No wonder was þou hire was wo,   f. 5ᵇ
Sche sau hire ferli fode,
His blisful bodi blodi an blo,
Wol reuli rent on þe rode.   76

Prei we alle þat precious þing,
Of þraldom þat mad us fre—
Wif, mayden, & moder so ying,
Was neuere non but sche.   Amen.   80

58. *A Song of the Blessed Virgin and Joseph.*

Advocates Lib. 18. 7. 21.

ALs i lay vp-on a nith   f. 5^b
I lokede vp-on a stronde,
I be-held a mayden brith,
a child sche hadde in honde.   4

Hire loking was so loueli,
Hire semblant was so suete,
Of al my sorwe sikerli
Sche mithte my bales bete.   8

I wondrede of þat suete with,
& to my self i sayde,
Sche hadde don mankindde vnrith,
but ȝif sche were a mayde.   12

Be hire sat a sergant
þat sadli seide his sawe,
He sempte be is semblant
a man of þe elde lawe.   16

His her was hor on heuede,
His ble be-gan to glide,
He herde wel wat i seyde,
& bad me faire abide.   20

' Þu wondrest,' he seyde, 'skilfuli
On þing þu hast be-holde,
& i dede so treuli
Til tales weren me tolde.   24

Hou a womman sulde ben þan,   (col. 2)
Moder an maiden þore ;
& with-outen wem of man
þe child sulde ben bore.   28

Al-þou i vnworþi be
Sche is marie, my wif ;
God wot sche hadde neuere child be me—
I loue hire as my lif.   32

But or euere wiste i
Hire wombe be-gan to rise ;
I telle þe treuthe treuli,
In wot neuere in wat wyse.   36

I troste to hire goodnesse,
Sche wolde no þing mis-do ;
I wot et wel i-wisse,
For i haue founden et so,   40

Þat raþere a maiden sulde
With-outen man conceyue,
Þan marie mis-don wolde
& so Ioseph deceyue.   44

Þe child þat lith so poreli
In cloutes al be-went
& bounden so misesli—
fro heuene he is i-sent.   48

His fader is king of heuene,
& so seide gabriel,
To wam þat child is euene,
O emanuel.'   52

But þis child þat i sau þan,
& as Ioseph seyde,
I wot þe child is god & man
& is moder mayde.   56

I þankid him of his lore
With al myn herte mith,
Þat þis sith i sau þore
　　Als i lay on a nyth.　　　　　　　　60

Þis child þanne worchipe we　　　　f. 6ᵃ
Boþe day an nith,
Þat we moun his face se
　　In ioyʒe þat is so lith.　　Amen.　　64

59. *Christ weeps in the Cradle for Man's Sin.*

Advocates Lib. 18. 7. 21.

Lullay, lullay, litel child, qui wepest þu so sore?

LUllay, lullay, litel child,　　　　　f. 6ᵃ
　　Þu þat were so sterne & wild,
Nou art be-come meke & mild,
　　To sauen þat was for-lore.　　　　4

But for my senne i wot it is
Þat godis sone suffret þis;
Merci lord! i haue do mis,
　　I-wis i wile no more.　　　　　　8

Aʒenis my fadris wille i ches
An appel with a reuful res;
Werfore myn heritage i les,
　　& nou þu wepist þer-fore.　　　　12

An appel i tok of a tre,
God it hadde for-boden me;
Werfore i sulde dampned be,
　　ʒef þi weping ne wore.　　　　　16

Lullay for wo, þu litel þing,
Þu litel barun, þu litel king;
Mankindde is cause of þi murning,
　　Þat þu hast loued so ʒore.　　　20

For man þat þu hast ay loued so
ȝet saltu suffren peines mo,
In heued, in feet, in hondis to,
     & ȝet wepen wel more.   24

Þat peine vs make of senne fre,
Þat peine vs bringge ihesu to þe,
Þat peine vs helpe ay to fle,
     Þe wikkede fendes lore.   Amen.   28

60. *The Blessed Virgin's Appeal to the Jews.*

Advocates Lib. 18. 7. 21.

WY haue ȝe no reuthe on my child?   f. 24ᵘ
    Haue reuthe on me ful of murni⟨n⟩g,
Taket doun on rode my derworþi child,
Or prek me on rode with my derling.   4

More pine ne may me ben don
Þan laten me liuen in sorwe & schame ;
Als loue me bindet to my sone,
so lat vs deyȝen boþen i-same.   8

61.   *A Song of Mercy.*

Advocates Lib. 18. 7. 21.

MErci abid an loke al day,   f. 85ᵃ
   Wan man fro senne wil wende awey.
ȝef senne ne were, merci ne were non ;
ȝef merci be cald, he comet a-non ;   4
Merci is redi þer senne is mest,
& merci is lattest þer senne is lest.
Lord, ȝef me grace my senne to se,
Þat nith & day I mov hem fle,   8
& comen to þat iche blisse to,
Þat euere sal lesten with-outen wo.   Amen,

62.   *Christ's Prayer in Gethsemane.*

Advocates Lib. 18. 7. 21.

A Sory beuerech it is & sore it is a-bouth   f. 119ᵇ
    Nou in þis sarpe time þis brewing hat me brouth
fader, if it mowe ben don als i haue be-south,
Do awey þis beuerich, þat i ne drink et nouth.   4

& if it mowe no betre ben, for alle mannis gilth,
Þat it ne muste nede þat my blod be spilth,
Suete fader, i am þi sone, þi wil be ful-filt!
I am her þin owen child, I wil don as þu wilt.   8

63.   *Jesus, Man's Champion.*

Advocates Lib. 18. 7. 21.

I Am iesu, þat cum to fith   f. 119ᵇ
    With-outen seld & spere,
Elles were þi det i-dith
ȝif mi fithting ne were.   4
Siþen i am comen & haue þe broth
A blisful bote of bale,
Vndo þin herte, tel me þi þouth,
Þi sennes grete an smale.   8

64.   *Lamentacio dolorosa.*

Advocates Lib. 18. 7. 21.

S Uete sone, reu on me, & brest out of þi bon-
      dis;   f. 120ᵃ
For nou me þinket þat i se, þoru boþen þin hondes,
Nailes dreuen in-to þe tre, so reufuliche þu honge⟨s⟩.
Nu is betre þat i fle & lete alle þese londis.   4

Suete sone, þi faire face droppet al on blode,
& þi bodi dounward is bounden to þe rode ;
Hou may þi modris herte þolen so suete a fode,
Þat blissed was of alle born & best of alle gode !   8

Suete sone, reu on me & bring me out of þis liue,
for me þinket þat i se þi detȝ, it neyhit suiþe ;
Þi feet ben nailed to þe tre—nou may i no more þriue,
Foɪ al þis werd with-outen þe ne sal me maken bliþe.   12

65.   *A Lullaby to Christ in the Cradle.*

Advocates Lib. 18. 7. 21.

Lullay, lullay litel child, child reste þe a þrowe, f. 120ᵃ
Fro heyȝe hider art þu sent with us to wone lowe ;
Pore & litel art þu mad, vnkut & vnknowe,
Pine an wo to suffren her for þing þat was þin owe.   4
    Lullay, l⟨ullay⟩ litel child, sorwe mauth þu make ;
    Þu art sent in-to þis werd, as tu were for-sake.

Lullay, l⟨ullay⟩ litel grom, king of alle þingge,   7
Wan i þenke of þi methchef me listet wol litel singge ;
But caren i may for sorwe, ȝef loue wer in myn herte,
For suiche peines as þu salt driȝen were neuere non so
        smerte.
    Lullay, l⟨ullay⟩ litel child, wel mauth þu criȝe,
    For þan þi bodi is bleyk & blak, sone after sal
        ben driȝe.   12

Child, it is a weping dale þat þu art comen inne, f. 120ᵇ
Þi pore clutes it prouen wel, þi bed mad in þe binne ;
Cold & hunger þu must þolen as þu were geten in
        senne,
& after deyȝen on þe tre for loue of al man-kenne.   16
    Lullay, l⟨ullay⟩ litel child, no wonder þou þu care,
    Þu art comen amonges hem þat þi detȝ sulen ȝare.

Lullay, l⟨ullay⟩ litel child, for sorwe mauth þu grete,
þe anguis þat þu suffren salth sal don þe blod to suete;
Naked, bunden saltu ben, & seiþen sore bete,⁣   21
No þing fre vp-on þi bodi of pine sal be lete.
  Lullai, l⟨ullay⟩ litel child, it is al for þi fo,
   þe harde bond of loue longging þat þe hat bun-
    den so.⁣   24

Lullay, l⟨ullay⟩ litel child, litel child þin ore!
It is al for oure owen gilt þat þu art peined sore;
but wolde we ȝet kinde be, & liuen after þi lore,
& leten senne for þi loue, ne keptest þu no more.⁣   28
  Lullay, l⟨ullay⟩ litel child, softe slep & faste,
   In sorwe endet eueri loue but þin at þe laste.
            Amen.

66. *Christ's Love-song to Man.*

Advocates Lib. 18. 7. 21.

L Oue me brouthte,   f. 121ᵃ
 & loue me wrouthte,
Man, to be þi fere.
Loue me fedde,   4
& loue me ledde,
& loue me lettet here.

Loue me slou,
& loue me drou,   8
& loue me leyde on bere.
Loue is my pes,
For loue i ches,
Man to byȝen dere.   12

Ne dred þe nouth,
I haue þe south,
Boþen day & nith,
to hauen þe,   16
Wel is me,
I haue þe wonnen in fith.

67. *Dialogue between Jesus and the B. V. at the Cross.*

Advocates Lib. 18. 7. 21.

Ihesus

M Aiden & moder, cum & se,   f. 121[a]
    þi child is nailed to a tre;   (col. 2)
hand & fot he may nouth go,
his bodi is wonden al in wo.   4
Al abouten he is to-toren,
his heued is wreþen with a þorn,
his sides boþen on blode be,
with blod he's blent, he may nouth se.   8

Maria

Mi suete sone þat art me dere,
Wat hast þu don, qui art þu here?
þi suete bodi þat in me rest,
þat loueli mouth þat i haue kist,—   12
Nou is on rode mad þi nest.
Mi dere child, quat is me best?

Ihesus

Ion, þis womman for my sake,
Womman, to Ion, I þe be-take.   16
Alone i am with-oten make,
On rode i hange for mannis sake,
þis gamen alone me must pleyȝe,
For mannis soule þis det to deyȝe.   20
Mi blod is sched, my fles is falle,
Me þristet sore, for drink i calle:
þei ȝeuen me eysil medlid with galle.
For mannis senne in wo i walle,   24
ȝef þei weren kende to louen me outh,
Of al my peine me ne routh.

Fader, my soule I þe be-take!
Mi bodi deyȝet for mannis sake,   28
Senful soules in helle lake—
To hem i go awey to take.
Mannis soule, þu art my make;
Loue me wel, I þe nouth for-sake,   32
& my moder herteliche
For sche helpet þe stedfas⟨t⟩liche,
An þu salt comen þat blisse to,
Þer my fader is for euermo.   Amen.   36

68.   *Ecce sto ad hostium et pulso.*

Advocates Lib. 18. 7. 21.

VNdo þi dore, my spuse dere,   f. ⅃121ᵇ
    Allas! wy stond i loken out here?
    fre am i þi make.

Loke mi lokkes & ek myn heued   4
& al my bodi with blod be-weued
    For þi sake.

Allas! allas! heuel haue i sped,
For senne iesu is fro me fled,   8
    Mi trewe fere.
With-outen my gate he stant alone,
Sorfuliche he maket his mone
    On his manere.   12

Lord, for senne i sike sore,
Forȝef & i ne wil no more,
With al my mith senne i forsake,
& opne myn herte þe inne to take.   16
For þin herte is clouen oure loue to kecchen,
Þi loue is chosen vs alle to fecchen;
Min herte it þerlede ȝef i wer kende,
Þi suete loue to hauen in mende.   20
Perce myn herte with þi louengge,
Þat in þe i haue my duellingge.   Amen.

69. *Lovely Tear from Lovely Eye.*

Advocates Lib. 18. 7. 21.

Lu⟨u⟩eli ter of loueli eyȝe, qui dostu me so wo ?   f. 124ᵇ
Sorful ter of sorful eyȝe, þu brekst myn herte a-to.

Þᴜ sikest sore,
  Þi sorwe is more
Þan mannis muth may telle ;
Þu singest of sorwe,   4
Manken to borwe
Out of þe pit of helle.   Luueli &c.

I prud & kene,
Þu meke an clene,   8
With-outen wo or wile ;
Þu art ded for me,
& i liue þoru þe,
So blissed be þat wile.   Luueli &c. 12

Þi moder seet   (col. 2)
Hou wo þe beet,
& þerfore ȝerne sche ȝepte ;
To hire þu speke,   16
Hire sorwe to sleke—
Suet sute wan þin herte.   Luueli &c.

Þin herte is rent,
Þi bodi is bent,   20
Vp-on þe rode tre ;
Þe weder is went,
Þe deuel is schent,
Crist, þoru þe mith of þe.   Luueli &c. 24

18 MS. Suet suet.

70.   *Homo vide quid pro te patior.*

Advocates Lib. 18. 7. 21.

S Enful man, be-þing & se   f. 124ᵇ
    Quat peine i þole for loue of þe.   (col. 1)
Nith & day to þe i grede,
Hand & fotes on rode i-sprede.   4
Nailed i was to þe tre,
Ded & biriȝed, man, for þe ;
Al þis i drey for loue of man,
But werse me dot, þat he ne can   8
To me turnen onis is eyȝe,
Þan al þe peine þat i dryȝe.

71.   *I would be Clad in Christis Skin.*

Advocates Lib. 18. 7. 21.

G Old & al þis werdis wyn   f. 124ᵇ
    Is nouth but cristis rode ;   (col. 2)
I wolde ben clad in cristes skyn,
Þat ran so longe on blode,   4
& gon t'is herte & taken myn In—
Þer is a fulsum fode.
Þan ȝef i litel of kith or kyn,
For þer is alle gode.   Amen.   8

72.   *Popule meus quid feci tibi?*
[Micah vi. 3]

Advocates Lib. 18. 7. 21.

M I folk, nou ansuere me,   f. 125ᵃ
    an sey wat is my gilth ;
wat mitht i mor ha don for þe,
þat i ne haue fulfilth ?   4

Out of Egipte i brouthte þe,
þer þu wer in þi wo;
& wikkedliche þu nome me,
als i hadde ben þi fo.   8

Ouer al abouten i ledde þe
and oforn þe i ȝede;
& no frenchipe fond i in þe
wan þat i hadde nede.   1 2

Fourti wenter i sente þe
angeles mete fro heuene;
& þu heng me on rode tre,
& greddist with loud steuene.   16

Heilsum water i sente þe
out of þe harde ston;
& eysil & galle þu sentist me,
oþer ȝef þu me non.   20

Þe see i partid o-sunder for þe,
& ledde þe þoru wol wide;
& þe herte blod to sen of me,
þu smettest me þoru þe side.   24

Alle þi fon i slou for þe,
& made þe cout of name;
& þu heng me on rode tre,
& dedest me michil schame.   28

A kingges ȝerde i þe be-tok
til þu wer al be-forn;
& þu heng me on rode tre,
& corounnedist me with a þorn.   32

I made þin enemies & þe
for to ben knowen o-sunder;
& on an hey hil þu henge me,
al þe werld on me to wonder.   36

73.   *Christ's Love for Man's Soul.*

Advocates Lib. 18. 7. 21.

MI loue is falle vp-on a may,   f. 125ᵇ
　　For loue of hire i defende þis day.
Loue aunterus no man for-saket,
It woundet sore wan it him taket;   4
Loue anterus may hauen no reste,
Quare thouth is newe þer loue is faste;
Loue anterus with wo is bouth,
Þer loue is trewe it flittetȝ nouth.   8

74.   *O vos omnes qui transitis per viam.*

Advocates Lib. 18. 7. 21.

ȜE þat pasen be þe weyȝc,   f. 125ᵇ
　　Abidet a litel stounde !   (col. 2)
Be-holdet, al mi felawes,
ȝef ani me lik is founde.   4
To þe tre with nailes þre
Wol fast i hange bounde,
With a spere al þoru mi side
To min herte is mad a wounde.   8

75. *The Christ Child shivering with Cold.*

Advocates Lib. 18. 7. 21.

L Er to louen as i loue þe ;   f. 126^a
  On al my limes þu mith i-se
Hou sore þei quaken for colde ;
For þe i suffre michil wo.   4
Loue me, suete, an no-mo—
To þe i take & holde.

Ihesu, suete sone dere,
In porful bed þu list nou here,   8
& þat me greuet sore ;
For þi credel is als a bere,
Ox & Asse ben þi fere—
Wepen may i þer fore.   12

Ihesu, suete, be nout wroth,
I haue neiþer clut ne cloth
Þe inne for to folde ;
I ne haue but a clut of a lappe,   16
Þerfore ley þi feet to my pappe,
& kep þe fro þe colde.

Cold þe taket, i may wel se.
For loue of man it mot be   20
Þe to suffren wo,
For bet it is þu suffre þis
Þan man for-bere heuene blis—
Þu most him biȝen þer-to.   24

syþen it most nedes þat þu be ded
To sauen man fro þe qued,
Þi suete wil be do.
But let me nouth duellen her to longe ;   28
After þi det me vnderfonge
To ben for eueremo.   Amen.

76.   *Christ's Three Songs to Man.*

Advocates Lib. 18. 7. 21.

Primus cantus

WAter & blod for þe i suete,   f. 126ᵃ
   & as a þef i am i-take ;
I am i-bounden, i am i-bete,
& al it is, man, for þi sake.   4

I suffre iewes on me to spete,
& al nith with hem i wake,
To loken wan þu woldest lete
Þi senne for loue of þi make.   8

Secundus cantus

Mi bodi is as red as ro,
Þornes prikken myn hed fol sore,
Mi visage waxit wan an blo,
I haue so bled i may no more.   12

Min herte is for-smite a-to,
al, mankinde, for loue of þe,
To loken wan þu woldest go
Fro þi senne for loue of me.   16

Tertius cantus

Þou þu wil nouth louen me,
Siþen i þe my lowe schewe,
Nedes i mot louen þe,
Ne be þu neuere so vntrewe.   20

Þe nailes, þe scourges, & þe spere,
Þe galle, & þe þornes sarpe—
Alle þese moun witnesse bere
Þat i þe haue wonnen with myn harte.   24

77.   *Homo Vide quid pro Te Patior.*

Camb. Univ. Dd. 5. 64, III.

Vnkynde man, gif kepe til me   f. 34ᵃ
   and loke what payne I suffer for þe.   f. 34ᵇ
Synful man on þe I cry,
alanly for þi lufe I dy.   4
Behalde, þe blode fra me downe rennes,
noght for my gylt bot for þi synnes.
My hende, my fete, with nayles er fest;
syns & vayns al to-brest;   8
þe blode owt of my hert-rote,
loke, it falles downe to my fote.
Of al þe payne þat I suffer sare,
with-in my hert it greues me mare   12
þe vnkyndenes þat I fynd in þe,
þat for þi lufe þus hynged on tre.
Alas! why lufes þou me noght,
and I þi lufe sa dere hase boght?   16
Bot þou me lufe þou dose me wrang
sen I haue loued þe lang.
Twa & thyrty ȝere & mare
I was for þe in trauel sare   20
with hungyr, thirst, hete, & calde;
For þi lufe bath boght & salde,
Pyned, nayled, & done on tre—
All, man, for þe lufe of þe.   24
Lufe þou me als þe wele aw,
And fra syn þou þe draw,
I gyf þe my body with woundes sare;
And þare-to sall I gyf þe mare,   28
Ouer all þis I-wysse,
In erth mi grace, in heuen my blysse.   Ihc̄ Amen.

78. *Christ pleads with His Sweet Leman.*

Camb. Univ. Dd. 5. 64, III.

L O! lemman swete, now may þou se   f. 34^b
   þat I haue lost my lyf for þe.
     What myght I do þe mare?
For-þi I pray þe speciali   4
þat þou forsake ill company
     þat woundes me so sare;

And take myne armes pryuely
& do þam in þi tresory,   8
     In what stede sa þou dwelles,
And, swete lemman, forget þow noght
þat I þi lufe sa dere haue boght,
     And I aske þe noght elles.   12

79. *A Lament over the Passion.*

Camb. Univ. Dd. 5. 64, III.

M Y trewest tresowre sa trayturly was taken, f. 34^b
   Sa bytterly bondyn wyth bytand bandes,
How sone of þi seruandes was þou forsaken,
And lathly for my lufe hurld with þair handes.   f. 35^a

My well of my wele sa wrangwysly wryed,   5
Sa pulled owt of preson to pilate at prime;
þaire dulles & þaire dyntes ful drerely þou dreed
Whan þai schot in þi syght bath slauer & slyme.   8

My hope of my hele sa hyed to be hanged,
Sa charged with þi crosce & corond with thorne,
Ful sare to þi hert þi steppes þa stanged—
Me thynk þi bak burd breke; it bendes for-borne. 12

My salue of my sare sa saryful in syght,
Sa naked and nayled þi ryg on þe rode,
Ful hydusly hyngand, þay heued þe on hyght,
Þai lete þe stab in þe stane all stekked þat þar stode.

My dere-worthly derlyng, sa dolefully dyght,   17
Sa straytly vpryght streyned on þe rode ;
For þi mykel mekenes, þi mercy, þi myght,
Þow bete al my bales with bote of þi blode.   20

My fender of my fose, sa fonden in þe felde,
Sa lufly lyghtand at þe euensang tyde ;
Þi moder and hir menȝhe vnlaced þi scheld—
All weped þat þar were, þi woundes was sa wyde.   24

My pereles prynce als pure I þe pray,
Þe mynde of þis Myrour þou lat me noght mysse ;
Bot wynd vp my wylle to won wyth þe ay,   27
Þat þou be beryd in my brest & bryng me to blysse.
                                              AmeN.

80.   *A prayer to Jesus.*

Camb. Univ. Dd. 5. 64, III.

IHesu, als þow me made & boght,   f. 35ᵃ
  þou be my lufe & all my thoght,
and help þat I war to þe broght—
with-owten þe may I do noght.   4

Ihesu, als þou may do þi wille,   f. 35ᵇ
and nathyn⟨g⟩ es þat þe may lette,
With þi grace my hert fulfill,
my lufe & my lykyng in þe sette.   8

Ihesu, at þi wille I pray þat I mote be ;
All my hert fulfill with perfyte lufe to þe.
Þat I haue done ill, Ihesu, forgyf þow me,
And suffer me neuer to spill, Ihesu, for þi pyte. 12
                                              Amen.

26 MS. þi.

81.   *A Song of Mortality.*

Camb. Univ. Dd. 5. 64, III.

WHen adam delf & eue span, spir, if þou wil
      spede,   f. 35ᵇ
Whare was þan þe pride of man þat now merres his
      mede.
Of erth & slame als was adam maked to noyes & nede.
Ar we als he maked to be, whil we þis lyf sal lede.   4
      With I & E, born ar we, als salomon vs hyght,
         To trauel here whils we ar fere, als fouls to þe
            flight.

In worlde we ware kast for to kare to we be broght to
      wende
Til wele or wa, an of þa twa, to won with-outen ende.
For-þi whils þou may helpe þe now, amend þe & haf
      mynde   9
When þou sal ga he bese þi fa þat are was here þi
      frende.
      With E & I, I rede for-þi þou thynk apon þies
         thre :   11
      What we ar, & what we ware, & what we sal be.

War þou als wyse praysed in pryce als was salomon,
Fayrer fode of bone & blode þen was absalon,
Strengthy & strang to wreke þi wrang als euer was
      sampson,   15
Þou ne myght a day, na mare þen þai, dede withstand
      allon.   f. 36ᵃ
      With I & E, dede to þe sal com als I þe kenne ;
         Þou ne wate in what state, how, ne whare, ne
            when.

Of erth aght þat þe was raght þou sal not haue, I hete,
Bot seuen fote þer-in to rote, & þi wyndyng-schete. 20
For-þi gyf whils þou may lyf, or all gase þat þou gete—
þi gast fra god, þi godes olod, þi flesch fowled vndur
    fete.
    With I & E, syker þow be þat þi secutowrs
    Of þe ne wil rek, bot skelk & skek ful boldly in
        þi bowrs. 24

Of welth & witt þis sal be hitt, in world þat þou here
    wroght,
Rekken þou mon, & ȝelde reson of thyng þat þou here
    thoght.
May no fal⟨a⟩s help in þis case, ne cownsel getes þou
    noght;
Gyft ne grace nane þare gase, bot brok als þou hase
    boght. 28
    With I & E, þe boke biddes þe, man, be ware of
    þi werkes;
    Terme of þe ȝere hase þou nan here—þi mede bese
    þer þi merkes.

What may þis be þat I here se? þe fayrehede of þi face,
þi ble sa bryght, þi mayn, þi myght, þi mowth þat miri
    mas? 32
Al mon als was to powder passe, to dede when þow
    gase,
A grysely geste bese þan þi breste, in armes til en-
    brase.
    With I & E, syker þou be þare es nane, I þe hete,
    Of al þi kyth wald slepe þe with, a nyght vnder
    schete. 36

82.   *A Song of Mercy.*

Camb. Univ. Dd. 5. 64, III.

Mercy es maste in my mynde,   f. 36^b
  for mercy es þat I mast prayse;
Mercy es curtayse & kynde,
fra al mischeues he mai me rayse.   4
Allas! sa lang I haue bene blynd
& walked will al-wayse.
Mercy walde I fayne fynd
to lede me in my last dayse.   8
    Mercy, lede me at þe last,
    When I owt of þis world sal wende.
    To þe cryand, I trayst fast
    þat þou saue me fra þe fende.   12

Mercy es trew as any stele
when it es ryght vp-soght;
Wha-sa will mercy fele,   f. 37^a
seke it, for it fayles noght.   16
Mercy es syght of al my hele,
þerfore I haue it mast in thoght.
Mercy likes me sa wele
for thorogh mercy was I boght.   20
    I ne wate what I may do or say
    til mercy, þat es ay sa gode:
    þou graunte mercy þat mercy may,
    þat es my solace & my fode.   24

Mercy walde I fayne honowre,
it es sa swete vnto my syght;
It lyes in my creatoure,
þat made vs of his awen myght.   28

Mercy es al my socoure,
til lede me to þe land of lyght,
And bring me til þe rial toure
whare I mai se mi god sa brygh⟨t⟩.   32
    God of al, lorde & keyng,
    I pray þe, ihesu, be my frende,
    Sa þat I may þi mercy syng
    in þi blys with-owten ende.   36

Mercy es sa hegh a poynt,
þar may na syn it suppryse ;
To þi mercy es my hert ioynt,
for þer-in al my likyng lyse.   40
Lord, lat it noght be aloynt,
when þou sal sett þi gret assyse.
With þi mercy my sawle anoynt,
when I sal come to þi Iugise.   44
    Til þe juge sal I come,
    bot I wate noght my day ;
    Mercy es bath al & some,
    þar-in I trayst & after pray   48

83.   A Song of Love-longing to Jesus.

Camb. Univ. Dd. 5. 64, III.

I Hesu, god sone, lord of mageste,   f. 37ᵃ
  Send wil to my hert anly to couayte þe.
Reue me lykyng of þis land, my lufe þat þou may be ;
Take my hert in-till þi hand, sett me in stabylte.   4

Ihesu, þe mayden sone, þat wyth þi blode me boght,
Thyrl my sawule wyth þi spere, þat mykel luf in men
    hase wroght ;
Me langes lede me to þi lyght, & festen in þe al my
    thoght ;
In þi swetnes fyll my hert, my wa make wane till
    noght.   8

39 MS. noynt.

H 2

Ihesu my god, ihesu my keyng, forsake noght my
    desyre,
My thoght make it to be meke, I hate bath pryde
    and Ire.   f. 37ᵇ
Þi wil es my ʒhernyng, of lufe þou kyndel þe fyre,
Þat I in swet louyng with aungels take my hyre.   12

Wounde my hert with-in, & welde it at þi wille;
On blysse þat neuer sal blyn, þou gar me fest my
    skylle;
Þat I þi lufe may wyn, of grace my thoght þou fylle,
And make me clene of syn, þat I may come þe tylle.

Rote it in my hert, þe memor of þi pyne;   17
In sekenes & in qwert, þi lufe be euer myne;
My ioy es al of þe, my sawle take it as þine;
My lufe ay waxand be, sa þat it neuer dwyne.   20

My sang es in syghyng, whil I dwel in þis way;
My lyfe es in langyng, þat ·byndes me nyght & day;
Til I come til my kyng, þat I won with hym may,
And se his fayre schynyng, & lyfe þat lastes ay.   24

Langyng es in me lent, for lufe þat I ne kan lete;
My lufe it hase me schent, þat ilk a bale may bete;
Sen þat my hert was brent in cryste lufe sa swete,
Al wa fra me es went, & we sal neuer mete.   28

I sytt & syng of lufe-langyng þat in my hert es bred;
Ihesu, my keyng & my ioyng, why ne war I to þe
    led?
Ful wele I wate in al my state in ioy I sulde be fed.
Ihesu, me bryng til þi wonyng, for blode þat þou hase
    sched.   32

14 MS. me skylle.

Demed he was to hyng, þe faire aungels fode ;
Ful sare þai gan hym swyng when þat he bunden
  stode,
His bak was in betyng & spylt hys blissed blode,   35
Þe thorn corond þe keyng þat nayled was on þe
  rode.   f. 38ª

Whyte was his naked breste, & rede his blody syde,
Wan was his faire face, his woundes depe & wyde ;
Þe iewyis wald not wande to pyne hym in þat tyde—
Als streme dose of þe strande, his blode gan downe
  glyde.   40

Blynded was his faire ene, his flesch blody for-bette,
His lufsum lyf was layde ful low & saryful vmbesette.
Dede & lyf began to stryf wheþer myght maystre
  mare,
When aungels brede was dampned to dede to safe
  oure sauls sare.   44

Lyf was slayne & rase agayne, in faire-hede may we
  fare ;
And dede es broght til litel or noght, & kasten in end-
  les kare ;
On hym þat þe boght hafe al þi thoght, & lede þe in
  his lare ;
Gyf al þi hert til crist þi qwert, & lufe hym euer-
  mare.   48

84.   *A Song of the Love of Jesus.*

Camb. Univ. Dd. 5. 64, III.

(L)Uf es lyf þat lastes ay, þar it in criste es
        feste ;   f. 38ᵃ
For wele ne wa it chaunge may, als wryten has men
    wyseste.
Þe nyght it tournes in-til þe day, þi trauel in-tyll reste;
If þou wil luf þus as I say, þou may be wyth þe beste.

Lufe es thoght wyth grete desyre, of a fayre louyng ; 5
Lufe I lyken til a fyre, þat sloken may na thyng ;
Lufe vs clenses of oure syn, lufe vs bote sall bryng ;
Lufe þe keynges hert may wyn, lufe of ioy may syng. 8

Þe settel of lufe es lyft hee, for in-til heuen it ranne ;
Me thynk in erth it es sle, þat makes men pale and
    wanne ;
Þe bede of blysse it gase ful nee—I tel þe as I kanne.
Þof vs thynk þe way be dregh, luf copuls god &
    manne.   12

Lufe es hatter þen þe cole, lufe may nane be-swyke ;
Þe flawme of lufe wha myght it thole, if it war ay
    I-like ?   f. 38ᵇ
Luf vs confortes & mase in qwart & lyftes tyl heuen-
    ryke ;
Luf rauysches cryste in-tyl owr hert—I wate na lust
    it lyke.   16

Lere to luf if þou wyl lyfe when þou sall hethen fare ;
All þi thoght til hym þou gyf, þat may þe kepe fra
    kare ;
Loke þi hert fra hym noght twyn if þou in wandreth
    ware ;   19
Sa þou may hym welde & wyn and luf hym euer-mare.

Ihesu þat me lyfe hase lent, In-til þi lufe me bryng ;
Take til þe al myne entent, þat þow be my ȝhernyng ;
Wa fra me away war went & comen war my couay-
  tyng,   23
If þat my sawle had herd & hent þe sang of þi louyng.

Þi lufe es ay lastand fra þat we may it fele ;
Þare-m make me byrnand þat na thyng gar it kele ;
My thoght take in-to þi hand & stabyl it ylk a dele,
Þat I be noght heldand to luf þis worldes wele.   28

If I lufe any erthly thyng þat payes to my wyll,
& settes my ioy & my lykyng when it may come me
  tyll,
I mai drede of partyng þat wyll be hate and yll ;
For al my welth es bot wepyng, when pyne mi saule
  sal spyll.   32

Þe ioy þat men hase sene es lyckend til þe haye,
Þat now es fayre & grene and now wytes awaye.
Swylk es þis worlde, I wene, & bees till domes-daye,
All in trauel & tene—fle þat na man it maye.   36

If þou luf in all þi thoght and hate þe fylth of syn,
and gyf hym þi sawle þat it boght, þat he þe dwell
  with-in,
Als crist þi sawle hase soght & þer-of walde noght
  blyn,   39
Sa þou sal to blys be broght & heuen won with-in.
         f. 39ᵃ

Þe kynd of luf es þis, þar it es trayst and trew,
To stand styll in stabylnes & chaunge it for na new ;
Þe lyfe þat lufe myght fynd or euer in hert it knew,
Fra kare it tornes þat kyend & lendes in myrth &
  glew.   44

   23 MS. cõne.

For now lufe þow, I rede, cryste, as I þe tell,
And with aungels take þi stede—þat ioy loke þou
    noght sell.
In erth þow hate, I rede, all þat þi lufe may fell ;
For luf es stalworth as þe dede, luf es hard as hell.   48

Luf es a lyght byrthen, lufe gladdes ȝong and alde,
Lufe es with-owten pyne, als lofers hase me talde,
Lufe es a gastly wynne þat makes men bygge & balde,
Of lufe sal he na thyng tyne, þat hit in hert will halde.

Lufe es þe swettest thyng þat man in erth hase tane,   53
Lufe es goddes derlyng, lufe byndes blode & bane ;
In lufe be owre lykyng, I ne wate na better wane,
For me & my lufyng lufe makes bath be ane.   56

Bot fleschly lufe sal fare as dose þe flowre in may,
And lastand be na mare þan ane houre of a day,
And sythen syghe ful sare þar lust, þar pryde, þar
    play,
When þai er casten in kare til pyne þat lastes ay.   60

When þair bodys lyse in syn, þair sawls mai qwake &
    drede ;
For vp sal ryse al men and answer for þair dede.
If þai be fonden in syn, als now þair lyfe þai lede,
Þai sal sytt hel with-in & myrknes hafe to mede.   64

Riche men þair handes sal wryng, & wicked werkes
    sal by
In flawme of fyre, bath knyght & keyng, with sorow
    schamfully ;   f. 39^b
If þou wil lufe þan may þou syng til cryst in melody ;
Þe lufe of hym ouer-coms al thyng—þar-to þou traiste
    trewly.   68

⟨I⟩ sygh & sob bath day & nyght for ane sa fayre of
    hew,
Þar es na thyng my hert mai light bot lufe þat es ay
    new ;
Wha-sa had hym in his syght or in his hert hym knew,
His mournyng turned til ioy ful bryght, his sang in-til
    glew.   72

In myrth he lyfes nyght & day þat lufes þat swete
    chylde—
It es ihesu, forsoth I say, of all mekest & mylde ;
Wreth fra hym walde al a-way þof he wer neuer sa
    wylde,
He þat in hert lufed hym, þat day fra euel he wil hym
    schylde.   76

Of ihesu mast lyst me speke þat al my bale may bete ;
Me thynk my hert may al to-breke when I thynk on
    þat swete.
In lufe lacyd he hase my thoght þat I sal neuer for-
    gete ;
Ful dere me thynk he hase me boght with blodi hende
    & fete.   80

For luf my hert es bowne to brest, when I þat faire
    behalde ;
Lufe es fair þare it es fest, þat neuer will be calde ;
Lufe vs reues þe nyght rest, in grace it makes vs
    balde ;
Of al warkes luf es þe best, als haly men me talde. 84

Na wonder gyf I syghand be, & sithen in sorow be
    sette,
Ihesu was nayled apon þe tre & al blody for-bette.
To thynk on hym es grete pyte, how tenderly he
    grette ;
Þis hase he sufferde, man, for þe, if þat þou syn wyll
    lette.   88

Þare es na tonge in erth may tell of lufe þe swetnesse;
Þat stedfastly in lufe kan dwell, his ioy es endlesse.
God schylde þat he sulde til hell þat lufes & lang-
   and es, 91
Or euer his enmys sulde hym qwell, or make his luf be
   lesse. f. 40ᵃ

Ihesu es lufe þat lastes ay, til hym es owre langyng ;
Ihesu þe nyght turnes to þe day, þe dawyng in-til
   spryng ;
Ihesu, thynk on vs now & ay, for þe we halde oure
   keyng ;
Ihesu, gyf vs grace, as þou wel may, to luf þe with-
   owten endyng. 96

85. *A Salutation to Jesus.*

Camb. Univ. Dd. 5. 64, III.

HEyle! ihesu my creatowre, of sorowyng medi-
   cyne, f. 40ᵃ
Heyle! ihesu mi saueowre, þat for me sufferd pyne,
Heyle! ihesu, helpe & sokowre, my lufe be ay þine.
Heyle! ihesu, þe blyssed flowre of þi moder virgyne. 4

Heyle! ihesu leder to lyght, In saule þou ert ful swete;
Þi luf schynes day & nyght, þat strenghes me in þis
   strete.
Lene me lángyng to þi sight, & gif me grace til grete,
For þou, ihesu, hase þat myght þat al my bale may
   bete. 8

Ihesu, þi grace my hert enspyre, þat me til blis mai
   bryng ;
On þe I sett al my desyre, þou ert my luf-langyng ;
Þi luf es byrnand als þe fyre, þat euer on he wil spryng ;
Far fro me put pride & Ire, for þam I luf na-thyng. 12

Heile ! ihesu, price of my prayer, lorde of mageste,
Þou art ioy þat lastes ay, all delyte þou art to se ;
Gyf me grace, als þou wel may, þi lufer for to be ;   15
My langyng wendes neuer a-way, til þat I come· til þe.

Ihesu to lufe ay be me lefe, þat es my gastly gode.
Allas ! my god es als a thefe nayled til þe rode ;
Hys tender vayns begyns to brest, al rennes of blode ;
Handes & fete with nayles er fest, þat chawnges mi
    mode.   20

Ihesu mi keyng es me ful dere, þat with his blode
    me boght ;
Of spittyng spred es al þat clere, to dede with betyng
    broght ;   f. 40ᵇ
For me he tholed þies payns sere, þe whilk wreche he
    wroght ;
For-þi þai sitt my hert ful nere, þat I forgete þam
    noght.   24

Ihesu, fortune of ilk a fyght, þou graunt me grace to
    spede,
Þat I may lufe þe ryght & haue þe to my mede ;
Þi luf es fast in ilk a fandyng, & euer at al owre nede ;
Als thurgh þi grace art my ȝhernyng, In-til þi lyght
    me lede.   28

86. *Thy Joy be in the Love of Jesus.*

Camb. Univ., Dd. 5. 64, III.

THy ioy be ilk a dele to serue þi god to pay,   f. 42ᵃ
   For al þis worldes wele þou sees wytes a-way,
Þow fande his lufe to fele þat last with þe will ay,
And þi kare sal kele, þi pyne turne þe to play.   4

20 MS. ert.

In crist þou cast þi thoght, þou hate all wreth and
    pryde,
And thynk how he þe boght with woundes depe &
    wyde;
When þou hym-self hase soght, wele þe sal be-tyde;
Of ryches rek þe noght, fra hell bot he þe hyde.   8

Do als I þe rede, lyftand vp þi hert,
And say til hym was dede, 'cryste, myne hele þou ert!'
Syn synkes as lede, & fer downe fals fra qwert;   11
Þarfore stabyl þi stede þar smy-tyng may noght smert.

In cryste knyt þi solace, hys lufe chawnge þi chere,
With ioy þou take his trace & seke to sytt hym nere;
Ever sekand his face, þou make þi sawle clere:
He ordans hegh þi place, yf þou his lufe will lere.   16

Þou kepe his byddyngs ten, hald þe fra dedely synne,
Forsake þe ioy of men, þat þou his lufe may wynne;
Þi hert of hym sal bren with lufe þat neuer sal twynne,
Langyng he wil þe len heuen to won with-Inne.   20

Þou thynk on hys mekenes, how pore he was borne;
Behalde his blody flesch es prikked wit thorne;
Þi lufe lat it noght lesse; he saued þat was forlorne.
To serue hym in swetnes, all haue we sworne.   f. 42ᵇ

If þou be in fandyng, of lufe þou hase grete nede,   25
To stedde ⟨þe⟩ in stallyng & gyf þe grace to spede;
Þow dwell ay with þi kyng—in hys lufe þe fede;
For lityll haue I connyng to tel of his fairhede.   28

Bot luf hym at þi myght whils þou ert lyuand here,
And loke vnto þi syght þat nane be þe so dere;
Say to hym bath day & nyght: 'when mai I negh þe
    nere?
Bryng me to þi lyght þi melodi to here.'   32

In þat lyfe þe stedde þat þou be ay lyuand,
And gyf hym lufe to wedde þat þou with hym wil
    stand.
Ioy in þi brest es bredde, when þou ert hym lufand;
Þi sawle þan hase he fedde in swete lufe brennand.   36

87.   *A General Confession.*

Burton MS. (Prebendary John R. Burton, Ludlow).

[Text within brackets supplied from Camb. Univ. MS. Ii. 6. 43.]

    SWete ihesu crist, to þe,   (verso, col. 1)
      copable wrecche ich ȝelde me,
of sennes þat ich habbe ydo
yn al my lyue hider-to,   4
In pride, yn wraþþe, in vyl enuye,
yn glotonye, yn lecherye,
yn sleuþe, lord, yn þy seruyse,
And of þis wordles couetyse.   8
To ofte ich habbe yn myne lyue
y-senȝed wit my wittes fyue,
Wit eren yhered, wit eȝen syȝt,
Wit senfol speche dey & nyȝt,   12
Wit cleppinges, wit kessenge also,
Wit hondes yhandled, wit fet ygwo,
Wit herte senfolliche yþoȝt,
Wit al my body euele ywroȝt;   16
And of al my folye
Mercy, lord, mercy ich crye.
Al-þaȝ ich senȝede euere,
Lord ich for-soc þe neuere,   20
⟨Ne oþer god took y noon,
Fadyr of heuen, but þe oon.
There-fore, lorde, y þe beseche
Wit ryȝt hertly speche,⟩   24

ʒef þou me none med⟨e⟩   (col. 2)
Efter my senful dede,
Ak efter, lord, þy grete ⟨pyte⟩.
Lord ihesu, asoyle þou me,   28
And send me ofte er ⟨y dyʒe⟩
Sorʒe of herte and teres o⟨f yʒe⟩,
For sennes þat ich habbe ⟨do⟩
yn al my lyue hider-⟨to⟩ ;   32
And let me neuere b⟨egynne⟩
To do no maner dede⟨ly synne⟩ ;
So þat ich at myn end⟨e daye⟩
Clene of senne deye ⟨maye⟩,   36
Srifte and housele at ⟨myn ende⟩,
Þat my saule mote ⟨wende⟩
yn-to þat blisse of ⟨þyn empyre⟩
Þer þou regnest lo⟨rde & syre.   Amen.⟩   40

88.   *Hand by Hand We Shall us Take.*

MS. Bodley 26.

HOnnd by honnd we schulle ous take,   f. 202ᵇ
    & ioye & blisse schulle we make,
for þe deuel of elle man haʒt for-sake,
& godes sone ys maked oure make.   4

A child is boren a-mo⟨n⟩ges man,
& in þat child was no wam ;
þat child ys god, þat child is man,
& in þat child oure lif bygan.   8
    Honnd by honnd þanne schulle ous take, &c.

Senful man be bliþe and glad,
for your mariage þy peys ys grad,
    wan crist was boren :   12

com to crist, þy peis ys grad,
for þe was hys blod ysched,
    þat were for-loren.
        Honnd by honnd þanne schulle ous take 16
        & ioye & blisse schu⟨lle⟩ we make, &c.

Senful man be bliþe & bold,
for euene ys boþe boȝt & sold,
    euereche fote: 20
com to crist, þy peys ys told,
for þe he ȝahf a hondre fo⟨l⟩d,
    hys lif to bote.
        Honnd by honnd, &c.   24

89.   *Iesu Dulcis Memoria.*

Hunterian Museum MS. V. 8. 15.

IHesu, swete is þe loue of þee,   f. 33ᵃ
  Noon oþir þing so swete may be ;
No þing þat men may heere & see
Haþ no swetnesse aȝens þee.   4

IHesu, no song may be swetter,
No þing in herte blisfullere,
Nouȝt may be feelid delitfullere,
Þan þou, so sweete a louere.   8

IHesu, þi loue was vs so fre
Þat it fro heuene brouȝte þee ;
For loue þou dere bouȝtist me,
For loue þou hynge on roode tre.   12

IHesu, for loue þou þoledist wrong,
Woundis sore, & peynes strong ;
Þin peynes weren ful long—   15
No man may hem telle ne song.   f. 33ᵇ

        22 MS. far þe ȝe.

IHesu, for loue þou bood so wo
Þat blody stremys runne þe fro ;
Þi whyte sydes woxen blw & blo—
Oure synnes it maden so, wolawo!   20

IHesu, for loue þou steiȝ on roode,
For loue þou ȝaf þin herte blode ;
Loue þee made my soules foode,
Þi loue vs bouȝte til al goode.   24

IHesu my loue, þou were so fre,
Al þat þou didest for loue of me.
What schal I for þat ȝelde þee ?
Þou axist nouȝt but loue of me.   28

IHesu my god, ihesu my kyng,
Þou axist me noon oþir þing,
but trewe loue & herte ȝernyng,
And loue teeris with swete mornyng.   32

IHesu my loue, ihesu my lyȝ⟨t⟩,
I wole þee loue & þat is riȝt ;   f. 34ᵃ
Do me loue þee wiþ al my myȝt,
& for þee moorne boþe day & nyȝt.   36

IHesu, do me so ȝerne þee
Þat my þouȝt euere vpon þee be ;
Wiþ þin yȝe loke to me,
And myldely my nede se.   40

IHesu, þi loue be al my þouȝt,
Of oþir þing ne recche me nouȝt ;
Þanne haue I þi wille al wrouȝt,
Þat hauest me ful dere bouȝt.   44

90.   *Christ's Gift to Man.*

Hunterian Museum MS. V. 8. 15.

C Rist makiþ to man a fair present,   f. 34ᵃ
  His blody body wiþ loue brent ;
Þat blisful body his lyf haþ lent,
For loue of man þat synne haþ blent.   4
    O Loue, loue, what hast þou ment ?
    Me þinkeþ þat loue to wraþþe is went.

Þi loueliche hondis loue haþ to-rent,
And þi liþe arme(s) wel streit itent ;   f. 34ᵇ
Þi brest is baar, þi bodi is bent,   9
for wrong haþ wonne & riȝt is schent.

Þi mylde boones loue haþ to-drawe,
Þe naylis þi feet han al to-gnawe ;   12
Þe lord of loue loue haþ now slawe—
Whane loue is strong it haþ no lawe.

His herte is rent, / his body is bent
    vpon þe roode tre ;   16
Wrong is went, / þe deuel is schent,
    crist, þurȝ þe myȝt of þee.

For þee þat herte is leyd to wedde ;
swych was þe loue þat herte vs kedde,   20
Þat herte barst, þat herte bledde—
Þat herte blood oure soulis fedde.

Þat herte clefte for treuþe of loue,
Þerfore in him oon is trewe loue ;   24
For loue of þee þat herte is ȝoue—
Kepe þou þat herte & þou art aboue.

Loue, loue, where schalt þou wone?
Þi wonyng-stede is þee bi-nome,   28
For cristis herte þat was þin hoome—
He is deed, now hast þou noone.
    Loue, loue, whi doist þou so?
    Loue, þou brekist myn herte a-two.   32

Loue haþ schewid his greet myȝt,
For loue haþ maad of day þe nyȝt;
Loue haþ slawe þe kyng of ryȝt,
And loue haþ endid þe strong fiȝt.   36

So Inliche loue was neuere noon;
Þat witiþ wel marie & Ioon,
And also witen þei euerychon,
Þat loue wiþ hym is maad at oon.   40

Loue makiþ, crist, þin herte myn,
So makiþ loue myn herte þin;
Þanne schulde myn be trewe al tym,
And loue in loue schal make it fyn.   44

91. *Ihesu that hast me dere I-boght.*

Longleat MS. 29, Art. 19.

IN seiynge of þis orisoun stynteth & bydeth at euery cros & þynketh whate ye haue seide. For a more deuout prayere fond I neuer of the passioun who-so wolde deuoutly say hitte.

I Hesu þat hast me dere I-boght,
  Write þou gostly in my þoȝt,
Þat I mow with deuocion
Þynke on thy dere passioun: 4
For þogh my hert be hard as stone,
ȝit maist þou gostly write þer-on
With naill & with spere kene,
And so shullen þe lettres be sene.   8

Write in my hert with speches swete,
Whan Iudas þe traytour can þe mete—
That traitour was ful of þe feende,
And yit þou caldest hym þy frende.　　　　12
Swete ihesu, how myȝt þou soo
Cal hym þy frend so fel & foo?
Bot sethen þou spake so louely
To hym þat was þyn enemy,　　　　16
how swete shulle þi speches be
To ham þat hertely louen the,
Whan þey in heuyn with the shal dwelle,
Iwis þer may no tonge telle.　　　　20

Write how þou were bounde sore
& drawen forth pilate byfore,
And how swetly þou answard þo
To hym þat was þy fel foo.　　　　24

Write how þat fals enqueste
Cried ay with-outen reste:
'honge hym on þe rode tre,
For he wil kynge of Iewes be'.　　　　28

Write vp-on my hert boke
þy faire & swete louely loke,　　　　(col. 2)
For shame of har hiddous crie
þat wolden of þe haue no mercy.　　　　32

Write how, whan þe cros was forth bro⟨ȝt⟩
And þe nayll of Iren wroȝt,
how þou began to cheuer & quake—
thyn hert was woo þoȝ þou ne spake.　　　　36

Write how dounward þou can loke
whan Iewes to þe þe cros betoke.
þou bare hit forth with reuthly chere;
þe teres ran doun by þy lere.　　　　40

Ihesu, write in my hert depe
how þat þou began to wepe
þo þy bak was to þe rode bent,
With rogget nayll þy handes rent.   44

Write þe strokes with hameres stout,
With þe blood rennynge a-bowt,
how þe naill stynt at þe bone
Whan þou were ful wo-begone.   48

Ihesu, yit write in my hert
how bloode out of þy woundes stert;
And with þat blode write þou so ofte,
Myn hard hert til hit be softe.   52

Ihesu þat art so myche of myȝt,
Write in my hert þat reuthful syȝt,
To loken on thy modyr fre
When þou were honget on roode tre.   56

Write þy swete moderes woo
Whan sho saw þe to [þe] deth goo : (verso, col. 1)
Iwis thogh I write al my lyue,
I sholde neuer hir woo discryue.   60
In myn hert ay mot hit be,—
þat hard knotty rode tree,

The naill & þe spere also
þat þou were with to deth do,   64
The croun & þe scourges grete
þat þou were with so sore I-bette,

Thy wepynge & þy woundes wide,
þe blode þat ran doun by thy syde,   68
The shame, þe scorne, þe grete despite,
þe spottel þat defoulet þy face so white,

42 MS. swete.   53 MS. þᵗ *interlined above.*

The eysel & þe bittyr galle,
And oþer of þy peynes alle,— 72
For while I haue ham in my þoȝt
þe deuyl I hope shal dere me noȝt.

Ihesu, write þis þat I myȝt knowe
how mychel loue to þe I owe ; 76
For þoȝ þat I wold fro þe flee
þou folwest euer to saue me.

Ihesu, whan I þynke on the,
how þou were bound for loue of me, 80
Wel owe I to wepe þat stounde
þat þou for me so sore were bounde.
bot þou þat bare vpon þy handes
For my synnes so bitter bandes, 84
with loue bandes bynd þou so me
þat I be neuer departed fro the.

Ihesu þat was with loue so bounde,
þat soffred for me dethes wounde, 88
At my deiynge so visite me
And make þe fend away to flee. (col. 2)

Ihesu, make me glad to be
Sympil & pouer for loue of þe, 92
And let me neuer for more ne lasse
loue good to myche þat sone shal passe.

Ihesu þat art kynge of lyf,
Tech my soule þat is þy wyf 96
To loue best no þynge in londe
Bot þe, ihesu, hir dere housbonde.
For oþer blesse & oþer beaute
Be hit foule & sorow to see ; 100
For oþer ioy & oþer blisse
Woo & sorow for-soth hit is,
And lesteth bot a lytel while
Mannys sowle for to begyle. 104

86 MS. neuer be

[Ihesu] let me fele what ioy hit be
To suffyre wo for loue of þe,
how myry hit is for to wepe,
how softe in hard cloþes to slepe.   108
lat now loue his bow bende
& loue arowes to my hert send,
þat hit mow percen to þe roote,
For suche woundes shold be my bote.   112

Whan I am lowe for þy loue
þan am I moste at myn aboue,
Fastynge is feest, murnynge is blis,
For þy loue pouert is richesse.   116
þe hard here shold be more of pris
þan softe sylk or pelur or bys ;
Defaut for þi loue is plente,
And fleishely lust wel loth shold be.   120

Whan I am with woo be-stadde   (recto, col. 1)
For þy loue, þan am I glad ;
To suffre scornys & grete despite
For loue of þe is my delite.   124

Ihesu, make me oo nyȝt to wake
& in my þoȝt þy name to take ;
And wheþer þe nyȝt be short or longe,
Of þe, ihesu, be euer my songe.   128
let þis prayere a chayne be
To draw þe doun of þy se,
þat I mow make þe ⟨a⟩ dwellynge
In my hert at þy lykynge.   132

Ihesu, I pray þe for-sake nat me
Thogh I of syn gylty be,
For þat þef þat henge þe by
Redyly þou yaf hym þy mercy.   136

109 MS. loue now.

Ihesu þat art so corteysly,
Make me bold on þe to cry;
For wel I wot with-out drede
þy mercy is more þan my mysdede.   140

Ihesu þat art so lef & dere,
Hyre & spede þis pouer prayere;
For poul, þat was so fel & wode
To spil cristen mennys blode,   144
To the wold he no prayere make,
& þou woldest nat hym forsake—
þan maist þou noȝt forsake me,
Seþen þat I pray þus ⟨to⟩ þe.   148
At my deynge I hop I-wis
of þy presens I shal noȝt mysshe.

Ihesu, make me þan to ryse   (col. 2)
From deth to lyue, on such a wise   152
as þou rose vp on estre day,
In ioy & blisse to lyue aye.
      Amen.

92.   *Oracio de sancta Maria.*

Camb. Univ. MS. Ii. 6. 43.

HEyle be þou ladye so bryȝt!   f. 88ᵃ
  Gabriel þat seyde so ryȝt,
    Cryst ys wyth þee.'
Swettyst & swotyst in syȝt,   4
Modyr and mayde of myȝt,
    Haue mercy on mee.

Hayle be þou fynest to fonde!
Ihesu þy sone, y vndyrstonde,   8
  Of þe borne he was;
Glad were þou, lef in londe,
Tho þou haddyst in honde
  The prynce of oure pees.   12

Heyle, ladye, flower of alle þynges!
Ryally .3. ryche kynges,
  Derely dy3t,
Comely wyth knelynges,   16
Brou3ten þi sone þree þynges—
  The sterre was ly3t.

Hayle, gladdyst of alle wyue!
Aryse fro deþ to lyue,   20
  Thy sone þo þou sy3e,
Blyssyd be þoo woundys fyue,   f. 88ᵇ
That made mannys soule to þryue
  In heuen so hy3e.   24

Heyle, ioye in hert & in y3e!
Wyth y3e þy sylf þoo þou sy3e
  On holy þursdaye
Ihesu þi sone all vp-sty3e   28
hoom in-to heuen so hy3e,
  The apostles to paye.

Heyle, ladye, full of all blys!
Þo þat þou wentyst wysse   32
  To blys soo bry3t—
That blys god lete vs neuer mysse,
Marye, þou vs wysely wysse
  Be daye and be ny3t.   AmeN.   36

93.   *An Orison to the Trinity.*

B.M. Addit. MS. 37787.

Fadur & sone & holygost,   f. 143ᵇ
    Lord, to þe I cri and calle ;
Studfast god of miȝthes most,
My synful lif is steken in stalle ;   4
I preye þe, lord, þat þou þe hast   f. 144ᵃ
Me to helpe þat I ne falle,
And make my soule clene & chast
Of dedly synne and vuelus alle.   8

Lord, haue merci on my synne
And bringe me out of al my care ;
Vuel to do wol I now blynne,
I haue wrouht aȝeynes þi lare.   12
Þou rewe of me out and Inne,
And helpe me of my wondes sare ;
Lord þat al þis world schal wynne,
Hele me ar I founde and fare.   16

Fadur in heuene þat wel may,
I preye þe, lord, þat þou me lede
In riht weyes of stable fay,
At myn endyng whon I haue drede.   20
Þi grace I aske nyht and day,
And ȝif me mercy of my mysdede ;
Of myn askynge say not nay,
But helpe me, lord, at al my nede.   24

Swete Ihesu þat for me was borun,   f. 144ᵇ
Þou here my preyere loude & stille,
For pine þat me is leide bi-forun ;
Ofte I sike & wepe my fulle,   28
Ofte so haue I ben forsworen,
Whon I haue don aȝeynes þi wille ;
Suffre neuer þat I be loren,
Lord, for my dedus ille.   32

Þe holigost, I preye to þe
Niht & day in good entent ;
In al my serwe cumfort me,
Þi holi grace þou me sent ;   36
And schilde me ȝif þi wille be
From dedly synne þat I ne be schent ;
For mary loue, þat mayden fre,
In whom þou lyhtest verrayment.   40

I preye þe, lady, meke and mylde,
Þat þou preye for my mysdede,
For loue of þi swete childe
As þou hym sauȝ on rode blede.   44
Euer ȝete haue I beon wylde,   f. 145ᵃ
My synful soule ys euer in drede,
Mercy leuedy, þou me schilde
And helpe me euer at al my nede.   48

MErcy, mary mayden clene,
Þou let me neuer in synne dwelle,
Prey for me þat hyt be sene,
And schilde me from þe pyne of helle ;   52
For certes, leuedy, riht wel I wene
Þat alle my fomen may þou felle ;
For-þy my serwe to þe I mene,
Wyt ferful mood my tale I telle.   56

BE-þenke þe, leuedy, euer and ay
Of alle wymmen þou berest þe flour ;
For synful mon, as I þe say,
God hathe do þe gret honour.   60
Receyue my preyere nyht & day,
Whon I þe byseche in eny a our ;
Helpe me, leuedy, so wel þou may,
Me by-houcþ þat þou be my counselour.   64

Off counseil, leuedi I preye to þe   f. 145^b
Niht and day in wele and wo,
Of al my serwe cumforte me,
And be my schelde aȝeynes my fo ;   68
For certes ȝif þi wille hyt be
Alle my fomen may þou slo.
Helpe me, leuedi hende and fre,
Þou take þat þe is fallen fro.   72

AT myn endyng þou stonde by me,
When I schal heþen founden & fare,
When þat I quake and dredful be
And alle my synnes I rewe hem sare ;   76
As euer my hope haþ ben in þe,
Þenke þer-on, leuedi, & helpe me þare
For loue of þat swete tre
Þat Ihesu spradde his bodi bare.   80

Ihesus, for þat þulke stonde
Þat þou woldest on rode blede,
At myn endyng whon I schal fonde,
Þou haue mercy of my mys-dede,   84
And hele of my dedly wonde,   f. 146^a
And helpe me in þat muchel nede,
Whon dethe me takeþ & bryngeþ to gronde—
Þen schal I, lord, þi domus drede.   88

LOrd, for my synnes to do penaunce—
For my dede þou grant hit me—
A space of uerray repentaunce
In serwe of hert I praye to þe.   92
In þi merci is myn affiaunce,
Of my foli þou haue pite,
Þat þou of me ne take uengaunce,
Lord, for þi benignite.   96

83 MS. fonge.

LOrd, as þou art ful of miht,
And as þou alle þingus wost,
My lif a-mende, my dedus riht,
For maryus loue, þat maydenes host ;   100
And brynge me sone in-to þat liht
Wiþ-outen ende þer ioye is most,
On þe to se þat swete siht,
Fadur & sone & holigost.   Amen.   104

94.   *A Prayer to Jesus.*

Stonyhurst Coll. MS. XLIII.

I Hesu, for þi wurthy wounde   f. 96^b
    That went to þin hert-rote,
For synne þat hath my soule bounde.
Lete þi blyssyd blod be my bote.   4

Ihesu, for þi wundys smerte
Of þe feet & of þe handyn twoo,
Make me meke & lawe of hert,
& þe to loue as I schuld doo.   8

Ihesu, for þoo doolful teerys
That þou weptyst for my gylt,
Here and spede my preyeȝerys,
And spare me þat I be not spylt.   12

Ihesu, þat art heuene Kyng,
Sothfast god & man also,
ȝeue me grace of good endyng,
And hem alle þat I am holdyn to.   16

Ihesu lord, þat madyst me
& wyth þi blyssed blod me bouȝt,
Forȝeue me þat I haf greuyd þe
Wyth wurd, worke, wyl, and thouȝt.   20

Ihesu, in qwam is alle my trost,
Þat dey⟨d⟩st upon þe rode-tre,
Wythdrawe my hert fro fleschly lust,
From coueityse & from vanyte.   24

Ihesu Cryst, to þe I calle
Þat art fadyr ful of myȝth,
Kepe me þat I ne falle
In fleschly synne as I haue tyȝt.   28

Ihesu, for þi blyssed blode,
Bryng þe sowlys into blysse
Of qwom þat I haue ony goode,
& spare hem þat haue doo amysse.   32

95. *Mercy Passes All Things.*

Vernon MS.

BI west, vnder a wylde wode-syde,   f. 407ᵃ
   In a launde þer I was lente,   (col. 1)
Wlanke deor on grounde gunne glyde,
   And lyouns Raumping vppon bente,   4
Beores, wolues wiþ Mouþes wyde,
   Þe smale Beestes þei al to-rente.
Þer haukes vn-to heore pray þei hyde,
   Of whuche to on I tok good tente—   8
    A Merlyon, a Brid had hente
     And in hire foot heo gan hit bringe;
    Hit couþe not speke, but þus hit mente,
     How Merci passeþ alle þinge.   12

Merci was in þat Briddes muynde,
   But þerof kneuȝ þe Hau⟨e⟩k non,
For in hir foot heo gan hit bynde,
   And heold hit stille as eny ston;   16

Heo dude after þe cours of kynde,
    And fleiȝ in-to a treo anon.
Þorw kuynde þe Brid gan Merci fynde,
    For on þe morwe heo let hit gon.   20
Ful stille I stod my-self al-on,
      To herken hou þat Brid gan synge :
A-wey wol wende boþe Murþe and moon,
      And Merci passeþ alle þinge.   24

How Merci passeþ strengþe & riȝt,
    Mony a wyse seo we may ;
God ordeyned Merci most of miht,
    To beo aboue his werkes ay.   28
Whon deore Ihesu schal be diht
    To demen vs at doomes-day,
Vr sunne wol beo so muche in siht,
      We schul not wite what we schul say ;   32
Ful fersliche Riȝt wol vs affray,
      And blame vs for vr mis-lyuing :
Þen dar non prese for vs to pray,
      But Merci þat passeþ alle þing.   36

Riht wolde sle vs for vr synne,
    Miht wolde don execucion ;
And Rihtwyse god þen wol be-gynne
    Forte reherce vs þis resoun :   40
' I made þe, Mon, ȝif þat þou minne,
    Of feture lich myn owne fasoun,
And after crepte In-to þi kinne,
    And for þe suffred passioun ;   44
Of þornes kene þen was þe croun,
      Ful scharpe vppon myn hed standyng ;
Min herte-blood ran from me doun,
      And I for-ȝaf þe alle þing.   48

' Myn herte-blood for þe gan blede
    To buye þe from þe fendes blake,
And I for-ȝaf þe þi mis-dede—
    What hast þou suffred for my sake?   52
Me hungred, þou woldest not me fede;
    Ne neuer my furst ne woldestou slake;
Whon I of herborwe hedde gret nede,
    Þou woldest not to þin hous me take;   56
    Þou seȝe me a-mong todes blake,
        Ful longe in harde prison lyng.
    Let seo what onswere constou make,
        Wher weore þou kynde in eny þing?   60

  And hou I quenched al þi care,
    Lift vp þin eiȝe and þou maiȝt se
Mi woundes wete, blodi, al bare,
    As I was rauȝt on Roode-tre.   64
Þou seȝe me for defaute forfare,
    In seknes and in pouerte;
ȝit of þi good woldestou not spare,
    Ne ones come to visyte me;   68
    Al eorþli þing I ȝaf to þe,
        Boþe Beest and fisch & foul fleoyng,
    And tolde þe hou þat charite
        And Merci passeþ alle þing.   72

' Hou mihtou eny merci haue
    Þat neuer desyredest non to do?
Þou seȝe me naked and cloþes craue,
    Barehed and Barefot gan I go;   76
On me þou vochedest no þing saue,
    But beede me wende þi wones fro.
Þou seȝe me ded a⟨nd⟩ bou⟨n⟩e to graue,
    On Bere seuen dayes and mo;   80

      79 and boune: MS. aboue.

For luitel dette I ouȝte þe þo,   f. 407ᵃ
    Þou forbed my buriȝing.   (col. 2)
Þi Pater noster seyde not so,
    For Merci passeþ alle þing.'   84

Þeos are þe werkes of Merci seuene,
    Of wȝuche crist wol vs areyne,
Þat alle schul stoney wiþ þat steuene
    Þat euer tresoun miȝte a-teyne;   88
For heer but ȝif we make vs euene,
    Þer may no miht ne ȝiftes ȝeyne.
Þenne to þe kyng of heuene,
    Þe Bok seiþ þat we schul seyne :   92
    ' Wher hastou, lord, in prisoun leyne?
        Whonne weore þou in eorþe dwellyng?
    Whon seȝe we þe in such peyne?
        Whon askedest þou vs eny þing?'   96

' Whon ȝe seȝe ouþer Blynd or lame
    Þat for my loue asked ȝou ouȝt ;
Al þat ȝe duden in myn name,
    Hit was to me, boþe deede & þouȝt ;   100
But ȝe þat hated cristendame,
    And of my wraþþe neuer ne rouȝt,
ȝour seruise schal ben endeles schame,
    Hellefuir þat slakes nouȝt.   104
    And ȝe þat wiþ my blood I bouȝt,
        Þat loued me in ȝoure lyuynge,
    ȝe schul haue þat ȝe haue souȝt,
        Merci þat passeþ alle þinge.'   108

Þis tyme schal tyde—hit is no nay—
    And wel is him þat haþ þat grace
For to plese his god to pay,
    And Merci seche while he haþ space.   112

For beo vr mouþ crommed with clay,
  Wormes blake wol vs enbrase—
Þen is to late, Mon, in good fay,
  Te seche to A-Mende of þi trespace.   116
  With mekenes þou may heuene purchase,
    Oþer Meede þar þe non bring,
  But knowe þi god in vche a case,
    And loue him best of any þing.   120

To god an mon weore holden meste
  To loue and his wraþþe eschuwe.
Now is non so vnkuynde a beeste
  Þat lasse doþ þat weore him duwe ;   124
For Beestes and foules, more & leeste,
  Þe cours of kynde alle þei suwe ;
And whonne we breken Godes heste,
  Aȝeynes kuynde we ben vn-trewe.   128
  For kuynde wolde þat we him knewe,
    And dradde him most in vre doing ;
  Hit is no riht þat he vs rewe,
    But Merci passeþ alle þing.   132

Now harlotrye for murþe is holde,
  And vertues tornen in-to vice,
And Symonye haþ chirches solde,
  And lawe is waxen Couetyse ;   136
Vr feiþ is frele to flecche & folde,
  For treuþe is put to luytel prise ;
Vre God is glotenye and golde,
  Dronkenes, Lecherye and dyse.   140
  Lo ! heer vr lyf and vre delyce,
    Vr loue, vr lust, and vre lykyng ;
  ȝet ȝif we wole repente and ryse,
    Merci passeþ alle þinge.   144

121 an] MS. and.

Vn-lustily vr lyf we lede,
  Monhod and we twynne in two;
To heuen ne helle take we non hede,
  But on day come, a-noþer go.   148
Who is a mayster now but meede,
  And pruide þat wakened al vr wo?
We stunte neiþer for schame ne drede
  To teren vr god from top to to,   152
  For-swere his soule, his herte also,
    And alle þe Menbres þat we cun Mynge,—
  Ful harde vengeaunce wol falle on þo,
    But merci passeþ alle þinge.   156

And corteis knihthod and clergye,
  Þat wont were vices to forsake,
Are nou so Rooted in Ribaudye
  Þat oþur merþes lust hem not make.   160
A-wei is gentyl cortesye,   f. 407ᵃ
  And lustines his leue haþ take;   (col. 3)
We loue so slouþe and harlotrie,
  We slepe as swolle swyn in lake;   164
  Þer wol no worschupe wiþ vs wake
    Til þat Charite beo mad a kyng,—
  And þen schal al vr synne slake,
    And Merci passeþ alle þing.   168

I munge no more of þis to ȝou,
  Al-þauȝ I couþe ȝif þat I wolde,
For ȝe han herd wel whi & hou
  Bi-gon þis tale þat I haue tolde.   172
And þis men knowen wel I-nouh,
  For Merlyons feet ben colde,
hit is heor kynde on Bank and bouh
  A quik Brid to hauen and holde,   176
  From foot to foot to flutte and folde,
    To kepe hire from clomesyng,—
  As I an hauþorn gan bi-holde,
    I sauȝ my self þe same þing.   180

Whon heo hedde holden so al niht,
 On Morwe heo let hit gon a-way.
Wheþer gentrie tauȝt hire so or nouȝt,
 I con not telle ȝou, in good fay.   184
But God, as þou art ful of miȝt,
 Þouȝ we plese þe not to pay,
Graunt vs repentaunce and respiȝt,
 And schrift and hosel or we day;   188
As þou art God and mon verray,
 Þou beo vr help at vre endyng,
Bi-fore þi face þat we mai sai:
 'Now Merci passeþ alle þinge.'   192

96.   *Deo Gracias.*   *I.*

Vernon MS.

IN a Chirche, þer I con knel   f. 407ᵃ
 Þis ender day in on Morwenynge,   (col. 2)
Me lyked þe seruise wonder wel,
 For-þi þe lengore con I lynge.   4
I seiȝ a Clerk a book forþ bringe,
 Þat prikked was in mony a plas;
Faste he souȝte what he scholde synge,
 And al was *Deo Gracias.*   8

Alle þe queristres in þat qwer,
 On þat word fast gon þei cri:
Þe noyse was good, & I drouȝ neer
 And called a prest ful priueli,   12
And seide: 'sire, for ȝor curtesi
 Tel me, ȝif ȝe habbeþ spas,
What hit meneþ, and for-whi
 Ȝe singe *Deo Gracias.*'   16

8 al *interlined by corrector.*
K 2

In selk þat comeli clerk was clad,
    And ouer a lettorne leoned he ;
And wiþ his word he maade me glad,
    And seide : 'sone, I schal telle þe.   20
    Fader and sone In Trinite,
        Þe holy gost, ground of vr graas,
    Also oftesiþe þonke we
        As we sei *Deo Gracias.*   24

'To þonke & blesse him we ben bounde
    With al þe murþes þat mon mai Minne ;
For al þe world in wo was wounde
    Til þat he crepte in-to vr kinne,—   28
    A louesum buirde he liȝte with-Inne,
        Þe worþiest þat euer was—
    And schedde his blod for vre sinne,
        And þerfore *Deo Gracias.*'   32

Þen seide þe Preost : 'sone, be þi leue
    I moste seie forþ my seruise,—
I preye þe tak hit nouȝt in greue,
    For þou hast herd al my deuise—   36
    Bi-cause whi hit is clerkes wyse
        And holychirche muynde of hit maas,
    Vnto þe prince so muchel of prise,
        Forte synge *Deo Gracias.*'   40

Out of þat chirche I wente my way,
    And on þat word was al my þouȝt,
And twenti tymes I con say,
    'God graunte þat I for-ȝete hit nouȝt.'   44
    Þouȝ I weore out of bonchef brouȝt,
        what help weore to me to seye 'allas !'
    In þe nome of god, what-euer be wrouȝt,
        I schal seie, '*deo gracias.*'   48

        20 seide *interlined by corrector.*

In Mischef and in bonchef boþe,   f. 407ᵇ
  Þat word is good to seye and synge,
And not to wayle ne to bi wroþe,
  Þauȝ al be nouȝt at vre lykynge;   52
For langour schal not euer lynge,
    And sum tyme plesaunse wol ouer-pas,
But ay in hope of a-mendynge
    I schal seye, '*Deo Gracias.*'   56

A-mende þat þou hast don amis,
  And do wel þenne, and haue no drede,
Wheþer-so þou beo In bale or blis;
  Þi goode suffraunce schal gete þe mede,   60
ȝif þou þi lyf in lykyng lede,
    Loke þou beo kuynde in vch a cas;
Þonk þi god, ȝif þou wel spede,
    Wiþ þis word, *Deo Gracias.*   64

ȝif god haþ ȝiue þe vertues mo
  Þen he haþ oþure two or þre,
Þenne I rede þou rule þe so
  Þat men may speke worschupe bi þe.   68
Be fert of pruide & bost þou fle,
    Þi vertues let no fulþe de-faas,
But kep þe clene, corteis, & fre,
    And þenk on *Deo Gracias.*   72

ȝif þou beo mad an Offycer,
  And art a Mon of muche miht,
What cause þou demest, loke hit be cler,
  And reue no mon from him his riht.   76
ȝif þou beo strong and fers to fiht,
    For envye neuer mon þou chas,
But drede þi god boþe dai & niȝt,
    And þenk on *deo gracias.*   80

ȝif we þis word in herte wol haue,
  And ay in loue and leute leende,
Of crist bi couenaunt we mow craue
  Þat Ioye þat schal neuer haue ende,   84
    Out of þis world whon we schul wende,
    In-to his paleys for to paas,
  And sitte a-mong his seintes hende,
    And þer synge *Deo Gracias.*   88

97.   *Against my Will I take my Leave.*

Vernon MS.

NOu Bernes, Buirdus bolde and blyþe,   f. 407ᵇ
  To blessen ow her nou am I bounde ; (col. 1)
I þonke ȝou alle a þousend siþe,
  And prei god saue ȝou hol and sounde ;   4
Wher-euer ȝe go, on gras or grounde,
  He ow gouerne with-outen greue.
For frendschipe þat I here haue founde,
  A-ȝeyn mi wille I take mi leue.   8

For frendschipe & for ȝiftes goode,
  For Mete & Drinke so gret plente,
Þat lord þat rauȝt was on þe Roode,
  He kepe þi comeli cumpayne ;   12
On see or lond wher þat ȝe be,
  He gouerne ow wiþ-outen greue.
So good disport ȝe han mad me,
  Aȝein my wille I take my leue.   16

Aȝein mi wille al-þauȝ I wende,
  I may not al-wey dwellen here ;
For eueri þing schal haue an ende,
  And frendes are not ay I-fere ;   20
Be we neuer so lef and dere,
  Out of þis world al schul we meue ;
And whon we buske vn-to vr bere,
  Aȝeyn vr wille we take vr leue.   24

And wende we schulle, I wot neuer whenne,
  Ne whoderward þat we schul fare ;
But endeles blisse or ay to brenne,
  To eueri mon is ȝarked ȝare.   28
  For-þi I rede vch mon be-ware,
    And lete vr werk vr wordes preue,
So þat no sunne vr soule forfare
    Whon þat vr lyf haþ taken his leue.   32

Whon þat vr lyf his leue haþ lauht,
  Vr bodi lith bounden bi þe wowe,
Vr richesses alle from vs ben raft,
  In clottes colde vr cors is þrowe.   36
  Wher are þi frendes ho wol þe knowe?
    Let seo ho wol þi soule releue.
I rede þe, mon, ar þou ly lowe,
    Beo redi ay to take þi leue.   40

Be redi ay, what-euer bi-falle,   f. 407[b]
  Al sodeynli lest þou be kiht ;   (col. 2)
Þou wost neuer whonne þi lord wol calle,
  Loke þat þi laumpe beo brennynge briht ;   44
  For leue me wel, but þou haue liht,
    Riht foule þi lord wol þe repreue,
And fleme þe fer out of his siht,
    For al to late þou toke þi leue.   48

Nou god þat was in Bethleem bore,
  He ȝiue vs grace to serue him so
Þat we mai come his face to-fore,
  Out of þis world whon we schul go ;   52
  And for to amende þat we mis-do,
    In Clei or þat we clynge and cleue,
And mak vs euene wiþ frend and fo,
    And in good tyme to take vr leue.   56

Nou haueþ good dai, gode men alle,
　　Haueþ good dai, ȝonge and olde,
Haueþ good day, boþe grete and smalle,
　　And graunt-Merci a þousend folde !　　　60
ȝif euere I miȝte ful fayn I wolde
　　Don ouȝt þat weore vn-to ȝow leue ;
Crist kepe ow out of cares çolde,
　　For nou is tyme to take my leue.　　　64

98.　　　　*Deus Caritas Est.*

Vernon MS.

*D**Eus caritas est,*—　　　　　　f. 407^b
　　A ! deore god omnipotent,　　　　　(col. 2)
lord, þou madest boþe foul & best—
　　On eorþe to mon þou here hit sent.　　4
I warne ȝow alle, boþe more & lest,
　　Charite I rede þat ȝe hent,
For hit is cristes hest,
　　Þat schal come to þe Iugement.　　　8

For whon he comeþ a domes-day,
　　Þat al þis world hit schal wel se,
Þe wikked he biddeþ to gon heor way,
　　In bitter penaunce for euere to be ;　　12
And to þe goode wol þat lord say :
　　' ȝe schul alle wende wiþ me
In-to þe blisse for euere and ay ;
　　Et qui manet in caritate.'　　　16

God þat made boþe heuene & helle,
　　Vre swete lord of Naȝareþ—
Adam þat was so feir of felle,
　　For his folyes he suffred deþ.　　　20
In God forsoþe he schal dwelle,
　　In charite ho-so geþ.
Hit is soþ þat I ou telle,
　　Bi-hold and seo, *In deo manet.*　　　24

Crist was toren vch a lim,
 And on þe Roode he was I-do ;
Þe fend þat was so derk and dym,
 To þe crois he com þo.   28
Crist—al charite is in him—
 Þere he ouer-com vr fo.
Charite I rede þat þou nym,
 And þenne *Deus est in eo*.   32

Let Charite nou awake,
 And do hit þer neod is.
Heuene, forsoþe, þen maiȝt þou take,
 And come to þat riche blis.   36
Nou crist, for his Moder sake,
 Let vs neuere þis place mis,
And schild vs from þe fendes blake,
 And *Sit deus in nobis*.   40

And charite I rede þat we be-ginne,
 As bi-fore alle oþer games,
And schriue vs clene of vre synne,
 For so dude Peter, Ion, and Iames ;   44
And þerfore god hem dwelled with-Inne,
 For þei weoren alle with-outen oþer blames.
Crist, let vs heuene wynne,
 E⟨t⟩ *nos in ipso maneamus*.   48

God þat dwelleþ in gret solas
 In heuene, þat riche regnyng,
And for vs þolede gret trespas
 Wonder muche at vre muntyng—   52
On þe Roode don he was,
 In gret dispyt I-cleped a kyng.
Þenkeþ nouþe On *Deus caritas*,
 And bring vs alle to good endyng.   56

99.   *Deo Gracias.   II.*

Vernon MS.

MI word is *Deo gracias*,   f. 407^b
   In world wher me be wel or wo.   (col. 3)
Hou scholde I lauȝwhe or sigge 'Allas'?
   For, leeue me wel, hit ⟨ne⟩ lasteþ o,   4
   And þouȝ hit greue, hit wol ouer go
As þouȝt chaungeþ, for such is graas.
   Þerfore, wher me beo wel or wo,
I sey not But *deo gracias*.   8

Þouȝ I beo riche of gold so red,
   And liht to renne as is a Ro,
Anoþur is boun to begge his bred
   Wiþ brestes blak and bleynes blo.   12
Whon I seo good de-parted so,—
     To sum Mon God sent gret solas
And sum Mon ay to liuen in wo—
   Þen sei I *Deo Gracias*.   16

Þou he beo pore and lyue in peyn,
   Anoþer mon proudeþ as doþ a poo,
Whon murþe is his & Mourning myn;
   As may be-falle to me and mo,   20
   ȝif fortune wolde be so my fo
     From me to turne hir freoly faas.
Seþþe god may sende boþe weole & wo,
   I sei not but *Deo Gracias*.   24

A lord of worchup ȝif I ware,
   And weore falle doun in a wro,
Siknesse sitteþ me so sare,
   And serwe wol neiȝ myn herte slo.   28
Þus am I bounde from top til to
     And I-turmente so for my trespas—
   ȝif God may loose me of þat wo,
   And þenne I sey *Deo Gracias*.   32

Whon I hedde spendyng her be-forn,
　　þer wolde no felauschip fonde me fro ;
But herkne & hiȝe to myn horn,
　　For in myn hond þer stod non ho.　　　　36
　　Nou a-peereþ non of þo—
　　　　So pouert a-peired haþ my plas.
　　Ho may haue wele with-oute wo?
　　　　þerfore I sey *Deo gracias.*　　　　40

Almihti, corteis, Crouned kyng,
　　God graunt vs grace to rule vs so
þat we may come to þi wonyng,
　　þer is wele wiþ-outen wo.　　　　44
　　Milde Mayde, prey þi sone also,
　　　　þat he for-ȝiue vs vre trespas,
　　And afterward in-to heuene go,
　　　　þer to synge *Deo gracias.*　　Amen.　　48

100. Each Man ought Himself to Know.

Vernon MS.

IN a Pistel þat poul wrouȝt　　　　f. 407ᵇ
　　I fond hit writen & seide riht þis :　(col. 3)
Vche cristne creature knowen himself ouȝt
　　His oune vessel ; and soþ hit is.　　　　4
Nere help of him þat vs deore bouȝt,
　　We weoren bore to luytel blis.
Whon al þi gode dedes beþ þorw-souȝt,
　　Seche, and þou schalt fynden Amis.　　8
Eueri mon scholde I-knowen his,
　　And þat is luitel, as I trowe ;
　　To teche vs self, crist vs wis,
　　　　For vche mon ouȝte him-self to knowe.　12

Knowe þi-self what þou ware,
    Whon þou were of þi moder born,
Ho was þi moder þat þe bare,
    And ho was þi fader þer-bi-foren.   16
Knowe hou þei beþ forþ-fare,
    So schaltou þeiȝ þou hed sworen;
Knowe þou come hider wiþ care,
    Þou nost neuer, ȝif þou byde til morn,   20
    Hou lihtly þou maiȝt be forlorn,
        But þou þi sinne schriue & schowe;
    For lond or kiþ, Catel or corn,
        Vche mon oute him-self to knowe.   24

Knowe þi lyf, hit may not last,
    But as a blast blou⟨t⟩h out þi breth,—
Tote and bi a-noþer mon tast—
    Riht as a glentand glem hit geth.   28
What is al þat forþ is past?
    hit fareþ as a fuir of heth;
Þis worldes good a-wey wol wast.
    For synnes seeknesse þi soule sleþ,   32
    And þat is a ful delful deþ;   f. 408
        To saue þi soule, ar þou be slowe,   (col. 1)
    Wiþ þi Maystrie medel þi meþ,
        For vche mon ouȝte him-self to knowe. 36

Ȝif þou þi-self knowe con,
    Sit doun, and tac Countures rounde:
Seþþe furst þou monnes wit bi-gon,
    Hou ofte sunne þe haþ I-bounde?   40
And for vch a synne lei þou doun on,
    Til þou þi synnes haue I-souȝt vp sounde.
Counte þi goode dedes euerichon;
    Abyd þer a while and stunte a stounde;   44

34 MS. and þou.

And ȝif þou fele þe siker and sounde,
  Þonk þou þi god as þou wel owe;
And ȝif þou art In sunne I-bounde,
  Amende þe, and þi-self knowe.   48

Knowe what god haþ for þe do :—
  Made þe after his oune liknes ;
Seþþe he com from heuene also,
  And diȝede for þe with gret distres ;   52
For þe he soffrede boþe pyne and wo.
  Knowe þou him and alle his ;
Who-so greueþ him Is worþi to go
  To helle-fuir, but he hit red⟨r⟩es,   56
And he be demed bi rihtfulnes.
    But his grace is so wyde I-sowe,
  From his wraþþe I rede vs bles—
    For vche mon ouȝte him-self to knowe. 60

Knowe þi-self, þat þou schalt dye,
  But what tyme þou nost neuer whenne ;
Wiþ a twynklyng of an eiȝe,
  Eueri day þou hiȝest þe henne.   64
Þi fleschly foode þe wormes wol fye—
  Vche cristen mon ouȝte þis to kenne.
Loke a-boute and wel a-spye,
  Þis world doþ bote bi-traye menne ;   68
  And beo war of þe fuir þat euer schal brenne,
    And þenk þou regnest her but a þrowe ;
  Heuene-blisse þou schal haue þenne,
    For vche mon ouȝte him-self to knowe. 72

Knowe þi flesch, þat wol rote ;
  For certes, þou maiȝt not longe endure ;
And nedes dye, hennes þou mote,
  Þei þou haue kyngdam and Empyre ;   76

76 MS. kyngdan.

And sone þou schalt beo for-gote,
　So schal souereyn, so schal syre.
Hose leeueþ not þis, I trouwe he dote,
　For eueri mok most in-to myre.　　　80
　　Preye we to god vr soules enspire
　　　Or we ben logged in erþe lowe,
　　Heuene to haue to vr huire—
　　　For vche mon ouȝte him-self to knowe. 84

Knowe þi kuynde Creatoure,
　Knowe what he for þe dide;
Knowe þis worldly honoure,
　Hou sone þat hit is forþ I-slyde;　　88
Ende of Ioye Is her douloure,
　Strengþe stont vs in no stide,
But longyng & beoing in laboure.
　　Vr Bost, vr Brag is sone ouerbide;　92
　　Arthur and Ector þat we dredde,
　　　Deth haþ leid hem wonderly lowe;
　　Amende þe, Mon, euene forþ-mide,
　　　For vche mon ouȝte him-self to knowe. 96

Þi Concience schal þe saue and deme,
　Wheþer þat þou beo ille or good;
Grope aboute and tak good ȝeme,
　Þer maiȝt þou wite, but þou beo wood;　100
Þer schalt þou þe same seone.
　Aske Merci wiþ Mylde mood,
Amende þe—þou wot what I mene—
　　Vche creatur þat beres bon and blood.　104
　　Preye we to god þat dyed on Rode,
　　　Ar vre breþ beo out I-blowe,
　　Þat cristes face mai ben vr foode.
　　　For vche mon ouȝte him-self to knowe. 108

101. *Think on Yesterday.*

Vernon MS.

WHon Men beoþ muriest at heor Mele,   f. 408ᵃ
⟨w⟩iþ mete & drink to maken hem glade, (col. 1)
⟨W⟩iþ worschip & with worldlich wele,
  þei ben so set þey conne not sade ;   4
þei haue no deynte for to dele   f. 408
  With þinges þat ben deuoutli made ;   (col. 2)
þei weene heor honour & heore hele
  Schal euer laste & neuer diffade ;   8
  But in heor hertes I wolde þei hade,
    Whon þei gon ricchest men on aray,
  Hou sone þat god hem may de-grade,
    And sum tyme þenk on ȝuster-day.   12

þis day, as leef we may be liht,
  Wiþ al þe murþes þat men may vise,
To Reuele wiþ þis buirdes briht,
  Vche mon gayest on his gyse ;   16
At þe last hit draweþ to niht,
  þat slep most make his Maystrise.
Whon þat he haþ I-kud his miht,
  þe morwe he boskeþ vp to rise,   20
  þen al draweþ hem to fantasy⟨s⟩e.
    Wher he is bi-comen, con no mon say—
  And ȝif heo wuste þei weore ful wise—
    For al is tornd to ȝester-day.   24

Whose wolde þenke vppon þis
  Mihte fynde a good enchesun whi
To preue þis world, al-wei I-wis
  Hit nis but fantum and feiri.   28

Þis erþly Ioye, þis worldly blis
    Is but a fikel fantasy,
For nou hit is and nou hit nis,
    Þer may no mon þer-inne affy;   32
    Hit chaungeþ so ofte & so sodeynly,
        To-day is her, to-morwe a-way—
    A siker ground ho wol him gy,
        I rede he þenke on ȝuster-day.   36

For þer nis non so strong in stour,
    Fro tyme þat he ful waxen be,
From þat day forþ, euer-vch an hour,
    Of his strengþe he leost a quantite.   40
Ne no buyrde so briht in bour,
    Of þritti wynter, I enseure þe,
Þat heo ne schal fade as a flour,
    Luite and luite leosen hire beute—   44
    Þe soþe ȝe may ȝor-self I-se
        Beo ȝor eldres in good fay.
    Whon ȝe ben grettest in ȝour degre,
        I. rede ȝe þenke on ȝesterday.   48

Nis non so fresch on fote to fare,
    Ne non so fayr on fold to fynde,
Þat þei ne schul a bere be brouȝt ful bare.
    Þis wrecched world nis but a wynde,   52
Ne non so stif to stunte ne stare,
    Ne non so bold Beores to bynde,
Þat he naþ warnynges to beo ware,
    For god is so corteys and so kynde.   56
    Bi-hold þe lame, þe bedrede, þe blynde,
        Þat bit ȝou be war whil þat ȝe may.
    Þei make a Mirour to ȝor mynde,
        To seo þe schap of ȝester-day.   60

Þe lyf þat eny mon schal lede,
   Beþ certeyn dayes atte last;
Þen moste vr terme schorte nede,
   Be o day comen a-noþer is past;   64
Her-of and we wolde take good hede
   And in vr hertes a-countes cast,
Day bi day, wiþouten drede,
   Toward vr ende we draweþ ful fast;   68
Þen schal vr bodies in erþe be þrast,
   Vr Careyns chouched vnder clay.
Her-of we ouȝte beo sore agast,
   And we wolde þenke on ȝester-day.   72

Salamon seide in his poysi,
   He holdeþ wel betere with an hounde
Þat is lykyng and Ioly,
   And of seknesse hol and sounde,   76
Þen be a Leon, þouȝ he ly
   Cold and ded vppon þe grounde.
Wher-of serueþ his victori,
   Þat was so stif in vche a stounde?   80
Þe moste fool, I herde respounde,
   Is wysore whil he lyue may,
Þen he þat hedde a þousend pounde
   And was buried ȝuster-day.   84

Socrates seiþ a word ful wys: f. 408
   Hit were wel betere for to se   (col. 3)
A Mon þat nou parteþ and dys,
   Þen a feste of Realte.   88
Þe feste wol make his flesch to ris,
   And drawe his herte to vanite;
Þe Bodi þat on þe Bere lys,
   Scheweþ þe same þat we schal be.   92
Þat ferful fit may no mon fle
   Ne wiþ no wiles win hit a-way;
Þerfore a-mong al Iolyte,
   Sum tyme þenk on ȝuster-day.   96

95 MS. a mon.

But ȝit me mcruevles ouer al
　Þat God let mony mon croke and elde,
Whon miht & strengþe is from hem fal,
　Þat þei may not hem-self a-welde ;　　　　100
And now þis beggers most principal,
　Þat good ne profyt may non ȝelde.
To þis purpos onswere I schal,
　Whi god sent such men boote & belde :　　104
Crist, þat Made boþe flour & felde,
　　Let suche men lyue, forsoþe to say,
Whon a ȝong mon on hem bi-helde,
　　Scholde seo þe schap of ȝester-day.　　　108

A-noþur skile þer is for-whi
　Þat God let such men liue so longe :
For þei beþ treacle and remedi
　For synful men þat han do wronge.　　　112
In hem þe seuen dedes of Merci
　A Mon may fulfille a-monge ;
And also þis proude men may þer-bi
　A feir Mirour vnderfonge.　　　　116
　For þer nis non so stif ne stronge,
　　Ne no ladi stout ne gay,—
Bi-hold what ouer hor hed con honge,
　　And sum tyme þenk on ȝuster-day.　　120

I haue wist, sin I cuþe meen,
　Þat children haþ bi candel liht
Heor schadewe on þe wal i-sen,
　And Ronne þer-after al þe niht ;　　　124
Bisy a-boute þei han ben
　To cacchen hit with al heore miht,
And whon þei cacchen hit best wolde wene,
　Sannest hit schet out of heor siht ;　　128
Þe schadewe cacchen þei ne miht,
　For no lynes þat þei couþe lay.
Þis schadewe I may likne a-riht
　To þis world and ȝuster-day.　　　132

In-to þis world whon we beþ brouȝt,
　　We schul be tempt to couetyse,
And al þi wit schal be þorw-souȝt
　　To more good þen þou may suffyse.　　　136
Whon þou þenkest best in þi þouȝt
　　On Richesse fo⟨r⟩te regne and ryse,
Al þi trauayle turneþ to nouȝt,
　　For sodeynly on deþ þou dyese.　　　140
Þi lyf þou hast I-lad wiþ lyȝes,
　　So þis world gon þe be-tray;
Þerfore I rede þou þis dispys,
　　And sum tyme þenk on ȝuster-day.　　　144

Mon, ȝif þi neiȝebor þe Manas,
　　Oþur to culle or to bete;
I knowe me siker in þe cas
　　Þat þou wolt drede þi neiȝebores þrete,　　148
And neuer a day þi dore to pas
　　Wiþ-oute siker defense and grete,
And ben purueyed in vche a plas
　　Of sikernes and help to gete.　　　152
Þin enymy woltou not for-ȝete
　　But ay beo a-fert of his affray.
Ensaumple her-of I wol ȝou trete,
　　To make ȝou þenke of ȝuster-day.　　　156

Wel þou wost wiþ-outen fayle
　　Þat deþ haþ manast þe to dye,
But whon þat he wol þe a-sayle,
　　Þat wost þou not, ne neuer may spye.　　160
Ȝif þou wolt don be my counsayle,
　　Wiþ siker defence beo ay redye;
For siker defence in þis batayle
　　Is clene lyf, parfyt and trye;　　　164
Put þi trust in Godes Mercye,　　f. 408ᵇ
　　Hit is þe beste at al assay,
And euer a-mong þou þe en-nuye
　　In-to þis world and ȝuster-day.　　　168

Sum men seiþ þat deþ is a þef,
 And al vnwarned wol on him stele,
And I sey nay, and make a pref,
 Þat deþ is studefast, trewe, and lele,   172
And warneþ vche mon of his greef,
 Þat he wol o day wiþ him dele.
Þe lyf þat is to ow so leof,
 He wol ȝou reue, and eke ⟨ȝ⟩or hele;   176
 Þis poyntes may no mon him repele,
  He comeþ so baldely to pyke his pray—
When men beoþ murgest at heor Mele,
  I rede ȝe þenke on ȝuster-day.   180

102. Keep well Christ's Commandments.

Vernon MS.

I Warne vche leod þat liueþ in londe, f. 408^b
 And do hem dredles out of were, (col. 1)
Þat þei most studie and vnderstonde,
 Þe lawe of crist to loue and lere.   4
 Þer nis no mon fer ne nere
  Þat may him-seluen saue vn-schent,
 But he þat casteþ wiþ concience clere
  To kepe wel Cristes Comaundement. 8

Þow most haue o God and no mo,
 And serue him boþe with mayn and miht;
And ouer alle þinges loue him also,
 For he haþ lant þe lyf and liht.   12
 Ȝif þou beo nuyȝed day or niht,
  In peyne be meke and pacient;
 And rule þe ay be reson riht,
  And kep wel Cristes Comaundement. 16

And let þi neiȝhebor, frend and fo,
　Riht frely of þi frendschupe fele,
In herte þat þou wilne hem so
　　Riht as þou woldest þi-self weore wele ;　　20
　And help to sauen hem from vncele,
　　So þat heore soules beo not schent ;
　And also heore care þou helpe to kele,
　　　And kepe wel Cristes comaundement.　　24

In Idel Godes nome tak þou nouȝt,
　But cese and saue þe from þat synne ;
Swere bi no þing þat God haþ wrouht ;
　Be war his wraþþe lest þou hit wynne,　　28
　But bisy þe her bale to blynne,
　　þat blaberyng are wiþ oþes blent,—
　Vncouþe & knowen & of þi kynne——
　　　And kep wel cristes comaundement.　　32

In clannes and in cristes werk
　Haue mynde to holden þin haly day ;
And drauh þe þenne from dedes derk,
　Wiþ al þi meyne, Mon and may ;　　36
　And men vnsauȝte loke þou assay
　　To sauȝten hem þenne at on assent ;
　And pore and seke þou plese & pay,
　　　And kepe wel cristes Comaundement.　　40

þi Fader, þi Moder, þou worschupe boþe
　ȝif þou wolt boteles bale escheuwe ;
With counseil cumforte hem, with mete & cloþe,
　As þou sest hem neodeþ newe ;　　44
　And ȝif þei talke of tales vn-trewe,
　　þou torn hem out of þat entent ;
　And cristes lawe help þat þei knewe,
　　　And kep wel cristes Comaundement.　　48

Sle no mon wiþ wikked wille;
  Be war and vengeaunce tak þou non,
In word ne dede, loude ne stille.
    Bakbyte þou no mon, blod ny bon,   52
    But ay let gabbynges glyde and gon
      A-wey wher þei wol glace or glent;
    And help þat alle men ben aton,
      And kep wel cristes comaundement.   56

Stele þou nouȝt þi neiȝebors þing,
  Nouþur with stillenes ne wiþ strif,
Nor with no maner wrong getyng—
    Þi self, þi seruaunt, child, ne wyf;   60
    To sulle & buye ȝif þou be ryf,
      Wayte al-way þat wrong be went;
    As þou wolt lyue þe lastyng lyf,
      Þou kepe wel cristes comaundement.   64

Fals witnesse loke þow non bere,   f. 408ᵇ
  ȝif þow wolt in blisse a-byde,   (col. 2)
Þi neiȝebore wityngly to dere,
    Ne no mon nouþer in no syde;   68
    But loke þat no mon be anuyȝed,
      And þou may him from harmes hent,
    And help þat falshede beo distruiet,
      And kep wel cristes comaundement.   72

Sunge þou not in lecherie;
  Such lust vn-leueful let hit pas.
Consente þou not to such folye,
    Þat founden is so foul trespas,   76
    And loke þat nouþer more ne las
      Þi lykyng on þat lust be lent,
    Leste þou synge þis songe, 'allas!
      For brekyng of cristes comaundement.'   80

Þi neiȝhebors wyf coueyte þou nouȝt
  Vnleuefully, a-ȝeynes þe lawe
Wiþ hire to sunge in word ne þouȝt ;
  And from þat deede euer þou þe drawe,   84
  And neuer sey to hire no sawe
    To make hire to synne assent ;
  Ne plese hire not with no mis-plawe,
    But kep wel cristes comaundement.   88

Þi neiȝhebors hous, wenche, ne knaue
  Vnskilfully coueyte þou nouht,
Ne ȝit his good with wrong to haue,
  For hit lest þou to bale be brouht ;   92
  For whon þe soþe schal vp be souht,
    ȝif þou in-to þis sunnes assent,
  Ful bitterly hit mot be bouȝt,
    For brekyng of cristes Comaundement.   96

Vche mon þat wol þis lessun lere
  And loueþ a laweful lyf to lede,
He may not misse on none manere
  Þe merþe of heuene to his mede ;   100
  For crist him here wol helpe & hede
    And heþene in-to heuene hent ;
  For-þi I preye þat crist vs spede
    Kuyndely to kepe his comaundement.   104

103. Who says the Sooth, He shall be Shent.

Vernon MS.

Þᴇ Mon þat luste to liuen in ese,   f. 408ᵇ
   Or eny worschupe her to ateyne,   (col. 2)
His purpos I counte not worþ a pese,
Witterli, but he ordeyne   4
Þis wikked world hou he schal plese
Wiþ al his pouwer and his peyne :
ȝif he schal kepe him from disese,
He mot lerne to flatere and feyne ;   8
Herte & mouþ loke þei ben tweyne,
Þei mowe not ben of on assent ;
And ȝit his tonge he mot restreyne,
For hos seiþ þe soþe, he schal be schent.   12

Þus is þe soþe I-kept in close,
And vche mon makeþ touh and queynte ;
To leue þe tixt and take þe glose,
Eueri word þei coloure and peynte.   16
Summe þer aren þat wolden suppose
For no tresour forte ben teynte :
Let a mon haue not to lose,
He schal fynde frenschipe feynte :   20
Summe þat semen an Innocent,
Wonder trewe in heore entent,
Þei beoþ a-gast of eueri pleynt,
For hos seiþ þe soþe, he schal be schent.   24

Þe wikked wone we may warie,
Þat eueri mon þus Inward bledes.
Let a lord haue his Corlarie,
He schal wel knowe of al his dedes,   28

14 mon *interlined by corrector.*

Þauȝ he be next his sacratarie ;
Wiþ flaterynge his lord he fedes,
And with sum speche he most him tarie,
And þus with lesynges him he ledes ;   32
To gabben his lord most him nedes,
And with sum blaundise make him blent,—
To leosen his offys euere he dredes,
For ȝif he þe soþe seiþ, he schal be schent.   36

And al is wrong, þat dar I preue ;
For let a mon be sore I-wounde,
Hou schulde a leche þis mon releeue,
But ȝif he miȝte ronsake þe wounde ?   40
For þauȝ hit smerte & sumdel greue,   (col. 3)
ȝit most he suffre a luitel stounde.
ȝif he kneuh of his mischeue,
With salues he miȝte make him sounde.   44
Were grace at large, þat liþ i-bounde,
Hap and hele mihte we hent ;
Lac of leche wol vs confounde,
For hos seiþ þe soþe, þe schal be schent.   48

For let a frere in Godes seruise
Þe pereles to þe peple preche,
Of vre misdede & vre queyntise,
Þe trewe tixt to telle and teche ;   52
Þauȝ he beo riht witti and wyse,
ȝit luytel þonk he schal him reche ;
And summe þer ben þat wol him spise,
And bleþely wayte him with sum wreche.   56
Þis pore prechour þei wolen apeche
At counseyl and at parliment ;
But ȝif he kepe him out of heore cleche,
For his soþ sawe he schal be schent.   60

45 MS. lippe.

Seþþe þe tyme þat god was boren,
Þis world was neuer so vntrewe;
Men recchen neuer to ben for-sworen,
To reuen þat is hem ful duwe;   64
Þe peynted word þat fel bi-foren,
Be-hynde, hit is anoþer hewe.
Whon Gabriel schal blowe his horn,
His feble fables schul hym rewe: 68
Þe tonges þat such bargeyn gon brewe,
Hit weore non harm þouȝ þei were brent.
Þus þis gyle is founde vp of newe,
For hos seiþ soþ, he schal be schent.   72

Siþen þe soþe dar no mon say,
For drede to geten him a fo,
Best I holde hit, in good fay,
Let o day come, a-noþer go,   76
And mak as murie as we may,
Til eueri frend parte oþur fro.
I drede hit draweþ to domes-day,
Such saumples we han, & oþer two: 80
Now knowes a child boþe weole & wo,
Þat scholde ben an Innocent,
Whil hit is ȝong, is norissched so,—
But hos seiþ soþ, he schal be schent.   84

Þis world wol han his wikked wone,
For soþe hit wol non oþer be;
His cursede cours þat is bi-gonne,
Þer may no mon from hit fle   88
Þat haþ longe a-mong vs ronne,
His oune defaute mai he not se.
Þe fader trust not to þe sone,
Ne non to oþer in no degre;   92
Falshede is called a sotilte
And such a nome hit haþ hent.
Þis lesson lerneþ alle at me:
Ho seiþ þe soþe, he schal be schent.   96

104. *Fy on a faint Friend!*

Vernon MS.

FRenschipe faileþ & fullich fadeþ,   f. 408^{b}
  Feiþful frendes fewe we fynde,   (col. 3)
But glosers þat vche mon gladeþ
    Wiþ feire bi-heste and wordes as wynde;   4
  But let a mon ones be cast be-hynde
    And with þis world turmented & tenet,
He schal ful sone ben out of mynde—
    And þere fy on a feynt frend!   8

Þe while þat þou ledest þi lyf in ese
  And goodlich gouernest þyn a-state,
Þe fyndest I-nouwe þat wol þe plese
    And folwe þi wil boþe erliche & late;   12
  ȝif þi los bi-gynne to abate
    And þy good from þe gon wende,
Þei schul be þe furste þat þe wol hate—
    And þer fy on a feynt frende!   16

Þus þou schalt, ar þou haue nede,
  Al þi frendes folly I-knowen
And seyen heo dor not helpen þe
    For drede, for fere þei lost her owen.   20
  Þei þat sum tyme wente ful lowe,
    Hem luste no lengore with þe to lende,
Beo-hynde þi bak heo makeþ a Mouwe—
    And þer fy on a feynt frende!   24

4 wynde: MS. wylde.

To þi-self trust al-wei best,   f. 409
  For as þou dost so schaltou haue ;   (col. 1)
Brek þe leste bouȝ of þi nest,
  Þou tyndest I-nouwe wol hit þe bi-raue,   28
    And wole dispise þe and repraue,
      And sakeles wayte þe schame and schende
    In such a cas, so god me saue—
      And euere fy on a feynt frende !   32

ȝif þou wolt not ben frendles,
  Lern to kepe þat þou hast ;
Loke þou be not penyles,
  Ne spend þou nouȝt þi good in wast.   36
  Or þou haue nede, þi frendes a-tast,
    Wȝuche be stif & wȝuche wol bende,
    And þer þou fynde bouwynde or bast—
      And euer fy on a feynt frende !   40

In feiþ þat Frendschip hold I nouȝt,
  To profer þe whon þou hast no nede ;
But ȝif þou weore in daunger brouȝt,
  Hose helpeþ þe þenne is worþi meede ;   44
  Hose wolde þe nouþur profre ne beode,
    He serueþ þonk wiþ-outen ende—
    Such frendes are fewe I-laft in leode,
      And þerfore fy on a feynt frende !   48

Ho⟨u⟩ scholde eny frendschupe ben I-founde ?
  Good feiþ is flemed out of þis londe ;
Þer is more treuþe in an hounde
  Þen in sum mon, I vnderstonde ;   52
  Knackes & mowes þei han In honde,
    Witterli to plese þe fende.
  He þat furst þat frendschip fonde,
    Euer fy on him for a feynt frende !   56

28 Þou: MS. Þe.   37 MS. frendest.

Eueri mon I counseile
　　To gouerne him in such a wyse,
if hit so beo þat frendschup fayle,
　　His owne deden wol maken him ryse.　　60
Hold him In a mene a-syse—
　　Euer to beo corteys and hende,
þen baldely may he dispise.
　　Euere fy on a feynt frende !　　64

þi lessun loke þat ȝe leore,
　　Whon ȝe haþe soþe souȝt and seid:
Trust on non such frendschup here—
　　Ho sannest do is tytes bi-trayed—　　68
Loke al ȝor loue on him beo leyd,
　　For vs on Rode was prikket & prenet.
Do we so þat crist beo payet,
　　And þenne we hauen a syker frend.　　72

105.　*Ever more Thank God of All.*

MS. Ashmole 343.

BY a way wandry⟨n⟩g as I went,　　f. 169[a]
　　For sorow sore I sykyt sadde ;
Hard happis me haþe hent,
And morny⟨n⟩g made me al madde ;　　4
Tyl a lettre of loue me lede,
þat was wyrtyn on a wall.
A blesful worde þer I rede
And euer I þank my god of all.　　8

5 Tyll a lettre: MS. Tyl aȝt.

ȝit I rade wel furþyre more—
Ful trew atent I tok me till—
cryst may euer ous restore,
Hit is noȝt to stryue a-ȝenyus his wyll.   12
Cryst may ous boþe saue & spill ;
Þynk ryȝt well we ben his þrall.
What vo oþer blys cum ous tyll,
euer we þank oure god of all.   16

ȝyf þou wex blyne or lame,
oþer any sekenys be on ȝow set,
Þynk ryȝt wel hit is no schame,
Þe gras of god þat þe haþ gret.   20
ȝyf þou be in sorowis knette   f. 169ᵇ
And þi prosperite be-gyn to fall,
I can red þe no bette,
Bot euer more þank god of all.   24

ȝif þou weld þis worldis gode
And ryaly þou leuyst þi lyf in rest,
Fayre of face, fre of mode,
Is none þi pere be hest ne west ;   28
God may sen al as him lyst—
Reches tornyþ as a ball.
In al maner I hold it best
Euer more þank þi god of all.   32

ȝif þi godys be fro þe pasce
And þou wexist a pore man,
Hold vp þi hed & bere gode face
And þynk on him þat al gode wan ;   36
Þynk of god al gode be-came,
He may rew boþe boure & hall,
ȝit þe best rede þat I canne :
Euer more þank þi god of all.   40

18 on: MS. ou.

ȝyth þynk on Iop þat was so ryche,   f. 170ᵃ
How he wax pore fram day to day ;
Hys bestis deyt in euery dyche,
His cattel fanchyt all a-way;   44
He was powt in pore aray
In purpure noþer in pall,
In sympil wedys, clerkys say,
And euer he þankyt his god of all.   48

For goddys loue so do we,
And þynk on him þat all schall make ;
Wat wo oþer care we in be,
He haþe myȝt oure sorowys to slake ;   52
Ful gode amennys he wol ous make
and we ⟨wiþ⟩ gode hert on him call.
Þi tyme with gode entent þou take
And euer more þank þi god of all.   56

ȝyf þou be in presoun cast
Oþer eny distres men wol þe   bede,
For godis loue be stydefast
And euer more þink on þi crede.   60
Be war þow falsym neuer at nede,   f. 170ᵇ
Þat derwarte duk schal deme ous all ;
In wel oþer wo ȝe tak gode hede
And euer more þank þi god of all.   64

ȝif þi frenchep fro þe faylle
And depe be-rewyt ham hare lyfe,
Warto schuldistou wepe oþer waylle ?
Hit is not gode with god to strywe ;   68
For god haþe made boþe man & wyfe,
And ȝaf ham wytte boþe gret & smal.
Of al my mysdedis i ham to-scrywe
And euer I þank my god of all.   72

54 him call: MS. him to call.   63 MS. hete.   64 more] MS. noþ.

Cryst, sende ous gras & powste
So to rewl oure sowlys þroȝt-out.
Þe blys of heuyn, lord, grant me
Þer to dwelle in & out.   76
Þan dar I say with-outyn dowte,
In heuyne blys schal be oure stall,
Pore & ryche þat lowyþ to lowte,
And euer þay þankyt haþ god of all.   80

106. This World fares as a Fantasy.

Vernon MS.

I Wolde witen of sum wys wiht   f. 409ᵃ
  Witterly what þis world were :   (col. 3)
Hit fareþ as a foules fliht,
  Now is hit henne, now is hit here,   4
Ne be we neuer so muche of miht,
  Now be we on benche, nou be we on bere ;
And be we neuer so war and wiht,
  Now be we sek, now beo we fere,   8
  Now is on proud wiþ-outen peere,
    Now is þe selue I-set not by ;
  And whos wol alle þing her⟨t⟩ly here,
    Þis world fareþ as a Fantasy.   12

Þe sonnes cours, we may wel kenne,
  Aryseþ Est and geþ doun west ;
Þe Ryuers in-to þe séé þei renne,
  And hit is neuer þe more al-mest ;   16
Wyndes Rosscheþ her and henne,
  In snouȝ and reyn is non arest ;

Whon þis wol stunte, ho wot or whenne,
  But only god on grounde grest?   20
  Þe eorþe in on is euer prest,
    Now bi-dropped, now al druyȝe;
  But vche gome glit forþ as a gest,
    Þis world fareþ as a Fantasye.   24

Kunredes come, & kunredes gon,
  As Ioyneþ generacions;
But alle hee passeþ euerichon,
  For al heor preparacions;   28
Sum are for-ȝete clene as bon
  A-mong alle maner nacions;
So schul men þenken vs no-þing on
  Þat nou han þe ocupacions;   32
  And alle þeos disputacions
    Idelyche all vs ocupye,
  For crist makeþ þe creacions,
    And þis world fareþ as a fantasye.   36

Whuch is Mon, ho wot, and what,
  Wheþer þat he be ouȝt or nouht?
Of Erþe & Eyr groweþ vp a gnat,
  And so doþ Mon whon al his souht;   40
Þauȝ mon be waxen gret and fat,
  Mon melteþ a-wey so deþ a mouht.
Monnes miht nis worþ a Mat,
  But nuyȝeþ him-self and turneþ to nouȝt.   44
  Ho wot, saue he þat al haþ wrouȝt,
    Wher mon bi-comeþ whon he schal dye?
  Ho knoweþ bi dede ouȝt bote bi þouȝt?
    For þis world fareþ as a fantasye.   48

Dyeþ mon, and beestes dye,
  And al is on Ocasion;
And alle o deþ bos boþe drye,
  And han on Incarnacion;   52

51 bos: MS. hos.

Saue þat men beoþ more sleyӡe,
  Al is o comparison.
Ho wot ӡif monnes soule styӡe,
  And bestes soules synkeþ doun?   56
  Who knoweþ Beestes entencioun,   f. 409ᵇ
    On heor creatour how þei crie,   (col. 1)
  Saue only god þat knoweþ heore soun?
    For þis world fareþ as a fantasye.   60

Vche secte hopeþ to be saue,
  Baldely bi heore bi-leeue;
And vchon vppon God heo craue—
  Whi schulde God wiþ hem him greue?   64
Vchon trouweþ þat oþur Raue,
  But alle heo cheoseþ God for cheue,
And hope in God vchone þei haue,
  And bi heore wit heore worching preue.   68
  Þus mony maters men don meue,
    Sechen heor wittes hou and why;
  But Godes Merci vs alle bi-heue⟨þ⟩,
    For þis world fareþ as a fantasy.   72

For þus men stumble & sere heore witte,
  And meueþ maters mony and fele;
Summe leeueþ on him, sum leueþ on hit,
  As children leorneþ for to spele.   76
But non seoþ non þat a-bit,
  Whon stilly deþ wol on hym stele.
For he þat hext in heuene sit,
  He is þe help and hope of hele;   80
  For wo is ende of worldes wele,—
    Vche lyf loke wher þat I lye—
  Þis world is fals, fikel and frele,
    And fareþ but as a fantasye.   84

73 MS. wittes.

Whar-to wilne we forte knowe
   þe poyntes of Godes priuete?
More þen him lustes forte schowe
    We schulde not knowe in no degre;   88
And Idel bost is forte blowe
   A Mayster of diuinite.
Þenk we lyue in eorþe her lowe,
    And God an heiȝ in Mageste;   92
   Of Material Mortualite
    Medle we & of no more Maistrie.
Þe more we trace þe Trinite,
    Þe more we falle in fantasye.   96

But leue we vre disputisoun,
   And leue on him þat al haþ wrouȝt;
We mowe no⟨t⟩ preue bi no resoun
    Hou he was born þat al vs bouȝt;   100
But hol in vre entencioun,
   Worschipe we him in herte & þouȝt,
For he may turne kuyndes vpsedoun,
    Þat alle kuyndes made of nouȝt.   104
   Whon al vr bokes ben forþ brouht,
    And al vr craft of clergye,
   And al vr wittes ben þorw-out souȝt,
    ȝit we fareþ as a fantasye.   108

Of fantasye is al vr fare,
   Olde & ȝonge and alle I-fere;
But make we murie & sle care,
    And worschipe we god whil we ben here;   112
Spende vr good and luytel spare,
   And vche mon cheries oþures cheere.

87 MS. lustnes.

M 2

Þenk hou we comen hider al bare,—
   Vr wey wendyng is in a were—   116
  Prey we þe prince þat haþ no pere,
    Tac vs hol to his Merci
  And kepe vr Concience clere,
    For þis world is but fantasy.   120

Bi ensaumple men may se,
  A gret treo grouweþ out of þe grounde ;
No þing a-bated þe eorþe wol be
  Þauȝ hit be huge, gret, and rounde.   124
Riht þer wol Rooten þe selue tre,
  Whon elde haþ maad his kuynde aswounde ;
Þauȝ þer weore rote suche þre,
    Þe eorþe wol not encrece a pounde.   128
  Þus waxeþ & wanieþ Mon, hors, & hounde,
    From nouȝt to nouȝt þus henne we hiȝe ;
  And her we stunteþ but a stounde,
    For þis world is but fantasye.   132

107.   *Merci God and graunt Merci.*

Vernon MS.

AS I wandrede her bi weste   f. 409^b
   Faste vnder a Forest syde,   (col. 1)
I seiȝ a wiht went him to reste,
  Vnder a bouȝh he gon a-byde ;   4
Þus to crist ful ȝeor⟨n⟩e he criȝede,   f. 409^b
  And boþe his hondes he held on heiȝ :   (col. 2)
  'Of pouert, plesaunce & eke of pruide,
    Ay Merci, God, And graunt-Merci !'   8

129 MS. wāteþ.

God, þat I haue I-greuet þe
　In wille & werk, in word and dede,
Almihti lord, haue Merci of me
　Þat for my sunnes þi blod gon schede!　　12
Of wit & worschupe, weole & wede
　I þonke þe, lord, ful Inwardly;
Al in þis world, hou-euere I spede,
　Ay Merci, god, And graunt Merci!　　16

Graunt Merci, god, of al þi ȝifte,
　Of wit & worschupe, weole & wo;
In-to þe, lord, myn herte I lifte,
　Let neuer my dedes twynne vs a-two.　　20
Merci þat I haue mis-do,
　And sle me nouȝt sodeynly!
　Þouȝ Fortune wolde be frend or fo,
　Ay Merci, God, And graunt Merci!　　24

I am vnkuynde, and þat I knowe,
　And þou hast kud me gret kuyndenes;
Þerfore wiþ humbel herte and lowe,
　Merci and for-ȝiuenes　　28
Of Pruyde and of vnboxumnes!
　What euer ⟨þ⟩i sonde be, þus sey I,
In hap and hele, and in seknes,
　Ay Merci, god, And graunt Merci!　　32

Graunt Merci, God, of al þi ȝrace,
　Þat fourmed me with wittes fyue,
With Feet and hond, & eke of face
　And lyflode, whil I am alyue:　　36
Siþen þou hast ȝiue me grace to þryue,
　And I haue Ruled me Rechelesly,
I weore to blame and I wolde striue—
　But Merci, God, And Graunt Merci!　　40

30 euer þi: MS. eueri.

Merci þat I haue mis-spent
  Mi wittes fyue! þerfore I wepe.
To dedly synnes ofte haue I a-sent,
  þi Comaundemens couþe I neuer kepe ;   44
  To sle my soule In sunne I slepe,
    And lede my lyf in Lecheri ;
  From Couetyse couþe I neuere crepe—
    Ay Merci, God, And Graunt Merci !   48

Of oþes grete and Glotony,
  Of wanhope and of wikked wille,
Bacbyte my neiȝhebors for enuy,
  And for his good I wolde him culle,   52
  Trewe men to Robbe and spille,
Of Symony and with surquidri—
  Of al þat euere I haue don ille
    Ay Merci, God, And graunt Merci !   56

Bi lawe I scholde no lengor liue
  þen I hedde don a dedly synne ;
Graunt Merci þat ȝe wolde forgiue,
  And ȝeue me space to mende me Inne !   60
  From wikked dedes & I wolde twynne,
    To Receyue me ȝe beo redi
  In-to þi blisse þat neuer schal blynne ;
    Nou Merci, God, And graunt Merci !   64

Graunt Merci, for þou madest me,
  Merci, for I haue don a-Mis !
Min hope, Min help is hol in þe,
  And þou hast ȝore bi-heiht me þis :   68
  Whos-euere is Baptiȝed schal haue Blis,
    And he Rule him Rihtwysli.
  To worche þi wille, lord, þou me wis—
    Nou Merci, God, And graunt Merci !   72

Soþfast god, what schal I say?
  how schulde I amendes make,
Þat plesed þe neuere in-to þis day,
  Ne schop me nouȝt mi sunnes forsake?   76
    But schrift of mouþe mi sunnus schal slake,
      And I schal sece and beo sori;
    And to þi Merci I me take—
      Nou Merci, God, And Graunt Merci!   80

Fader & sone and holigost,
  Graunt Merci, God, wiþ herte liht,
For þou woldest not þat I weore lost.
  Þe Fader haþ ȝiuen me a miht,   84
  Þe sone a science and a siht,   f. 409ᵇ
    And wit to welde me worschupely,   (col. 3)
  Þe Holigost vr grace haþ diht.
    Nou Merci, God, And graunt Merci!   88

Þis is þe Trone þat twynned neuere,
  And preued is persones þre,
Þat is and was and schal ben euere,
  Only God in Trinite: 92
    help vs, Prince of alle pite,
    Atte day þat we schal dy,
  Þi swete face þat we may se.
    Nou Merci, God, And Graunt Merci!   96

108.   T*r*uth is Best.

Vernon MS.

HOse wolde him wel a-vyse   f. 409ᵇ
  Of þis wrecched world I weene,   (col. 3)
I hope ful wel he schulde dispise
  þe foule falshede þat þer-in bene.   4
Sertes, sum day schal beo sene
    Much eorþly labour schal be lest;
Whon good and vuel vr dedes schal deme,
    We schal wel fynde þat treuþe is best.   8

Treuþe is best for kyng and kniht,
  Certes, hose riȝt wol rede;
Among þis ladyes feir and briȝt
  Hit schulde be loued in vch a leode;   12
þis Marchauns worþli vnder wede,
    To buyȝe & selle þei ben ful prest,
Among hem alle schuld no falshede,
    But vsen trouþe, þat euere i⟨s⟩ best.   16

Sikerli, I dar wel say,
  In al þis world nis heo ne he,
þat þei wolde fayn, ȝif þat þei may,
  Leden heore lyf in prosperite,   20
And als swiþe as þei schulde dyȝe,
    Til heuene þat þei mote come ful prest.
þat noble plase þei neiȝe ner neih
    But ȝif þei meyntene trouþe for best.   24

Trouþe schal deme vs alle be-dene,
  He wol do trewely and no wrong;
I hope we schal boþe seye and sene
  þat we han contraried him al to long.   28
And þerfore lordes, boþe stout and strong
    þat may deeme her riht as þé lest,
For Godes loue wis þou so among,
    þat trouþe be meyntened for þe best.   32

And þerfore haue þis in ȝour muynde,
  Hose medleþ wiþ þe lawe :
Let neuer falshed a-ȝeynes vn-kuynde
  Fordon trouþe ne soþ sawe ;   36
    For falshed euermore schal stonde awe
      Of trouþe þauȝ he be neuer so prest.
    For godes loue, let neuer gold þe drawe
      Aȝeynes trouþe þat euer is best.   40

Wolde we rule us al wiþ trouþe,
  And mak him hollych vr gouernour,
We schulde keuere out of synne & slouþe,
  And of Chiualrye bere þe flour ;   44
    For trouþe in were may most endour,
      And euer is biggest at þe lest.
    For godes loue, graunt we him socour,
      And mayntene trouþe þat euer is best.   48

Trouþe was sum tyme here a lord,
  wiþ him alle vertues, as I wene ;
ȝit Spayne, Brutayne wol bere record,
  And oþer diuerse londes be-dene,   52
  þat we endouwed hem as þei schulde bene,
    And made hem lordes to lyue in rest—
  Þer dorste no falshede with hem be sene,
    So loued þei trouþe, þat euer is best.   56

Wolde we ȝit lete trouþe a-ȝeyn
  Be lord and bere his heritage,
Al oþer londes schuld be ful fayn
  To don vs feute and homage ;   60
  Baldelych þis dar I wage,
    And falshede & his lore weore lest,
  þei schulde not dure vn-to a page
    To werre with trouþe, þat euer is best. 64

38 MS. On trouþe.

Falshed may wel regne a while
  þorw Meyntenaunce of couetise;
Atte last his grount wol him be-gyle,
  A while þouȝ he be neuer so wyse.   68
  Falshed haþ ben most in pris   f. 410ᵃ
    Boþe bi North and eke bi West;
We schul him hunte as Cat doþ mys,
    Whon trouþe him cheues þat euer is best. 72

109.   *Charity is no longer Cheer.*

Vernon MS.

Hose wolde be-þenke him weel   f. 410ᵃ
  Ou þis world is went, I-wis,   (col. 1)
And couþe enterly grope & feel
  þe foule falshede þat þer-in is,   4
I durste be bold, so haue I blis,
  þat mony good mon schuld haue mateere
Te mene & mourne and fare a-Mis,
  For charite is no lengor cheere.   8

Mony a Mon, riht as him seemeþ
  A þing þat he neuer kneuh ne wist,
Boþe lordes & Mene Men he demeþ,
  And spekeþ of hem riȝt as him list.   12
Allas! for ȝif a mon nou trist
  His broþer or his cosyn neere,
He schal be deceyued in his fist,
  For charite is no lengore cheere.   16

Þo þat spekeþ most, as I leeue,
  And demen men so, al a-boute—
Wher no faute vppon hem cleue?
  ȝus, be my trouþe, hit is no doute—   20
  Such Men may not ben wiþ-oute,
    No more þen hecgh wiþ-outen Brere;
  Envye is wiþ hem so stoute
    Þat charite is no lengore chere.   24

For þreo lettynges þat þer bene,
  A Mon mai not deeme rihtwislye:
Þe furste lettyng, as I wene,
  A þing þat is to fer from eiȝe;   28
  Or elles a þing may beo to neiȝ,
    Schal lette his siht þauȝ hit be clere;
  Þe þridde is, þat he demeþ bi,
    Whon charite is no lengore chere.   32

ȝe mai in feelde sum tyme i-se
  A bosck þat stondeþ ful fer þe fro,
Þat ȝe schal deme hit schal be
  Mon or Beest, hors, on of þo;   36
  And al is wrong to deeme hit so,
    Certes, as ȝe schal after lere.
  So demes a Mon ofte be his Fo,
    Whon charite is no lengore chere.   40

ȝif þou hast an huge envy,
  And hatest a mon wiþ al þi miht,
Liue þat mon neuer so rihtwisly,
  ȝit schaltou deme he liueþ not riht;   44
  Envye stoppeþ þer þi siht,
    And makeþ fer þat schulde be neere;
  And lac of loue letteþ þi liht,
    Whon charite is no lengore chere.   48

Vppon þin Eȝe-lide þer mai ley
 A spot or elles a mote I-wis,
And for bicause hit is so neiȝ,
  þou maiȝt not seo hit, so haue I blis,   52
  To deme treuly what hit is ;
   þerfore þi doom falleþ in a weere.
  So demeþ a mon ofte syþes a-mis,
   Whon þat his herte is set from cheere. 56

ȝif þou louest þi broþer so
 þat þi loue passeþ al a-syse,
What þat euer þi broþer do,
  Euel or wrong in eny wyse,   60
  Al is wel to þin a-vise,
   Bi-cause þou louest him so entere ;
  His defaute constou not spise,
   For þer þin herte is set to chere. 64

Let a lechour heere a-spye
 A ȝong mon with a wommon rage,
And nouþer of heom ne þenke folye
  But wel may falle of o linage,   68
  ȝit wol þat lechour þinke outrage,
   And deeme þei wolde do mis I-fere ;
  Such deemyng askeþ sliper wage,
   For charite þer is no-þing cheere. 72

And riȝt so fareþ hit, be my trouþe,
 Wiþ a proud Mon & a Couetous,
A wrecche þat liueþ al in slouȝþe,
  And eke a mon þat is vicyous ;   76
  He wenes vch mon þat is vertuous f. 410
   Vseþ his wyse and his maneere ; (col. 2)
  So fareþ Men þat beþ Envyous,
   Whon Charite is no lengor chere. 80

   56 þat *added above line by corrector.*
   67 ne *added above line by corrector.*

Let a trewe mon, bi þe Rood,
  Þat is good, honest, and sad,
He weeneþ þat vche mon be good,
    He nolde not demen a mon weore bad.   84
  But wrecched fooles þat beoþ mad,
    Þat con not wel heore tonge steere,
  To deme þe worste þei ben ful glad,
    Whon Charite is no lengor cheere.   88

I leeue þer beo no mon a-lyue,
  ȝif he his warison scholde winne,
Þat couþe enterliche knowe & skreue
    Þe lyf þat is sum mon wiþ-Inne;   92
  For summe þat semeþ most wiþ synne,
    In hap, of synne may beo most clere.
  Of such demyng I rede ȝe blynne,
    For Charite þer is no-þing chere.   96

And þo þat leouest is to lak,
  And demeþ men so al bideene,
Vn-bynt þe burþen on ȝor bak,
    And loke furst þat ȝor-self be clene.   100
  Al such demyng, as I wene,
    Schulde beo reseruet to godes pouecre;
  So me þinkeþ hit best to beone,
    For þen schal charite ben most cheere.   104

Certes, and ȝe loke ariht,
  A good word no more wol weye
Þat hit liþ on ȝor tonge as liht,
    As þe worste þat ȝe con seye.   108
  Such Idel wordes, I ou preye,
    ȝe louke hem faste in ȝoure forcere,
  And let concience bere þe keye,
    For þen schal charite be most chere.   112

110. *Of Women cometh this Worldes Weal.*

Vernon MS.

IN worschupe of þat Mayden swete,   f. 410ᵃ
  Mylde Marie, Moder and May,   (col. 2)
Alle gode wimmen wol I grete,
  þat god sende hem from vch afray;   4
With muche menske mote þei mete,
  And wel worþe alle wymmen ay!
Al vr Bale þei may beete,
  Serteynliche, I dar wel say;   8
And hose blameþ hem niht or day,
    Wiþ Bale mot heore tonge belle.
I preue hit wel, ho-euer seiþ nay,
    Of wimmen comeþ þis worldes welle.   12

But moni vn-witti wiht-is woode
  Vn-wysliche wimmen wol dispyse,
þat ben I-boren of wimmen blode.
  I-wis, such wihtes ben vn-wyse,   16
For þei defoule heor oune foode;
  Such grimly goostes may agryse
wiþ þulke þat dude god on þe Rode:
  At dredful dom such schal aryse,   20
  Be Iugged wiþ þe heiȝe Iustise
    To folewe þe false feendes fele,
  And rikene wiþ þe vnrihtwyse,
    þat of wymmen comeþ worldes welle.   24

Sum seiþ wimmen haþ be-gilt
  Adam, Sampson, and Salamon,
And seiþ þat wimmen haþ I-spilt
  Mony a wys, worþi mon.   28
þus þei greggen wymmens gilt
  Of Monnes riken þei neuer on;

And monnes falshed weore fulfild,
   I trowe þer weore twenti a-ȝeynes on,   32
Of Macabeus, Iudas, and Ion,
    Alisaundre and oþer feole,
   Þat with monnes gult was fordon—
     But of wimmen comeþ þis worldes wele.   36

And Iudas gentil Ihesu solde
   Þat saued alle þat was forlore ;
And monnes falsed weore I-tolde,
   Men miht rikene moni a score.   40
Wommon wrouȝte riht as god wolde—
   Þat gult made god to ben I-bore—
And þerfore beo ȝe neuer so bolde
    To blame wymmen neuer-more   44
   For nouȝt þat þei haue don bi-fore ;   f. 410[a]
    For monnes schome I rede ȝe hele.   (col. 3)
    Wimmen for Men ofte suffreþ sore—
     But of wymmen comeþ þis worldes wele.   48

Wimmen wrouȝte neuer no wrong
   But þorw Monnes entysement ;
Men secheþ wimmen so strong,
   And sei in Bale þei mote be brent ;   52
And ligge a-boute hem so long,
   To bringen hem til heore a-sent.
And þus þorw monnes false song,
    Ofte wymmen haþ be schent ;   56
   ȝif eny such be in present
    Stille holde him, I rede, he schell
    And preise wimmen in good entent,
     For of wymmen comeþ þis worldes wele.   60

---

58 schell : MS. stell.   59 in *interlined by corrector.*

God worschuped wimmen in his lyue,
 And kept hem in his cumpaygnyc,
Boþe widewe, wenche, and wyue,
 Þat was wiþ-outen vilenye.   64
Hose luste with wymmen striue,
 I rede he drede him for to dye,
And of þat synne sone him schriue,
 And to vr ladi Merci crye;   68
 And in worschip of Marie
  Such vn-Redines þat ȝe repele.
 Defendeþ ȝou alle from such folye,
  For of wymmen comeþ al þis worldis wele. 72

I holde þat Brid muche to blame
 Þat defouleþ his oune nest;
Þou wost wel a wommon was þi dame,
 I-Boren and fed of hire Brest.   76
But moni gabben on heore dame,
 To blame wymmen þei þinke hit best
Stunteþ for ȝor owne schame,
 Of such resouns I rede ȝe rest,   80
 To preyse wymmen þat ȝe be prest!
  Wymmen ben hende in hete and chele,
 Wimmen gladeþ vch a godly gest,
  For of wymmen comeþ þis worldes wele. 84

Wymmen wrappen vs in wede
 Whon we beo naked boren and bare,
And of hire flesch fostreþ and feede,
 And ȝarken vs whon we ben ȝare;   88
Whon we ben old, þei moste vs hede
 And keuere vs out of mony a care;
Whon we be nafti, nouȝt at neode,
 Neore wimmen help, hou schulde we fare?   92

At dredful dom, whon we schal dare
  For fere of false fendes feole,
Whon vche mon schal his speche spare,
  Þen wommon help is al vr weole.   96

For God and Mon was fer a-twinne
  Whon he made Monkuynde of Séé-flod.
I wolde wite, whon þat Eue gon spinne,
  Bi whom þat ȝoure gentrie stod?   100
Hou be-come ȝe godes kinne
  But barelych þorw þe wommones blod?
Allas, hou may men for synne
  Speke bi wymmen ouȝt bote good!   104
  Wimmen beoþ so mylde of mood,
    Louesum, loueli, lyf, and lele.
  Witnes on him þat died on Rood,
    Of wymmen comeþ þis worldes wele.   108

God þat made boþe sonne and Mone,
  To alle wymmen socour he sende!
In alle þe dedes þat þei haue done,
  Kepe hem from þe false fende!   112
And to Marie I bidde a bone:
  Warde wymmen, wher-so-euer þei wende,
From synne and serwe schylde hem sone,
  Wher in londe þat euer þei lende!   116
  I warne alle þat be wimmenes frende,
    I con not preise hem þe haluen-dele;
  Þouȝ I þus schortliche make an ende,
    Of wymmen comeþ þis worldes wele.   120

III. A song of Love to the Blessed Virgin.

Vernon MS.

OF alle floures feirest fall on,   f. 410^a
 And þat is Marie, Moder fre,   (col. 3)
Þat bar þe child of flesch and bon,
 Ihesu, Godes sone in Maieste.   4
A loue-likyng is come to me   f. 410^b
 To serue þat ladi, qwen of blis,   (col. 1)
Ay better and better in my degre,
 Þe lengor þat I liue, I-wis.   8

So hertly I haue I-set my þouȝt
 Vppon þat buyrde of buyrdes best ;
For al-þauh I seo hire nouȝt,
 Min herte schal fully wiþ hire be fest.   12
Ihesu, þat sek milk of hire brest,
 To ȝou boþe I be-heete,
Mi loue schal holly wiþ ȝou rest,
 Þauȝ I be not worþi ne meete.   16

Sertes, swete, on ȝou is al
 Min helpyng at myn endyng-day ;
Þat I be not þe fendes þral,
 Marie, to ȝor sone ȝe pray.   20
Hou schal I do, my swete may,
 But ȝif I loue ȝou souereynly ?
Elles miht men boldly bi me say,
 Daunger mad vnskilfuly.   24

Hose beþenkeþ him, I-wis,
 Of ȝor gret goodnesse and ȝor grace,
He scholde neuer wilne to don a-mis,
 Ne luste to loue in oþer place.   28
In hope to seo ȝor blessed face,
 And dwelle wiþ ȝou at myn endynge,
And haue relese of all trespace,
 Ladi, þauȝ I mourne, I synge.   32

Lentun-dayes, þei ben longe,
  And nou weor good tyme to amende
Þat we be-foren han do wronge.
    Þis world nis no-þing as I wende;   36
  In sori tyme my lyf Is spend;
    Þis world is fals and þat I feel.
  But Marie Moder me amende,
    A-Mis I fare and noþing wel.   40

But þat swete worþli wyf,
  Hire goodly loue þat I may gete,
Al my Ioye wol turne to strif,
    And I may syke with wonges wete.   44
  Whon þat I þenke on þat swete,
    Me þinkeþ hit is so good a þouȝt,
  I sey to eueri mon þat I meete:
    'Gode, go wey, and let me nouȝt!'   48

Loue me haþ in Bales brouȝt
  For on such þat I suppose,
Þat is so studefast in hire þouȝt,
    Þat couþe neuere gabbe ne glose;   52
  Hose hire loueþ he schal not lose,
    For ȝit be-giled heo neuer no wiht.
  I likne þat ladi to þe Rose—
    I-blessed beo þat buirde briht!   56

Me longede neuere so sore, so sore,
  To seo my loueli ladi deere;
ȝif heo neore, we neore but lore,
    Þat ladi lofsum most of lere.   60
  And wite hit wel wiþ-outen weere,
    Whon I þenk on hire semblaunt sad,
  Þer wol no wys mon blame me here,
    Þauȝ þat I go murie and glad.   64
        N 2

A louely lyf to loken vp-on,
   So is my ladi, þat Emperys;
Mi lyf I dar leye þer-vppon,
   Þat princesse is peerles of prys;   68
   So feir, so clene, so good, so wys,
      And þerto trewe as eny steel,
   Þer nis no such to my deuys—
      Lor God, þat I loue hire wel!   72

To þis newe ȝer, my ladi sweete,
   Wiþ al myn herte in good entent,
Wiþ fyue Aues I ow grete,
   And preye ou take þis feire present,   76
   And schape so þat I beo not schent,
      Seþþen of ȝou Merci gon springe.
   For al my loue is on ȝou lent,
      [Sweete] swettest of alles-kunnes þinge! 80

Þis is þe remenaunt of my lust,
   Þat I not wheþer my ladi mylde
To my loue haue inly trust,
   Bicause Monkuynde is frele and wylde. 84
   But, ladi, for ȝoure blisful childe,   f. 410^b
      Siþen al my loue is leyd on þe,   (col. 2)
   In heuene help me a boure to bylde,
      Ladi, ȝif þi wille be.   88

Þe loue þat I haue ȝeorned ȝore,
   Þe kyng of loue graunt hit me!
In eorþly loue is luytel store,
   For al þat nis but vanyte   92
   Wher I schal euer þat day I-se
      To plese my ladi ones to pay?
   Heo is of colour and beute
      As fresch as is þe Rose In May.   96

---

80 MS. alle skunes.   87 help] p *added by corrector.*

Hose lust not loue, let hym be-leue,
 For I wol holde þat I haue hiht;
þat lust schal no mon from me reue,
 þat I nul loue my ladi briht.   100
 Loue, loue, do me riht,
  Marie Mooder, Mayden clene,
 In heuene of þe to haue a siht,—
  Ladi, to þe my mone I mene!   104

112. *Maiden Mary and her Fleur-de-Lys.*

Vernon MS.

MArie Mayden, Moder Mylde,   f. 410^b
  þat blisful Bern in bosum beere,   (col. 2)
Cheef & chast, þou ches of chylde,
 Of alle wymmen In world þat were.   4
Saue vs sound and socur vs here,
  As princes is preised & proued for prys.
What leode þis lesson lykes to lere,
  Be token hit is þe Flourdelys.   8

þat freoli flour weore fair to fynde,
 what gome wolde go þer-as hit greuȝ—
As Maacer her-of made in his Mynde,
 þus kenned him Catoun, his craftes he kneuȝ— 12
 What segge on soil þat þat seed seuȝ,
  Hit is holy at myn a-vys;
 Aboue þe Braunches beþ Blosmes neu,
  þe lele cheses faire þe Flourdelys.   16

Þou lele ladi, I likne to þe
Þe flour, to þi semeli sone also,
Þe blisful Blosme þat euer mihte be,
 Treuly þat was be-twix ȝou to.   20
 Whon we weore wrapped al in wo,
  Þorw werkes þat we had wrouȝt wrongwys,
 Þi godnes gert vs graiþly go,
  Þorw vertu of þi Flourdelys.   24

Ful greiþli was þe graunted grace
 Whon Gabriel from god þe gret,
Þat fel to þi feet bi-fore þi face,
 Þe Murieste meetyng þat euer was met. 28
 So sittyngli hire sawes heo set,
  As a wommon boþe war and wys:
 'To-seo þi seruaunt and þi soget!'
  And þer bi-gon furst þi Flourdelys. 32

In hond þou haddest & heold vr hele,
 Þorw him þat hadde heiȝ heuene in holde;
What Murþe was mad no Mouþ miȝt mele,
 Whon þou þat worþly hed wonnen in wolde— 36
 He com to keuere vs of cares colde,
  His pepul he put in paradys—
 Þat tyde and tyme þe Angel tolde,
  Of þe schulde springe þe Flourdelys. 40

Þat Blisful Barn of þe was born,
 Þat suffred trauayle, boþe trey and tene,
Throly þhrusten & throng wiþ þorn
 Of his cunreden, vnkuynde and kene,— 44
 From top to-torn al bi-deene
  Þe Iewes þei Iugged his Iuwys—
 And dyȝed for Adam deedes bi-deene;
  And þenne was sprongen þe Flourdelys. 48

A studi steer þer stod ful steere
  For steeres-men þat bi stremes gun stray,
And neore his worþly wille weore,
    Þei wolde haue went a wilful way.   52
    No feyntysenes þei founden in fay,
      Þat burth was buried In Marbel bys,
    And whon god wolde he went his way,
      And þenne was sprad þe Flourdelys.   56

Where his worþli wilnyng was,
  Hit weore to wite whoder he went ;
Þe geynest gate greiþli he tas,
    Til derknes dipt, doun he decent ;   60
    Þe ȝates he russchede, and al to-Rent,   f. 410^b
      Þer Lucifer, þat luþure, lys ;   (col. 3)
    Adam and Eue bi hond he hent,
      And tauȝte hem faire þe Flourdelys.   64

Þus haþ þis heende herewed helle,
  Al Adames of-spring out haþ tan ;
Þe fend, þat was boþe fers and felle,
    He tiȝed til a stok, stille as stan.   68
    Vp of his graue þen is he gon,
      As God and Mon to-gedere gon Rys,
    Bodily boþe in blod and bon
      To þe Maudeleyn he schewed þe Flourdelys. 72

Þus purchased he þe pepul heor pees
  And goodly for-ȝaf hem al heore gilt,
And seide : ‘Adam, eft nou I þe sese
    In blisse, þat for blod was buld ;   76
    No wey wonde, but wurch what þou wilt.’
      Þus haþ he now bitauȝt þat wyse,
    And þus feole prophecies ben folfild,
      Of Marie wiþ þi Flourdelyse.   80

Of bounte berestou þe þe best,
  Was neuer no buirde such beute bare ;
Crist of þe com, vre cumfort to kest,
  To ȝelde þe þat we ȝerned ȝare.   84
    At his steiȝynge þei stod to stare
      How cleer in Clouden he cloumben is ;
    What wy in þat worþily wonyng ware,
      Þer miht he fynden þe Flourdelys.   88

Þus was al þis world in weere—
  Þen seide two wyȝes in weedes whyt :
'To heiȝ heuene what be-holde ȝe here ?
  Is Ihesu take from ȝow þus tyd ?   92
    Apeere he schal in propre plyt,
      As he in werk⟨e⟩ con vanys.'
    Her afturward hit weore to wite,
      Of hire þat bar þe Flourdelys.   96

So lelly his loue on þe was lent,
  Þi longyng, ladi, for to lete ;
So semely sondes after þe he sent,
  Be-sydes him-self to sitte in sete ;   100
    Þei song al samen with soun ful swete,
      As schewen and stand in þi storis.
    Wiþ more murþes miȝt neuer mon meete,
      But þer to fynde þe Flourdelys.   104

Siþen þou þi worþly wones hast wonnen,
  And wones In worschipe at þi wille,
Vre grith was graunted, vr grace bigunnen,
  For vs þat was ordeyned þertille.   108
    Puire dette proueþ bi proper skille
      Þou schalt vs socour in þi seruys,
    Þat greiþes⟨t⟩ was for greuaunce to grille,
      And for to bere þe flourdelys.   112

Of al þe floures bi Frith and Felde,
  Hit is þe freolokest for to fynde,
Þat weole & wit and wisdam welde,
    And al þis word haþ wrouȝt, In wynde   116
    Noũ, comely kyng, Corteis and kynde,
      Þat halp vs heere from vre enemys.
    Þe mon þat þis matere made in mynde
      Seide, non is lich to þe Flourdelys.   120

Hedde not Adam don þat dede,
  Vr bitter bales hed neuer ben bouȝt
On no maner, for no-kenes nede ;
    Ne for no werkes we schuld haue wrouȝt—   124
    Al þus I þenk hit in my þouȝt—
      Monkynde for vs bi-com so chys ;
    His Blisful blod þorw him þei souȝt—
      Vs ouȝte to prey to þe Flourdelys.   128

Nou Marie Mayden, Moder clene,
  Þi semeli sone þat beres þe Flour,
ȝif vs grace ow to qweme,
    And plese Ihesu, vr saueour.   132
    Bryng vs out of dette & dedly synne,
      To liue and dye in þi seruys,
    Heuene blisse þat we may wynne
      And wone þer wiþ þi Flourdelys.   136

113. *Verses on the Earthquake of 1382.*

Vernon MS.

Yit is God a Curteis lord,   f. 411[a]
  And Mekeliche con schewe his miht ; (col. 2)
Fayn he wolde bringe til a-cord
  Monkuynde, to liue in treuþe ariht.   4
Allas ! whi set we þat lord so liht,
  And al to foule wiþ him we fare ?
In world is non so wys no wiht,
  Þat þei ne haue warnyng to be ware.   8

We may not seye, but ȝif we lyȝe,
  Þat god wol vengaunce on vs stele ;
For openly we seo wiþ eiȝe,
  Þis warnynges beoþ wonder & fele.   12
But nou þis wrecched worldes wele
  Makeþ vs liue in sunne and care.
Of Mony Merueyles I may of Mele,
  And al is warnyng to be ware.   16

Whon þe Comuynes bi-gan to ryse,
  Was non so greṭ lord, as I gesse
Þat þei in herte bi-gon to gryse,
  And leide heore Iolyte in presse.   20
Wher was þenne heore worþinesse,
  Whon þei made lordes droupe & dare ?
Of alle wyse men I take witnesse,
  Þis was a warnyng to be ware.   24

Bi-fore, ȝif men hedde haad a graas,
　　Lordes mihte wondur weel
Han let þe rysing þat þer was,
　　But þat god þouȝte ȝit sumdel　　　　28
　　Þat lordes schulde his lordschup feel,
　　　　And of heore lordschipe make hem bare.
　　Trust þer-to as trewe as steel,
　　　　Þis was a warnyng to be ware.　　　　32

And also, whon þis eorþe qwok,
　　Was non so proud, he nas a-gast,
And al his Iolite for-sok,
　　And þouȝt on god whil þat hit last;　　36
　　And alsone as hit was ouer-past
　　　　Men wox as vuel as þei dude are.
　　Vche mon in his herte may cast,
　　　　Þis was a warnyng to be ware.　　　　40

For-soþe, þis was a lord to drede,
　　So sodeynly mad Mon agast;
Of gold & seluer þei tok non hede,
　　But out of her houses ful sone þei past.　44
　　Chaumbres, Chimeneys al to-barst,
　　　　Chirches & Castels foule gon fare,
　　Pinacles, Steples to grounde hit cast;
　　　　And al was warnyng to be ware.　　　48

Þe Meuyng of þis eorþe, I-wis,
　　Þat schulde bi cuynde be ferm & stabele,
A pure verrey toknyng hit is,
　　Þat Mennes hertes ben chaungable;　　52
　　And þat to falsed þei ben most Abul,　f. 411ᵃ
　　　　For with good feiþ wol we not fare.　(col. 3)
　　Leef hit wel wiþ-outen fabel,
　　　　Þis was a warnyng to be ware.　　　56

Þe Rysing of þe comuynes in londe,
  Þe Pestilens, and þe eorþe-quake—
Þeose þreo þinges, I vnderstonde,
    Beo-tokenes þe grete vengaunce & wrake   60
    Þat schulde falle for synnes sake,
      As þis Clerkes conne de-clare.
    Nou may we chese to leue or take,
      For warnyng haue we to ben ware.   64

Euere I drede, be my trouþe,
  Þer may no warnyng stande in sted ;
We ben so ful of synne and slouþe,
    Þe schame is passed þe sched of hed,   68
    And we liggen riht heuy as led,
      Cumbred in þe Fendes snare.
    I leeue þis beo vr beste Red,
      To þenke on þis warnyng & be ware.   72

Sikerliche, I dar wel saye,
  In such a plyt þis world is in,
Mony for wynnyng wolde bi-traye
    Fader and Moder and al his kin.   76
    Nou were heih tyme to be-gin
      To A-Mende vr mis & wel to fare ;
    Vr bagge hongeþ on a sliper pyn,
      Bote we of þis warnyng be ware.   80

Be war, for I con sey no more,
  Be war for vengauns of trespas,
Be war and þenk vppon þis lore !
    Be war of þis sodeyn cas ;   84
    And ȝit Be war while we haue spas,
      And þonke þat child þat Marie bare,
    Of his gret godnesse and his gras,
      Sende vs such warnyng to be ware.   88

114. *Love Holy Church and its Priests.*

Vernon MS.

CRist ȝiue vs grace to loue wel holichirch,   f. 411ᵃ
  Or elles, certes, we don riht nouht ;   (col. 3)
And let vs neuere aȝeynes hit worche,
  From þenne vre cristendom is brouht.   4
    Preostes weore at vre biginnynge,
      Wȝuche God haþ graunted hem pouste
    For vs to rede, I-wis, and synge ;
      Is non so gret a dignyte.   8

Þei ȝaf vs vre Cristenynge,
  And at vr buriinge þei moste be ,
To worschipe hem in alle þinge,
  Muchel þer-to holden beo we.   12
    Godus bodi may no mon make
      But preostes al-one, as we rede —
    Kyng ne Emperour I non out-take,
      For alle heore richesses of lond or leode.   16

Of alle Ordres he beres þe prys—
    Kyng, Duyk, oþer Emperour—
Þouh heo weren þe Flourdelys,
  Þat is richest of alle colour.   20
In Matynes and vres þei ben wys,
    To bringe vs to vr longe bour,
And vche day syngeþ a Masse to þis,
    And scheweþ vs Ihesus, vre sauiour.   24

In Matyns and Masse þei beren þe prys,
    And in heore orisons for vs þei pray ;
Þer is no mon þat is wys,
    Þat oþur record bi heom may say.   28
Hose loueþ þis ordre, I holde him wys,
    For certeyn soþ and in good fay,
In holy chirche þei don seruys
    Boþe bi nihtes and bi day.   32

But hose-euer wole þis ordre bere,
    Wys and witti moste he be,
Grete oþes may he non swere,
    Ne falshede nouþer don ne se.   36
By-fore þe Bisschop reseyueþ he þere
    And takeþ þe ȝok of chastite.
A-vyse him wel hou he hit were,
    Oþur elles him schal rewe oþer me.   40

Whon we ben falle in eny mischef,
    Wiþ serwe In dedly synne I-bounde,
Þen is þe prest vs ful leef,
    For he may helen vs of þat wounde.   44
For þer is non so strong a þeef   f. 411[b]
    Þat euer tok cristendom on godes grounde,
Þat he most haue a preest bi-foren his deþ,
    Or elles he schal warie þe stounde.   48

On domes-day whon we schul meete
    Þat dredful Iuge forte se,
Þen is schrift to vs ful seete—
    Þe prest þer-of record beres he ;   52
Of alle bales he may beete
    Vnder god In Trinite.
Þenne schrift & hosul is ful swete,
    And hit trewely holden be.   56

Þis ordre I rede þat we honoure,
  And so I counseyle þat we do,
And take penaunce for sunnes oure
  Whuche þe prest haþ Iuned vs to. 60
Þen schal we come to þat boure
  Þer euere is Ioye with-outen wo.
Ihesu, bring vs and socoure,
  Out of þis world whon we schal go! 64

115. *Always try to Say the Best.*

Garrett MS. (Princeton Univ.).

THe grete god so ful of grace f. 45ᵃ
  of whom al godnes growe ganne—
And alle þat listeneth me a space,
God childe hem from þe fende satanne! 4
A litil word in my hert ranne,
I wole hit synge, ʒif hit ʒou lest,
To gete þe loue of god & man—
And al-wey fonde to say þe best. 8

Speke non yuel in no place,
But rule þi tonge & get þi frende;
And let no wicked word out pace,
For hit is an eggement of þe fend. 12
ʒif þou with oon be sore atenede
And knowist him a wickid gest,
Be þou þi-silf curtese & hende,
And al-way fond to say þe best. 16

For eny anger, or eny hate,
Or eny enuy, be þe sette,
An ille word may sone make bate;
Let noȝt þi wille passe þi witte :   20
An ille word ful sore may sette,   f. 45ᵇ
That longe in hert is kepit faste :
Of þe worst commyth no profite,
And þerfore fond to say þe beste.   24

For cristis loue, þat bouȝte þe dere,
let noȝt þi tonge haue al his wille.
What art þou þe bet or þe nere
Þi neiȝbur wickedli for to spille ?   28
Ȝif man or woman com þe tille
To frayne yuel of any gest,
For cristis loue, holde þe stille,
And al-way fond to say þe beste.   32

In company ȝif þat þou be
Þer men speketh vilany,
Ȝyve þou be tempted ȝet turne þe,
And þan dost þou a gret gentri.   36
A bad tale is ribaudi,
Hit gete no worschip, est ne west,
For godis loue do cortesi,
And euer fond to say þe best.   40

Hoso wolde be-þenke him-silf ariȝt,   f. 46ª
A good wo⟨r⟩d, how good hit is,
I durst well swere be þis liȝt
He nol neuer willen to say amys.   44
For good word may gete heuen blisse,
And do þe lyue in ese & rest ;
For cristis loue, tak a-tent to þis,
And euer fond to say þe best.   48

Loke þat þou no man de-fame
With wicked wille, so haue þou blisse ;
For ho-so haþ a wicked name
Me semeþ for soþe half hongid he is ;   52
Þou maist not make amendis his
With al þe tresor in þi chest ;
For cristis loue þou þenke on þis,
And euer fond to say þe best.   56

I holde þat dede to dere a stre,
Don to do anoþer fame ;
I had as leue þou woldest him slee,
For þis is holde an endelis blame,   60
For þou myȝtist noȝt brynge aȝaine his name
Þrouȝ wicked wordis þat þou seist.   f. 46ᵇ
For maries loue, cristes dame,
Al-way fond to say þe best.   64

In halle or chau⟨m⟩ber þer þou gos,
What-euer þat þou here or see,
Al-way kepe þi tonge in clos,
ȝif eny man aske ouȝte of þe.   68
ȝif eny fiȝt or foli be,
Let not þi tonge a-mys be wrest ;
But for his loue þat died on tre,
Al-way fond to say þe best.   72

For godis loue, þenke on þis songe,
Man & woman faire of face,
And take þis in ȝoure hertis amonge,
Whare-euer ȝe go, or in what place.   76
Ihesus ȝou kepe in eueri cas,
And in heuene ȝou make a feste ;
For godis loue so ful of grace,
Al-way fond to say þe best.   80

54 MS. þi þresor.   59 MS. haþ.

116. *Tarry not till To-morrow.*

Vernon MS.

ILke a wys wiht scholde wake, f. 411ᵇ
  And waite with werk, heuen to wynne (col. 1)
Sadliche, for goddes sake,
  And set ȝoure soule sauely fro sinne. 4
  ȝif þou haue kynges of þi kynne, (col. 2)
    And in þi clos, catel and corn,
  Amende þi misses more and minne,
    And mak no tarijng til to-Morn. 8

Þou leod þat liues as lord in londe,
  Þenk hou lowe þou schalt aliht,
Þauȝ þou haue hundredus at þin honde
  To holde þin heste in herte has hiht. 12
  ȝif þou bragge for þi Beȝauns briht,
    Bi-holde hou bare þat þou was born ;
  Þis dai þou dresse þi dole and diht,
    Leste þat þou dye longe er to-Morn. 16

Þou freike þat art in frendschupe fast
  And þenkest no foot-mon is þi fere,
Whon þi pompe and pride is past,
  A pore penaunt schal beo þi pere. 20
  Loke in londe, and þou mai lere,
    Hou liȝtly þat þi lyf is lorn ;
  Whon þi bodi is brouht on bere, 23
    As þou hast browen, þou broukest to-Morn.

16 þat *interlined by corrector.*

Gome, er þou giue vp þi gost,
  Bi-greiþ ho schal gripe þi goode ;
He schal hit haue þou hatest most—
  So fares hit ofte, be myn hode,   28
  Þen al þi fee fonges but foode.
    For-þi ordeyne þi fare be-forn,
  And with a bone mende þi mis in mode—
    Hit wol þe menske aȝeyn to-Morn.   32

Parte with ȝor godes in priuete
  Vn-to þe pore with-outen pride ;
Hit wol þe brynge in blisse to be,
  Wiþ-outen bale to buylde & byde.   36
  Þou sette þi seketur fro þi syde,
    He wol þe swyke þouȝ he be sworn.
  Þin hord whon he may hent oþur hyde,
    Trust him not after to-Morn.   40

Þe sikernes of þi seketoure
  Þis is þe soþe to seo and say :
Þauȝ he for þi loue lurke and loure,
  Þat he has lauht he wol nouȝt lay,   44
  But skelpe and scrope al þat he may ;
    He lettes nouþer for skaþe ne skorn
  Þi goodes, whon he has geten a-way—
    Trust nouȝt on hem after to-Morn.   48

Mony a wiht wenes ful wel
  Out of þis world þei schal neuur wende ;
For feole lykinges þat þei feel,
  Þei make no fors of fo nor frende.   52
  Now trust riht wel þei schal be tenede,
    Ar bodi and soule a-two be torn.
  Of erþly ese þis is þe ende :
    Here to-day, a-wey to-morn !   56

O 2

Ihesus, þat on þe Rode was don,
  From wo and wondreþ þou vs wisse;
Gladly graunte us vre bone
  And bryng us blessedly to þi blisse.   60
  For vre loue, soþ hit is,
    Þi syde with scharpe spere was schorn;
  Þou saue us þat we ben not his
    Þat wolde þat we weore tynt to-Morn.   64

Marie.Moder, Mayden Mylde,
  On al mon-kuynde ȝe haue Merci.
In feole fulþes we ben fuylede;
  Þis world vseþ þe flessches foly.   68
  Vn-to þi sone þou calle and cry,
    Crist crounet wiþ kene þorn.
  He ȝiue vs grace to wone him by;
    Þen schal vs tyde no teone to-Morn.   72

117.   *Make Amends!*

Vernon MS.

BI a wode as I gon ryde,   f. 411^b
  Walkynge al mi-self alone,   (col. 2)
A boske of briddes bad me abyde,
  Bi-cause þer songe mo þen one.   4
  Amonge þo foules euerichone,
    To on gret hede I gan take,
  For he seyde with reuþful mone,
    'For þi sunnes a-Mendes make!'   8

'Make a-mendes, mon, trewely,'
  Seide þat foul with feþeres blake.
In myn herte i-went, wo was I,
  For he me bad amendes make.
  I stod and studied al þat day ;
    Þat resun made me a niht to wake :
  Þen fond I þreo skiles in good fay,
    Whi he me bad a-mendes make.

12
(col. 3)

16

Þe furste skile þat I gan fynde,
  As hit bi-semes in my witte,
Is a þing þat comes of kynde :
  Þat eueri mon schal haue a pitte.
  Whon top and to to-gedre is knitte,
    Þen schal þi proude wordes a-slake ;
  For-þi in eorþe er þou be ditte,
    Mon, of þi synnes a-mendes make !

20

24

Þat oþer skile is, þat þou schalt dye,
  Whuche tyme þou wost nere ;
And þou wustest, witerly,
  Þow woldest fle þi deþ for fere.
  Þi laste bour schal ben a Bere,
    ʒif þi frendes þe may take :
  Þerfore do wel while þou art here,
    And for þi sunnes a-Mendes make !

28

32

Þe þridde skile wol do þe wo
  Whon þou þenkest þer-on I-wis :
Whon þi lyf is clene I-go,
  Þou wost nere whoder to bale or blis.
  I fynde no clerk con telle me þis ;
    Þerfore my serwe bi-ginnes to wake.
  Whon þou þenkest to don a-mis,
    Haue mynde of þis & amendes make !

36

40

Ensaumple we may sen al day,
    As crist schewes a-mong vs alle ;
To-day ȝif þou be stout and gay,
    To-morn þou lyst ded bi þe walle.   44
    Merci þenne to crie and calle,
        Hit is to late þi leue to take.
    Be war of folye er þou falle,
        And for þi sunnes amendes make !   48

ȝif þou haue don a dedly synne
    wher-þorw þi soule scholde be schent,
Al þe ȝer þou wolt lye þer-Inne
    In derfnes til hit beo lent ;   52
    Þen a Frere þou wolt hent,
        Þi parisch prest for schame forsake.
    Of alle suche dedes, verament,
        I rede þe beo wys, & amendes make.   56

ȝif þou be kyng and croune bere,
    And al þis world be at þi wil,
ȝit schaltou be pore as þou was ere,
    And þat þou knowest bi puire skil :   60
    A schete schal þi body hule,
        And huyde þi cors for sinnes sake.
    Þerfore repente, þou hast do ille,
        And for þi synnes amendes make !   64

ȝif þou beo a fryk mon in þi floures,
    And haue vn-bouȝt boþe purpel & pal,
At Masse, ne Matyns, ne at houres,
    Þou kepes not come with-in þe chirche wal,   68
    Þer-in þi sauor is ful smal.
        Of sleuþe may þou nouȝt awake ;
    On day þou schalt leue hit al—
        Þerfore I rede, Amendes make.   72

            52 MS. derknes.

Þauȝ þou haue riches gret plente,
  In world while þou liuest here,
God made þi neiȝebur as wel as þe,
  And bouȝt ȝou boþe I-liche dere;   76
  Þauȝ he be nouȝt þi worldes pere,
    Do him no wrong, for synnes sake!
  To nouȝt shal turne þi proude chere:
    Þerfore I rede, þou amendes make.   80

Loke þou bere þe feir and euen,
  Þauȝ þou be lord, Bayli, oþur Meire,
For ofte men meten at vn-set steuen:
  Coueyte not þi neiȝebor to peyre,   84
  Þis world nis but a chirie-feire,
    Nou is hit in sesun, nou wol hit slake;
  To-day artou lord, to-morn is þin heire—
    Þerfore I rede, þou amendes make.   88

Nou god, þat was in bethleem boren,
  And siþen died vppon þe tre,
let vs neuer ben for-loren,
  Lord, ȝif þi wille be.   92
  Marie Moder, Mayden briht,   f. 412ᵃ
    Preye for vre synnes sake,   (col. 1)
  In heuene of þi sone to haue a siht,
    And heer in eorþe, Amendes make.   96

118. Suffer in Time and that is Best.

Vernon MS.

WHon alle soþes ben souht and scene,   f. 412ª
  Euerichone at heore deuys,   (col. 1)
Euer a-mong in tray and tene,
  Murþe is mey⟨n⟩t wiþ malys: 4
Aʒeynes cumfort comeþ cares kene,
  Aʒeynes vche a uertu is a vys.
Of alle þe vertues þat þer beone,
  To suffre, hit is a þing of prys.   8
 Þerfore he þat wol be wys
  And loue to rule him siker in rest,
 Loke þat he beo not to nys,
  But suffre in tyme, and þat is best.   12

Ʒif þou beo mon of mene a-syse
  Of gret lord in duresse,
And þi stat may not suffise
  Of þi wronge to gete red⟨r⟩esse,   16
Þen mostou worchen on þis wyse,
  And schewe to him such boxumnesse,
Þat rouþe in his herte may ryse
  And wiþ-drawe his grete distresse;   20
 Ʒif he be Mesured wiþ Mekenesse,
  Þen pite in him hit wol be preste.
 A-mong alle þing, as I gesse,
  To suffre in tyme and þat is beste.   24

Ʒif þou be mon of gret degre,
  And a pore mon in his place
Ful wrongfully has greued þe,
  And don þe gref wiþ his trespace,   28
Þe cuntrey con wel knowe and se,
  Þou mai be venget in þat case;

14 Of: MS. or.

ȝif þou be perset wiþ pite,
  ȝit woltou spare him for a space.   32
  ȝif þou so goodly schewe þi grace,
    Þe holigost is in þe feste ;
  Þen godes blessyng schaltou in-brace,
    And suffre ⟨in⟩ tyme and þat is beste.   36

Hit is luytel worþ, seiþ Socrates,
  A glasen pot is wayk and liht
To puiten him self to fer in pres
  A-ȝeynes a caudrun for to fiht.   40
  Þe soþe al day is seene in siht,
    Þe weikest ay bi-neoþe is cast ;
  Þerfore sei I, bi god almiht,
    To suffre ⟨in⟩ tyme and þat is best.   44

Mon, ȝif þou wolt þi state meyntene,
  Wiþ lordes In counseil forte sitte,
Þer eueri mon moste in certeyne
  Schewe his wisdom and his witte,   48
Þen, what-so-euer hapnes þe to seyne,
  Let al þi wordes to wisdam knitte,
Or summe of þi feeres wol taken in-deyne,
  And for pruyde reson hitte.   52
  ȝif þou here hem so chyde or flitte,
    Þer wol no reson in hem reste ;
  Holt þi tonge and þi mouþ ditte,
    And suffre ⟨in⟩ tyme and þat is beste.   56

And aftur, whon þou woldest not wene,
  Whon alle soþes ben souȝt and sayd,
Þi wordes þei wole take by-deene,
  And of þi speche þei wol holde hem payd.   60
Þen schul þei abassched beone,
  And of heor errours ben dismayed,

Whon þi wisdam schal be set and sene,
  And alle heore folys ben displayed.   64
Hasti men ben ofte outrayede
  Whon heore tonges ben to preste;
Hose haþ ben ofte of sore hokes braide,
  Soffre ⟨in⟩ tyme and þat is beste.   68

ʒif hit bi-tideþ be niht oþer day
  To falle in-til a cumpaignye
Þer nyse folk wiþ folyes play,
  And out of reson þei ʒelle and crie,   72
Þen mostou worchen wiþ þis assay,
  And holde vp 'oyl' by and by,
Til þou mowe priuely go þi way;
  Þen kuiþest þou wel þat þou art slih.   76
I holde hit riht a gret foly   (col. 2)
  To schewe reson þer non wol reste;
Þer, bi God and vre ladi,
  Suffre in tyme and þat is beste.   80

119.   *Mane nobiscum, Domine.*

Vernon MS.

IN Somer bi-fore þe Ascenciun   f. 412ᵃ
  At Euensong on a Sonundai,   (col. 2)
Dwellyng in my deuociun,
  For þe pees fast gon I prai;   4
I herde a Reson to my pai,
  Þat writen was with wordes þre,
And þus hit is, schortly to say:
  Mane nobiscum, domine!   8

What þis word is forte mene
  On Englisch tonge, I schal ȝou telle.
In Concience and we be clene,
  Digne þe, lord, with vs to dwelle,   12
  þe feondes pouste for to felle.
    þat for vs diȝede vppon þe tre,
  In wit and worschipe, wei and welle,
    Mane nobiscum, domine!   16

Whon þou from deth was risen and gon,
  þen as a Palmere forþ gon pas,
þo met þou pilgrimes makyng moon,
  But ȝit þei wust neuur who þou was.   20
  þus þen Carpes Cleophas:
    'þe Niht is neih as we may se,
  þe liht of þe dai is waxen las,
    Mane nobiscum, domine!'   24

Dwelle with vs, vr fader dere!
  þi bidyng is in heuene blis,
And euure þi name be halewed here,
  þi kyngdom let vs neuere mis.   28
  In heuene þi wille folfuld is,
    And heere in eorþe þat hit so be,
  þe Rihtwys weyes ȝe wolde vs wis—
    Mane nobiscum, domine!   32

Vr bred, vr vche dayes foode,
  Drihten deore, þou vs diht!
Vr dette, God þat is so goode,
  For-ȝiue vs for þi muchele miht,   36
  As we schul heom wiþ herte liht
    þat in vr dette or daunger be.
  Leste we Rule vs not a-riht,
    Mane nobiscum, domine!   40

12 MS. þi.   19 MS. þou *corrected from* I.

Dwelle wiþ vs, lord, leste we haue teene,
   Lede us to no temptacion,
In eny synne, ʒif we beo seene,
    We prey þe of Merci and pardoun;   44
    Wiþ al þe Mekenes þat we moun,
      We schal crye, knelyng on kne:
   'Vppon bere whon we beo boun,
    Mane nobiscum, domine!'   48

Lord, dwelle with vs in al ur neode,
   Wiþ-outen þe we haue no miht
Vr hondes vp til vr hed to beode;
    Wit nor weole sauereþ no siht.   52
    In eny caas ʒif we ben cliht,
      We con not, but we crie to þe
In al vr neode, boþe day and niht,
    Mane nobiscum, domine!   56

Ho dwelleþ wiþ þe, þar haue no doute
   For no synne ne sodeyn chaunce;
But ay þe fend is fast aboute
    To putte vs, lord, fro þi plesaunce.   60
    Whon we beoþ out of gouernaunce,
      Vr flesch is frele, we can not fle;
Keep us out of al cumbraunce,
    Mane nobiscum, domine!   64

Dwelle wiþ us, lord of loue and pes,
   And make þi wonynge vs wiþ-inne,
In Charite þat we encres,
    And kep vs out of dedly synne;   68
    Torn neuere þi face from us to twynne,
      For Marie loue þat Mayden fre.
Whon we schal eny werk beo-gynne,
    Mane nobiscum, domine!   72

Mane nobiscum, domine!
 Wiþ-outen þe we ben riht nouht.
What Ioye or Blis weore þat to þe,
  To þeose þat þou hast deore abouht ? 76
  In word, In wille, In herte, and þouht, (col. 3)
   We schul preye to þe Trinite:
   'Out of þis world whon we be brouȝt,
    Mane nobiscum, domine!' 80

120. But thou say Sooth thou shalt be Shent.

B.M. Addit. 22283.

WHo-so loueth endeles rest, f. 134ᵃ
 Þis false world þen mot he fle, (col. 1)
And dele þer-wiþ bot as a gest,
And leue hit not in no degre. 4
Hit is but trouble & tempest,
Fals fantasye, & vanite ;
In þat þraldom who-so is I-þrest
Him mot eschewe al charite. 8
  Þat day þat eueri mon schal se
  His dedes schewed & his entent ;
  What maner mon so þat he be,
  But he sey soth, he schal be schent. 12

Seyth now dauid in his sawe
In þe sauter book openly,
Þat whoso to þe worldus lust drawe,
In his lyf is leef to lye, 16
Þat he ne leueþ not on godus lawe,
But forsakeþ hit wylfully.
And for him stont of god no awe,
In bremful bale he schal hit by, 20
  When concience his werk schal wrye ;
  And as he doþ, he dom schal hente
  Whit-outen rescores or remedye,—
  But he sey soth he schal be schente. 24

    23 MS. restores.

A lesyng is, with-outen doute,
Wel worse þen som men taken hede,
For haue þe tonge onus told hit oute,
A-brod þen schal hit sprynge & sprede,   28
And renne ful ryf in eueri route ;
And be hit onus so blowen on brede,
Þey men wolden aftur knele & loute,
Men may not stoppe hit with no mede.   32
  Such lesyngus þen I rede ȝe drede,
  Lest ȝe in bittur bales ben brent
  For þer nis non so styf on stede,
  But he sey soth he schal be schent.   36

Þou miht als chep robbe a mon
As with a lesyng lese his name ;
What-so þou spekest, where, or whanne,
Loke þat þou no mon diffame.   40
Sey þe sothe, ȝif þat þou kan,
Þou suppose to here a blame ;
Ful sore þe stonde elles schal þou ban
When truthe þi tales schal a-tame.   44
  To greue god, hit is no game,
  Þat lust & lykyng haþ þe lent.
  For outh þat þou const forge or frame,
  But þou sey soth þou schalt be schent.   48

ȝif þou be þrat to take þe deth
For seyng soth, be not agast ;
Let not þe sothe be set be-neth,
But truþe to mayntene, be ay studefast.   52
Þenke þi lyf is but a breth,
Þenke þou schalt passen, as mo han past.
Clottes of clay þi cors schal cleth,   (col. 2)
Þi careyne vn-to wormes cast.   56
  When Gabriel schal blowe his blast,
  For soth sawe schaltou neuer repent ;
  Þen leue hit lely, at þe last,
  But þou sey soth, þou schalt be schent.   60

Alas! what corsed lyf is þis,
Þat men dreden more þe world now here
Þen him þat wrouȝte þe world I-wys,
And al þing haþ in his pouwere!   64
As men in questus seyn ofte a-mys,
And stoppen quereles o trewe & clere,—
Such men þenkeþ not on heuen blys,
Þat ȝeuen verdites in such manere.   68
     Truthe & kuyndenesse knyt in fere,
     God askeþ of vs non oþer rent.
     Þenne wyte hit wel with-oute were,
     But þou sey soth, þou schalt be schent.   72

Þey þou kacche blame a þrowe
For seyng sooþ more or lasse,
Þenne aftur, when þe treuþe is I-knowe,
Among goode men, as I gesse,   76
Þou schalt be leef—vch mon to trowe
And worschyp—for þi sothfastnesse.
Þerfore I rede boþe hye and lowe,
Sey soth, and lette for no dystresse.   80
     Þyn owne wordus schul bere witnesse
     A-ȝeyn þe at þi Iuggement;
     When grete god þat doom schal dresse,
     But þou sey soth, þou schalt be schent.   84

Hold vp no monnus 'oyl', I rede,
When he wenduþ out of þe wey,
For such glosyngus makeþ mony quede,
When non þe soþe dar to him say.   88
Such flaterynge schal luyte stond in stude
When god þe grete doom schal aray;
And he þat best now here con plede,
I leue he schal be lewede þat day.   92
     Whan crist schal his woundes dysplay,
     Þat for vs was on rode I-rent,
     And vche mon schal take his pay,   95
     But þou sey soth, þou schalt ⟨be⟩ schent.

For seyng soþ, þou miht not synne,
But ȝif þou sclaundre eny wyȝth ;
Sclaundre no mon more ne mynne,
For sclaundre stynkeþ in godus syȝth.   100
Elles, what quarel þou art ynne,
Sey þe soþe, ay meynteyne þe ryȝth,
And on þis wyse þou miht wynne
Þe blysse a-boue þat blesseþ bryȝth,   104
    And endeles lyf þat lasteþ lyȝth
    Þus I am sure þat þou miht hent,
    And elles, when deþ þi doom schal dyȝth,
    But þou sey soþ, þou schalt be schent.   108

121. *The Bird with Four Feathers.*

MS. Bodley 596.

Here bygynnith the tretys of *Parce michi domine.*

BY a forest syde walking, as I went   f. 21ᵇ
    Disport to take In o mornyng,
A place I fond, schaded with bowes ybent,
Iset a-boute with flowrs so swete smellyng   4
I leyde me down vpon that grene,
And kast myn eyȝen me aboute :
I fond there breddes with fedres schene,
Many on sitting vpon a rowte.   8
O brid þer-by sat on a brere,
Hir fedres were pulled, sche myght not fle ;
She sat and song with mornyng chere,
    Parce michi domine.   12

'Spare me, lord, kyng of pytee,'
Thus sang þis bryd in pover array,
'My myrthe is goo & my Iolyte ;
I may not flee as othir may,   16
My fedres schene ben pulled me fro ;
My ȝowthe, my strengthe, & my bewte,
Wher-thorgh I take þis song me too :
    Parce michi domine.'   20

When I herd þis mornyng song,
I drew þis brid nere and nere,
And asked who had don þis wrong
And brought here in so drowpyng chere,   24
And who had pulled here fedres away
That schuld here bere from tre to tre,
And why sche song in her lay,
    Parce michi domine.   28

The bryd answerd and seid me till :
'Man, be In pees for cristes sake !   f. 22ᵃ
ȝif I schewe the myn hertis will,
Peynes sore me wolle awake ;   32
ȝif thow wilt take my word in mynde,
Ther shal no sorow be my letting,
That I nyl holy myn herte vnbynde,
And sothly telle the thyn asking :—   36
Which were myn fedres þat were so clere,
And who hath pulled hem alle fro me,
And why I sitte singging on brere,
    Parce michi Domine.   40

'Fedres fowre I had ywis,
The two were set on euery wynge ;
Thei bare me breme to my blys,
Where me lust be at my lykyng :   44
The first was ȝowthe, þe secunde bewte,
Strengthe and ryches þe other two ;

          23 MS. askesd.

And now þei ben, as thow maist se,
Alle foure fedres Ifalle me fro.   48
My principal fedre ʒowthe it was,
He bare me ofte to nysete,
Wherfore my song is now, " allas!
  Parce michi Domine !"   52

' In ʒowthe I wrowth folies fele,
my herte was set so hye in pride ;
To synne I ʒaf me euery dele,
Spared I neither tyme ne tyde ;   56
I was redy to make debate,
my lyf stood ofte in mochel drede ;
And my lyking, to walke late,
And haue my lust of synful dede :   60
I was now here, I was now there,
Vnstable I was In al degre,—   f. 22ᵇ
To him I crye þat marie bare,
  Parce michi domine !   64

' For Salamon seith in his poyse,
Thre weyes ther beth ful hard to knowe :
Oon is a schep þat sailleth in the see,
An Egle in hey, a worm in lowe ;   68
And of þe ferthe, telle he ne can,
It is so wondirful in his hering—
The weyes of a ʒong man,
Whiche þat ben here at her lyking.   72
And now hath age Ismyte me fro
My pryncypal fedre of Iolyte ;
For al þat euer I haue misdoo,
  Parce michi domine !   76

' My Secunde fedre heith bewte ;
I held my self so clere of schap,
That al the peple scholde loke on me,
And worschip me with hoode & cap ;   80

' My rud was reed, my colour clere,
me þought neuer non so faire as I
In al a contre, feer no nere,
In fetewrs & schap so comely,   84
My forhed large, my browes bent,
Myn eyȝen cleer, and corage bolde ;
My schap ne myght no man ament,
Me thought my self so fayre to be-holde.   88
And ȝet I was begyled in syght,
The myrrour, lorde, desceyued me,
Wher-fore I aske, lord, of þi myght
    Parce michi domine!   92

' This fedir me bare ful ofte to synne,
And principally to leccherye ;
Clipping and kessing cowth I not blynne,.
me thought it craft of curteseye.   f. 23ᵃ
 A cusse it is þe deuel-is gynne,   97
Oft of it ariseth woo & wrake ;
The deuel with cusse many doth wynne,
I counseil the thow synne forsake.   100
Sampson lost his strengthe þer fore,
Dauid his grace for Bersabee,
Til he cried with wordes sore,
    Parce michi domine!   104

' Salamon, þat worthy king,
Ful fayr he was from top to too ;
Wher-fore in his age ȝyng,
He was *amabilis domino* ;   108
And after he fel fowle & sore,
For lust of women þat was him neygh ;
Thei fonned him in his age hore,
That he forsoke his god on heygh.   112

'Nought onlich þise but many moo,
bewte hath be-giled I-wys:
I woot wel I am on of thoo,
I can þe better telle þis.   116
Now hath age y-smyte me fro
My secunde Fedre, þat height bewte;
For al þat euer I haue misdoo,
　　Parce michi domine!   120

'My thridde fedre strengthe height;
My name was knowe on euery syde,
For I was man of mochel myght,
And many on spak of me ful wide: 124
To prike and praunce I was ful preste,
My strengthe to kepe In euery place;
And euer more I had the beest—
Such was my hap, such was my grace.   128
My strengthe ful ofte me drowgh amys,   f. 23ᵇ
And torned me, lord, clene fro the;
Now kyng corowned In heuenne blys,
　　Parce michi domine!   132

'This feder me bare be-ȝonde the see,
To gete me name In vncowth londe,
To robbe and slee had I deyntee,
Ne spared I neither fre ne bonde;   136
Of holy chirche took I no ȝeme,
Bokes to take ne vestement;
Ther myght no þing so moche me queme
As robbe, or see an abbey brent.   140
With strengthe I gat me gret aray,
Precious clothes, gold, and fee:
I thougth ful litel on thilke day—
　　Parce michi domine!   144

128 MS. *inverts* grace *and* hap.　　　133 feder: MS. fader.

'When Nabugodonosor, fers in fight,
Ierusalem had thought to wynne;
And so he dede with mayn & myght,
And brent þe temples þat were þer Inne;   148
And al the gold þat he there founde
He toke with him and hom gan ryde;
Him thought þer schold no þing withstonde.
His herte was set so heigh In Pryde: 152
Till þe king of myghtes most
Browght him þere þat lowest was,
And caught him from his real oost,
And drof him to a wildirnesse;   156
And there he lyued with erbe & rote,
Walkyng euer on foot & on honde,
Till god of mercy dede him bote,
And his prison out of bonde: 160
Thanne seide þis kyng thise wordes, Iwis:
" Al thing be, lord, at thi powste,   f. 24ᵃ
Mercy I crie; I haue do mys—
        Parce michi domine!"   164

'While I had my strengthe at will,
Ful many a man I dede vnrest;
Thei þat wolde not my heste fulfill,
My knyf was redy to his brest;   168
And now I sitte here blynde and lame,
And croked beth my lymes alle.
I was ful wilde, I am now tame.
This Fedre of strengthe is fro me falle;   172
And now hath age ysmyte me fro
My thridde fedre of Iolyte:
For al þat euer I haue misdo,
        Parce michi domine!   176

' My ferthe feder ryches was;
To make it schyne I trauailled sore,

' I went in many a perilous place,
Wel oft my lyf was neigh for-lore;   180
By dale, by downe, by wode syde,
I bood many a bitter schowr;
In salt see I sailled wel wide,
For to multiplie my tresowr: 184
With fals sleightes I gat my gode,
In couetise I grownded me,—
Ihesus, for thi precious blood,
    Parce michi domine!   188

' Whan I was siker of gold ynow,
I gan to ride a-boute wel fast;
I purchaced moche, & god wot how;
I wende þis lyf wolde euer haue last;   192
I let me bilde castell and towres,
With-out I-warded with stronge dyche,
With-Inne I-bildet halles and bowres.
Ther was no towr my castel liche,   f. 24^b
In this was yset al my lyking,   197
And turned me, lord, holich from the—
To the I crye now, heuen king,
    Parce michi domine!   200

' Whan I was most in al my flours,
and had aboute me wif and childe,
I lost my catel and my tours;
Thanne wex my herte in party mylde;   204
Catell fel fro me sodeynly,
Ryght as it come it went away:
men seith, good gete vntrewly,
the thridde heire broke it ne may.   208
I was ful wilde, I am now tame;
fortune hath pulled ryches me fro:
ȝowre wreche, lord, I can not blame—
    Parce michi domine!   212

194 MS. dyches.

' Iob was richer þanne euer was I,
of gold, siluer, & other good ;
it fel hym fro, and þat scharply
As dede þe water owt of the flood ;   216
Hym was not left so mochel a clothe
his naked body for to hille ;
Hym lakkyd crostes of a loffe,
When him lest ete In tyme of mele :   220
And ȝet he held vp thanne his honde,
And seide, " heigh god in mageste,
I thank the of thy swete sonde !
    Parce michi domine ! "   224

' Now *parce michi domine !*
My Ioye, my merthe, is al agoon ;
ȝowthe, Strengthe, and my bewte,
My fetheres faire, be falle me froo.   228
Wher-to is a man more liche
Þanne to a flowr þat springis In may ?
Alle that lyueth, bothe powre and ryche,
Shal deye vnknowyng of her day.'   232

I sette me down vp-on my knee,
And thanked this bryd of here gode lore ;
It thought me wele this word ' *Parce* '
Was bale and bote of gostly sore.   236
Now *parce*, lord, and spare thow me !
This is a worde þat sone gat grace,
And ' *Parce* ' geteth godis pyte,
And scheweth to vs his blessed face. **Amen.** 240

122. *A Prayer by the Five Joys.*

MS. Rawlinson liturgical g. 2.

MArie moder, wel the be,
   Marie mayde, þenk on me!   f. 4^b
Moder and mayde was neuer non
To-geder, ladi, bote þou alon.   4

Marie moder, mayde clene,
Schilde me fro sorwe & tene!
Marie, out of synne help þou me,
And out of dette for charite.   8

Marie, for thine ioies .v.,
Help me to leue in clene lyue,
For þe teres þou lete under þe rode,   f. 5^a
  Sende me grace of liues fode,   12

Wher-with i may me clothe & fede
And in treuthe mi lijf lede.
Help me, ladi, & alle myne,
And schilde us alle fro helle pyne.   16

Schilde me, ladi, fro uelanye,
And fro alle wikkede companye ;
Schilde me ladi fro wikked schame,
And fram alle wikkede fame.   20

Swete ladi, thou me were,
That the fend nouȝth ⟨me⟩ dere ;
Bothe bi day and bi nyȝth,   23
Help me, ladi, with thi riȝth.   f. 5^b

For myne frendes i bidde the,
That hiȝ mote amended be,
Bothe to soule & to lyue,
Marie, for thyne ioies fyue.   28

For myne fomen i bidde also,
That they mote heer so do
That they in wrathe hy ne deye,
Swete lady, ich the preye.   32

Hy that ben in goode lyue,
Marie, for thine ioies fyue ;
Swete ladi, ther-Inne hem holde,
Bothe the ȝonge & the olde.   36

And that ben in dedlich synne,   f. 6ᵃ
ne lete hem neuere deie ther-Inne :
Marie, for thine ioies alle,
Lete hem neuere in helle falle.   40

Swete ladi, thou hem rede,
That thei amendi of here misdede ;
Bysek thi sone, heuene kyng,
That he me graunte good endyng,   44

And sende me, as he wel may,
Schrift & hosel at myn endyng day ;
And that we mote thider wende,   47
Ther ioie is with-outen ende. Amen Amen.

123. *A Prayer to be delivered from the Deadly Sins.*

MS. Rawlinson liturgical g. 2.

IHesu, for þi precious blod,   f. 19ᵃ
  þat þou bleddest for oure good
    in circumcisioun,
Of þe, crist, ich aske mercy   4
to chaste my lecherous bodi
    fro dampnacioun.   *Pater nr. Aue Maria.*

Ihesu, for þi dropes swete,
þat þou bleddest on oliuete   8
    out of þi fayre face,
late me neuere in wratthe falle,
but loue my emcristone alle—   11
    oure lord, ȝif me grace!   *Pater n̄r. Aue*

Ihesu, for þi blodi dropes,   f. 19ᵇ
þat þe scourge & þe ropus
    Made hem to renne a-doun,
Fede me wit mete & drinke,   16
þat i neuere in synne sinke—
    Haue mercy on me, glotoun!
        Pater n̄r Aue m̄a.

Ihesu, for þi blodi heued,
þat wit thornes was beweued,   20
    longe, scharp, & kene,
chast me þat am so wilde;
Make my herte mek & mylde,   23
    to be þi seruaunt clene.   f. 20ᵃ
        Pater n̄r Aue

Ihesu, for þi blodi strondes,
þat ran out of ȝoure handes—
    þe nayles þer-inne i-driue—
fro couetyse drawe me þouȝt,   28
more þan me nedeȝ ȝef me nouȝt,
    wiles þat i schal leue.   *Pater nr*

Ihesu, for þi blod so swete,
þat ran out of ȝoure fete   32
    for synful mannes sake,
ȝif me grace good werkes to worche,
to loue god & holy cherche,   f. 20^b
    þat no slowthe me take.   *Pater noster.*
               Aue Maria 36

Ihesu, for þi woundes smarte,
whan þi blood ran fro þi herte
    & watur menged to-gedure,
Make me styf in charite ;   40
& to heuene bringe me,
    and alle men þedur.

124. *A Prayer for Three Boons.*

MS. Rawlinson liturgical g. 2.

FAdur and sone & holy gost,   f. 58^a
  þat i clepe & calle most,
On god in trinite,
To þe, lord, i clepe & calle,   4
for me synfol, & for ous alle,
    þou graunte me bones thre.

The firste bone þus i by-ginne :
lord, haue mercy up-on my synne,   8
    þat i haue don seth y was born ;
wit word, wit wylle, wit herte, y-thouȝt ;
wit flesch, wit blod, wit handes, wrouth ;   f. 58ᵇ
    wit mouþ spoken, & be-for sworn.   12

In my thouȝt & my heued,
Mytte i neuer my with weld ;
    Euere to synne day were redy ;
wel swyft i was to don ful ylle,   16
wel slow to worche godes wille,
    Ther-of y crie ihesu mercy.

don i haue sinnes seuene,
Bereued men of þe blysse of heuene,   20
    i-broke þe ten comaundementes ;   f. 59ᵃ
Al my synnes wol i for-sake,
to ihesu crist wol i me take,
    to don amendemens.   24

y crie, ihesu, thyn hore !
for þi peynes & for þi woundes sore ;
    þou syttest al in thi trone,
late & herliche, nyth & day,   28
Mercy, ihesu, i crie ay—
    þis is my ferste bone.

Þat other bone of my askinge,
y the praie, heuene kyn⟨g⟩,   32
    þat y mowe haue grace,   f. 59ᵇ
þat i mowe my sinne lete
Or deth & i to-gydur mete,
    lord, ȝeue me miȝt & spase.   36

19 MS. fyue.

And of my lord, to loue þe swo—
war i sytte or war i go—
    þat þou be euir in my sythe
þat i mowe euere ȝow see,   40
þe better my synnes for to fle,
    þat þu kepe me day & nyth.

Alle þat mai to synne drawe,   43
Word, or werk and oþir plawe,   f. 60ᵃ
    Kepe me, lord, þer-fro !
In good lyf to stande fast,
To do þi seruise longe to last,
    Fro þis day euere mo.   48

Ihesu, for þi holi grace,
ȝef me myth & gyf me space,
    And kepe me fro þe quede ;
Þat i neuere falle in no synne,   52
wit-outen repentaunse to deye þer-inne,
    Schilde me fro soden dede.

Ihesu lord, he me wise & rede,   f. 60ᵇ
Holy lyf to leuen & lede,   56
    Þat made sonne & mone ;
And do me, lord, to knowe þi wille,
Þat in dede i mowe fulfille—
    Þis is my oþer bone.   60

Þe þridde bone to þe, ihesu, i praie,
Þat i mowe haue þe rith waie
    To þe blisse of my deth daye :
Ful wel i wot my lyf haueþ ende,   64
Whan out of þis world schal wende,
    Þat tyme wite me may !   f. 61ᵃ

43 MS. þⁿ   44 MS. plawge.   54 MS. deth.
                59 MS. deþe.

Þer-fore, ihesu, me graunte a þrawe,
Þat i mowe my sinnes knawe, 68
  Clene me to schriue ;
Of prestes hondys houseled to be
By-for my deth, be grant-hit me,
  Lord, for þi woundes fyue. 72

Wit stodefast thouȝt þou me sette,
Þat þe fend me neuer lette
  wit his foule syth ;
whan mi herte schal cleue & brest, 76
Þow take my sowle in-to þi reste, f. 61ᵇ
  Þar day is wit-owten nyth.

At domesday, whan wikked schal drede,
whan þai seeþ þi woundes blede, 80
  Ihesu, þanne on me rewe ;
And do me lord up-on þi rith hond,
In-to þat blisse, þat riche lond,
  Þar ioie and blisse is euere newe. 84

Þat ioie & blysse ȝe graunte to me
Now þou woldys þi woundes schede, f. 62ᵃ
  For senfol man & for me ;
Þou graunte me þis bones þre, 88
And alle þo þat cristen bee,
  Amen, pur charite.

76 MS. berst. 84 MS. Þat.

125. **The Knight of Christ.**

MS. Bodley 416.

Fadur & sone & holi gost, o god in tr⟨i⟩nite, f. 105ᵃ
  To þe y make my mone, þouȝ y unworþi be ;
I am but myn one, & fomen haue y þre—
þe fend, þe world, myn owne flesh—him mai y not
  fle.   4

   þe fend me tempteþ dai & nyȝt,
   he wol me reue heuene briȝt,
     þat he les þorw his pride ;
   swete ihesu, y am þi knyȝt,   8
   aȝenus him y take þe fiȝt,
     stifli him to abide.

   At þe y mot myn armes borwe,
   Mi sheld shal be þe swerd of sorwe,   12
     marie þat stong to þe herte ;
   þe holi cros my baner biforn,
   myn helm þi garlond of sharpe þorn,
     Mi swerd þi scourges smerte.   16

   Mi plates shullen þi nailes be,
   myn acotoun þat spere tre,
     þat stong þi swete syde.
   Now y am armed þus wel,   20
   nel y him fle neuere a del,
     tyde what bi-tyde !

   þe wordle me haþ long lif bihet,   f. 105ᵇ
   and biddeþ me murie make ;   24
   whanne i am olde and of unmyȝt
   to penaunce forte take :
   it haþ be shewed to oure syȝt,
   þenne is al to late ;   28

he haþ deseyued king and knyȝt,
& many man brouȝt to wrake.
swete ihesu, ful of myȝt,
þou here my bone & do me riȝt,   32
him here to forsake.

Holi fadur, y herie þe
for þe loue þat þou hast shewed me,
    siþ þat þou furst bigan ;   36
for loue þou came from heuene blisse,
& madest for loue to þi liknes,
    oure fadur adam :
he as unwise þyn heste brak,   40
whanne he of þat appel at,
    In sorwe to mony man.

For loue adoun þou sendest þi sone,
In swete marie bosome to wone,   44
    here wiþ us to dwelle :
Ihesu, for loue þou lettest take
wiþ foule iewes ȝolewe & blake,
to lede þe bifore pilate,   48
    as holi writ us telle.

Swete ihesu, for loue of me,
þou henge upon þe rode tre,
harde fastned wiþ nailes þre,   52
    þi swete bodi by-swonge ;
for loue þou þoledest woundes depe,
þin hondes þerled, and eke þi fete ;   f. 106ᵃ
þy modir blodi teres lete—   56
    she sauȝ þi herte stoonge,
þi swete bodi al on a flod,
out of þi syde water & blod
      60
    and ran doun to grounde.

Swete ihesu, for loue of me þus was þi bodi shent,
wiþ ropis and wiþ nailes, wiþ þornes al to-rent :
was neuere body in erþe at suche a turment.　　64
Swete ihesu, siþþen to helle for oure soules wente,
þe prisones out to fecche þat weren wiþ peynes blent.

　　Swete ihesu, curteys & fre,
　　þou3 y wrecche unworþy be,　　68
　　wiþ al myn herte y þonke þe
　　þat þou woldest on rode tre
　　peynes stronge suffre for me,
　　and to þi blisse bigge me,　　72
　　wiþoute ende to wone wiþ þe :
　　to þat blisse þou us brynge,
　　þat woldest of a maide springe.
　　So be it pur scinte charite !　　76

126.　*Jesus Pleads with the Worldling.*

MS. Bodley 416.

　　IHesus doþ him bymene,　　f. 106ᵃ
　　　and spekeþ to synful mon :
　　' Þi garland is of grene,
　　of floures many on ;　　4
　　Myn of sharpe þornes,
　　myn hewe it makeþ won.

　　' Þyn hondes streite gloued.
　　white & clene kept ;　　8
　　Myne wiþ nailes þorled,
　　on rode & eke my feet.

　　' A-cros þou berest þyn armes,　　f. 106ᵇ
　　whan þou dauncest narewe ;　　12
　　To me hastou non awe.
　　but to worldes glorie :

Myne for þe on rode,
wiþ þe iewes wode,   16
wiþ grete ropis to-draw.

' opyne þou hast þi syde,
spaiers longe & wide,
for ueyn glorie & pride,   20
and þi longe knyf a-strout—
þou ert of þe gai route:
Myn wiþ spere sharpe
y-stongen to þe herte ;   24
My body wiþ scourges smerte
bi-swongen al aboute.

' al þat y þolede on rode for þe,
To me was shame & sorwe ;   28
Wel litel þou louest me,
and lasse þou þenkest on me,
an euene & eke a-morwe.

' Swete broþer, wel myȝt þou se   32
þes peynes stronge in rode tre
haue y þoled for loue of þe ;
Þei þat haue wrouȝt it me
mai synge welawo.   36
be þou kynde pur charite,
let þi synne & loue þou me,
heuene blisse y shal ȝeue þe,
þat lasteþ ay & oo.'   40

127. *Jesus appeals to Man by the Wounds.*

MS. Harley 2339.

Wiþ scharpe þornes þat weren ful kene,   f. 117ᵇ
   Myn heed was crowned, ȝe moun wel sene ;
The blood ran doun al bi my cheke,
Þou proud man, þerfore be meke.   4

Iff þou be wrooþ & wolt take wreche,   f. 118ᵃ
Biholde þe lessoun þat I þee teche :
Þoruȝ my riȝthond þe nail it gooþ,
Þerfore forȝeue & be nouȝt wrooþ.   8

In al my þirst vpon þe rode,
Men ȝauen me drinkis þat weren not gode,
Eysel & galle for to drynke ;
Glotoun, þeron I rede þee þenke.   12

Of a clene maiden I was born,
To saue mankynde þat was for-lorn,
To suffre deeþ for mannys synne.
Lecchour, þerfore of lust þou blynne.   16

Thoruȝ my lifthond a nail was dryue—
Þenke þou þeron if þou wolt lyue,
And helpe þe pore wiþ almesdede,
If þou in heuene wolt haue þi mede.   20

Wiþ a spere scharp, þat was ful grill,
Myn herte was persid—it was my wil—
For loue of man þat was ful dere ;
Enuyous man, of loue þou lere.   24

Arise up, vnlust, out of þi bed,
And biholde my feet, þat are forbled
And nailid faste upon þe tree ;
Þanke me þerfore, al was for þee.   28

Ihesu, for þi woundis fyue,
Þou kepe hem weel in al her lyue
Þat þese lessouns ouer wole rede,
And þerwiþ her soulis fede.   32

128. The Blessed Virgin to her Son on the Cross.

Balliol Coll. Oxford MS. 149.

Crisostomus et ymaginatur de planctu virginis quod beata virgo stat sub cruce dicens filio suo sic O fili agnosce matrem, &c.

A Sone! tak hede to me whas sone þou was,   f. 11^b
  and set me with þe opon þi crosse.
Me, here to leue, & þe, hennys þus go,
hit is to me gret care & endeles wo.   4
stynt now, sone, to be harde to þi moder,
þu þat were euer godliche to al oþir.   f. 12^a

Et sicut idem doctor ymaginatur ibidem filius matri conquerenti sic respondet—

stynt now, modir, & wep no more;
þi sorowe & þi disseise greuyþ me ful sore;   8
þou knowyst þat in þe i tok mannys kynde,
in þis for mani(s) synne to be þus pynde.
Be now glad, moder, & haue in þi þough(t)e,
þat manys hele is founde, þat i haue souȝt.   12
þou schalt noȝt now care what þow schalt done,
lo! Iohan, þi cosyn, schall be þi sone.

129. *I have Set my Heart so High.*

MS. Douce 381.

I Hafe set my hert so hye,
  me likyt no loue þat lowere ys ;
And alle þe paynes þat y may drye,
me þenk hyt do me good y-wys.   4

For on that lorde þat louid vs alle,
So hertely haue ı set my þow3t,
yt ys my Ioie on hym to calle,
for loue me haþ in balus brow3t.   8
    Me þenk yt do ⟨me good⟩ Iwys.

f. 20[a]

130. *The Spring under a Thorn.*

Magdalen Coll. Oxford MS. 60.

AT a sprynge-wel vnder a þorn,
  Þer was bote of bale, a lytel here a-forn ;
Þer by-syde stant a mayde,
fulle of loue y-bounde.   4
Ho-so wol seche trwe loue,
yn hyr hyt schal be founde.

f. 214[a]

129. 3 MS. dryue.

131. An Acrostic of the Angelic Salutation.

Camb. Univ. Gg. 4. 32.

> Heil! Marie, ful of grace,
> God is wiþ þe in eurich place;
> Blesced be þou ouer alle wymmen,
> And þe fruit of þin wombe, amen.

HEil! and holi ay be þi name,   f. 14ᵇ
 Fulsum leuedi, hende and swete;
To hem þat beþ þorgh sennes lame,
Hastif helpe þou bihete;   4
And schildest hem fram schendful schame,
Þat here sennes willeþ lete.
Help out of euerech blame
Senfulle þat þe willeþ grete.   8

Marie, mayde and moder milde,
Milce and merci was of þe boren,
To sauuen and fram helle schilde
Alle þo þat weren forloren;   12
For giltes of oure eldren wilde,
Adam and Eue her biforen,
Praie for vs to þine childe,   f. 15ᵃ
Þat we to his blisse be coren.   16

Fvl of eche þewes gode
Þou were, chaste and clene of þoghte,
Þou vnderfenge liues fode
Of Gabriel, þat hit te broghte,   20
And his gretinge wel vnderstode,
Þorgh what crist in þe wonder wroghte
Of manlich flessch and blode,
Þat he tok þat vs dere boghte.   24

Grace þou founde in god and loue,
Þo he so holilich þe dighte
Þat he wolde fro heuene aboue
So lowe into þin bodi lighte ;   28
Þorgh þe to sike is helþe iȝoue,
To lame limes, to blinde sighte ;
Out of heuene blisse ischoue
Nis non þat þe serueþ aplighte.   32

God is he þat iboren was,
Wiþoute eurich senful likinge,
Of þe, ase sonne þorgh glas
Schineþ wiþoute ani brekinge.   36
His birþe was blisful solas
To hem þat weren þorgh egginge
Forloren of Satanas—
Help vs to þi blisse to bringe !   40

With þe is eure, and þe aboute,
Michel mirþe and ioie and blisse
In heuene of angles route,
Þat þe worþschipeþ myde iwisse.   44
Wel owen we to þe aloute,
And preien þat þou vs wisse
And schilde fram deueles doute,
Þat non of þin helþe ne misse.   48

In euerech sor þat we hauen here,
Þorgh þe we finden liþing sone ;
For iesu crist, þin sone dere,
Nelle naght werne þe þin bone,   52
Whan þou bisext wiþ milde chere
For vs, þat weren dempt and fordone
As deueles into helle fere,
Þorgh sennes þat her beþ idone.   56

46 wisse : MS. schilde.   47 schilde : MS. wisse.

Place ches him, on forto reste
In þis world, crist godes sone,
In þin clene, blisful breste:
Wel likede him þer-in to wone,   60
And kenned was as brid in neste;
Of milce and merci þou him mone,
Þat he ʒiue vs soules reste,
And grace oure fon forto schone.   64

B⟨l⟩esced was þat ilke stounde
Þat god almighti on þe þoghte,
Þo he fram heuene to þe grounde
Lighte, and in þe lownesse soghte;   68
And þat was in þin herte ifounde,
Þorgh what we weren alle ibroghte
Out of sor and maked sounde,
Þat ferst yuele weren idoghte.   72

Be þou, leuedi, to al mankenne
Þat to þe clepeþ in here nede,
Right scheld and clensing of senne;
And to þin sone oure ernde bede,   76
Þat we, whan we wenden henne
Out of þis world, þin help ifrede,
Smartliche to renne
Þider, þer eche god haueþ mede.   80

Ouer alle angles in heuene heʒe,
Þe sette crist on his right side,
To helpen þo þat beþ onsleʒe,
And ek forloren þorgh senne of pride: 84
Wend toward vs þin milʒful eʒe,
So þat þorgh þe bet vs bitide,
Clense vs ar we deʒe   f. 15^b
Of senne þin blisce to bide.   88

The End of the Century. 233

Wymmen weren alle ischente,
In þraldom helde and onworþlie,
Þorgh eue þat þe deuel blente,
What iesu crist wiþ his maistrie 92
Þo lettres of hire name wente,
And made of eua aue marie,
And clansing sente
To wymmen of ech vileinie. 96

And þe fruit, þat to alle gode
Frouering is, and ek hem strongeþ,
And soules helþe and liues fode
Þat worþschipeliche hit vnderfongeþ, 100
Ripede in þin herte blode,
Ase appel þat on þe tre hongeþ.
So dede vpon rode
He to wham folk cristene longeþ. 104

Of þin wombe crist his halle
Maked, her among mankinde,
To driue awey þo deueles alle,
Þat mannes soules gonnen binde 108
Wiþ biterere pines þane ȝalle.
Help vs þat of þe makeþ mynde,
And doun beþ falle,
Þorgh þe reisinge to finde! 112

Amen! so mote hit euer be,
As y haue seid in my gretinge,
Þat iesu crist sente to þe
In þin worþschipe ouer alle þinge. 116
Help, leuedi, to maken vs fre,
Out of dedli senne to bringe,
Þat we þi blisse i-se
Moten, in heuenlich woniinge. Amen. 120

132. *Quia Amore Langueo.*

MS. Douce 322.

IN a tabernacle of a toure,   f. 8^b
 As I stode musyng on the mone,
A crouned quene, most of honoure,
Apered in gostly syght ful sone.   4
She made compleynt thus by hyr one,
For mannes soule was wrapped in wo:
' I may nat leue mankynde allone,
  Quia amore langueo.   8

' I longe for loue of man my brother,
I am hys vokete to voyde hys vyce;
I am hys moder—I can none other—
Why shuld I my dere chylde dispyce? 12
Yef he me wrathe in diuerse wyse,
Through flesshes freelte fall me fro,   f. 9^a
Yet must we rewe hym tyll he ryse,
  Quia amore langueo.   16

' I byd, I byde in grete longyng,
I loue, I loke when man woll craue,
I pleyne for pyte of peynyng;
wolde he aske mercy, he shuld hit haue. 20
Say to me, soule, and I shall saue,
Byd me, my chylde, and I shall go;
Thow prayde me neuer but my son forgaue,
  Quia amore langueo.   24

14 MS. Though.

'O wreche in the worlde, I loke on the,
I se thy trespas day by day,
With lechery ageyns my chastite,
With pryde agene my pore aray;　　　　　28
My loue abydeth, thyne ys away;
My loue the calleth, thow stelest me fro;
Sewe to me, synner, I the pray,
　　Quia amore langueo.　　　　　32

'Moder of mercy I was for the made;
Who nedeth hit but thow all-one?
To gete the grace I am more glade
Than thow to aske hit; why wylt þou noon?　36
When seyd I nay, tel me, tyll oon?
Forsoth neuer yet, to frende ne foo;
When þou askest nought, þan make I moone,
　　Quia amore langueo.　　　　　40

'I seke the in wele and wrechednesse,
I seke the in ryches and pouerte;
Thow man beholde where þy moder ys,
Why louest þou me nat syth I loue the?　　44
Synful or sory how euere thow be,
So welcome to me there ar no mo;
I am thy suster, ryght trust on me,
　　Quia amore langueo.　　　　　48

'My childe ys outlawed for thy synne,
Mankynde ys bette for hys trespasse;
Yet prykketh myne hert þat so ny my kynne
Shuld be dysseased, o sone, allasse!　　52
Thow art hys broþer, hys moder I was;
Thow sokyd my pappe, thow louyd man so;
Thow dyed for hym, myne hert he has,
　　Quia amore langueo.　　　　　56

31 MS. Shewe.

'Man, leue thy synne þan for my sake;
Why shulde I gyf þe þat þou nat wolde?
And yet yef thow synne, som prayere take
Or trust in me as I haue tolde.   60
Am nat I thy moder called?
Why shulde I flee the? I loue the soo,
I am thy frende, I helpe beholde,
  Quia amore langueo.'   64

'Now sone,' she sayde, 'wylt þou sey nay,
Whan man wolde mende hym of hys mys?
Thow lete me neuer in veyne yet pray:
Than, synfull man, see thow to thys,   68
What day þou comest, welcome thow ys,
Thys hundreth yere yef thow were ⟨me⟩ fro;
I take the ful fayne, I clyppe, I kysse,
  Quia amore langueo.   72

'Now wol I syt and sey nomore,
Leue and loke with grete longyng,
When [a] man woll calle I wol restore;
I loue to saue hym, he ys myne hosprynge;   76
No wonder yef myne hert on hym hynge,
He was my neyghbore; what may I doo?
For hym had I thys worshippyng,
  And therefore *Amore langueo.*   80

'Why was I crouned and made a quene?
Why was I called of mercy the welle?   f 9ᵇ
Why shuld an erþly woman bene
So hygh in heuen a-boue aungelle?   84
For þe, mankynde, þe truþe I telle;
þou aske me helpe, and I shall do
þat I was ordeyned, kepe þe fro helle,
  Quia amore langueo.   88

62 MS loo.

' Nowe man, haue mynde on me for-euer,
loke on þy loue þus languysshyng ;
late vs neuer fro other disseuere,
Myne helpe ys þyne oune, crepe vnder my wynge ; 92
Thy syster ys a quene, þy broþer [ys] a kynge,
Thys heritage ys tayled, sone come þer-to,
Take me for þy wyfe and lerne to synge,
     Quia amore langueo.' 96

133. Wretched Man, why art thou Proud?

MS. Laud Miscell. 111.

WRecche mon, wy artou proud, f. 65^a
   þat art of herth I-maked ?
hydyr ne browtestou no schroud,
bot pore þou come & naked. 4
Wen þi soule is faren out,
þi body with erthe y-raked,
þat body þat was so ronk and loud,
Of alle men is i-hated. 8

134.   Cur Mundus Militat.

Trin. Coll. Camb. MS. 181.

WHi is þe world biloued, þat fals is & vein ? f. 169^b
   Siþen þat hise welþis ben vncertein.

Al so soone slidiþ his power away
as doiþ a brokil pot, þat freisch is and gay. 4

Truste ȝe raþir to lettirs writen in þ'is,
þan to þis wrecchid world, þat ful of synne is.

90 þus] MS. þys.

It is fals in his biheste, and riȝt disceiueable ;
it haþ bigilid manie men, it is so vnstable.   8

It is raþer to bileue þe wageringe wiynd,
þan þe chaungeable world, þat makiþ men so blynd.

Wheþir þou slepe oþere wake, þou schalt fynde it fals,
boþe in his bisynessis & in his lustis als.   12

Telle me where is salamon, sumtyme a kinge riche?
or sampson in his strenkeþe, to whom was no man
    liche?

Or þe fair man absolon, merueilous in chere,
or þe duke ionatas, a weel biloued fere?   16

Where is bicome cesar, þat lord was of al?
or þe riche man cloiþd in purpur and in pal?   f. 170ᵃ

Telle me where is tullius in eloquence so swete?
or aristotil þe filisofre wiþ his witt so grete?   20

Where ben þese woriþi þat weren here to-foren—
boiþe kingis & bischopis, her power is al loren.

All þese grete princis, wiþ her power so hiȝe,
ben wanischid a-way in twinkeling of an iȝe.   24

Þe ioie of þis wrecchid world is a schort feeste ;
it is likned to a schadewe þat abidiþ leeste ;

And ȝit it drawith man from heudne-riche blis,
and ofte tyme makiþ hym to synne & do a-mys.   28

Calle no þing þin owen þerfore, þat þou maist her lese ;
þat þe world haþ lent þee, eft he wolde it cese.

Sette þin herte in heuen aboue, & þenke what ioie is
    þere,
& þus to dispise þe world, I rede þat þou lere.   32

Þou þat art but wormes mete, poudir, & dust,
to enhaunce þi silf in pride, sette not þi lust.

For þou woost not to-day þat þou schalt lyue to-
    morewe ;
Þerfore do þou euere weel, & þanne- schalt þou not
    sorewe.   36

It were ful ioiful & swete lordschip to haue,
if so þat lor⟨d⟩schip myȝite a man fro deeþ saue ;

But for as miche a man muste die at þe laste,
it is no worschip, but a charge, lordschip to taste.   40

135.   *Esto Memor Mortis.*

Camb. Univ. MS. Ee. 6. 29.

Esto memor mortis iam porta sit omnibus ortis
    Sepe sibi iuuenes accipit ante senes.

SYth all þat in þys wordle haþ been *in rerum
    natura,*   f. 17ᵃ
Or in þys wyde wordle was seen *in humana cura,*
Alle schalle passe wyþ-outen ween *via mortis dura* ;
God graunte þat mannys soule be cleen *penas non
    passura.*   4
    Whan þow leste wenys, *veniet mors te superare*:
    Þus þy graue greuys, *ergo mortis memorare.*

Vnde vir extolleris, þow schalte be wormes mete,
Qui quamdiu vixeris þy synnys wolte þou not lete ;   8
Quamuis diues fueris And of power grete,   f. 17ᵇ
Cum morte percuteris Helpe may þow noon gete.
    Si diues fias Do þyself gode, man, wyþ þy handis ;
    Post necis ergo uias Ful fewe wole lose þe of þy
        bandis.   12

34 enhaunce : MS. enchaunce.   38 if : MS. it.

Þys auȝt wele to fel þy pryde, *quod es moriturus*;
Þow knowest neþer tyme ne tyde *qua es decessurus.*
Wormes schalle ete þe bakke & syde, *inde sis securus* :
As þou hast wrouȝt in þys worlde wyde *sic es receptu-*
  rus.   16
  Þus deþe þe ledeþ, *terre tumilo quasi nudum* ;
  Deþe no man dredyþ, *mors terminat hiccine ludum.*

Nam nulli vult parcere Dethe þat ys vn-dere,
Pro argenti munere, Ne for noon fayre prayere ; 20
Sed dum rapit propere, He chaunges eche mannys
  chere,   f. 18ᵃ
In peccati scelere Yif he be fownden here.
  Set cum dampnatis Helle to þy mede þou wynnes,
  Þat neuyr blynnes *Pro peccatis sceleratis.* 24

When y þenk vp-on my dede, *tunc sum contristatus*,
And wexe as heuy as any lede *Meos ob reatus* ;
Dede torneþ into wrecchidhede *Viros magni status*,
Þan may no þynge stonde in stede *Mundi dominatus.* 28
  Wyþ full bare bonys *Mundi rebus cariturus*,
  Þus from þys wonys *transit numquam rediturus.*

Caro vermis ferculum, Þenk on þe pynes of helle ;
Mors habet spiculum Þat smyteþ man full felle; f. 18ᵇ
Te ponet ad tumilum Tyl domes day to dwelle. 33
Hic relinquis seculum ; Þere nys not ellis to telle.
  Mors cito cuncta rapit, Þerefor man þynk on þy
    werkys.
  Þus sey þees clerkys : *Mors cito cun⟨c⟩ta rapit.* 36

God þat deydest on þe tree *Pro nostra salute*,
And a-rose affter dayes three *Diuina uirtute*,
Yif vs grace synne to flee *Stante Iuuent⟨ut⟩e*,
On domysday þat we may see *Vultum tuum tute.* 40
  Delful dethe drede y the, *Veniet quia nescio*
    quando :
  Be redy þerefor y warne þe, *De te peccata fugando.*

  23 *Set cum dampnatis*] MS. *Sic cum dampnatus.*

NOTES

1. *Candet Nudatum Pectus.*

DIRECTLY translating lines which occur in the *Liber Medita-tionum*, a treatise ascribed in the Middle Ages to Augustine. For the Latin lines and their context see Migne, *Patrol. Lat.* xl, col. 906. In John Grimestone's Commonplace Book one finds the text of the Latin original together with the English verses (Advocates MS. 18. 7. 21, f. 117[a]):

Augustinus In quadam meditacione. Candet nudatum pectus. Rubet cruentum latus. Tensa [MS. tonsa] arent viscera. Decora languent lumina. Regia pallent ora. Procera rigent brachia. Crura dependent marmorea. Et rigat terebratos pedes beati san-guinis vnda. Anglice:

> With it was his naked brest & red is blodi side
> Bleike weren his leres his wondis depe & wyde
> Starke weren his armis spred vpon þe rode
> On fiue stedes vpon his bodi þe stremes ronnen on blode.

Another version, in six lines, occurs in B.M. Addit. MS. 11579 (early fourteenth century) at f. 35[b]:

> *Vne remembrance de la passion ihū crist, anglice.*
>
> Þwit was his naked brest. and red blodi his side.
> Hise faire eyen woxen dasewe. hyse armes weren spradde wyde.
> Hise leichende lyppes bycomen pale. and hys bodi al dreie.
> As cheld marbre hengen hyse lemes. þat blod was al a-weye.
> Hys fet were þerled þat weren so þwyte. hee bledde from fot til heued.
> Þere; for man he þchedde hys blod. ne was þer noust by-leued.

Version A. Written in an early fourteenth-century hand on a strip of vellum inserted in the Durham MS. Printed (from an inaccurate transcript by Rev. W. Greenwell) in *Pol. Rel. and Love Poems*, rev. ed., p. 243; and by Heuser, *Bonner Beitr.* xiv, 209.

[See S. Harrison Thomson, 'The Date of the Early English Translation of the "Candet Nudatum Pectus"', *Medium Ævum* iv, pp. 100–5: dated *ca.* 1230 on palæographical grounds.]

Version B. In the opinion of H. O. Coxe, formerly Librarian of the Bodleian, MS. Bodley 42 is to be dated between 1300 and 1320.

2. *Respice in Faciem Christi.*

Translated from a Latin meditation, the text of which immediately precedes the English lines in MS. Bodley 42 and New Coll. MS. 88 (printed by Heuser, *Bonner Beitr.* xiv, 208, 209). John Grimestone gives the Latin text only (Advocates MS. 18. 7. 21, f. 117ᵃ): '*Respice in faciem christi tui* [Ps. lxxxiii. 10] & inuenies eum in dorso flagellatum. Latere sauciatum. Capite spinis coronatum. Manibus perforatum. Pedibus confossum. Volue & reuolue dominicum corpus a latere vsque ad latus. A summa vsque deorsum & circumquaque inuenies dolorem & cruorem.' A slightly different version of this meditation is ascribed to St. Bernard by Ludolphus de Saxonia in his *Vita Christi* (Pars II, cap. lxv): 'Hec Bernardus: Contempleris etiam bene dominum et salvatorem tuum. Gira et regira, volve et revolve a latere in latus, *a planta pedis vsque ad verticem et non invenies in eo sanitatem* [*Isa.* i. 6] sed vndique dolorem vbique cruorem.' It is interesting to note that Richard Rolle inserts the '*Respice*' passage, with only a few verbal changes, in his *Incendium Amoris* (ed. Margaret Deanesly, p. 221).

A. Shorter Version.

Printed by Heuser, *Bonner Beitr.* xiv, 209.

3. *hi-pitz*: the word which this renders in the Latin version preceding it in the MS. is *uidebis*; the emendation is based on this and on palæographical considerations (the common confusion of þ with p and of *c* with *t*). *z* is here an AN. spelling for *st* or *s*.

8. *puend*: This appears to be a survival of the runic 'wyn' for *w*. It is not altogether certain whether the MS. actually reads p or þ. If it be the latter, then the scribe must have misread his copy, for *volve* in the Latin original shows that *wuend* is the form intended. Cf. the phrase *went and trent* in *Seuen Sages*, v. 2360 (Brunner, EETS. 191, 1933).

B. Longer Version.

In this one finds the *Respice ad faciem Chriṣti* combined with the *Candet nudatum pectus*, which supplies the basis for vv. 5–8. Another text of this version with sixteen lines occurs in Harley 913, f. 28ᵃ (printed by Furnivall, *Early Eng. Poems*, p. 20, and by Heuser, *Bonner Beitr.* xiv, 128). The Harley text preserves the order of the *Candet nudatum pectus* by making vv. 7–8 precede 5–6; moreover, in Harley, vv. 9–10 (lacking in the St. John's MS.)—

> His lenden so hangiþ as cold as marbre stone
> For luste of lechuri nas þer neuer none,

we have a clear reminiscence of the Latin, *crura dependent marmorea.*
Finally, the concluding couplet of Harley (not in the St. John's MS.)

> Turne him uppe, turne him doune, þi swete lemman,
> Ouer al þou findist him blodi oþer wan—

probably belonged to this lyric in its original form, for it closely
paraphraṣes the Latin.

On the other hand, the language of the St. John's text better
represents the original, on account of its preservation of older forms.
In Harley archaic words have been replaced: e.g. *neb* by *felle*,
desewet by *dimmiþ*, *blickied* [Lat. *candet*] by *bihold to*, *molde* by
heued. [See Thomson, *op. cit.*, p. 103, n. 1, for corrections in trans-
cription of B.]

5. *desewet.* See Supplementary Note on p. 288.

3. *Think, Man, of my Hard Stundes.*

The original suggestion for this appeal of Christ to man may
perhaps be recognized in the well-known passage in a sermon by
Caesarius of Arles, 'De Iudicio extremo' (Migne, *Patrol. Lat.* xxxix,
col. 2207), in which Christ is represented as reciting to sinners at
the Judgement the sufferings which He endured for their sake. It
was an easy matter to transfer this address from the Judgement
Day to the time of the Crucifixion itself; and this change in setting
naturally carried with it an important change in the tone: Christ's
recital becomes a pleading with man rather than merely a reproach
or an accusation.

The appeal of Christ to man inserted in the *Cursor Mundi* (vv.
17115-17178) is very closely related in thought to the present piece,
and even shows similarities of phrase. The *Cursor* text is in couplets
instead of strophes, and it may be significant that the author of this
lyric prefixes as a motto a couplet which directly recalls *Cursor*,
vv. 17151-2:

> I haf þus mani blodi wondes
> And sufferd her þis herd stondes.

4. *Look to Me on the Cross.*

Printed by Heuser, *Bonner Beitr.* xiv, 208. In structure and
arrangement this piece, like no. 2, is based upon the *Respice in
faciem Christi.* On the other hand, in the fact that Christ is repre-
sented as the speaker, these lines bear closer resemblance to no. 3,
as well as to the Appeal in the *Cursor Mundi.*

5. *Thole a Little!*

Printed by Heuser, *Bonner Beitr.* xiv, 208.

These lines are preceded in the MS. by the following passage from the *Confessions* of St. Augustine (Lib. VIII, cap. v), of which they are a direct translation: 'Non erat quid responderem tibi ueritate conuictus dicenti mihi. *Surge qui dormis & exurge a mortuis & illuminabit tibi* [sic] *Christus* [*Eph.* v. 14]. nisi uerba lenta & sompnolenta. modo ecce modo. sine paululum. sed modo & modo non habebant modum & sine paululum in longum ibat. similiter est de differentibus penitencie.'

6. *An Old Man's Prayer.*

Printed by T. Wright, *Spec. Lyr. Poetry*, Percy Soc., pp. 47–51; by Böddeker, *Alteng. Dicht.*, pp. 187–90; and by Patterson, *Mid. Eng. Penit. Lyr.*, pp. 61–4.

10–11. The punctuation and the interpretation it implies are supported by the syntactically similar ll. 27–8.

16. *fulle-flet*: i.e. 'fill-floor' in the sense of one always in the way, a useless encumbrance. For this suggestion I am indebted to Dr. C. T. Onions.

27. The emendation to *þat* is clearly required, and is supported by ll. 10–11. Prof. Brook (*The Harley Lyrics*, p. 81) invokes l. 41 in support of the MS. *þar*; but *þer* in l. 41 is apposite ('in those circles'), while in l. 27 it is not.

52–63. All the Deadly Sins are here introduced except Wrath; his place is taken by Liar. With this personification of the Sins may be compared the description in *Ancren Riwle* of the servants in the Devil's Court (ed. Camden Soc., pp. 210–16).

56. *lauendere*: Professor Krapp (*Mod. Lang. Notes*, xvii. 204) argues that this word has the significance of *meretrix*. In the present instance, however, it is clearly to be understood as 'laundress', though the dubious reputation of the laundress in mediæval times may have suggested this as the fitting office for Lechery.

63. *weneþ*: Böddeker emends to *wheneþ* (< OE. *hwænan*) in order to parallel the MS. reading *whene* in the following line. But, as Professor Klaeber has suggested to me, it is better to make the emendation in the latter case.

85. The meaning is: Dreadful Death, why do you lurk in concealment? Come and bring this body, &c.

7. *Suete Iesu King of blysse.*

Printed by T. Wright, *Spec. Lyr. Poetry*, Percy Soc., pp. 57–9;

by Böddeker, *Alteng. Dicht.*, pp. 191–3; and by Horstmann, *Richard Rolle*, ii. 9–11 (at the foot of the page).

The following text of stanza 3 alone is written on the upper margin of a leaf in a MS. (Anglo-French) preserved among the archives of the Wilton Corporation (Wiltshire):

> Swete Ihesu my saule bote
> One min herte sete a rote
> Of þi loue þat ys so swote
> And graunte þat hit springe mote.

Inasmuch as this MS. includes a copy of a letter from Edward I, dated in the thirty-fourth year of his reign, it cannot be earlier than 1306, but the lines just quoted cannot have been written much later, for, in the opinion of Dr. H. H. E. Craster, of the Bodleian Library, they are in a hand of the very early fourteenth century. I am indebted to Mrs. Herbert Richardson, who with the Rev. P. R. B. Brown is engaged in cataloguing the archives of the Wilton Corporation, for the opportunity of seeing these lines.

8. *Iesu Crist Heouene Kyng.*

Printed by T. Wright, *Spec. Lyr. Poetry*, Percy Soc., pp. 59–60; by Böddeker, *Alteng. Dicht.*, p. 194; and by Patterson, *Mid. Eng. Penit. Lyr.*, pp. 88, 89.

14. *iesse*: Clearly a scribal error for *iesu*.

9. *A Winter Song.*

Printed by Ritson, *Anc. Songs and Ballads*, 3rd ed., 1877, p. 56; by T. Wright, *Spec. Lyr. Poetry*, p. 60; by Böddeker, *Alteng. Dicht.*, p. 195; and by Chambers and Sidgwick, *Early Eng. Lyrics*, p. 169.

11–13. The figure appears to be based upon *John* xii. 24, 25: 'Nisi granum frumenti cadens in terram mortuum fuerit, ipsum solum manet; si autem mortuum fuerit, multum fructum affert.' Cf. the metrical homily on this text, printed by Horstmann, *Herrig's Archiv*, lxxxi. 83. See also *Pearl*, v. 31: 'For vch gresse mot grow of grayneȝ dede.' *Grene* and *faleweþ* as used here do not refer to colour but to vitality and decay.

10. *An Autumn Song.*

Printed by T. Wright, *Spec. Lyr. Poetry*, pp. 87–9; by Böddeker, *Alteng. Dicht.*, pp. 213–15; by Chambers and Sidgwick, *Early Eng. Lyr.*, pp. 97–9; and by Patterson, *Mid. Eng. Penit. Lyr.*, pp. 98–100.

11. *petres-bourh*: Peterborough. A significant indication that this piece originated in East Midland territory.

34. i.e. from Caithness (the most northern county of Scotland) to Dublin. Cf. Robert of Glouc. *Chron.* vv. 176–8:

> Þe verþe is mest of al. þat tilleþ fram totenas
> Fram þe on ende of cornewaille. anon to cattenas
> Fram souþwest to þe norþest to engelondes ende.

51–60. One line is here lacking according to the rime-scheme of the other stanzas: *aabaab*[*c*]*bcb*. Through this omission v. 59 is left without a rime line. Böddeker assumes that this was an intentional change on the part of the poet, but in view of his ease in handling the 10-line stanza this seems unlikely.

11. *A Song of the Five Joys.*

Printed by T. Wright, *Spec. Lyr. Poetry*, pp. 94–6; by Wülker, *Alteng. Lesebuch*, i. 48, 49; and by Böddeker, *Alteng. Dicht.*, pp. 218, 219.

25–60. The enumeration of the Five Joys agrees closely with that in the hymn *Primum fuit gaudium*, which is found in the *Scala Caeli* (text in Dreves, *Anal.* xxxi. 175).

33. See G. L. Brook, *The Harley Lyrics*, no. 27, 33, note, who adopts the suggestion of Sister Mary Immaculate (*A Note on 'A Song of the Five Joys'*, *Modern Language Notes* lv, 1940, 249–54): *lay* 'light' (OMerc. *lēg*), *poro* adj. 'perfect'. This is at least an advance on earlier ones.

34. Cf. the corresponding line of the Latin hymn: 'Et erranti populo lucem protulisti'.

35. *þe ster*: Wright, Wülker, and Böddeker misread as *þestri*.

12. *Hostis Herodes impie.*

Printed by 'N. H.', *Rel. Ant.* i. 86–7.
The English verses are based directly on the well-known hymn by Sedulius (Daniel, *Thes. Hymn.* i. 147). In the MS. each stanza is headed by the opening phrase of the Latin text.

13. *Vexilla Regis prodeunt.*

Printed by 'N. H.', *Rel. Ant.* i. 87–8.
Based directly on the celebrated hymn by Venantius Fortunatus. For the Latin text see Daniel, *Thes. Hymn.* i. 160, and Dreves, *Anal.* ii. 45. The second stanza ('confixa clauis viscera') is omitted in the

English translation. As in the preceding hymn, each stanza is headed in the MS. by the opening phrase of the Latin.

16. *op-bere*: MS. *oup*, with dots under the *u* for deletion.

14. *Gloria Laus et Honor.*

Printed by Halliwell, *Rel. Ant.* ii. 225.

This is a translation of the first twelve lines of the Latin hymn by Bishop Theodulphus, which were regularly sung in the Palm Sunday Procession. (See the thirteenth-century *Sarum Graduale.*) For the Latin text see Daniel, *Thes. Hymn.* i. 215, and Dreves, *Anal.* l. 160.

12. *mylsful kyng*: Altered in margin from *kyng of mylse*.

15. *Popule meus quid feci tibi?*

Printed by Halliwell, *Rel. Ant.* ii. 225–6.

The Latin text which is here translated was known as the *Improperia*, or Reproaches of Christ, and was sung in the service for Good Friday. The first three verses are found in the thirteenth-century *Sarum Graduale* (p. 101); two additional verses are given in the text in the *Liber Sacerdotalis* (Venice, 1523) as reprinted by Karl Young, *The Dramatic Associations of the Easter Sepulchre* (Univ. of Wisconsin Studies in Lang. and Lit. x, pp. 57, 58). For the complete text of the *Improperia* see *The Liturgical Year*, by Abbot Gueranger, O.S.B., tr. by D. L. Shepherd, O.S.B., New York, 1911, vi. 491. As the starting-point from which the *Improperia* developed, one may refer to the 'Responsorium' for the Fourth Sunday in Lent, according to the *York Breviary* (ed. Surtees Soc., i, col. 334), in which the 'Popule meus' consists simply of a recital of benefits conferred upon the people of Israel, without any mention of the pains of the Passion.

For a later and freer rendering of the 'Popule meus' see no. 72.

15. MS. *vedde wel*, with dots under *wel* for deletion.

22. *sullest*: MS. *soldest*, corrected in margin to *sullest*.

24. *ledest*: MS. *laddest*, corrected in margin to *ledest*.

30. *betest*: MS. *boete*; *betest* interlined above.

32. *ȝyfst*: MS. *ȝeue*; *ȝyfst* interlined above.

34. *hongest*: Altered in MS. from *henge*.

The change from preterite to present tense, which has been carried through consistently, adds to the dramatic vividness of these verses.

16. *An Orison to the Blessed Virgin.*

Printed by Halliwell, *Rel. Ant.* ii. 227–8.

In the introductory stanzas of this Orison one recognizes phrases which have been appropriated without essential change from such hymns as *Virgo gaude speciosa* (Mone, ii. 47, Dreves, *Anal.* x. 73). Thus (vv. 13–32):

> Hic ignotus apud patrem
> nobis notus fit per matrem;
> noster ergo factus frater
> per te, virgo, facta mater.

> Deus deum genuit
> absque matre,
> virgo deum protulit
> sine patre.

> O quam mira genitura!
> creatorem creatura
> peperit cum gloria.
>
> .   .   .

> Virgo mater, o Maria,
> tantus frater prece pia
> nos sua clementia
> emundatos a delictis
> simul iungat cum electis
> in caelesti gloria.

The central figure in this Orison, however—that of the charter executed by Christ on the Cross—does not appear to have been suggested by the Latin hymns. For the history of this figure of the Charter see M. Caroline Spalding, *The Middle English Charters of Christ*, Bryn Mawr Monographs, xv, 1914 (cf. especially pp. lviii–lxi).

5. MS. *and ek hyre broþer*; *ek* dotted for deletion.

6. MS. *non oþer nas*; *non* dotted for deletion.

7–12. This stanza is added at the bottom of the page, and marked for insertion at this point.

7. MS. *and my moder*; *my* dotted for deletion.

8. MS. *sone ys my broþer*; *ys* dotted for deletion.

24. MS. *And þe enke*; *And* dotted for deletion.

32. MS. *help me at þe noede*; *me* dotted for deletion.

42. At the end of this line is written *Amen*, showing that the

Orison originally ended at this point. The two stanzas which follow are added at the bottom of the page.

48. *mi*: originally written *þy* and altered to *mi*.

17. *Aue Maris Stella.*

Printed by Halliwell, *Rel. Ant.* ii. 228–9.

For the Latin original see Daniel, *Thes. Hymn.* i. 204, and Dreves, *Anal.* ii. 39. For a later version see below, no. 45. A translation of a portion of this hymn combined with two stanzas of *Quem terra, pontus, aethera*, and the Antiphon, *Alma redemptoris mater*, will be found in no. 41.

25. MS. *To þe uader cryst and to þe holy gost*, with dots under *þe* and *to þe* for deletion.

18. *Veni creator spiritus.*

Printed by Halliwell, *Rel. Ant.* ii. 229.

For the Latin text of this hymn see Daniel, *Thes. Hymn.* i. 213, Mone, *Lat. Hymn.* i. 241, Dreves, *Anal.* ii. 93 (from the *Moissac Hymnary*). Dreves's text alone lacks the concluding stanza ('Sit laus patri cum filio'). For another English version see below, no. 44.

12. MS. *To leue þat in boþe þou euer boe woninge.* Interlined above *in* is *uul of*, and above *woninge* is *louinge*.

13. *to þe vader*: *þe* interlined above.

14. MS. *And also þes holy gost euer worshipe and los*: *to* has been interlined after *also*: under *s* in *þes* is a dot for deletion: *euer* has been altered to *ay boe*.

19. *Alma redemptoris mater.*

For the Latin text of this Antiphon, which is ascribed to Hermann Contractus (†1054), see Daniel, *Thes. Hymn.* ii. 318, Dreves *Anal.* l. 317. For notes on its popularity see C. Brown, *A Study of the Miracle of Our Lady told by Chaucer's Prioress*, Chauc. Soc., second ser., 45, pp. 122–5.

To Herebert's translation of the *Alma redemptoris* is appended the following outline of the miracle of the little clerk slain by the Jews:

Hic nota de filio vidue qui semper eundo ad scolas et redeundo de scolis consueuit istam antiphonam decantare: propter quod a iudeis per quos transitum fecit 'puer marie' dicebatur. quem ipsi tandem occiderunt et in cloacam proiecerunt, qui tamen a cantu non cessauit, &c.

For a discussion of this analogue of *The Prioresses Tale* see *Mod. Lang. Notes* xxxviii, 92–4.

20. *Conditor alme siderum.*

For the Latin text of this hymn see Daniel, *Thes. Hymn.* i. 74, Mone, *Lat. Hymn.* i. 49, and Dreves, *Anal.* ii. 35 (from the *Moissac Hymnary*). Herebert's version follows closely the arrangement of the hymn in the Moissac MS.

10. MS. *to alende*; *o* dotted for deletion.

11. MS. *Into on*; *to* dotted for deletion.

13. This line translates the 'honestissima . . . clausula' of Daniel's text instead of the 'honestissime' in the text of Dreves.

14. MS. *to oure*; second *o* dotted for deletion.

23. This line agrees with Daniel's text, 'Hostis a telo perfidi', rather than with Dreves, 'Noctis a telo perfidi'.

21. *Christe redemptor omnium.*

The Latin text is printed by Daniel (*Thes. Hymn.* i. 78) from an ancient MS. (col. A) and from the *Roman Breviary* (col. B); cf. also Dreves, *Anal.* li. 49.

1. Daniel (A), 'Christe redemptor gentium'; (B), 'Iesu redemptor omnium'. Dreves, 'Christe redemptor omnium'.

7. *volk*: Daniel (A), 'famuli'. Dreves and Daniel (B). 'servuli'.

13. *pys day*: Dreves, 'Hic . . . dies'; Daniel (A), 'Sic . . . dies'; (B), 'hoc . . . dies'.

25–8. This concluding stanza occurs only in Daniel (B).

22. *Tu Rex glorie Christe.*

A paraphrase of vv. 14–20 of the *Te Deum Laudamus* (Daniel, *Thes. Hymn.* ii. 276). It will be observed that stanzas 5 and 6 offer alternative versions of the Latin, 'Te ergo quaesumus, famulis tuis subveni, quos pretioso sanguine redemisti'. In the MS. opposite stanza 6 is written : 'Alit*er* sic'. The phrasing in the second English version, it is to be noted, translates the Latin more closely.

23. *Make Ready for the Long Journey.*

In the MS. these verses are headed by the line: 'Vous purveez en cete vye'. The direct source of Herebert's poem is found in a collection of Anglo-Norman verse (for the most part by Nicholas Bozon, who, like Herebert, was a Franciscan), which is included in the earlier portion of the MS.[1] The text of the Anglo-Norman poem as it stands in this MS. is here printed for the first time:

[1] For an account of the Anglo-Norman material in Phillipps MS. 8336 see P. Meyer, *Romania*, xiii. 497 ff.

fol. 84ᵃ.   *Vous purveez en ceste vie*
       De soustenaunce en l'autre vie.

1. Pus ke homme deit morir
  E de ceo secle departyr
  E aillurs saunz fyn meyndra
  Bone serreyt ke chescun trossat
  Les bens ke il put en soun sak
  Kar Iammes ne revendra
      Enpense checun de espleyter
       Ki il ne perde le grant louher
       Ke deu promis nous a.

2. Ceste vie nest for dolur
  a peyne auera Ioye vn Iour
  ke de sa fyn ben pensera
  homme ho dolour de mere nest
  e en dolour icy est
  e ho dolour departira
      Enpense checun de espleyter
       Ke yl ne perde le grant louheur
       Ke deu promis nous a.

3. Ke vaut pouher e hautesce
  Ke vaut auer hou richesce
  Or e argent sen irra
  Le corps ert mys en grose heyre
  e li alme sen va en heyre
  hou ceo ke cy glene a
      Enpense checun de espleyter
       Ke il ne perde le grant louher
       Ke deu promis nous a.

4. Savise chescun e fra ke sage
  auaunt ke veygne au passage
  en queu bens safyera
  Les benfez ke auera fet icy
  prest les tornera deuaunt ly
  kaunt du secle departyra
      Enpense checun de espleyter, &c.

5. Ke si cum cely ke ben fet
  le cecle pur louher
  cum promis est receuera
  Ansi cely ke sa vie
  degaste en pecche e vylenye
  en enfern demorra
      Enpense checun de espleiter, &c.

6. Ke fray li Reys baroun e counte
   ke ne seuent ren de acounte
   kaunt acounter couendra
   Mes certes plusurs [fol. 84^b] auerount hounte
   kaunt nul contour put par counte
   pur ewus pleider la.
       Enpense checun de espleyter, &c.

7. Ke fray le prestre e li esueke
   ly sage clerk ly erseueke
   ke taunt de acountes apris a
   kaunt la soumme ert souztrete
   de despensis e de recete
   ly plus sage fou se tendera
       Enpense checun de espleyter, &c.

8. Seyt homme veuz hou enfaunz
   ja si fort ne wayllanz
   ke il ne mourra
   La mort tapit dedenz se gaunz
   ke ly ferra de sa launz
   kaunt meynz quyde le prendera
       Enpense checun de espleyter, &c.

9. Meuz vaut vn ben devaunt la mort
   ke dis apres e plus confort
   l'alme kant sen irra
   kant l'alme ert departye
   ne auera dounkes amy ne amye
   allas en ky safiera
       Enpense checun de espleyter, &c.

10. Pur œo checun se puruee
    e ceo ke ay dit ne descreye
    kar tout yssi serra
    Ceo ke homme auera cy ouere
    ayllours ly ert guerdoune sen fet
    sen louher receuera
        Enpense checun, &c.

11. Aust sygnefie ceste vie
    Le sage en aust fet sa quillie
    par vnt en l'an apres viuera
    E la petite formye
    en este ne se oblie
    ben seyt ke yuer apres vendra
        Enpense checun, &c.

12. Checun pense en sun corauge
    Li ieuene e li ueil de age
    en queus bens se afiera
    checun pense quey ad glene
    e queus bens ad entasse
    e ques bens o ly menera
        Checun enp., &c.

These Old French verses have already been printed from two other MSS., (1) Lambeth 522 (by Reinsch, *Archiv*, lxiii. 76), and (2) Sloane 1611 (by P. Meyer, *Romania*, xl. 533). Instead of the twelve stanzas printed above, these MSS., however, offer a text of ten stanzas, rearranged in the following sequence (the numbers denote their position in Phillipps): 1, 11, 12, 2*, 3, 8*, 6, 7, 5*, 9. Stanzas marked with (*) show a radical modification of the text according to the Phillipps MS.

In Herebert's paraphrase the first four stanzas correspond to the first four of the Old French version printed above. This in itself would indicate almost beyond a doubt that Herebert used as his basis the text in the Phillipps MS. But there is even more conclusive evidence. On the lower margin of fol. 84ᵇ appear the following lines of English, written with a plummet in Herebert's hand (some portions are no longer legible):

?   ne cacheþ in hys snare
...e mon ȝong be he old Ne be so strong ne wel ytold þat deþ
        gloue   houe   and make
Deþ ys hud wythinne his þat shal hym smyte wyth ys
...ere þe deþ is bet' e o dede þen tene after and more of
...........................Be þe soule vrom vles..
...................................sh..ed.....

If we compare this passage in pencil with vv. 28–41 of Herebert's poem we see that they represent a trial draft of this portion—marking probably the beginning of his attempt to render the French verses into English.

2. MS. *nede mot deȝen*; *mot* dotted for deletion.

41. *sheued*: a crux. The context suggests some such sense as 'dispersed' or 'stripped'. A verb 'sweep clear (of chaff)' is conceivable as a formation on *sheave* (*shive*) sb.² 'husk; particle of chaff, etc.', but semasiologically unlikely. Accommodation of ON. *skæva* ' to go quickly ' is improbable for the same reason.

24. *Iesu Nostra Redempcio.*

For the Latin original of this hymn see Daniel, *Thes. Hymn.* i. 63, and Dreves, *Anal*. ii. 49; see also *York Breviary*, Surtees Soc., i. 480. The three pairs of short lines (vv. 5–6, 14–15, 19–20) were no doubt intended as single lines broken by medial rime.

25. *Quis est iste qui uenit de Edom?*

A paraphrase of *Isaiah* lxiii. 1–7, one of the *Lectiones* for Wednesday in Holy Week. It would appear that in the Service Book used by Herebert verse 5 was directly followed by verse 7. Herebert noted the omission of verse 6, and supplied it in the concluding couplet of his paraphrases.

10. *won*: 'hope', 'available means'. Cf. Robt. of Gloucester's *Chron*., v. 275: 'þo he ne sey oþer won'; also 'The Husbandman's Lament', v. 5: 'Nou we mote worche, nis þer non oþer won' (Böddeker, *Alteng. Dicht*., p. 102).

26. *An Orison of the Five Joys.*

This orison occurs also in the Vernon MS., fol. 115[b] (*Minor Poems Vernon MS.*, pp. 30–2), Royal MS. 17 ˙A. xxvii, fol. 81[a], and Lambeth MS. 559, fol. 15[b]. The *Aue Maria* in Lambeth MS. 853, p. 26 (*Hymns to Virg. and Christ*, pp. 6, 7) borrows three stanzas (1, 8, and 11).

5. *Heil*: Royal, *lady*.

11. *in bok*: Royal omits.

13. *gladful*: Royal, *ioyful*.

16. *Help*: Royal, *þou bringe*.

20. *help*: Royal, *bringe*.

23–4. Royal: *þow ȝiue me grace in erþe my sines to bete/and þat i may in heuen sitte before þi fet.*

25. *trewe in alle nede*: Royal, *redy in gode dede*.

26. *redi in goud dede*: Royal, *rede in al nede*.

Stanzas 9 and 10 transposed in Royal.

40. *ioyes*: Royal, *þat ioy*.

41. *þat sittest*: Royal, *þat heie settest*.

44. *þat heye kyng*: Royal omits *heye*.

47. Royal: *þow ȝyue me grace to come into þat liȝte.*

51. *help*: Royal, *bringe*.

Stanza 14 lacking in Royal.

27. *The Four Foes of Mankind.*

Printed by D. Laing, *Owain Miles and other inedited fragments*, Edinb., 1837, No. IV; and by E. Kölbing, *Engl. Stud*. ix, 441–2.

82. Evidently refers to lending money at interest. The miser and the usurer come in together appropriately.

lyowen: i.e. *lyopen*. Although a form of pp. with *w* is not recorded in OE. *līon, lēon*, it can be posited on the strength of *siwen*, and since -*w*- would be the historically correct development of Gmc. *ʒ*ʷ. An ONth. -*iǫ*- in the pp. would likewise be historically regular, and is supported by *āseowen* (beside *āsiwen*, after other verbs in class I whose pp. stems did not contain *w*).

95–6. Evidently a proverb: *mock* (lit. *muck*) is used for 'wealth', 'riches', as in *Sarmun*, v. 81 (Heuser, *Bonn. Beitr.* xiv, 91), Wyclif's *Works*, EETS., p. 147 (last line), Gower, *Conf. Am.*, v. 4855, Hoccleve's *De Reg. Princ.*, vv. 1124, 1632; see also below, no. 100, v. 80.

104. *on bendes*: in the MS. the *t* suprascript is squeezed in between the *u* and the *b*, and was probably not intended as an abbreviation, but was a scribal afterthought and an attempted emendation prompted by the miswriting of *n* as *u*.

28. *Lollai litel child whi wepistow so sore?*

Printed by Wright, *Rel. Ant.* ii. 177–8; by Heuser, *Bonn. Beitr.* xiv, pp. 174–5; and by Chambers and Sidgwick, *Early Eng. Lyrics*, p. 166.

This is the earliest known example of the 'Lullay' song, of which we find a considerable group in the later fourteenth and the fifteenth centuries. It is exceptional in being the song of a human mother. All the other 'Lullay' songs deal with the Blessed Virgin and her Child. The present piece should be compared particularly with no. 65, which is composed in the same measure, and seems to be a direct adaptation.

Stanza 1. The rimes in this stanza could easily be restored by amending vv. 3 and 4 to 'þer-fore' and 'wore'. Moreover, this would avoid the awkwardness of beginning and ending v. 3 with the same word.

Stanza 4. The source of this stanza is the separate quatrain on Lady Fortune and her Wheel (see no. 42).

29. *worp*: (< OE. *weorpan*), i.e. 'wove', 'prepared'; cf. *Midelerd for mon wes mad*, v. 65: 'wo him wes ywarpe ʒore' (Böddeker, *Alteng. Dicht.*, p. 183). The same thought is repeated below in v. 35.

29. *An Orison to the Trinity.*

This and the two following pieces are insertions in the *Cursor Mundi*. The orison to the Trinity occurs in three MSS. (printed *Cursor Mundi*, EETS., vv. 25403–86).

59. *ta me wit*: 'Take ... wíth' = receive, accept.

60. *Fott was þe fallen fra*: Göttingen MS., *Fott þe was fallen fra*; Fairfax MS., *focche me was fallin þe fra*. The obscurity arises from the omission of the rel. pron. Fetch [that which] was fallen away from thee. Note the parallel phrase in 93. 72: 'þou take þat þe is fallen fro'.

30. *The Matins of the Cross.*

This, like the preceding piece, occurs in three MSS. of the *Cursor Mundi* (ed. EETS., vv. 25487–618). It is the earliest English text of the 'Hours of the Cross', of which other examples are nos. 34 and 55. See the Notes by Canon Simmons, *Lay Folk's Mass Book*, EETS., pp. 346 ff.

31. *A Song of the Five Joys.*

This piece occurs in only a single MS. of the *Cursor Mundi*, and is here reprinted from the EETS. ed. (vv. 25619–83) without collation of the original.

32. *Marye, mayde mylde and fre.*

By William of Shoreham.

Printed by Wright, *Poems of Wm. of Shoreham*, Percy Soc., xxviii. 131–4; and by Konrath, EETS., Extra Ser., lxxxvi. 127–9.

5. MS. *fet vn on clene*, with dots under *vn* for deletion.

5–6. An obvious allusion to the story of 'Dainties in a foul dish', which is of frequent occurrence in the collections of Miracles of Our Lady. In Ward's *Catal. of Romances*, vol. ii, four instances of this story are recorded in MSS. in the British Museum (Royal 5 A. viii, no. 6; Arundel 406, no. 29; Egerton 1117, no. 28; Addit. 33956, no. 9).

20. *rytte sarray*: The legitimate wife, Sarah, as opposed to Hagar. Sarah was often used as a type of the Blessed Virgin.

21. *out of cry*: out of range, out of calling distance.

68–70. Cf. *Apoc.* xii. 1 'mulier amicta sole, et luna sub pedibus eius, et in capite eius corona stellarum duodecim.'

33. *An Orison to the Blessed Virgin.*

This orison, written as prose, stands at the conclusion of the *Ayenbite of Inwyt*. Dan Michel evidently adapted these lines from the first stanza of the macaronic prayer preserved in Harley 2253, fol. 83ᵃ (Böddeker, *Alteng. Dicht.*, p. 220).

34. *The Hours of the Cross.*

Printed by Morris, *Legends of the Holy Rood*, EETS., pp. 222–4, and by Horstmann, *Min. Poems Vernon MS.*, pp. 37–42 (at foot of page). For the complete text of the Latin original see *Lay Folk's Mass Book*, EETS., pp. 85 and 87. For an English version of the 'Hours' with the prayers in prose see *The Prymer*, EETS., pp. 15 ff. For other metrical versions (independently tr. from the Latin) see *Min. Poems Vernon MS.*, pp. 37 ff. and also no. 55, below.

6. *dare*: Horstmann emends to *dede* on the basis of the Latin: 'defunctis veniam et requiem'.

15. *day on rode*: Horstmann's emendation, 'do Ihesu on rode', spoils the metre. The form *day* implies a pronunciation [dai], which is amply attested in ME. rhymes, as [wrai] is in the parallel case of *wreȝen*, *wrye* < OE *wrēgan*. The [ai] was levelled into the infinitive from the 2 and 3 pr. sing. indicative.

17. This line, which evidently ended with *kinge*, has been omitted by the scribe: no gap in MS.

35. *Jesus Have Mercy on Me.*

These English verses, written as prose, occur in a homily on the text 'Ihesu, fili dauid, miserere mei'. Miss E. G. Parker informs me that fol. 64, with which Art. 11 of the Merton Coll. MS. begins (see the description in Coxe's *Catal. Cod. MSS. qui in Coll. Aulisque Oxon. . . .*, i. 96), has the heading in a faint hand: 'Mauleuerer videlicet ad folium 17 vbique'. The Mauleverer family was established at Wothersome, near Leeds, and in other parts of Yorkshire, from the beginning of the thirteenth century (cf. Whitaker, *Hist. and Antiq. of Craven*, pp. 296, 443 f.; Wm. Brown, F.S.A., 'Ingleby Arncliffe', *Yorksh. Arch. Journal*, xvi. 184 ff. Burton's *Monast. Eboracense* records many benefactions to religious houses by this family). Thomas M. was a senior monk in St. Mary's Abbey at York in 1390 (cf. M. Deanesly, *Incendium Amoris*, p. 77 n.). Bp. Sheppey may therefore have borrowed the sermon from someone of Yorkshire family. Such a person would hardly have written the English lines, which are in southern dialect. May it be that Bp. Sheppey himself added them?

It will be observed that these verses are arranged as a roundel, and that the second series of verses corresponds roughly to the first, and introduces the same refrain lines. [For further information on this MS. see Sir Maurice Powicke's *The Medieval Books of Merton College* (1931), p. 171, no. 545.]

36. *How Christ shall Come.*

At the heading of fol. 139 is written: 'Stanschaue', apparently the name of the author from whom the sermon which follows was borrowed.

5–8. The original of these lines is a passage in the Latin text found on the preceding page of the MS. (fol. 139[a], col. 2):

Vnde venis. Set ad has 4[or] causas huius questionis inesse ratio potuit per 4[or] notas solucionis. Venio inquit de thalamo ut sponsus dulcissimus. venio de prelio ut Miles strenuissimus. venio de foro ut mercator ditissimus. venio de longinquo ut peregrinus extraneus. & sic a 4[or] partibus mundi ad eos veniebat.

6. *vo*: MS. *enemy*; *vo* interlined above.

Immediately following in the MS. are the following lines based on the Vision of the Four Horsemen (*Apoc.* v. 2–5):

> He Rod vpon a whit hors in þet
> þet he be-cam man vor þe.
> He Rod on a red hors in þet
> þet he was i-nayled to þe Rode tre.
> He Rod on a blak hors in þet
> þet he þe deuel ouer cam.
> He rod on a dun hors in þet
> þet þe cloude hym vp nam.

He Rod on a whit hors & hadde a boȝe in his hond
in toknyng þet he was skyluol.
He þet Rod on a Red hors hadde a sverd in his hond
in toknyng þet he was medful.
He þ[t] rod on þe blake hors hadde a weye in his hond
in toknyng þe⟨t⟩ he was riȝtful.
He þet rod on þe dunne hors hadde Muchel uolk þ[t] hym volwede
in tokning þet he was Miȝtful.

37. *Aurora lucis rutilat.*

For the text of the Latin hymn of which the first two stanzas are here translated see Mone, *Lat. Hymn.* i. 190; Daniel, *Thes. Hymn.* i. 83; and Dreves, *Anal.* ii. 47. In the MS. the Latin text immediately precedes the English lines.

38. *O gloriosa domina excelsa.*

On fol. 146[a], on the left-hand margin, at the beginning of a sermon, is written the name 'Oliver', possibly a clue to the author of the sermon which follows.

The lines which are here translated form stanzas 5–7 of the hymn

Quem terra pontus aethera (Daniel, *Thes. Hymn.* i. 172, Dreves, *Anal.* ii. 38). These three stanzas frequently occur separately, as in Mone, *Lat. Hymn.* ii. 129. Stanzas 5 and 6 are incorporated in no. 41, below.

39. *The Evils of the Time.*

16. Immediately following this line is written:

De Mundo

lex lyis done ofuer al quia fallax fallit ubique
and loue es bot smal quia gens se gestat inique.

Cf. vv. 13–14 of the macaronic verses printed by Wright, *Pol. Songs* (Camd. Soc.), p. 251. Cf. also the excerpt of four lines among the sentences printed by Horstmann, *Richard Rolle*, ii. 65.

17–20. Cf. Harley MS. 2316, fol. 26ᵃ:

Men hem bimenin of litel trewthe
It is ded and ȝat is rewthe
Lesing livet and is above
And now is biried trewthe and love.

(*Rel. Ant.* ii. 121.)

And Hatton MS. 107, fol. 1ᵇ:

Me⟨n hem com⟩pleynes of vntrewyth
la⟨we e⟩s dede and þat es Rewth
trechery es al oboue
and grauen he as trewlouf.

40. *Crux fidelis.*

This is a translation of stanza 8 of the celebrated hymn, *Pange lingua gloriosi*, by Venantius Fortunatus (Daniel, *Thes. Hymn.* i. 163). This stanza was sung separately in the service for Good Friday: see the text as given in the *Sarum Graduale* (thirteenth century). Sometimes this stanza was repeated as a refrain between the several stanzas of *Pange lingua gloriosi* (see Mone, *Lat. Hymn.* i. 131).

41. *Ave Maris Stella.*

These verses represent an amalgamation of three well-known hymns: (1) *Ave Maris Stella* (see above, no. 17), (2) *Quem terra pontus aethera* (see above, no. 38), (3) *Alma redemptoris mater* (see above, no. 19).

1–16. Cf. stanzas 1, 2, 5, and 4 of the *Ave Maris Stella*.
17–24. Cf. stanzas 5 and 6 of *Quem terra*, &c.
25–34. Cf. *Alma redemptoris mater*.

42. *Lady Fortune and her Wheel.*

Printed by Heuser, *Bonner Beitr.* xiv, 173.

These verses are written on a parchment roll (*ca.* 1325) containing genealogies of English kings. Among scraps of Latin, French, and English verse on the last page of MS. 317, in the Library of the University of Ghent (printed by H. Logemann, *Archiv*, lxxxvii. 432), one finds these lines in both French and English versions:

> la dame de fortune estraungement fest sun pas
> A tous hom ele est commune de tourner haut en bas
> Sa vy nest pas une diuersement fest sun pas
> Quy creyst a fortune sowent dirra allas.

> the leuedy dame fortune scho ys both frend and fo
> ye riche sco makes pore and pore ryche als so
> Scho tournes wo intyl wele and wele intyl wo
> Noman trou dam fortune for algates yt thar be so.

These lines are also incorporated in the *Fasciculus Morum,* a fourteenth-century compilation by a Franciscan (see note on no. 133, below). I have noted the occurrence of this quatrain in the following copies: Laud Misc. 213, Bodley 410, Rawl. C. 670, Durham Univ. Cosin V. iv. 2. They also appear, with slight variations, as stanza 4 of the 'Lullay' poem (see above, no. 28).

43. *All is Phantom.*

Printed by Halliwell, *Rel. Ant.* ii. 20.

These lines occur also on a fly-leaf at the beginning of Royal MS. 17 B. xvii (late fourteenth century) and in B.M. Addit. MS. 8151, fol. 200b (fifteenth century). They have been printed from the latter by Furnivall, *EETS.*, Ex. Ser., viii. 85.

44. *Veni Creator Spiritus.*

Printed by Heuser, *Anglia*, xxix. 409.

For Herebert's version of this hymn, and references to the Latin original, see above, no. 18.

12. *richand protes*: Lat. *ditans guttura.*

13. Lat. *Accende lumen sensibus.*

16. The scribe has omitted all of this line except the last word, which he has written as the first word of v. 17.

25–8. This stanza is not found in Herebert's version nor in the earliest MSS. of the Latin hymn. It properly forms the concluding stanza of the hymn *Beata nobis gaudia* (Daniel, *Thes. Hymn.* i. 6; Mone, *Lat. Hymn.* i. 241).

27. *þi sinnes*: Clearly a scribal error: probably we should emend *þi* to *nou* in accordance with the Latin: 'dimitte nunc peccamina'.

45. *Ave Maris Stella.*

Printed by Heuser, *Anglia*, xxix. 411.

For an earlier version of this hymn, and references to the Latin original, see above, no. 17.

46. *Abide, Ye Who Pass By.*

This piece and no. 47 are found also in Cotton MS. Galba E. ix, fol. 51ᵇ (col. 1), from which they have been printed by Horstmann, *Richard Rolle*, ii. 457, and by Hall, *Engl. Stud.* xxi, 207-9. In the Cotton MS. (written between 1400 and 1420) these verses are headed by Latin riming lines:

> Vos qui transitis. si crimina flere uelitis.
> Per me transite. qui sum ianua vite.

The suggestion for the English verses was taken, of course, from *Lam.* i. 12 'O vos omnes, qui transitis per viam, attendite, et videte si est dolor sicut dolor meus.'

For another treatment of the same theme see no. 74, below.

1. Cott. MS. *Bides a while and haldes ȝoure pais.*

14. The scribe originally wrote: *my mysdedes*, and then erased the *y* of *my* without substituting another letter. Cott. MS. reads *þi misdedes*.

47. '*How Crist Spekes tyll Synfull Man of His Gret Mercy.*'

This piece, like the preceding, occurs also in Cotton MS. Galba E. ix. In the Cotton MS. these verses are headed:

> In cruce sum pro te. qui peccas desine pro me.
> Desine do ueniam. dic culpam corrige uitam.

These Latin lines are frequently found alone, as, for example, in Corp. Christi Coll. Camb. MS. 277, fol. 141ᵇ. In other cases they are followed by a close translation into two English couplets, as in Grimestone's Commonplace Book (Advocates MS. 18. 7. 21, fol. 125ᵇ):

> Vpon þe rode I am for þe
> þat þu sennest let for me
> I þe for-ȝeue lat ben þi strif
> Be-knou þi senne & amend þi lif.

In all probability these Latin lines also furnished the suggestion for the more expanded version of Christ's appeal to man in the six stanzas before us.

48. *The Sweetness of Jesus.*

Of this piece no less than fifteen MSS. (complete or fragmentary) survive, of which the one here printed is the earliest. Rawl. Poet. 175 is the only one besides the Thornton MS. which offers a Northern text of the poem. Horstmann has noted that the rimes indicate that the poem was of Northern origin.

The other MSS. containing these verses are: Vernon (*V*) (*Minor Poems Vernon MS.*, i. 45), Ashmole 41 (*A¹*) (vv. 1–92 wanting), Ashmole 750 (*A²*) (first stanza only), Rawlinson A. 389 (*R*), Douce 141 (*D¹*), Douce 322 (*D²*), Harley 1706 (*H¹*), Harley 2339 (*H²*), Sloane 963 (*S*), Lambeth 853 (*L*) (*Hymns to Virgin and Christ*, p. 8), Thornton (*T*) (*Relig. Pieces*, rev. ed., p. 92, Horstmann, *Richard Rolle*, i. 368), Gurney MS., fol. 185ᵇ, Advocates 19. 3. 1, fol. 170ᵇ, Hunterian Museum V. 8. 23 (*Hu*). The readings of all except the Gurney and Advocates MSS. have been compared, and significant variants noted below.

1. *A Ihesu*: All other MSS. omit *A*.

2. *langyng*: All other MSS., *knowyng*.

3. *lust*: All other MSS., *loue*.

bytter sall: *T*, *sulde bitter*. All other MSS., *bytter schulde*.

10. *sadly se*: So also *D¹*, *D²*, *H¹*. *soþly se*, *V*, *H²*, *R*, *L*, *Hu*. *soþe se*, *S*. *hertly se*, *T*.

14. *So fast*: *T*, *D¹*, *D²*, *H¹*, *so harde*.

16. *H²*, *R*, *L*, *V*, *Hu*, *S*, *þat no þing likede me but he.*

23. *Als fader of fude*: So also *T*. All other MSS. (essentially), *As fader he fondeþ.*

27. *strynd*: Changed to *kynde* in *L*, *V*, *H²*, *Hu*, *R*, *S*.

41–8. This stanza omitted in *T*.

41. *Bot oft þis*: *H²*, *R*, *L*, *V*, *Hu*, The loue of him. *S*, *þe loue of þe*. *D¹*, *Bot loue of þe spouse*. *H¹*, *D²*, *Loue off that lorde*.

43. *spouse*: changed to *lorde* in *D²*, *H¹*.

48. *full sare*: *H²*, *R*, *L*, *V*, *Hu*, *S*, *for*.

49. *me bihoues*: *T*, *me bude*. *H¹*, *D²*, *me shulde*. *L*, *Hu*, *me þenkiþ*. *D¹*, *I moste*.

50. *me*: *T*, *R*, *L*, *V*, *Hu*, *myn*.

55. *Pouert . . . payns*: *T*, *D²*, *H¹*, *Pouert . . . penaunce*. *R*, *V*, *Peynes . . . pouert*.

59. Following this line *T* adds: *And þat my saule sulde sauede bee*, thus making a 9-line stanza.

67. *perched*: Changed to *pirled* in D^1.

68. *rewfull*: D^1, D^2, H^1, H^2, L, S, *rewli.* T, *bludy.* V, Hu, *wyde*.

71. *His ded*: T, D^1, D^2,˙H^1, *His dulefull dede*.

burd to me be: T, *burde do me.* D^2, H^1, *shulde do me.* D^1, *ouȝt do me.* H^2, L, Hu, *schulde be to me ful.* S, *ouȝte be to me ful.* R, V, *most be to me ful*.

73. *burd*: D^2, H^1, L, Hu, *schulde.* D^1, S, *ouȝt.* H^2, R, V, *most*.

78. *tholed*: So also T. All other MSS., *suffrede*.

82. *ouercomen*: T, D^1, R, V, *venqwyste.* H^2, *vencusid.* S, *venchyd.* D^2, H^1, *endyd*.

92. *do*: So also T, H^2, V. All other MSS., *kype*.

94. *lely*: So also T, D^1. L, *hertily*; all other MSS., *trewely*.

95. *wordes*: All other MSS., *werkes*.

96. *þat he lered*: T and almost all other MSS., *That he me leryde*.

97. *hert*: T and almost all other MSS., *werkes*.

98. *wirk*: T and almost all other MSS., *wreche*. In Hu this word has been altered to *wu^rche*.

99. *do*: All other MSS., *wirke*.

101. *faes*: T, *Enemyse*.

102. *frele*, the reading of all other MSS., has been adopted here in place of R's *frely*.

107. *boght*: T, H^2, R, L, V, Hu, S, *made*.

108. *spouse*: As in A^1, D^1. T, *sun*; D^2, H^1, *frende*. All other MSS., *childe*.

114. *whare I*: T, *when I sall*. All other MSS., *when I henne*.

49. *All Other Love is like the Moon.*

These verses are written in pencil on a page left nearly blank at the end of the text of Vegetius, *De Re Militari*. The hand, in the opinion of Dr. James, Provost of Eton, is very little later than 1350. I am under the greatest obligations to Dr. James for his kindness in calling my attention to these verses and also for his patience in assisting me to decipher some of the lines which have become almost illegible.

50. *The Tower of Heaven.*

Written on the lower margin of the last leaf of a treatise by Bp. Grosseteste, *De Veritate Theologie*.

51, 52, 53, 54.

These pieces have been printed by T. Wright, *Rel. Ant.* ii, 119-20. They are written as prose in a hand of the second half of the fourteenth century. The scribe always writes *ȝ* for *þ*.

55. *The Hours of the Cross.*

For other metrical versions of the 'Hours' and references to the Latin original see above, no. 34.

56. *Dialogue between the Blessed Virgin and her Child.*

Fragmentary texts of this 'Lullay' are found in three other MSS.: (1) Harley 2330 (on a fly-leaf at the end), stanzas 1–5 (printed by H. E. Sandison, *Chanson d'Aventure in Middle English*, Bryn Mawr Monographs, xii, p. 103); (2) St. John's Camb. 259, fol. 4ᵃ, stanzas 1–9 (printed by James and Macaulay, *Mod. Lang. Rev.*, viii. 72–3); (3) Camb. Univ. Add. 5943, no. 11, stanza 1 only (printed by L. S. M., *Music, Cantilenas, Songs*, &c., Lond. 1906). As all of these are much later than the Advocates MS. and the texts are in every way inferior, collation of variant readings seems fruitless.

57. *A Song of the Nativity.*

No other MS. of this piece is known.

74. *ferli fode*: We should expect *freli fode*: cf. *Sir Tristram*, vv. 193 and 369.

58. *A Song of the Blessed Virgin and Joseph.*

MS. Selden B. 26, in the Bodleian (*c.* 1450), contains the first eleven stanzas of this song, with musical notation (printed in *Early Bodleian Music*; text reprinted by F. M. Padelford, *Anglia*, xxxvi. 102–4). In MS. Selden the stanzas occur in the following order: 1, 2, 4, 6, 8, 10, 3, 5, 7, 9, 11—to the serious detriment of the sense. Obviously the Selden scribe copied from a MS. written in double-column in which the stanzas were arranged as follows:

	1	
2		3
4		5
6		7
8		9
10		11

But instead of reading across from the left-hand to the right-hand column the scribe stupidly copied *down* the columns.

59. *Christ weeps in the Cradle for Man's Sin.*

The first six stanzas of this piece are found also in MS. Harley 7358, fol. 12ᵇ (fifteenth century), from which they have been printed by Heuser, *Bonner Beiträge*, xiv. 211. The text in the Harley MS.

has suffered much corruption. This 'Lullay' song differs notably from the others of its type in that it is addressed to Christ by a penitent instead of by the Blessed Virgin.

60. *The Blessed Virgin's Appeal to the Jews.*

No other text of these verses is known.

Immediately above these lines in the MS. is the following sentence: 'Quare ut ait B. [? Bernardus] in persona uirginis ad Iudeos. Si non placet compati filio compatimini matri.' The English verses appear to be based on a passage in the *Liber de Passione Christi et Doloribus et Planctibus Matris Eius* (Migne, *Patr. Lat.* clxxxii, col. 1133 ff.; for another text see Kribel, *Engl. Stud.* viii, 85 ff.) usually ascribed to St. Bernard. Cf. Kribel's text, lines 94–100. This treatise appears to supply the basis also for nos. 67 and 128.

61. *A Song of Mercy.*

MS. Harley 2316 (see above, nos. 51, 52, 53, 54) contains a definition of Mercy (printed *Rel. Ant.* ii. 120) in three couplets of which the first two are identical with vv. 5, 6, 1, 2 of the present piece.

Another definition of Mercy in three couplets is found in MS. Harley 7322 (second half fourteenth century) from which they have been printed by Furnivall (*Pol. Rel. Love Poems*, rev. ed., p. 263). These three correspond to vv. 3, 4, 5, 6, 1, 2 in the Advocates MS. The last four lines in the Advocates text have no counterpart in the other MSS., and may perhaps be an addition. The arrangement of the lines in the Advocates MS. is the best, though possibly the original sequence may have been 5, 6, 1, 2.

62. *Christ's Prayer in Gethsemane.*

In the MS. these lines are headed: 'Pater si fieri possit, &c. Et iterum Si uis vt bibam', &c. Cf. *Mark* xiv. 35 and *Matt.* xxvi. 42.

63. *Jesus, Man's Champion.*

The theme of this piece is developed more fully in the Anglo-Norman verses, 'Coment le fiz Deu fu armé en la croyz', in Phillipps MS. 8336, fol. 90b. (See the description by P. Meyer, *Romania*, xiii. 530–1.) Note also the figure of Jesus as champion introduced in no. 48, vv. 81–92.

64. *Lamentacio dolorosa.*

Immediately above these lines in the MS. is written: 'Beda. Audi cum Maria quae dixit.' A general (though not a verbal) parallel for this Lament occurs in the 'De Meditatione Passionis Christi per Septem Diei Horas Libellus' sometimes ascribed to Bede: 'O Fili dulcissime, quid facit haec misera et moestissima, cui me miseram commendatam relinquis, fili mi dulcissime? Memento mei et omnis familiae tuae, quam sic desolatam dimittis, memento omnium qui tibi serviunt, fili mi . . . O Pater, in manus tuas commendo filium meum, imo et Dominum meum, in quantum possum, et non in quantum debeo, quia non possum, quia deficio et hoc desidero ante filium in conspectu tuo mori' (Migne, *Patr. Lat.* xciv, col. 568).

65. *A Lullaby to Christ in the Cradle.*

For another 'Lullay' poem in the same measure, and having a very similar refrain, see above, no 28.

66. *Christ's Love-song to Man.*

With these verses may be compared four lines which occur elsewhere in the same MS. (fol. 19ᵃ; copied again on fol. 119ᵃ):

Loue made crist in oure lady to lith
& loue broutte crist in-to mannis sith ⎫ Amore
Loue made crist wᵗ þe deuel to fith ⎬ langueo
& loue made detȝ to iesu crist ful lith ⎭

67. *Dialogue between Jesus and the B.V. at the Cross.*

This is the earliest English version of this Dialogue; the next is that in seven 4-line stanzas, found in Sloane MS. 2593 (printed by T. Wright, *Songs and Carols from a MS. in the B.M.*, Warton Club, pp. 65, 66). In two later versions a refrain has been added: Bodl. MS. Eng. poet. e. 1 (printed by Wright, *Songs and Carols*, Percy Soc., xxiii. 38, 39), and Balliol MS. 354 (printed by Dyboski, EETS., Ex. Ser. ci. 13, 14). A comparison of these several versions affords an interesting opportunity to observe the tendencies in lyrical development.

Although in the MS. 'Ihesus' is written opposite the first section of this piece, it is clear that in vv. 1–8 the speaker is another person. These lines might be assigned to John, as is actually done in the

Sloane text, but it should be noted that the rôle of observer at the Cross is not unlike that assumed by the author in the treatise *De Passione Christi*, &c. (see note on no. 60), of which this poem shows unmistakable influence.

2–10. Cf. the Latin (Kribel's text, lines 210–15) in which, however, these lines follow the Descent from the Cross.

14. Cf. the Latin: 'O fili mi, ultra quid faciam?' (Kribel, line 111).

15–23. Cf. Kribel's text, lines 115–20, 148–9.

69. *Lovely Tear from Lovely Eye.*

19–24. This stanza reappears in no. 90 (stanza 4) although the metre establishes it as belonging originally to no. 69.

70. *Homo vide quid pro te patior.*

These lines are found also in a MS. owned by Wilfred Merton, Esq., Crawford Cottage, Richmond Hill, Surrey. In both MSS. the English verses are preceded by the text of the Latin original, which is ascribed to the 'Cancelarius parisiensis'. The Chancellor in question was Philippe de Grève (†1236), as my friend Prof. Jean B. Beck first pointed out to me. The Latin lines are preserved in a number of MSS., and have been printed by Dreves (*Anal.* xxi. 18). For an Anglo-Norman version preserved in Phillipps MS. 8336 see *Romania*, xiii. 518.

The English text in the Wilfred Merton MS. shows the following variants:

1. be-*þing*: *bihold*.
2. *þole*: *drehe*.
5, 6. omitted.
7. *loue of*: *sinful*.
9. *To me turnen*: *Tornen to me*.

71. *I would be clad in Christis Skin.*

The figure of hiding one's self in the wound in the side of Christ is frequently met with in Latin hymns. Cf., for example, Daniel, *Thes. Hymn.* ii. 371:

> Dignare me, O Iesu, rogo te
> In cordis vulnere abscondere
> Permitte me hic vivere
> In tuo latere quiescere.

One may refer also to the 'Salutatio ad latus domini' (Mone, *Lat.*

Hymn. i. 166; Migne, *Patrol. Lat.* clxxxiv, cols. 1321-2), especially the lines:

> Plaga rubens aperire,
> fac cor meum te sentire,
> sine me in te transire,
> vellem totus introire,
> pulsanti pande pauperi.
>
> .   .   .
>
> O quam dulcis sapor iste!
> qui te gustat, Iesu Christe.

Cf. also the following passages in homilies doubtfully attributed to St. Augustine and St. Bernard: Migne, *Patrol. Lat.* xl, col. 706, § 9, col. 961 (cap. xxiii); clxxxiv, col. 753.

72. *Popule meus quid feci tibi?*

Cf. the earlier version of the 'Popule Meus' by William Herebert, no. 15, above.

A later and much corrupted text of the present version is found in Jesus Coll. Camb. MS. 13 (fifteenth century) at fol. 84ᵃ, where the speaker is designated as 'mater ecclesia in persona Christi cantans'. The Jesus Coll. text consists of eleven stanzas arranged as follows (the numbers indicate the corresponding stanzas in the Advocates MS., the letters, stanzas peculiar to the Jesus MS.): 1, 2, 3, 6, 4, 7, A, B, 5, C, D. The Jesus Coll. text in its second, third, and fifth stanzas degenerates into ballad metre through the loss of the rimes uniting the first and third lines.

7. Jesus Coll., *thow dyȝthest a cros now for my deth*. This is an interesting case of reversion to the Latin: *parasti crucem saluatori tuo*.

74. *O vos omnes qui transitis per viam.*

In the MS. an express reference to the Scriptural source [*Lam.* i. 12] stands at the head of these lines. For another (quite independent) treatment of the same theme see no. 46, above.

75. *The Christ Child shivering with Cold.*

In the MS. vv. 7-30 are written in column 1, and vv. 1-6 are written at the top of col. 2 with a row of dots to indicate their proper position as the first stanza.

The first three stanzas occur also in MS. Harley 7322 at fol. 135ᵇ. The verses from the Harley MS. have been printed (*Pol. Rel. Love Poems*, p. 255) as though they were two separate pieces although they are clearly connected by the line of Latin which stands between stanzas 1 and 2: 'Et reuera mater sua nichil habuit vnde posset eum induere, inde dixit sibi'. Notice also that the metre of the three stanzas is the same.

Stanzas 4 and 5 are peculiar to the Advocates MS.

15. The Harley text inserts after this verse an extra (and wholly redundant) line: 'þe on to folde ne to wrappe.'

77. *Homo Vide quid pro Te Patior.*

[On pieces 77–86 see H. E. Allen, *Writings ascribed to Richard Rolle*, pp. 294–301.]

Printed from this MS. by Horstmann, *Richard Rolle*, i. 71. A southernized version of this piece, still unprinted, occurs in the Vernon MS., fol. 334ᵃ (col. 1). These verses are an expansion of the well-known Latin lines by Philippe de Grève (see note on no. 70, above). Still another (unprinted) English version (fourteen lines), which seems to be verbally related to that in these two MSS., is preserved in Camb. Univ. Ii. 1. 2, fol. 126ᵇ, and Harley 4012, fol. 94ᵃ.

  2. *loke*: seo *V.*

  11. *suffer*: byde *V.*

  12. *it*: ȝit *V.*

  17, 18. These lines in reverse order in *V.*

  18. *And I have loued þe so longe V.*

  24. *Al for þe loue I hedde to þe V.*

  26. *And from þi sinnes V.*

  29. *I-wyse*: ȝit I-wisse *V.*

78. *Christ pleads with His Sweet Leman.*

Printed by Horstmann, *Richard Rolle*, i. 71.

79. *A Lament over the Passion.*

Printed by Horstmann, *Richard Rolle*, i. 72.

80. *A Prayer to Jesus.*

Printed by Horstmann, *Richard Rolle*, i. 72.

81. *A Song of Mortality.*

Printed from this MS. by Horstmann, *Richard Rolle*, i. 73. This piece occurs also in the Thornton MS. (Lincoln Cath. A. 5. 2) at fol. 213ᵃ, from which it is printed by Horstmann (*op. cit.*, p. 367); by Heuser, *Anglia*, xxvii. 307–10; and also in *Relig. Pieces in Prose and Verse*, EETS., rev. ed., pp. 88–91.

Between stanzas 3 and 4, and again between 4 and 5, the Thornton text includes a stanza not found in the Camb. MS. In both cases, however, these extra stanzas appear to be additions to the original text. The Judgment Day (Thornton, st. 4) comes in oddly out of place in its present position; and in Thornton, st. 6, the phrase in the refrain has been altered, doubtless for convenience of rime, to 'with E and O'.

22. *olod*: see C. T. Onions, *Medium Ævum* i. 206-8, ii. 73.

24. The second *k* in *skelk* (along with ʒ *skek*) is written on an erasure, in what seems to be a different hand. This gives further point to Prof. Menner's proposal to read *skelt* 'hasten' (*Mod. Lang. Notes* lv (1940), p. 248). But the striking resemblance of ll. 21-4 to 116. 33-48 (where *sekutowr* recurs in the alliterative conjunction with *syker*) suggests that *skelp* or a synonym would be equally possible; see note on 116. 45. Thornton reads *skikk and skekke*.

25. *T*: Of will and witt þat vesettis it in worde and þat we wroghte.

82. *A Song of Mercy*.

Printed by Horstmann, *Richard Rolle*, i. 74.

83. *A Song of Love-longing to Jesus*.

Printed by Horstmann, *Richard Rolle*, i. 75. This piece is also found as an insertion in a southern recension of no. 84, preserved in Lambeth 853 and Longleat 29. For the text of the insertion see vv. 137-228, according to the numbering in the EETS. ed. (*Hymns to Virgin and Christ*, pp. 26-9).

84. *A Song of the Love of Jesus*.

Printed by Horstmann, *Richard Rolle*, i. 76-8. A southern recension of this piece occurs in combination with no. 83, in Lambeth MS. 853 (printed in *Hymns to Virgin and Christ*, EETS., pp. 22-31) and also in Longleat MS. 29, fol. 49ᵃ.

Miss Hope Allen (*Mod. Lang. Rev.*, xiv. 320) points out the interesting fact that vv. 1-60 of this piece are direct translations of passages in Rolle's *Incendium Amoris*. The following references are to Miss Margaret Deanesly's edition of the *Incendium* (Manchester, 1915):

1-4. Cf. p. 267: Est enim amor . . . et solidatur, etc.

5-8. Cf. p. 268: Est enim amor . . . amabilis, etc.

9-12. Cf. p. 270: Sedes siquidem amoris in altum quoniam usque in celestia cucurrit . . . Unde et ad quietem eterne glorie propius accedit, etc.

13–16. Cf. p. 271: Amor enim . . . est carbone ignito, etc.

17–20. Cf. p. 272: Disce igitur amare . . . transieris, etc.

21–4. Cf. p. 272: O bone Ihesu qui mihi uitam tribuisti, etc.

25–8. Cf. p. 272: Amor tuus in nobis . . . maneat, etc.

29–32. Cf. p. 272: Si enim amauero aliquam . . . mundi huius, etc.

33–6. Cf. p. 273: Omne itaque oblectamentum quod homines in hoc exilio aspexerunt feno comparatur, etc.

37–40. Cf. p. 273: Tu autem Christum . . . iniquitatis, etc.

41–4. Cf. p. 273: Amoris autem fidelis et . . . hec est, etc.

45–8. Cf. p. 274: Igitur amare consulo sicut . . . locum tuum, etc.

49–52. Cf. p. 274: Amor enim est leuis sarcina, etc.

53–6. Cf. p. 274: Amor igitur res dulcissima est, etc.

57–60. Cf. p. 275: Uerumtamen carnalis dileccio prosperabitur et peribit quemadmodum, etc.

69. MS. *Sygh & sob.* The pronoun is added on the authority of the reading in the Lamb. MS.

85. *A Salutation to Jesus.*

Printed by Horstmann, *Richard Rolle*, i. 78–9.

86. *Thy Joy be in the Love of Jesus.*

Printed from this MS. by Horstmann, *Richard Rolle*, i. 81–2. This piece is found also in the Thornton MS. (Lincoln Cath. A. 5. 2), fol. 222ª (from which it is printed by Horstmann, *op. cit.*, i. 370–2, and in *Rel. Pieces in Prose and Verse*, EETS., rev. ed., pp. 107–13), and in Longleat MS. 29, fol. 50ª, still unprinted.

87. *A General Confession.*

The 'Burton MS.' is a single leaf of vellum, found in the binding of a book printed at Antwerp, 1535. Printed by Furnivall (*Archiv*, xcviii. 129, and *Min. Poems Vern. MS.*, p. 785), with the exception of four lines at the foot of col. 1, which have been trimmed away. This metrical paraphrase of the General Prayer of Confession exists in numerous MSS., which are divided into two main groups by certain differences in the order of the Deadly Sins and by the reading in the second line of *copable* in one group and *gulti* in the other. Of the *copable* group the Burton MS. is the earliest; of the *gulti* group the earliest is the Vernon MS.

To the *copable* group belong (besides the Burton MS.) Camb. Univ. MS. Ii. 6. 43, fol. 88ᵇ, and Douce MS. 306 (Audelay's MS.), fol. 12ᵇ, col. 1. To the *gulti* group belong the Vernon MS. fol. 114ᵇ (printed *Min. Poems Vern. MS.*, pp. 19–20), Camb. Univ. Dd. 8. 2, fol. 5ª,

Camb. Univ. Dd. 14. 26, fol. 42ᵇ, Harley 210, fol. 34ᵇ, B.M. Addit. 37787, fol. 14ᵃ. The fragments of text in Lambeth 559, fol. 14ᵃ, and Edinb. Univ. MS. Laing 32, fol. i, are too brief to enable one to determine their classification.

5–8. The Vernon text arranges the sins differently: Pride, Envy, Lechery, Sloth, Wrath, Gluttony, Covetyse.

8. Following this line the Vernon MS. inserts two couplets not found in the Burton MS.:

> I-broken Ichaue þi Comaundemens
> Aȝeynes myn owne Conciens,
> And not iserued þe to queme:
> Lord, Merci, ar þu domis deme.

88. *Hand by Hand We Shall us Take.*

This piece should have been included among the 'Miscellaneous Lyrics before 1350'. It occurs in a series of sermon outlines by a Franciscan in a hand hardly later than 1350. The notes are in Latin, but here and there English phrases and riming lines are interspersed. The homily in which these verses occur begins on fol. 201ᵇ with an exposition of the four locks by which the heart of the sinner is closed, of the several keys which will open these locks, and then of the banquet which Christ offers to those who will open the door to him:

... pro 3° panes operis satisfaccione dabit 3ᵐ ferculum gaudiorum omnium plenitudinem & iocunditatem & hoc est cena de qua in apoc. [xix. 9] beati qui ad cenam agni vocati sunt; ad quam cenam specialiter vocat deus 3ᵃ hominum genera sicud alibi, &c.

The English verses follow immediately. The last stanza of this piece is found also in a Latin homily in a fourteenth-century MS. at Helmingham Hall (MS. LJ. 1. 7, fol. 140ᵃ [now p. 287], col. 2).

89. *Iesu Dulcis Memoria.*

These eleven stanzas (according to the Hunterian MS.) are continued to the extent of forty-nine stanzas in Harley MS. 2253 (ed. Böddeker, *Alteng. Dicht.*, pp. 198–205). The first two stanzas very clearly depend upon the opening lines of the well-known Latin hymn ascribed to St. Bernard, but denied to him by the editors of Migne's *Patrologia* (clxxxiv, cols. 1317–20). From the beginning of stanza 3, however, the English verses show only traces here and there of verbal resemblance to the Latin.

The Hunterian text, though found in a MS. late in the fourteenth century, is independent of the text in Harley 2253. For example, in v. 3, Hunt. agrees more closely with the Latin: 'Nil auditur iucundius' than does Harl.: 'al þat may wiþ eȝen se'. Again, in v. 8, 'a louere' (Hunt.) is certainly right, where Harl. reads 'alu-mere'. In this case, also, the reading in Hunt. is confirmed by the later poem, 'Swete Ihesu now wol I synge', which is really a com-bination and expansion of nos. 7 and 89; these expanded versions agree with Hunt. in reading 'so swete a louyere' (cf. *Min. Poems Vern. MS.*, EETS., p. 451, v. 12). Further evidence that Harley 2253, though the oldest of the extant MSS., was not the source of the later texts appears from the Harley scribe's omission of vv. 49, 50 (Böddeker, p. 200) and the strange corruption in v. 51 of 'croune' into 'bac'. Since the later MSS., which combine nos. 7 and 89, show no trace of these errors, it is clear that they do not derive from Harley 2253.

90. *Christ's Gift to Man.*

This poem is written, for the most part, in the same measure as the 'Iesu Dulcis Memoria' (no. 89), which in the Hunterian MS. (*H*) immediately precedes, with nothing to indicate the line of division. 'Christ's Gift to Man' is preserved in two other fourteenth-century MSS., (*T*) Trinity Coll. Camb. B. 15. 17 (no. 353 in James's Cata-logue), from which it is printed in *Rel. Ant.* i. 166, and (*P*) Powis MS. (Lot 327, Sotheby Sale Cat., Mar. 20–2, 1923), purchased by Mr. Rosenbach, and now in the Huntington Library, Pasadena, California. In both *T* and *P* these verses directly follow the text of Richard Rolle's *Form of Perfect Living* (ed. Horstmann, i. 3–49). Moreover, a collation of the three MSS. shows that *T* and *P*, where they differ from *H*, agree in almost every instance with each other.

1. *makiþ*: TP, *made*.
3. *lent*: TP, *sent*.
12. *þe naylis*: TP, *þi nailes*. HP, *han al to*. T, *ben al to*.
14. *it haþ*: TP, *loue haþ*.
15. HP, *is bent*. T, *is blent*.
23. *clefte*: P, *he left*. T, *he yef*.
29. *cristis herte*: PT, *cristes* (*herte* omitted).
34. *of day þe nyȝt*: P, *day of nyȝt*. T, *day of þe nyȝt*.
37. *So Inliche*: P, *So moche*. T, *so muchel*.
38. *witiþ wel*: PT, *weteþ ful wel*.
40. HT, *is maad*. P, *haþ made*.
43. *schulde*: PT, *schal*. *trewe al tyme*: PT, *trewe & fin*.
44. *make it fyn*: PT, *make fin*.

The readings of *H* are manifestly better in almost all cases: in v. 34, where *PT* reverse the sense, the reading of *H* seems an allusion to the darkness from the sixth to the ninth hour, and is further confirmed by v. 35, with which the reading of *PT* is hardly consistent. The occurrence (*tym*: *fyn*) of assonance in place of rime finds a parallel in vv. 27–30.

91. *Ihesu that hast me dere I-boght.*

The text of this poem (complete or fragmentary) is preserved in ten MSS., Bodleian S.C. 2604 (*B*), 3657 (*M*), 29110 (*A*), in Pepys 2125 (vv. 1–70) (*P*), in Sloane 963 (vv. 87 to end) (*S*), in B.M. Addit. 39574 (*W*), in Lambeth 559 (vv. 1–12), in Gurney MS. (*G*), and in Longleat MSS. 29 (*L*) and 30 (*X*).

This poem has been printed by Dr. Charlotte D'Evelyn (*Medit. on Life and Passion*, EETS., Or. Ser. 158, pp. 60–4) from *A* with collations from *B* and *M*.

L and *M* show such special agreements in their readings that the relationship between these two MSS. must have been particularly close. *S* offers a notably good text, but unfortunately through the cutting out of a leaf from this MS. vv. 1–86 have been lost.

7. *LM, naill*: *ABGPWX, nailis.*

14. *LM, fel & foo*: *ABGPW, fel a foo.*

34. *LM, nayll*: *ABGPWX, naylis.*

42. *LM, to swete*: *ABGPWX, to wepe.*

94. Immediately following this verse *S* inserts six unique lines paraphrasing the *O vos omnes*, etc.

> Ihesu þat seydest on þe crosse hanggynge
> To all þat were þat wey passynge
> O all ȝe þat passe be the wey
> Abyde and here what I sey
> By-holde and se if sorwe & pyne
> Be any lyk vn-to myne.

105. *ALM, Ihū let*: *BGSWX, omit Ihū.*

107. *AGLM, for to weep*: *BSWX, for the to wepe.*

109. *LM, let love now*: *ABSWX, lete now love*: *G, Lat now þy love.*

131. *LMX, dwelling*: *ABGSW, a dwellinge.*

137. *LM, Ihū þat art so corteysly*: *ABGSW, Ihū þat grete cortesye*: *X, Ihū for þat grete curtesye.*

146. *LM, And*: *AGSWX, And ȝitte*: *B, ȝit.*

148. *L, þus þe*: *ABGMSWX, þus to þe.*

For the figure of inscribing the details of the Passion in the heart cf. *Lib. Meditationum* (*Patrol. Lat.* xl, col. 931 ff.): 'Scribe digito tuo in pectore meo dulcem memoriam tui melliflui nominis nulla unquam oblivione delendam. Scribe in tabulis cordis mei voluntatem tuam et iustificationes tuas: ut te immensae dulcedinis Dominum et praecepta tua semper et ubique habeam prae oculis meis', etc.

For the figure of the 'love arrows' (vv. 109–12) cf. col. 935 'Tu sagitta electa, et gladius acutissimus, qui durum scutum humani cordis penetrare tua potentia vales, confige cor meum iaculo tui amoris', etc.

93. *An Orison to the Trinity.*

Besides the text here printed from B.M. Addit. 37787 (*A*), this orison is preserved in the Vernon MS. (*V*) (printed by Horstmann, *Min. Poems Vern. MS.*, EETS., pp. 16–19, and by Patterson, *Mid. Eng. Penit. Lyric*, pp. 82–5) and in Thornton MS. (*T*) (printed *Relig. Pieces* EETS., rev. ed., pp. 83–6, and Horstmann, *Richard Rolle*, i. 365–6). *A* has connexions with Worcestershire: on ff. 182 v., 183 r. there is inscribed a statement to the effect that the book belonged to one John Norþewode, and that he entered on a novitiate at Bordesley on S. Augustine's day [26 May] 1386.

A and *V*, being southerly in dialect, agree in most readings, against *T*, which is northerly. *A* in several places shows more correct readings than *V* (e.g. in v. 12 'lare' not 'lawe', in v. 25 'þat for me' instead of 'for me', and in v. 81 'þulke' instead of 'ille'), and accordingly is not to be regarded as derived from *V*.

The poem was originally composed in the northern dialect, as is shown, for example, by the concluding stanza. In *T* the alternate lines present the rimes *taste*: *chaste*: *maste*: *Gaste*. In *V* these are altered to *wost*: *chost*: *most*: *gost*: and in *A* they appear as *wost*: *host*: *most*: *gost*. Evidently v. 100 presented difficulties to the reviser which forced him to such expedients as 'maiden chost' and 'maydenes host'.

94. *A Prayer to Jesus.*

Printed by W. H. Hulme, *Harrowing of Hell*, EETS., p. xxxviii. This same prayer occurs also in the Vernon MS. (*Min. Poems Vern. MS.*, pp. 48, 49), but stanzas 1–3 are here transposed to follow stanza 8. The arrangement in the Stonyhurst MS. beginning with the personal petitions seems on the whole preferable to that of the Vernon MS.

This hymn of eight stanzas was expanded into twelve (or fourteen) stanzas by Richard de Caistre and in this form circulated widely (see Rev. D. Harford, *Norfolk and Norwich Arch. Soc. Proceedings*, xvii. 221–44).

95. *Mercy Passes All Things.*

Printed from this MS. by Varnhagen (*Anglia*, vii (2). 282–7); also in *Min. Poems Vern. MS.*, pp. 658–63. Occurs also in B.M. Addit. 22283 (*S*), fol. 128ᵇ (printed by Furnivall, *Early Eng. Poems*, pp. 118–24) and B.M. Addit. 31042 (*A*), fol. 123ᵇ (printed by Brunner, *Archiv*, cxxxii. 323–7).

26. *Mony a wyse*: *A*, *One many a wyse*.

35. *A*, *Es none so priste for us dare praye*.

37. *sle*: *A* reads *fleme*, which better represents the Scriptural basis; cf. also vv. 103, 104, which carry out the thought of banishment rather than death as the punishment of sinners.

54. *furst*: the reading of *A* is *þurst*.

63. *wete*: *A* reads *wyde*, which is the adjective one expects.

76–79. These four lines are omitted in *S*.

79. *and boune*: the emendation is supported by *& bownn* in *A*. Corruption might have proceeded from some such form of text as *ā boūe* (*ā* for *an*, as a form of *and*).

80–2. These lines recall the folk-tale of 'The Grateful Dead', which has been traced through mediæval literature by Professor G. H. Gerould (*Pubs. Folk-Lore Soc.*, lx, 1908).

88. *tresoun*: *A* reads *to resone*.

121. The reading of *V*, *To god and mon weore holden meste*, is certainly corrupt. The reading of *S* is preferable: *To god a man were holden meste.* In *A*, vv. 121, 122 read:

> To God are we halden moste
> To loue hym, and his wrethe ethechewe.

124. *A* reads *Ne lesse dose þat hym es dewe*.

133–140. These lines show the influence of the Twelve Abuses of the Age, concerning which cf. C. Brown, *Herrig's Archiv*, cxxvii. 72 ff.

136. *waxen*: *A* reads, *ledde by*, which has the advantage of alliteration.

183. *or nouȝt*: *A*, *or Righte* (preferable in meaning and correct in rime).

96. *Deo Gracias I.*

Printed from this MS. by Varnhagen (*Anglia*, vii (2). 287–9); also in *Min. Poems Vern. MS.*, pp. 664–6. Occurs also in B.M. Addit. 22283, fol. 129ᵃ (printed by Furnivall, *Early Eng. Poems*, pp. 124–6), and in a Northern version in Advocates MS. 19. 3. 1, fol. 93

(printed by Turnbull, *Visions of Tundale*, &c., pp. 161–3). The text in the Advocates MS. lacks stanzas 4 and 5.

53. *langour*: Adv., *angur*.
54. *plesaunse*: Adv., *dysplesaunce*.
70. *vertues*: Adv., *wittes*.

97. *Against my Will I take my Leave.*

Printed from this MS. by Varnhagen (*Anglia*, vii (2). 289–91); also in *Min. Poems Vern. MS.*, pp. 666–8. Occurs also in B.M. Addit. 22283, fol. 129ᵃ (collated by Varnhagen).

98. *Deus Caritas Est.*

Printed from this MS. by Varnhagen (*Anglia*, vii (2). 291–2); also in *Min. Poems Vern. MS.*, pp. 668–70. Occurs also in B.M. Addit. 22283, fol. 129ᵇ (printed by Furnivall, *Early Eng. Poems*, pp. 127–8). The Latin phrases in the first four stanzas stand in the same sequence in 1 *John* iii. 16. On the other hand, those in stanzas 5 and 6 are not scriptural, but are probably taken from the liturgy.

99. *Deo Gracias II.*

Printed from this MS. by Varnhagen (*Anglia*, vii (2). 293–4); also in *Min. Poems Vern. MS.*, pp. 670–1. Occurs also in B.M. Addit. 22283, fol. 129ᵃ (printed by Furnivall, *Early Eng. Poems*, pp. 128–30).

100. *Each Man ought Himself to Know.*

Printed from this MS. by Varnhagen (*Anglia*, vii (2). 294–7); also in *Min. Poems Vern. MS.*, pp. 672–5. Occurs also in B.M. Addit. 22283, fol. 129ᵇ (printed by Furnivall, *Early Eng. Poems*, pp. 130–3).

The basis of these verses is the scriptural text: 'vt sciat vnusquisque vestrum vas suum possidere in sanctificatione & honore' [1 *Thess.* iv. 4]. Apparently the English versifier separated the first six words from their context.

31. *wast*: B.M. MS. reads *hast*.

101. *Think on Yesterday.*

Printed from this MS. by Varnhagen (*Anglia*, vii (2). 297–301 ff.); also in *Min. Poems Vern. MS.*, pp. 675–80. Occurs also in B.M. Addit. 22283, fol. 129ᵇ (printed by Furnivall, *Early Eng. Poems*, pp. 133–8).

95. *a-mong*: The reading of the B.M. MS.
176. *ȝor hele*: The reading of the B.M. MS.

102. *Keep well Christ's Commandments.*

Printed from this MS. by Furnivall (*Hymns to Virgin and Christ*, pp. 106–12); also in *Min. Poems Vern. MS.*, pp. 680–3. Occurs also in B.M. Addit. 22283, fol. 130ª, in Lambeth 853, p. 49 (*Hymns to Virgin and Christ*, pp. 107–13), in Pepys MS. 1584, Art. 9, and in Harley 78, fol. 86ª (begins and ends imperfectly).

It will be observed that according to the Vernon text the commandments against stealing and bearing false witness precede the command against adultery. In Lambeth and Harley, on the other hand, vv. 73–80 precede v. 57 so that the commandments stand in their proper order.

103. *Who says the Sooth, He shall be Shent.*

Printed from this MS. by Varnhagen (*Anglia*, vii (2). 301–4); also in *Min. Poems Vern. MS.*, pp. 683–6. Occurs also in B.M. Addit. 22283, fol. 130ª (collated by Varnhagen), and in Trinity Coll. Camb. MS. 1450, fol. 23ª. In this latter MS. the stanzas occur in the following order: 1, 2, 6, 5, 7, 8—stanzas 3 and 4 being omitted.

27. *Corlarie*: Properly *corolarie* (< Lat. *corollarium*). The 'o' of the interior syllable was probably elided for metrical reasons, the line being accented thus: Lét a lórd have hís Corlárie. The word is here employed in the unusual sense of 'sycophant', 'flatterer'.

29. *sacratarie*: Here used in the sense of a place rather than of a person. Cf. *Prompt. Parv.*: 'Secretary, place of privyte or cowncel: *secretarium*, ij : neut. 2.' The Latin word is so employed in one of the Hymns to the B.V.: 'Ave, secretarium exauditionis' (Dreves, *Analecta*, xxxiv. 158).

71. *gyle*: Trinity, *gyse*. This may be correct; cf. the character 'Newegyse' in the Moralities.

104. *Fy on a faint Friend!*

Printed from this MS. by Varnhagen (*Anglia*, vii (2). 304–6); also in *Min. Poems Vernon MS.*, pp. 686–8. Occurs also in B.M. Addit. 22283, fol. 130ᵇ (collated by Varnhagen).

4. *wylde*: Prof. Menner has pointed out (*Mod. Lang. Notes* lv (1940), p. 248) that the Simeon MS. reads *wynde*, which he would therefore adopt here as an emendation.

18–20. Possibly corrupt.

39. *bast*: the identity of this word is established by the existence of an alliterative phrase *bow or burst*; cf. *Dream of the Rood* 36, and *NED. burst* v, 1 c.

105. *Ever more Thank God of All.*

Text from MS. Ashmole 343, end of fourteenth century, hitherto unprinted. The text from the Vernon MS. (fol. 409ᵃ) has been printed by Varnhagen (*Anglia*, vii (2). 306–9) and is found in *Min. Poems Vern. MS.*, pp. 688–92. This piece occurs also in B.M. Addit. 22283, fol. 130ᵇ (collated by Varnhagen), in Cotton Calig. A. ii, fol. 68ᵇ (Halliwell, *Lydgate's Minor Poems*, Percy Soc., pp. 225–8), in Sloane MS. 2593, fol. 19ᵇ (T. Wright, *Songs and Carols*, Warton Club, pp. 56–9, and B. Fehr, *Archiv*, cix. 59–62), in the Garrett MS., Princeton University, fol. 47ᵃ (R. K. Root, *Eng. Stud.* xli, 374–6), and in Trinity Coll. Camb. MS. 1450, fol. 25ᵇ.

Comparison of the several MSS. enables us to distinguish three stages, at least, in the development of this lyric:

1. Of twelve stanzas: Cotton, Ashmole (stanzas 10, 11 lost), Garrett (stanza 12 lost).

2. Adds a new concluding stanza, but drops stanza 11 (acc. to Cotton numbering): Trinity Camb., Sloane (which has also lost stanza 8).

3. Seventeen stanzas: Vernon, B.M. Addit. 22283. These MSS. rearrange the poem by transferring stanza 2 to the end, and by inserting five new stanzas between stanzas 6 and 7. They agree with Trinity and Sloane in retaining the concluding stanza which first appears in those MSS.; they differ, on the other hand, by retaining also stanza 11 which Trinity and Sloane lack.

That the five new stanzas in the Vernon version (stanzas 6–10) represent an insertion is evident from the much better connexion when the line *ffor goddes loue so do we* follows directly after the example of Job.

61. *falsym*: = fals hym, i.e. prove false to Him (the *derwarte duk* of the next line). The Vernon MS. gives a widely different reading: *þenk God feyleþ þe neuer at neode.*

106. *This World fares as a Fantasy.*

Printed from this MS. by Varnhagen (*Anglia*, vii (2). 310–13); also in *Min. Poems Vern. MS.*, pp. 692–6. Occurs also in B.M. Addit. 22283, fol. 130ᵇ. On the content of the piece, see Fr. Gerald Sitwell, 'A Fourteenth-Century English poem on *Ecclesiastes*', *Dominican Studies*, iii (1950), 284–90. Ll. 13–17 are a reminiscence of *Eccl.* i. 5–7, ll. 25–6 of i. 4, and ll. 29–30 of i. 11.

11. *hertly*: The reading of the B.M. MS.

73. *witte*: The reading of the B.M. MS.
99. *not preue*: The reading of the B.M. MS.

107. *Merci God and graunt Merci.*

Printed from this MS. by Varnhagen (*Anglia*, vii (2). 313–15);
also in *Min. Poems Vern. MS.*, pp. 696–9, and Patterson, *Mid. Eng.
Penit. Lyr.*, pp. 54–7. Occurs also in B.M. Addit. 22283, fol. 131ᵃ,
and in Balliol MS. 354, fol. 145ᵃ (printed by Flügel, *Anglia*, xxvi.
160–2, and by Dyboski, EETS., Ex. Ser., ci. 54–7). The first twelve
lines only occur also in Advocates MS. 19. 3. 1, fol. 91ᵃ.
5. *ȝeorne*: The reading of the B.M. MS.

108. *Truth is Best.*

Printed from this MS. in *Min. Poems Vern. MS.*, pp. 699–701.
Occurs also in B.M. Addit. 22283, fol. 131ᵃ.

109. *Charity is no longer Cheer.*

Printed from this MS. in *Min. Poems Vern. MS.*, pp. 701–4.
Occurs also in B.M. Addit. 22283, fol. 131ᵇ.

110. *Of Women cometh this Worldes Weal.*

Printed from this MS. in *Min. Poems Vern. MS.*, pp. 704–8.
Occurs also in B.M. Addit. 22283, fol. 131ᵇ.

111. *A Song of Love to the Blessed Virgin.*

Printed from this MS. in *Min. Poems Vern. MS.*, pp. 708–11.
Occurs also in B.M. Addit. 22283, fol. 131ᵇ.
41, 42. Anacoluthon. The meaning is: 'Unless I may get the
goodly love of that sweet, worthy woman.'

112. *Maiden Mary and her Fleur-de-Lys.*

Printed from this MS. in *Min. Poems Vern. MS.* pp. 711–15.
Occurs also in B.M. Addit. 22283, fol. 132ᵃ.
11. *Maacer*: i.e. Aemilius Macer, the author of the hexameter poem
De Viribus Herbarum, which was regarded in the later Middle Ages
as an authoritative treatise on botanical science.
76. *buld*: if *blod* here is 'race, stock' (with preceding *þi* under-
stood), *buld* may mean instituted' (OE. *byld(ed)*). The editor's
original gloss was 'overthrown' (with an etymological reference to
ON. *bylta*, wrongly printed *bytta*).
90–4. A direct paraphrase of the scriptural account (*Acts* i. 10, 11).
94. *in werke*: 'in fact'; adv. phr. similar to 'indeed'.
111. Cf. Sermon of St. Bernard on the Passion: 'O mater mollis

ad fluendum [Migne, *Patr. Lat.* clxxxii, col. 1133: flendum] mollis ad dolendum' (Kribel's text, *Eng. Stud.* viii, 95).

113. *Verses on the Earthquake of 1382.*

Printed from this MS. by J. J. Conybeare, *Archæologia*, xviii. 26–8; also in *Min. Poems Vern. MS.*, pp. 719–21. Occurs also in B.M. Addit. 22283, fol. 132ᵇ (printed by T. Wright, *Polit. Poems and Songs*, Rolls Ser., i. 250–2), and in Peniarth MS. 395, Art. 4 (Nat. Lib. of Wales). The Peniarth MS. contains a unique extra stanza.

114. *Love Holy Church and its Priests.*

Printed from this MS. in *Min. Poems Vern. MS.*, pp. 721–3. Occurs also in B.M. Addit. 22283, fol. 132ᵇ. This piece is written from the point of view of a secular priest. The same point of view appears again in no. 117 (stanza 7), where confession to a friar instead of to the parish priest is discouraged.

37, 38. *reseyueþ . . . And takeþ*: Two verbs denoting the same action.

115. *Always try to Say the Best.*

Two versions of this piece exist: (1) seven stanzas in the Vernon MS. (fol. 411ᵇ) and B.M. Addit. 22283 (fol. 132ᵇ), printed in *Min. Poems Vern. MS.*, pp. 723–5; (2) ten stanzas preserved in Cotton Calig. A. ii, fol. 68ᵃ, and in the Garrett MS., Princeton Univ., fol. 45ᵃ (R. K. Root, *Eng. Stud.* xli, 371–4). Stanzas 2, 4, and 9 of the Cott.-Garrett version = stanzas 2, 3, and 5 of the Vernon version, but the remaining stanzas are wholly different. Clearly we have in this case a conscious refashioning of the poem in one or the other of these two texts. Unfortunately there is no sure means of determining which of the two was the original.

116. *Tarry not till To-morrow.*

Printed from this MS. in *Min. Poems Vern. MS.*, pp. 725–7. Occurs also in B.M. Addit. 22283, fol. 133ᵃ.

37–48. This has a distant but undeniable resemblance to *Ecclesiasticus* xii, 10–18: *Non credas inimico tuo in æternum* (cf. ll. 40–1); *et si humiliatus vadat curvus* (cf. l. 43); *non statuas illum penes te nec sedeat ad dexteram tuam, ne forte conversus in locum tuum . . .* (cf. ll. 37–40). Consequently l. 45 probably echoes *Eccles.* xii, 18 (cf. especially *commutabit vultum suum*).

45. *Skelk* 81. 24, since it must be referred to ON. *skelkja* 'to mock' (there being no other known word of corresponding form),

gives further grounds for interpreting *skelpe* as a vb. formed on ON. *skelpa* 'wry face'; see 81. 24, note, and 37–48 above, note. The glosses on these and *scrope* in the original edition imply a series of risky assumptions (*skelk* a corruption of *skolk*; *scrope* a form of *scrape*, or a corruption of *screpe*; and *skelpe* a formally inexplicable adoption of L. *scalpere*). If the revised interpretations are correct, all three words are ἅπαξ λεγόμενα, and remarkable examples of Nse. influence.

117. *Make Amends!*

Printed from this MS. in *Min. Poems Vern. MS.*, pp. 727–30. Occurs also in B.M. Addit. 22283, fol. 133ᵃ, in Cotton Calig. A. ii, fol. 69ᵃ (printed by Halliwell, *Lydgate's Minor Poems*, Percy Soc., pp. 228–32), and in the Garrett MS., Princeton Univ., fol. 49ᵃ (printed by R. K. Root, *Eng. Stud.* xli, 376–9).

Though the number of stanzas is the same in all four MSS. they are somewhat differently arranged in Cotton-Garrett and in Vernon-Addit. 22283. The order of the stanzas in the Cotton and Garrett MS. is as follows (using the stanza numbers in Vernon for comparison): 1, 2, 3, 4, 5, 8, 9, 6, 7, 11, 10, 12. On the whole the order in Cotton-Garrett seems preferable. According to the Vernon order, stanza 7, coming between stanzas which warn of the imminence and uncertainty of death, makes a decided break in the thought.

3. *A boske of briddes*: Cott.-Garrett, *A blisse of briddes*.

9–16. In this stanza the rime-scheme changes from the normal *ababbcbc* to *ababcbcb*. The rimes in Cott.-Garrett, on the other hand, are: truli, gray, I, say, day, wake, fay, make—thus preserving the normal scheme.

89–96. In this stanza the rime-scheme is again altered and a fourth rime is introduced: *ababcdcd*. The rimes in Cott.-Garrett are: bore, tree, lore, be, fre, sake, se, make—thus preserving in this stanza also the normal rime-scheme.

118. *Suffer in Time and that is Best.*

Printed from this MS. in *Min. Poems Vern. MS.*, pp. 730–3. Occurs also in B.M. Addit. 22283, fol. 133ᵃ.

4. *meynt*: the emendation is based on the assumption that the word was at some stage in the transmission of the text written *meȳt*, and that the titulus was then overlooked.

37–44. This stanza lacks four lines of the normal twelve. The most likely place for the omission is between v. 37 and v. 38, where there seems to be a break in the construction.

74. *holde vp* '*oyl*': i.e. confirm the assertion of another person. Note the recurrence of this phrase in no. 120, v. 85.

119. *Mane nobiscum, Domine.*

Printed from this MS. in *Min. Poems Vern. MS.*, pp. 733-5, and by Patterson, *Mid. Eng. Penit. Lyr.*, pp. 125-8. Occurs also in B.M. Addit. 22283, fol. 133ᵇ.

These verses appear to have been suggested by the moralization on this scriptural text in the pseudo-Bernardian homily printed in Migne, *Patrol. Lat.* clxxxiv, col. 977.

120. *But thou say Sooth thou shalt be Shent.*

This piece does not occur in the Vernon MS., but is found only in B.M. Addit. 22283. It has been printed in *Min. Poems Vern. MS.*, pp. 740-3.

66. Cf. 96. 75: 'What cause þou demest, loke hit be clere.'

121. *The Bird with Four Feathers.*

Printed from Douce MS. 322 (fol. 15ᵃ) by Kail, EETS., Orig. Ser., 124, pp. 143-9. Occurs also in the following (still unprinted) MSS.: Trinity Camb. 601, fol. 34ᵃ, and 1450, fol. 24ᵃ, Harley 1706, fol. 16ᵃ, Royal 18 A. x, fol. 119ᵇ, Stonyhurst College, xxiii, fol. 60ᵇ.

A much shortened version of this poem, in 8-line stanzas (*ababbcbc*), occurs in Harley 2380, fols. 72ᵇ-74ᵃ.

122. *A Prayer by the Five Joys.*

Printed from Camb. Univ. MS. Ff. 5. 48 (fol. 74ᵇ) in *Rel. Ant.* ii. 212-13, and from Harley 2382 (fol. 86ᵇ) by Patterson, *Mid. Eng. Penit. Lyr.*, pp. 139-41. Occurs in no less than thirty-five other MSS. still unprinted. The extensive circulation of this prayer to the B.V. was due in large part to its inclusion in the *Speculum Christiani*, a treatise of instruction which was widely popular.

123. *A Prayer to be delivered from the Deadly Sins.*

The wounds, it will be observed, are arranged in this text in chronological sequence. But it was possible to rearrange these stanzas according to the order of the Deadly Sins against which these petitions were uttered; this has actually been done in another text introduced later in this same MS. (Rawl. liturg. g. 2, fol. 62ᵃ), which begins with the line 'Ihesu for þi blodi heued' (stanza 4), and arranges the Sins in the following order: Pride, Envy, Covetyse, Sloth, Gluttony, Lechery, and Wrath. Clearly, however, the text printed from the Rawl. MS. gives the prayer according to its original arrangement. Lambeth MS. 559, fol. 33ᵇ also gives this prayer line for line as it stands in the Rawl. text. The arrangement in the Rawl. text is further confirmed by an Orison of the Wounds in Balliol MS. 316 A, fol. 108ᵃ, and Cotton Calig. A. ii, fol. 70ᵇ, which begins:

> Ihesu for the blode þou bleddest
> And in the firste tyme þou sheddest.

Though this Orison shows no verbal parallels to the Rawl. text, it is written, like the other, in 6-line stanzas, and is identical in content and order. Both, no doubt, are translated from a common original.

The influence of the Rawl. text appears also in certain variant versions. A text in St. John's Camb. 237, p. 33, agrees verbally with the Rawl. MS. except for the transposition of stanzas 6 and 7, but extends the prayer to the length of ninety lines by adding eight stanzas, in the same measure, on the Hours of the Cross (see notes on no. 34, above). An even more distorted version occurs in MS. Bodley 789, in which the third stanza has been dropped, but the number seven is preserved by devoting one stanza each to the right and left hand. In the second stanza the petition is against gluttony instead of wrath, but wrath is introduced in the stanza devoted to the right hand. Finally, by repeating at the beginning of each stanza the couplet,

> Ihesu for þi precious blood
> Þat þou schaddist for our good,

the number of lines in each is increased from six to eight. This version offers a notable example of elaborate tinkering—and its melancholy consequences.

124. *A Prayer for Three Boons.*

This piece occurs also in B.M. Addit. 37787 (early fifteenth century) at fol. 142ᵃ.

125. *The Knight of Christ.*

23. *bihet*: In the interest of both grammar and rime this should be emended to *bihiȝt*.

126. *Jesus Pleads with the Worldling.*

18–20. With this reference to the fashion of long and wide slits in clothing, one may compare the injunction of Pride in 'The

Mirror of the Periods of Man's Life' (*Hymns to Virgin and Christ*, p. 62):

> Loke þi pockettis passe þe lengist gise;
> Slatre þi clothis boþe schorte & side
> Passinge alle oþere mennis sise (vv. 130–2).

See also Dr. Furnivall's references in regard to this custom in his Preface, pp. viii–ix.

127. *Jesus appeals to Man by the Wounds.*

This piece occurs also in Camb. Univ. Ff. 2. 38, fol. 33[a], in Pepys MS. 1584, Art. 15, and in B.M. Addit. 37049, fol. 30. Stanzas 4 and 8 only are found in Sloane MS. 2275, fol. 245[a]. A late and somewhat degenerate text of these verses is preserved in Ashmole 61, fol. 150[b]; in this stanzas 2 and 6 have been transposed.

128. *The Blessed Virgin to her Son on the Cross.*

Occurs also in Worcester Cath. MS. F. 10, fol. 25 (printed by Floyer and Hamilton, *Cat. of MSS. in Libr. of Worcester Cath.*, p. 6).

I have not been able to find the Latin original of these lines among the works of Chrysostom, but it is to be recognized in the following passage from the Sermon on the Passion attributed (doubtfully) to St. Bernard:

O fili carissime, o benignissime nate, miserere matri tuae et suscipe preces eius! Desine nunc mihi esse durus, qui cunctis semper fuisti benignus! Suscipe matrem tuam in cruce, ut vivam tecum post mortem semper. . . .

O mater mollis ad fluendum [Migne: flendum] mollis ad dolendum, tu scis quia ad hoc veni et ad hoc de te carnem assumpsi ut per crucis patibulum saluarem genus humanum . . . desine flere et dolorem depone. . . . Congratulare mihi, quia nunc inueni ovem errantem quam tam longo tempore perdideram. . . .

Interim Iohannes, qui est nepos tuus, reputabitur tibi filius, curam habebit tui, etc.

(Text printed by Kribel, *Eng. Stud.* viii, 93–6; cf. also Migne, *Patrol. Lat.* clxxxii, col. 1136.)

129. *I have Set my Heart so High.*

These verses are accompanied in the MS. with the musical notes. For a facsimile reproduction see *Early Bodleian Music*, &c., ed. Sir John Stainer, ii. 51. Words only printed by Chambers and Sidgwick, *Early Eng. Lyr.*, p. 155.

130. *The Spring under a Thorn.*

These English lines occur in a Latin exemplum, 'de confessione', included in a miscellaneous collection of 'Exempla moraliter exposita'.

Cf. the somewhat similar song in Balliol MS. 354, printed by Dyboski, EETS., Ex. Ser., ci. 12.

131. *An Acrostic of the Angelic Salutation.*

Printed from this MS. by Heuser, *Anglia*, xxvii. 326–9. Occurs also in Cotton Cleop. B. vi, fol. 204ᵇ (printed by T. Wright, *Rel. Ant.* i. 22), and, in a variant text, in Emmanuel Coll. MS. 27, fol. 162ᵃ (col. 1).

132. *Quia Amore Langueo.*

It is singular that this, justly one of the most admired lyrics in Middle English, should have been printed hitherto only from Lambeth MS. 853, p. 4. (*Pol. Rel. and Love Poems*, EETS., pp. 177–9), especially as this MS. gives an inferior and much altered text. The following table exhibits the number and order of the stanzas in each of the six extant MSS. of this piece:

	1	2	3	4	5	6	7	8	9	10	11	12
Douce 322 (Text)	1	2	3	4	5	6	7	8	9	10	11	12
Harley 1706 (*H*)	1	2	3	4	5	6	7	8	9	10	11	12
Douce 78 (*D*)	1	2	3	4	5	6	[ ]	8	[ ]	10	11	12
Rawl. C. 86 (*R*)	1	2	3	4	5	6	7	8	9	10	11	[ ]
Ashmole 59 (*A*)	1	2	3	5	4	6	7	8	9	10	11	[ ]
Lambeth 853 (*L*)	1	2	3	5	4	[ ]	7	A	B			

Stanza 11, occurring separately, is also found in Rylands MS. 18932, fol. 138ᵃ.

In the above table the stanzas denoted by A B are peculiar to *L*. Douce 322 and Harley 1706 are sister manuscripts, and their readings show only the most trifling scribal variations.

1. *tabernacle*: *A*, *tourret*.
3. *crouned*: *A*, *comly*.
4. *R*, *I saw sittande high in a trone*. *L*, *Me þouȝte y siȝ sittinge in trone*.
11. *DR*, *y am his mediatrice & his modur*.
15. *we rewe*: *RA*, *me rew* (preferable reading).
18. *I loue, I loke*: *R*, *And busy I loke*.
21. *soule*: *R*, *sonne*.
23. *my son forgaue*: *RAL*, *I forgaue*.
31. *R*, *Shew to me love sonne I the pray*.

50. *R, My chylde is bet for þy trespas. L, His body was beten for þi trespase.*

53. *hys moder: R, þy moder.*

Stanza 7 has caused some confusion on account of the change in the person addressed. It seems best to regard the speech as far as the middle of line 4 as addressed to Man (following the readings of *R* or *L*) and the remainder of the stanza as the plea addressed to her Son in Man's behalf.

62. *DRA, Why schuldest þou fle? y loue þee, lo!* (preferable to the reading in the text).

63. *I helpe: A, þy helpe.*

70. *were me fro: A, were foo.*

95. *for þy wyfe: D, for þi modure.*

[Prof. Wrenn kindly points out that another copy of this piece, in MS. Anglais 41 (Supplément Français 819) of the Bibliothèque Nationale, has been published and discussed by S. Segawa, *Paris Version of 'Quia Amore Langueo'*, Kanazawa 1934. In the order of the first six stanzas it agrees with *L*; but in place of stanzas A and B in *L* it has four others, which all occur (in a different order) in H, A, and Douce 322.]

133. *Wretched Man, why art thou Proud?*

These lines occur in the treatise of popular instruction in morals, compiled by an English Franciscan, under the title *Fasciculus Morum*. Some twenty-nine MSS. of the *Fasciculus* survive. (See the account of this treatise by Mr. A. G. Little, *Studies in English Franciscan History*, Univ. of Manchester Hist. Series, xxix, 1917, pp. 139–57.)

These lines appear later in some of the MSS. of 'Erthe upon Erthe' (B-version), into which they have been incorporated as stanza 6 (cf. the texts of Lambeth 853, Laud Misc. 23, Cotton Titus A. xxvi, and Trin. Camb. B. 15. 39, printed by Miss Hilda Murray, EETS., Orig. Ser., 141).

134. *Cur Mundus Militat.*

A free translation of the celebrated Latin poem, variously ascribed, which begins with this phrase. For the Latin text see T. Wright, *Poems of W. Mapes*, Camd. Soc., p. 147, Daniel, *Thes. Hymn.* ii. 379, and Dreves, *Anal.* xxxiii. 267. See also the 'Rhythmus de Contemptu Mundi' in Migne, *Patrol. Lat.* clxxxiv, col. 1313. Migne's text differs from the others in arrangement, the last four stanzas, according to the usual order, being transferred to the beginning.

The English version has already been printed from Harley 1706, fol. 150ᵃ (Horstmann, *Richard Rolle*, ii. 374–5), and from Lambeth 853, p. 32 (Furnivall, *Hymns to Virgin and Christ*, pp. 86, 87; Wülker, *Alteng. Lesebuch*, ii. 14, 15). It occurs also in the following seven MSS., which are still unprinted: Laud Misc. 23, fol. 112ᵇ; Bodley 220, fol. 106ᵃ; Ashmole 59, fol. 83ᵃ; Ashmole 1524, fol. 11ᵃ (vv. 1–30 only); Camb. Univ. Mm. 4. 41, fol. 137; B.M. Addit. 37788, fol. 81ᵇ; Sir Israel Gollancz MS., fol. 13ᵃ.

4. *A¹, As a fresshe flowre in somer certayne.*

9. *wageringe*: BLd, *wauering.*

17–20. *A¹* changes the rimes of these lines.

19. *eloquence*: The reading of *B. A²Ld, eloquens.* Trin. Coll. MS., *eloquente.*

22. *A¹, Boþe spirituell and temporell þe lordes be lorne.*

26. *schadewe*: *A¹, swalowe.*

135. *Esto Memor Mortis.*

Printed from this MS. by Halliwell, *Rel. Ant.* i. 138–9. Occurs also in Trin. Camb. MS. 365, fol. 195, in Sloane MS. 1609, fol. 56ᵃ, and in Douce MS. 126, fol. 91ᵇ (a defective text, omitting vv. 5–6, 17–30, and ending with v. 34).

Heading. *accipit ante senes*: T, *mors rapit ante senes.* DS, *mors rapit atque senes.*

7. *þow schalte be*: ST, *and schal be.* D, *þat schalt be.*

23. *Set cum dampnatis*: The reading of *ST*, which restores the rime with *sceleratis.*

30. *transit*: ST, *transis* (the correct reading).

39. *Yif*: ST, *Lene.*

40. *þat we may see*: S, *that semly we se.* T, *þat semyly to se.*

Supplementary Note

2 B 5 *desewet*: the form with root-vowel *-e-* (not recorded in *NED.*, Mätzner, or Bradley-Stratmann) is shown to be authentic by another example in Horstmann, *Richard Rolle*, i. 157, l. 7. It suggests etymological reference to OE. *dwǣsian* 'be foolish' (with an unusual but not incredible metathesis of *w* in the ME. form). For the semantic pattern which this would imply, cf. L. *hebes* (which the adj. *dwǣs* is used to gloss in OE.) and the early uses of *blunt.*

GLOSSARY

The attempt has been made to include in the Glossary all words which occur in the Texts, and to record the variant spellings of each. It has been impossible, however, to cite more than a single occurrence of any form. The reference given is ordinarily to the earliest instance in which a given form appears.

Verbs are entered under the form of the infinitive, except in a few cases where the infinitive does not occur in the Texts. Where other forms than the infinitive are cited this fact is expressly indicated. The abbreviations of grammatical terms are too obvious to require explanation.

Proper names have not been included for the reason that these consist for the most part of scriptural names which are readily recognizable. Proper names which call for comment have been treated in the Notes.

a, *interj.*; *ah! O!* 13. 25.

a, *prep.* (OE on); *in, with* 4. 6; *at* 49. 25.

abakward, *adv.*; *backward* 17. 8.

abassched, *pp.*; *abashed* 118. 61.

abate, *vb.*; *diminish* 104. 13; *pp.* a-bated 106. 123.

abide, *vb.*; (1) *abide* 58. 20; *pr.* 3 *s.* abid 61. 1, abit 106. 77; *imp.* abyd 100. 44; *pl.* abidet 74. 2, abyde 46. 1. (2) *experience* 10. 8.

a-bouth, *pp.*; *paid for* 62. 1.

aboue, *adv.*; *above* 18. 8; abouen 57. 37.

a-brod, *adv.*; *abroad* 120. 28.

abul, *adj.*; *disposed* 113. 53.

abuten, *adv., prep.*; *about, around* 4. 8; abouten 72. 9, a-bute 30. 54, aboute 25. 16.

ac, *conj.*; *but* 32. 52; ak 49. 16.

a-cord, *sb.*; *accord* 113. 3.

acotoun, *sb.*; *a sleeveless tunic* 125. 18.

a-countes, *sb.*; *accounts, reckonings* 101. 66.

a-cros, *adv.*; *crossed* 126. 11.

adoun, *adv.*; *down* 34. 27.

adreynt, *pp.*; *drowned* 25. 23.

a-fert, *ppl. adj.*; *frightened* 101. 154.

affiaunce, *sb.*; *trust* 93. 93.

affy, *vb.*; *trust* 101. 32.

affray, *vb.*; *attack* 95. 33.

afray, *sb.*; *attack* 110. 4.

after, *prep., adv.*; *after* 7. 51; aftur 118. 57.

agan, *vb.*; *disappear, pass away*; *pr. pl.* agas 27. 5.

agast, *adj.*; *aghast, alarmed* 12. 2.

age, *sb.*; *old age* 121. 73.

a-ʒeyn, (1) *prep.*; *against* 6. 76; aʒein 97. 16, agene 132. 28. (2) *adv.*; *again, back* 108. 57; a-gayne 41. 8, ogayne 48. 56, againe 45. 8, aʒaine 115. 61.

aʒeynest, *prep.*; *against* 14. 7;

aȝeynes 93. 12, aȝens 32. 81, aȝenis 59. 9, aȝenus 125. 9, a-ȝenyus 105. 12.

aght, *sb.* (OE ǣht); *property, possessions* 29. 65.

aght, *sb.* (OE āht).—See *ouȝt.*

aght, *vb. pt.*—See *owe.*

agryse, *vb.*; *impers. be filled with horror* 110. 18.

ai, *adv.*—See *ay.*

ak, *conj.*—See *ac.*

al, *adj.*; *all* 3. 9; *pl.* alle 6. 42, halle 49. 7.

al, *adv.*; *wholly* 2 B. 2.

alanly, *adv.*; *only, solely* 77. 4.

ald, *adj.*—See *old.*

aleggance, *sb.* (OF alegeance); *relief* 46. 16.

alende, *vb.*; *take up one's abode* 20. 10.

aleyd, *pp.*; *subdued, tamed* 32. 64.

aliht, *vb.*; *alight, descend* 116. 10; *pt.* 2 s. alyhteṣt 21. 15.

aliues, *adv. phr.*; *alive* 28. 4.

alkine.—See *alles-kunnes.*

allas, *interj.*; *alas!* 49. 25; allasse 132. 52, hallas 39. 17.

alles-kunnes, *adj. phrase*; *of every sort* 111. 80; alkine 45. 12.

almesdede, *sb.*; *alms-deed* 127. 19.

almyhti, *adj.*; *almighty* 24. 3; almiht 118. 43, almith 56. 52.

al-one, *adj., adv.*; *alone* 20. 12; al . . . on 25. 9, al-on 95. 21, allon 81. 16, allane 48. 4.

aloute, *vb.*; *bow down, do homage* 131. 45. See also *loute.*

aloynt, *ppl. adj.*; *far removed, absent* 82. 41.

als, *adv.*; *as* 29. 82. See also *as.*

also, *adv.*; (1) *just as* 9. 7; alse 6. 84. (2) *also* 18. 14; alsua 29. 19, all-sa 48. 79.

alsone as, *adv. phrase*; *as soon as* 113. 37.

al-þaȝ, *conj.*; *although* 87. 19; al-þou 58. 29, al-þauȝ 95. 170, al-þauh 111. 11.

al-wei, *adv.*; *always* 101. 27; al-wey 115. 8, alway 115. 16, alwayse 82. 6.

al-wher, *adv.*; *everywhere, wherever* 8. 6.

amende, *vb.*; (1) *reform: trans.* 26. 43; *intr.* 122. 42. (2) *improve on:* ament 121. 87.

amendemens, *sb. pl.*; *amends* 124. 24.

amendis, *sb.*; *amends* 115. 53; amennys 105. 53.

amendynge, *vbl. sb.*; *mending, improvement* 96. 55.

among, (1) *prep. among* 17. 18; a-mang 45. 18, amonges 65. 18, amongus 57. 2. (2) *adv. besides* 8. 5; *from time to time* a-monge 101. 114.

amys, *adj., adv.*; *amiss* 32. 11; amis 96. 57.

an, *prep., adv.*; *on, in* 1 B. 4, 2 A. 2, 41. 5.

an, *indef. pron.*; *one* 26. 38; ane 31. 35.

an, *conj.*; *and* 1 B. 2, 4. 5, 33. 3. See also *and* and *ant.*

ancele, *sb.* (Lat. ancilla); *handmaid* 31. 19.

and, *conj.*; (1) *and* 1 A. 1. (2) *if* 101. 65, 110. 39. See also *an* and *ant.*

an-fald, *adj.*; *single* 29. 4.

anguisse, *sb.*; *anguish* 2 B. 12; anguis 65. 20.

an-honged, *pp.*; *hanged* 13. 4.

ani, *adj.*; *any* 27. 19; ony 94. 31. See also *eny.*

anly, *adv.*; *only* 83. 2.

a-non, *adv.*; *straightway* 10. 9.

anoynt, *vb.*; *anoint* 82. 43. See also *enoint.*

ansuere, *vb.*; *answer* 72. 1; *pt.* 1 s. ansuarede 5. 2; *pt.* 2 s.

answard 91. 23. See also
onsuere.

ant, *conj.*; *and* 1 A. 2. See also
an and *and*.

anuyȝed, *pp.*; *injured* 102. 69.
See also *nuyȝed*.

apeche, *vb.* (AN apechier);
bring charges against 103. 57.

apeired, *pp.*; *impaired* 99. 38.

apel, *sb.*; *appeal* 16. 36.

apere, *vb.*; *appear* 16. 43; apeere
112. 93; *pt.* 3 *s.* apered 132. 4.

aplighte, *adv.*; *truly, assuredly*
131. 32.

apon, *prep.*; *upon* 30. 27, 84.
86.

appel, *sb.*; *apple* 59. 10; apul 29.
32.

ar, *adv., conj.*; *ere, before* 100.
106; are 81. 10.

aray, *sb.*; *array* 101. 10.

aray, *vb.*; *prepare* 120. 90.

arere, *vb.*; *raise up* 24. 11.

arest, *sb.*; *cessation* 106. 18.

areste, *vb.*; *rest* 49. 8.

areyne, *vb.*; *call to account* 95.
86.

ariht, *adv.*; *aright* 101. 131;
aryht 7. 8.

a-ring, *adj.*; *continuous, un-
failing* 49. 12.

arli, *adv.* (see also *erliche*);
early 29. 17; arely 47. 18.

armed, *pp.*; *armed* 125. 20.

armes, *sb. pl.*; *arms* 1 B. 3;
arms 1 A. 3.

armes, *sb.*; *armour* 78. 7.

aromat, *sb.*; *spices* 34. 33.

arowes, *sb.*; *arrows* 91. 110.

aryse, *vb.*; *arise*; *pr.* 3 *s.* aryseþ
106. 14; *pt.* 3 *s.* aros 11. 46;
pp. aryse 92. 20.

as = *has* 39. 11.

as, *adv.* and *conj.* (see also *als*);
as, 26. 50; ase 6. 27, has 41.
32.

a-sayle—See *assail*.

a-sent—See *assent*.

aske, *vb.*; *ask* 78. 12; *pr.* 2 *s.*
axist 89. 28; *pr.* 3 *s.* askeþ
109. 71; *pt.* 1 *s.* asked 121.
23; *pt.* 2 *s.* askedest 95. 96.

a-slake, *vb.*; *slacken, abate* 117.
22.

asoyle, *vb.*; *absolve (imp.)* 6. 6.

a-spye, *vb.*; *espy* 100. 67.

assail, *vb.*; *assail* 48. 84; a-sayle
101. 159.

assay, *sb.*; (1) *assay, trial* 101.
166. (2) *policy* 118. 73.

assay, *vb.*; *try to prevail on* 102. 37.

asse, *sb.*; *ass* 75. 11.

assent, *sb.*; *accord* 102. 38;
compliance with a desire 110.
54.

assent, *vb.*; *consent* 102. 86.

a-state, *sb.*; *estate* 104. 10.

aste = *haste*.

a-strout, *adv.*; *sticking out* 126.
21.

astu = *as þu*.

aswounde, *part. adj.*; *feeble* 106.
126.

asyse, *sb.*; (1) *court of judgement*
23. 23; 82. 42. (2) *measure*
109. 58. (3) *social position*
104. 61; 118. 13.

at, *prep.*; (1) *at* 2 B. 11. (2) *to*
(with infin.) at lite 27. 53, at
hald 30. 43.

at (*vb.*).—See *ete*.

a-tame, *vb.*; *puncture* 120. 44.

a-tast, *vb.*; *make trial of* 104. 37.

ate = *at the* 34. 31.

atenede, *pp.*; *angered, vexed*
115. 13. See also *tenede*.

atent, *sb.*; *heed, attention* 105.
10; 115. 47.

ateyne, *vb.*; (1) *attain* 103. 2.
(2) *corrupt, infect* 95. 88.

at-gon, *vb.*; *disappear, depart*;
pr. 3 *s.* at-goht 6. 42.

a-þrist, *adj.*; *athirst* 55. 17.

atte = *at the* 32. 35.

a-tuo, *adv.*; *in two* 6. 49; a-to
69, heading; a-two 90. 32.

a-twinne, *adv.*; *apart* 110. 97.
auhte, *vb. pt.*—See **owe.**
aungel, *sb.*; *angel* 26. 6; angel
57. 57; ?*gen.* aungels 83. 33;
pl. aungles 7. 51, angles 37.
2, aungelle 132. 84; *gen.*
angeles 72. 14, aungeles 15. 9.
a(u)nterus, *adj.*; *daring in feats
of arms* 73. 3, 73. 5, 73. 7.
auter-ston, *sb.*; *altar-stone* 32.
35.
aue, *interj.*; *Ave* 17. 5.
a-uonge, *pp.*; *taken* 32. 46.
a-vys, *sb.*; *opinion, judgement*
112. 14; avise 109. 61.
a-vyse, *vb.*; *refl. consider* 108. 1.
aw, *vb.*—See **owe.**
awake, *vb.*; *become active* 98. 33.
away, *adv.*; *away* 6. 12; awey 6.
45, oway 27. 32, a-wei 95.
161, a-wai 44. 17.
awe, *sb.*; *awe, fear* 108. 37.
awelde, *vb.*; (1) *control* 101. 100.
(2) *subdue, overcome* 24. 18;
pt. 3. *s.* awalde 24. 8.
awen, *adj.*—See **owen.**
ay, *adv.*; *ever* 20. 2; ai 29. 82,
hay 50. 7.

bad, *adj.*; *bad* 115. 37.
bagge, *sb.*; *bag* 113. 79.
bak, *sb.*; *back* 79. 12, 104. 23;
bake 57. 72, bakke 135. 15.
bakbyte, *vb.*; *backbite* 102. 52.
balde, *adj.*—See **bolde.**
baldely, *adv.*; *boldly* 101. 178.
bale, *sb.*; *pain, misery* 6. 88;
pl. bales 56. 111; balus 129.
8.
ball, *sb.*; *ball* 105. 30.
ban, *sb.*; *bone* 26. 39; bane 84.
54. See also **bon.**
ban, *vb.*; *curse* 120. 43.
bandes, *sb. pl.*—See **bond.**
baner, *sb.*; *banner* 48. 83; *pl.*
baneres 13. 1.
bank, *sb.*; *bank* 95. 175.

baptym, *sb.*; *baptism* 48. 27.
baraine, *adj.*; *barren* 56. 42.
bare, *vb.*—See **beren.**
bare, *adj.*; *bare* 6. 87; baar 90. 9.
barefot, *adj.*; *barefoot* 95. 76.
barehed, *adj.*; *barehead* 95. 76.
barelych, *adv.*; *wholly, solely*
110. 102.
bargeyn, *sb.*; *bargain, affair* 103.
69.
barn, *sb.* (< OE bearn); *child*
112. 41; bern 112. 2.
barst, *vb.*—See **brest.**
barun, *sb.*; *baron* 59. 18.
bast, *vb.* (OE berstan); *break,
collapse, fail: inf.* 104. 39.
bat, *adj.*—See **bath.**
batail, *sb.*; *battle* 48. 82; batayle
101. 163.
bate, *sb.*; *strife* 115. 19.
bath, *adj.*; *both* 29. 7; bat 30. 11.
See also **bo, bopen.**
bayli, *sb.*; *administrative officer*
117. 82.
be, *vb.*—See **ben.**
be, *prep.*; *by* 56. 52; beo 101. 46.
See also **bi.**
bed, *sb.*; *bed, couch* 10. 25.
bed, *sb.*; *prayer* 26. 30; *pl.* boedes
14. 8.
bede, *sb.*; *?resting-place* 84. 11
(see Note).
bede, beede, *vb.*—See **beode.**
be-dene, *adv.*; *straightway* 45.
22; by-dene 9. 12, bi-deene
109. 98.
bedrede, *adj.*; *bed-ridden* 101.
57.
bed-yuer, *sb.*; *bedfellow* 6. 62.
beelde, *vb.*; *encourage, hearten*
(*pr. subj.*) 34. 3.
beem, *sb.*; *beam (of light), ray,
pillar* 7. 14; bem 15. 23.
beest, *adj. supl.*—See **best,** adj.
begge, *vb.*; *beg* 99. 11.
beggers, *sb.*; *beggars* 101. 101.
be-gyle, *vb.*; *beguile* 91. 104;
pt. 3 *s.* be-giled 111. 54; *pp.*

be-giled 121. 114, bigilid 134.
8, be-gilt 110. 25.

behalde, *vb.*; (1) *behold, see
(imp.)* 77. 5; be-hald 46. 7,
bi-hald 46. 13, beheld 51. 9;
pl. beholdet 74. 3; *pt.* 1 *s.*
beheld 58. 3; *pp.* be-holde
58. 22. (2) *signify* beholde
(*pr.* 1 *s.*) 132. 63.

belde, *sb.*; *help, comfort* 101.
104.

be-leue, *vb.*; *refrain* 111. 97.

belle, *vb.* (ON bæla); *burn* 110.
10.

bemette, *pp.* (?*cf.* OE metian);
destined 28. 11.

ben, *vb.*; *be* 3. 4; bene 11. 52,
boen 16. 40, beone 109. 103,
beo 95. 28, bi 96. 51; *pr.* 1 *s.*
am 6. 8, ame 56. 92, ham 105.
71; *pr.* 2 *s.* art 7. 3, ert 31.
23, ertow 28. 6, es 29. 3, is 44.
10; *pr.* 3 *s.* is 5. 6, ys 6. 99,
hys 32. 8, es 29. 12, biis 2 B.
3, beet 69. 14, bies (*shall be*)
50. 2, bese 81. 10, bees 84. 35;
pr. pl. beoð 2 B. 8, beth 4. 5,
bueþ 6. 60, beoþ 10. 49,
boeth 17. 10, ar 30. 33, aren
103. 17, er 27. 13; *pr. subj.*
be 6. 5, boe 14. 1, bee 34. 34,
beo 95. 113, buen 7. 58; be
55. 34; *pr. p.* beoing 100. 91;
pt. 1 *and* 3 *s.* was 1 A. 1, wes
6. 7, wasce 56. 66; *pt.* 2 *s.*
were 7. 15; *pt. pl.* weren 3.
11, were 6. 59, waren 1 B. 3,
weorₑn 98. 46, ware 48. 36,
war 30. 55, wor 41. 20, was
79. 24; *pt. subj.* were 6. 45,
ware 84. 19, war 27. 85, wor
39. 16, wore 59. 16, weor 111.
34, weore 95. 121, 112. 51;
pp. ben 93. 29, beon 93. 45,
benₑ 82. 5.

benche, *sb.*; *bench* 106. 6.

bende, *vb.*; *bend* 91. 109; *pr.* 3 *s.*
bendes 79. 12; *pr. pl.* bend-

eth (*refl.*) 20. 17; *pp.* bent 69.
20, (*arched*) 121. 85, ybent
121. 3.

bₑndes, *sb. pl.*; *bonds* 27. 104.
See also *bonde*.

bene, *sb.* (OE bēn); *prayer* 7.
42.

benignitₑ, *sb.*; *benignity* 93. 96.

bente, *sb.*; *field* 95. 4.

beode, *vb.*; (1) *offer* 104. 45; *pr.*
1 *s.* bede 47. 3. (2) *stretch
forth* (*the hand*) 119. 51.

beores, *sb. pl.*; *bears* 95. 5.

bere, *sb.*; *bier* 66. 9.

bere, *sb.*; *bearing* (*gestation*) 32.
76.

beren, *vb.*; (1) *bear, carry*: *pr.*
3 *s.* berþ 16. 50, beres 100.
104; *imp.* bere 105. 35; *pt.*
3 *s.* ber 10. 2, bar 34. 18,
bare 41. 21, bere 6. 58. (2)
bear (witness): bere 76. 23;
pr. 3 *s.* berth 21. 13; *pr. pl.*
bereþ 11. 36; *pp.* i-bore 34.
12. (3) bere þe floure, *be un-
equalled*: bere 108. 44; *pr.* 2 *s.*
berest 93. 58. (4) *give birth
to*: beren 56. 28; *pt.* 1 *s.* bare
56. 49; *pt.* 2 *s.* bare 41. 30,
bere 16. 2, beere 112. 2; *pt.*
3 *s.* ber 8. 14; *pp.* boren 21.
3, borun 93. 25, borne 86.
21, bore 11. 28, born 31. 65,
i-born 57. 1, ibor 28. 25, y-
boren 21. 26, y-bore 7. 15.

bern, *sb.*—See *barn*.

berne, *sb.* (OE beorn); *man,
hero* 7. 45.

bernes, *sb. pl.*; *barns, store-
houses* 23. 41.

beryd, *pp.*—See *biriȝed*.

beryyng, *vbl. sb.*—See *buriinge*.

best, *sb.*; *beast* 98. 3; *pl.* beestes
95. 6.

best, *adj., adv. supl.*; *best* 7. 45;
beste 6. 26, beest 121. 127.

be-stadde, *pp.* (ON staddr);
beset 91. 121.

be-swyke, *vb.*; *deceive*, *betray*
84. 13.

bet, *adj.*, *adv. comp.*; *better* 75.
22; bette 105. 23. See also
betere.

betacht, *vb. pt.*—See *bi-teche*.

be-take, *vb.*; (1) *commit*, *deliver*
67. 16; *pt.* 3 *s.* be-tok 72. 29;
pt. pl. betoke 91. 38. (2)
accept, *receive*: *pr. subj.* be
take 41. 15.

bete, *vb.* (OE bētan); *tr. amend*,
relieve 6. 71; *absol. reform*
beete 110. 7.

bete, *vb.* (OE bēatan); *beat* 101.
146; *pr.* 2 *s.* betest 15. 30;
pt. 1 *s.* boet 15. 29, boeth 15.
18; *pp.* bete 65. 21, bette
132. 50, i-bete 76. 3, i-bette
91. 66, i-biten 4. 3.

betere, *adj. adv. comp.*; *better*
10. 31; betre 62. 5, better
124. 41. See also *bet*.

be-þing, *vb.*—See *by-þenche*.

be-toknen, *vb.*; *signify*: *pr. pl.*
beo-tokenes 113. 60.

be-tyde, *vb.*; *betide* 86. 7.

betyng, *sb.*; *beating* 83. 35.

beute, *sb.*; *beauty* 101. 44;
bewte 121. 18, beaute 91. 99.

beuerech, *sb.*; *beverage* 62. 1;
beuerich 62. 4.

be-ware, *vb.*; *beware* 97. 29.

be-went, *pp.*—See *bi-wnde*.

be-weued, *pp.*; *enveloped* 68. 5;
byweued 23. 43.

be-ȝonde, *prep.*; *beyond* 121.
133.

bezauns, *sb. pl.*; *besants* 116.
13.

bi, *prep.*; (1) *concerning* 6. 83.
(2) *with* 49. 5. See also *be*.

bicome, *vb.*; *become* 11. 27; (*pt.*
2 *s.*) 24. 6; *pt.* 3 *s.* bi-com 34.
26, by-com 17. 15; *pt. pl.* be-
come 110. 101; *pp.* bi-comen
101. 22, bicome 11. 42, by-
come 32. 62.

bidd, *vb.*; *bid*, *pray* 29. 49;
bydde 33. 6; *pr.* 1 *s.* bidde 7.
35, byd 132. 17; *pr.* 3 *s.*
biddeþ 98. 11, bit 101. 58,
biddes 81. 29; *pr. pl.* biddeth
8. 3; *pt.* 3 *s.* bad 56. 8.

bide, *vb.*; (1) *intr. wait*, *remain*
132. 17; *imp.* bydeth 91.
heading. (2) *tr. experience*,
live to see 56. 127; bide 131.
88, ?byde 132. 32; ?*pr.* 2 *s.*
bist 22. 4; *pt.* 1 *s.* bood 121.
82; *pt.* 2 *s.* bood 89. 17.

bi-dropped, *pp.*; *be-dewed* 106.
22.

bidyng, *sb.*; *abode* 119. 26.

bi-falle, *vb.*; *befall* 97. 41.

bi-fore, *adv.*, *prep.*; *before* 26.
11; by-fore 11. 35, before 56.
42, bifor 28. 12, be-for 29.
77, be-forn 55. 7, biforn 125.
14, bi-foren 103. 65, bi-forun
93. 27.

bigge, *vb.*—See *byȝen*.

bi-ginne, *vb.*; *begin*: be-ginne
56. 86, begynne 87. 33, begyn
48. 19, beo-gynne 119. 71;
pr. 3 *s.* bigint 49. 5; *pr. pl.*
begyns 85. 19; *imp.* bigin
2 B. 11; *pt.* 2 *s.* began 91. 35;
pt. 3 *s.* be-gan 58. 34, bygan
88. 8, bi-gan 95. 172; *pp.*
bigonne 103. 87, bigunnen
112. 107.

biginnyng, *sb.*; *beginning* 8. 4.

bi-greiþ, *vb.*; *prepare*, *arrange*
116. 26.

bi-haten, *vb.*; *promise*: *pr.* 1 *s.*
beheete 111. 14; *pp.* bihet
125. 23, bi-heiht 107. 68.

bi-heden, *vb.*; *guard*, *protect*: *pt.*
1 *s.* bihedde 15. 8.

bi-heste, *sb.*; *promise* 104. 4.

bi-heue, *vb.*; *be necessary*: *pr.*
3 *s.* biheue⟨þ⟩ 106. 71.

bi-hinde, *adv.*; *behind* 45. 11;
be-hynde 103. 66.

bihouen, *vb.*; *behove*, *befit*: *pr.*

3 s. bihoues 48. 49, by-houeþ
93. 64.

bilde, vb.; build 121. 193; bylde
111. 87; pp. i-bildet 121. 195.

bi-leeue, sb.—See byleue.

biloued, pp.; beloved 134. 1.

binden, vb.; bind: pr. 3 s. bindet
60. 7, byndes 83. 22; imp.
bynd 91. 85; pp. bonden 48.
14, bondyn 79. 2, ibounde
55. 4, y-bounde 6. 88, y-
bonden 34. 13.

bi-neoþe, adv.; beneath 118. 42;
be-neth 120. 51.

bi-niman, vb.; take away: pt.
2 s. by-nome 32. 40; pp. bi-
nome 90. 28.

binne, sb.; manger 65. 14; bynne
57. 24.

birdyn, sb.—See burþen.

bi-reue, vb.; bereave, rob (inf.)
bi-raue 104. 28; pr. 3 s.
berewyt 105. 66; pp. by-
reued 23. 37; bereued 124. 20.

biriȝed, pp.; buried 70. 6; byrid
39. 20, beryd 79. 28, buried
101. 84, i-biriȝed 55. 27.

biseche, vb.; beseech (pr. 1 s.)
26. 42, byseche 16. 37, be-
seche 87. 23; pr. 2 s. bisext
131. 53; pr. pl. bisecheth 19.
11; imp. bysek 122. 43; pt.
1 s. besohte 8. 15; pp. be-
south 62. 3.

bi-seme, vb.; beseem, befit: pr.
3 s. bi-semes 117. 18.

bi-spet, pp.; covered with spittle
2 B. 4; be-spat 55. 10.

bi-sprad, pp.; covered 36. 1.

bisschop, sb.; bishop 114. 37.

bisy, vb.; busy (oneself) (imp.)
102. 29.

bisy, adj.; busy 101. 125; comp.
bisier 27. 103.

bisynessis, sb. pl.; activities, em-
ployments 134. 12.

bite, vb.; bite: pr. 3 s. bites 27.
20; pr. p. bytand 79. 2.

bi-teche, vb. (OE betǣcan);
commit, deliver (pr. 1 s.) 31.
10; pt. 3 s. betacht 28. 36.

bi-traye, vb.; betray 100. 68;
be-tray 101. 142.

bitter, adj.; bitter 22. 10; bytter
48. 3, bittyr 91. 71; comp.
biterere 131. 109.

bitterly, adv.; bitterly: bytterly
79. 2.

bi-twixe, prep.; between 34. 20;
be-twixen 55. 16, by-tuexte
32. 16.

bi-wnde, pp.; wound about, en-
circled 2 B. 3; be-went (con-
taminated with bi-wende) 58.
46.

bla, adj.—See blo.

blaberyng, pr. p.; babbling 102.
30.

blak, adj. (OE blāc); pale 65.
12.

blake, adj. (OE blæc); black 95.
50.

blame, sb.; crime, fault, sin 115.
60; pl. blames 98. 46.

blame, vb.; blame, accuse 95. 34;
pr. 3 s. blameþ 110. 9.

blast, sb.; blast 28. 27.

blaundise, sb.; flattery 103. 34.

ble, sb.; colour, complexion 10.
55.

blede, vb.; bleed 26. 27; bled 29.
80; pr. 3 s. bledet 2 B. 7, blet
51. 3, bledes 103. 26; pt. 2 s.
bleddest 123. 2; pp. bled 76.
12.

blenden, vb.; make blind: pt. 3 s.
blente 131. 91; pp. blent 67.
8.

blent, pp.; ?morally blinded, led
astray 102. 30.

bless, vb.; (1) bless: pr. 3 s.
blesseþ 120. 104; pr. pl.
blissen 55. 5; pp. blessed 13.
17, blesced 131. 65, blissed
69. 12. (2) refl. bles from
guard against, avoid 100. 59.

blesse, *sb.*—See *blysse*.

blessedly, *adv.*; *blessedly* 116. 60.

bleþely, *adv.*; *gladly* 56. 45.

bleyk, *adj.* (ON bleikr); *pale, wan* 65. 12; bleyc 1 A. 2.

bleynes, *sb. pl.*; *blotches, pustules* 99. 12.

blickien, *vb.*; *glisten*: *pr.* 3 *s.* blickied 2 B. 7.

blinne, *vb.*; *cease* 3. 15; blynne 93. 11, blin 50. 4, blyn 83. 14; *pr. subj.* blyn 47. 19.

blisce, *sb.*—See *blysse*.

blisfol, *adj.*; *blissful* 21. 20; blisful 63. 6, blesful 105. 7; *comp.* blisfullere 89. 6.

þliþe, *adj.*; *blithe, happy* 37. 3; blyþe 17 24.

blo, *adj*; *livid* 57. 75; bla 48. 65.

blod, *sb.*; *blood*; blode 7. 32, blood 91. 46;? *race, stock* 112. 76 (see Note).

blody, *adj.*; *bloody* 16. 52; blodi 123. 13.

blosmes, *sb. pl.*; *blossoms* 112. 15.

blowe, *vb.*; (1) *intr. be exhaled (for the last time)*: *pr.* 3 *s.* blouth 100. 26, *pp.* i-blowe 100. 106. (2) *tr. blow* 103. 67. (3) *utter*: *pp.* blowen 120. 30; ~ bost *brag* 106. 89.

blw, *adj.*; *blue* 89. 19.

blynd, *adj.*; *blind* 17. 10; blynde 101. 57, blyne 105. 17.

blynded, *pp.*; *become blind* 83. 41.

blysse, *sb.*; *bliss* 7. 1; blys 8. 23, blisse 7. 50, blis 10. 8, blesse 91. 99, blisce 131. 88.

blyssed, *ppl. adj.*; *blessed* 85. 4.

blyue, *adv.*; *quickly* 10. 48.,

bo, *vb.* (OE behōfian); *to be necessary*; *pr.* 3 *s.* bos 106. 51.

bo, *adj. pron.*; *both* 7. 30. See also *bath*, *boþen*.

bodword, *sb.*; *message* 31. 17.

body, *sb.*; *body* 1 A. 4; bodi 1 B. 4; *pl.* bodys 84. 61, bodies 101. 69.

boffetes, *sb. pl.*; *buffets* 30. 5.

bok, *sb.*; *book* 16. 54; boke 81. 29; *pl.* bokes 121. 138.

bolde, *adj.*; *bold* 6. 19; balde 84. 51

bon, *sb.*; *bone* 11. 46; bone 28. 8; *pl.* boones 90. 11. See also *ban*.

bonchef, *sb.*; *well-being* 96. 45.

bond, *sb.*; *bond* (vinculum) 17. 9; *pl.* bonde 7. 24, bondis 64. 1. bandes 45. 9, bandis 135. 12.

bone, *sb.* (ON bón); (1) *prayer* 6. 1; bon 29. 6. (2) *boon* 7. 44; *pl.* bones 124. 6.

borwe, *vb.*; (1) *ransom* 69. 5; (2) *save pp.* i-boruhe 2 A. 9. (3) *borrow* 125. 11.

bosck, *sb.*; *bush* 109. 34; bosche 32. 19, boske 117. 3.

boskeþ, *vb.*—See *buske*.

bost, *sb.*; *boast* 96. 69; see *blowe*.

bosum, *sb.*; *bosom* 112. 2; bosome 125. 44.

bot, *prep., conj.*—See *but*.

bote, *sb.*; (1) *remedy* 6. 26; (2) *relief* boote 101. 104.

boteles, *adj.*; *irremediable* 102. 42.

boþen, *adj. pron.*; *both* 60. 8; boþe 11. 22, boiþe 134. 22. See also *bo*, *bath*.

bouȝ, *sb.*; *bough* 104. 27; bouh 95. 175; *pl.* bowes 14. 7.

boun, *adj.*; *ready, prepared* 119. 47; bowne 84. 81, boune 95. 79.

boun, *ppl. adj.*; *constrained* 99. 11.

bounte, *sb.*; *bounty, goodness* 112. 81.

bour, *sb.*; *bower, chamber* 6. 19; *pl.* boures 10. 53, bowrs 81. 24, bowres 121. 195.

bow, *sb.*; *bow* (arcus) 91. 109.

bowen, *vb.*; *bow, incline* 6. 71; bouwen 20. 20; *pr. p.* bouwynde 104. 39.

boxumnesse, *sb.*; *obedience* 118. 18.

brade, *adv.*; *broadly, fully* 48. 83.

brag, *sb.*; *brag, boast* 100. 92.

bragge, *vb.*; *brag (pr subj.)* 116. 13.

braide, *pp.* (OE bregdan + ME braid *sb. trick*); *snared, caught* 118. 67. See *broyden pp.*

braunches, *sb.*; *branches* 112. 15.

brayd, *sb.*; *moment* 27. 45.

breche, *sb.*; *breach, fracture* 32. 74.

bred, *sb.*; *bread* 7. 59.

brede, *sb.* (OE brǣdu); on ~ *abroad* 120. 30.

brede, *sb.*; *(one belonging to) a breed, race* 83. 44.

breden, *vb.*; *breed*: *pp.* bred 83. 29, bredde 86. 35.

breke, *vb.*; *break* 79. 12; *pr. 2 s.* brekst 69, heading, brekist 90. 32; *pr. 3 s.* brekeþ 6. 49; *pr. pl.* breken 95. 127; *subj. 3 s.* brek 104. 27; *pt. 3 s.* brak 37. 7.

brekyng, *vbl. sb.*; *contravening* 102. 96; *check* 131. 36.

breme, *adv.*; *fiercely, impetuously* 121. 43.

bremful, *adj*; *raging, dire* 120. 20.

brenne, *vb.*; *burn* 97. 27; bren 86. 19; *pr. p.* brennand 86. 36, byrnand 84. 26, brennynge 97. 44; *pp.* brent *kindled* 83. 27.

brere, *sb.*; *briar* 109. 22.

brest, *vb.*; *burst* 84. 81; *imp.* brest 64. 1; *pt. 3 s.* barst 90. 21. See also *bast.*

brest, *sb.*; *breast* 1 A. 1; breste 32. 66; *pl.* brestes 44. 4.

breth, *sb.*; *breath* 100. 26.

brewe, *vb.*; *brew* 103. 69; *pp.* browen 116. 24.

brewing, *sb.*; *brewing* 62. 2.

brid, *sb.*; *bird* 95. 9; bryd 121. 29; *gen.* briddes 95. 13; *pl.* briddes 117. 3, breddes 121. 7.

briht, *adj., adv.*—See *bryht.*

bringe, *vb.*; *bring* 11. 29; bringge 56. 6, brynge 115. 61; *pr. 3 s.* bringeþ 6. 97, brynkis 39. 15; *imp.* bring 7. 55, bryng 6. 87; *pt. 1 and 3 s.* brohte 11. 34, brouhte 15. 10, brout 57. 28, broute 32. 14; *pt. pl.* brouȝten 92. 17; *pp.* broth 63. 5, ybroht 6. 98.

briȝel, *adj.* (OE * brieþel); *frail* 53. 4.

broke, *vb.* (OE brūcan); *enjoy* 121. 208; *pr. 2 s.* broukest 116. 24; *imp.* 81. 28.

brokil, *adj.*; *brittle, frail* 134. 4.

brol, *sb.*; *child, offspring* 28. 10.

broþer, *sb.*; *brother* 16. 5; broder 16. 10.

browes, *sb. pl.*; *brows* 121. 85.

broyden, *pp.*; *?snatched off* 27. 45. See *braide pp.*

bryht, *adj., adv.*; *bright* 7. 41; bryȝt 26. 45, bryth 10. 55, brryht 20. 1, briht 11. 8; *comp.* bryhtore 7. 14.

bryhtnesse, *sb.*; *brightness, glory* 21. 5.

bufeten, *vb.*; *buffet*: *pr. 2 s.* bufetest 15. 26. ·

buggere, *vb.*; *buyer, redeemer* 19. 2.

buirde, *sb.*; *lady* 96. 29; buyrde 101. 41; *pl.* buirdes 101. 15, buyrdes 111. 10, buirdus 97. 1.

buld, *pp.* 112. 76: see note.

bunde, *?pp. a.* (ON búinn); *at hand* 19. 4.

bur, *vb.* (OE byrian); *ought,* *pt. 3 subj.* burd 48. 71, 73.

buried, *pp.*—See *biriʒed.*

buriinge, *vbl. sb.*; *burial* 114. 10; buriʒing 95. 82, beryyng 34. 31.

burth, *sb.*; *offspring, child* 112. 54.

burþen, *sb.*; *burden* 109. 99; birdyn 40. 7, byrthen 84. 49.

buske, *vb.*; (1) *tr. prepare, make ready pr.* 3 *s.* boskeþ 101. 20. (2) *intr. go* (*pr. pl.*) 97. 23.

but, *prep.*; (1) *without* 71. 2; boute 16. 1, bote 23. 10. (2) *except*: bute 2 B. 12, bote 9. 9.

but, *conj.*; (1) *except, unless*; bot 49. 28. (2) *but*; bute 5. 5, bot 91. 15.

but ʒif, *conj.*; *unless* 58. 12.

buye, *vb.*—See *byʒen.*

buylde, *vb.*; *dwell* 116. 36.

by, *vb.*—See *byʒen.*

by, *prep.* (see also *be, bi*); (1) *by* 7. 40. (2) *concerning* 6. 83.

bydde, *vb.*—See *bidd.*

byddyngs, *sb. pl.*; *commandments* 86. 17.

by-dene, *adv.*—See *be-dene.*

byʒen, *vb.*; *buy, redeem, pay for* 66. 12; by 84. 65, bigge 125. 72, biʒen 75. 24, buye 95. 50, byʒe 57. 68; *pt.* 1 *s.* bouthe 3. 2; *pt.* 2 *s.* bohtest 7. 31, bouhtest 13. 27, boutest 55. 6, bouʒtist 89. 11; *pt.* 3 *s.* bohte 10. 18, bowth 41. 26, bouhte 14. 1, buiʒt 34. 22; *pp.* boht 6. 100, bouth 22. 24, ibouʒt 34. 27, y-bouth 22. 20.

bygge, *adj.*; *strong, resolute* 84. 51; *supl.* biggest 108. 46.

by-glyde, *vb.* (OE biglīdan); *disappear, pass away* 10. 6.

by-gon, *pp.*; *clothed* ('amicta') 32. 68.

byleue, *sb.*; *belief* 20. 2; bi-leeue 106. 62, (*gen.*) byleues 22. 12.

bymene, *vb.* (OE bi-mǣnan); *complain* 126. 1.

byrnand, *pr. p.*—See *brenne.*

byrthen, *sb.*—See *burþen.*

bys, *sb.* (OF bysse); *fine linen* 91. 118.

bys, *adj.* (OF bis); *dark grey* 112. 54.

byseche, *vb.*—See *biseche.*

bysoeth, *vb.* (OE bisēon); *provide* (*imp. pl.*) 23, heading.

by-spreynd, *pp.*; *besprinkled* 25. 8.

by-ssad, *pp.*; *drenched* 36. 2.

by-swonge, *pp.*; *bescourged* 125. 53.

by-þenche, *vb.*; *consider*; *imp.* by-þench 23. 22, be-þing 70. 1; *refl.* by-þenche 25. 20, bi-þenke 93. 57.

cacchen, *vb.*; (1) *catch* 101. 126. (2) *chase pt.* 3 *s.* caught 121. 155. See also *kecchen.*

calde, *adj.* and *sb.* (see also *cold*); *cold* 84. 82, 77. 21.

calenge, *sb.*; *claim* 32. 22.

calle, *vb.*; *call* 6. 82; cal 91. 14; *pr.* 1 *s.* calle 8. 8, call 29. 2; *pr.* 3 *s.* calleþ 6. 16; *pr. pl.* kalle 21. 8; *imp.* call 47. 21; *pt.* 2 *s.* caldest 91. 12; *pp.* called 132. 61, cald 48. 12, kald 17. 6.

caluari, *prop. name*; Calvary 57. 71.

can, *vb.* (= gan); *did* 91. 10.

can, con, *vb.*; (1) ?*know*: *pr.* 3 *s.* canne 49. 23. (2) *can, be able*: *pr.* 1 *s.* can 33. 6, con 95. 184. *pr.* 2 *s.* const 120. 47, constou (= const þou) 95. 59; *pr. pl.* cun 95. 154, conne 101. 4; *subj.* 2 *s.* con 100. 37; *pt.* 1 *s.* couþe 95. 170, cuþe 101. 121; *pt.* 3 *s.* couþe 95. 11, couth 48. 10. See also *kan.*

candel-liht, *sb.*; *candle-light* 101. 22.

cannes, *sb. pl.*; *cans* 12. 11.

cap, *sb.*; *cape* 121. 80.

care, *sb.*; *care* 6. 89. See also *kare*.

careful, *adj.*; *full of care, anxious* 6. 89.

caren, *vb.*; *be anxious* 65. 9; *pr. pl.* care 43. 3.

careyne, *sb.*; *dead body* 120. 56; *pl.* careyns 101. 70.

carpe, *vb.*; *speak, talk*: *pr.* 3 *s.* carpes 119. 21.

cas, *sb.*; (1) *turn of events* 113, 84. (2) *difficult situation* caas 119. 53.

cast, *sb.*; *a cast, throw* 29. 78.

cast, *vb.*; (1) *cast, throw* (*imp.*) 86. 5; *pp.* casten (*staked*) 29. 78, ycast 6. 89. (2) *reckon* 101. 66. (3) *consider, reflect, plan* 113. 39; *pr.* 3 *s.* casteþ 102. 7. (4) *arrange*: *pp.* caste 56. 140. (5) *cast down, overthrow* 31. 53. (6) *doff*: cast 27. 34. See also *kast* and *kest*.

castel, *sb.*; *castle* 29. 66; castell 121. 193.

cat, *sb.*; *cat* 108. 71.

catel, *sb.*; *chattels, possessions* 100. 23; katel 23. 17.

Catenas, Caithness 10. 34.

caudrun, *sb.*; *cauldron* 118. 40.

certes, *adv.*; *certainly* 51. 16; sertes 108. 5.

cese, *vb.*; *cease* 102. 26.

cese, *vb.*; *seize* 134. 30. See also *sese*.

chapman, *sb.*; *merchant* 36. 7.

charge, *sb.*; *charge, burden* 134. 40.

charged, *pp.*; *burdened* 79. 10.

charite, *sb.*; *charity* 16. 51.

chartre, *sb.*; *charter* 16. 23.

chase, *vb.*; *chase, persecute*: *imp.* chas 96. 78.

chast, *adj.*; *chaste* 41. 12; chaste 17. 20.

chaste, *sb.*; *obscure* 44. 30.

chaste, *vb.*; *restrain by discipline* 123. 5; *imp.* chast 123. 22.

chastite, *sb.*; *chastity* 114. 38.

chaumbre, *sb.*; *chamber* 20. 12; *pl.* chaumbres 113. 45.

chaunce, *sb.*; *turn of events* 119. 58.

chaungable, *adj.*; *changeable* 113. 52.

chaunge, *vb.*; *change* 84. 2; *pr.* 3 *s.* chawnges 85. 20.

chaunpyoun, *sb.*; *champion* 25. 6.

cheaste, *?adj.*; *chaste* 32. 64.

cheef, *adj.*; *chief* 112. 3; cheue *Supreme Being* 106. 66.

cheere, *adj.* (AN cher); (1) *prized, valued* 109. 8, 16, 24, 32, 40, 48, 72, 80, 88, 96, 104, 112. (2) *loving* 109. 56, 64.

chele, *sb.*; *cold* 110. 82.

chep, *adv.*; *cheaply* 120. 37.

chepyng, *sb.*; *market-place* 36. 7.

chere, *sb.*; *state of mind* 26. 13; cheere 106. 114.

cheries, *vb.*; *cheer, gladden* 106. 114.

chese, *vb.*; *choose* 113. 63; *pr.* 3 *s.* cheses 112. 16; *pr. pl.* cheoseþ 106. 66; *pt.* 1 *s.* ches 59. 9; *pt.* 2 *s.* ches 112. 3; *pt.* 3 *s.* 29. 32; *pp.* chosen 68. 18, ychose 32. 45, coren 131. 16, ycoren 21. 1, y-kore 13. 15.

cheue, *vb.* (OF chever); *?flourish*: *pr.* 3 *s.* cheues 108. 72.

cheuer, *vb.*; *shiver* 91. 35.

childe, *vb.*—See *schylde*.

chimeneys, *sb. pl.*; *chimneys* 113. 45.

chirche, *sb.* (see also *kirk*); *church* 96. 1; cherche 123. 35; *pl.* chirches 95. 135.

chirie-feire, *sb.*; fair for selling cherries 117. 85.

chouched, *pp.*; *couched, laid* 101. 70.

chyde, *vb.*; *chide* 118. 53.

chyld, *sb.*; *child* 17. 15; child 28. 1, childe 33. 2; *pl.* chyldren 14. 2.

chyldynge, *sb.*; *child-bearing* 32. 30.

chys, *adj.* (OE cīs); *fastidious, proud* 112. 126.

clad, *pp.*—See *clothe.*

clannes, *sb.*; *purity* 102. 33.

clansing *sb.*; *cleansing* 131. 95.

clay, *sb.*; *clay* 27. 76; clei 97. 54.

cleche, *sb.*; *clutch* 103. 59.

cleer, *adv.*; *radiantly* 112. 86.

clene, *adj., adv.*; *clean* 13. 7; *pure* cleen 135. 4.

clense, *vb.*; *cleanse*: *pr.* 3 *s.* clenses 84. 7; *imp.* clens 30. 130.

clepie, *vb.*; *call* (*pr.* 1 *s.*) 8. 8; clepe 124. 2; *pr. pl.* clepeþ 11. 38; *pt.* 2 *s.* clepedest 5. 1; *pp.* cleped 18. 3, i-cleped 98. 54, y-cleped 12. 7.

clere, *adj.*; (1) ?*just* 96. 75. (2) *radiant* 85. 22.

clergye, *sb.*; *clergy* 95. 157.

clerk, *sb.*; *clerk* 96. 5; *pl.* clerkes 96. 37.

cleth, *vb.*; *envelop* 120. 55.

cleue, *vb.* (OE clēofan); *cleave, split* 124. 76; *pt.* 3 *s.* clefte 90. 23; *pp.* clouen 68. 17.

cleue, *vb.* (OE clifian); *intr.* (1) *be lodged*: *pr. pl.* 97. 54. (2) *attach to*: *pr. subj.* 109. 19.

cliht, *pp.* (*inf.* clicche); *caught* 119. 53.

clipping, *sb.*; *embracing* 121. 95; *pl.* cleppinges 87. 13.

clomesyng, *sb.*; *numbness* (from cold) 95. 178.

clos, *sb.*; *a* (*place of*) *confinement* 24. 12; kepe in ~ *hold captive, in restraint* 103. 13, 115. 67.

cloth, *sb.*; *cloth, clothing* 75. 14; cloht 6. 44, cloþe 102. 43; *pl.* cloþes 91. 108.

clothe, *vb.*; *clothe* 122. 13; *pt. pl.* cloþeden 55. 12; *pp.* cloiþd 134. 18, clad 71. 3.

clottes, *sb. pl.*; *clods* 97. 36.

cloude, *sb.*; *cloud* 15. 23; *pl.* clouden 112. 86.

cloumben, *pp.*; *climbed* 112. 86.

clut, *sb.*; *clout, rag* 75. 14; *pl.* clutes 65. 14, cloutes 58. 46.

clynge, *vb.*; *decay* 97. 54.

cofres, *sb. pl.*; *coffers* 23. 39.

cold, *adj.* and *sb.*; 65. 15, 101. 78; colde 75. 3. See also *calde.*

cole, *sb.*; *coal* (*of fire*) 84. 13.

colour, *sb.*; *colour* 111. 95.

coloure, *sb.*; *embellish* 103. 16.

coluere, *sb.*; *dove* 32. 13.

comely, *adj., adv.*; 6. 82, 92. 16; oomeli 96. 17.

comen, *vb.*; *come* 22. 15; com 28. 16, cum 29. 52; *pr.* 1 *s.* come 36. 5, cum 56. 11; *pr.* 2 *s.* comest 14. 4, comes 50. 8; *pr.* 3 *s.* comeþ 9. 4; commyth 115. 23, comet 61. 4; *pr. pl.* commiþ 28. 9; *imp.* com 18. 1, cum 44. 1; *pt.* 1 *s.* kam 56. 110; *pt.* 2 *s.* come 20. 14, com 28. 18; *pt.* 3 *s.* com 12. 7, cam 11. 26; *pt. pl.* comen 14. 7, come 11. 39; *pp.* comun 57. 3, icommen 28. 6.

coming, *vbl. sb.*; *coming* 53. 1; comynge 21. 19.

company, *sb.*; *company* 78. 5; companye 122. 18. See also *cumpaignye.*

comparison, *sb.*; *comparison* 106. 54.

compli, *sb.*; *compline* 30. 123. See also *cumplin.*

comuynes, *sb.*; *commons* 113. 17.

con, *vb.*—See *can*.

conceyue, *vb.*; *conceive* 58. 42; *pp.* conceyued 56. 43.

concience, *sb.*; *conscience* 100. 97.

conforte, *vb.*; *comfort*; *pr.* 3 *s.* confortes 84. 15; *imp.* cumfort 93. 35, cumforte 93. 67.

conforth, *sb.*; *comfort* 30. 67; cumfort 112. 83.

confounde, *vb.*; *destroy* 103. 47.

conning, *adj.*; *wise, able* 56. 102.

connyng, *sb.*; *skill* 86. 28.

contrarien, *vb.*; *oppose*: *pp.* contraried 108. 28.

copable, *adj.*; *guilty* 87. 2.

copul, *vb.*; *couple, unite*: *pr.* 3 *s.* copuls 84. 12.

corage, *sb.*; *spirit, temper* 121. 86.

coren, *pp.*—See *chese*.

corlarie (properly *corolarie*), *sb.*; lit. *gift, present*; possibly *sycophant, flatterer* 103. 27 (see Note).

corn, *sb.*; *corn, grain* 116. 6.

corounen, *vb.*; *crown*: *pt.* 2 *s.* corounnedist 72. 32; *pt.* 3 *s.* corond 83. 36; *pp.* corond 79. 10, crouned 99. 41, crounet 116. 70, i-corouned 55. 13.

cors, *sb.*; *corpse* 97. 36.

corsed, *adj.*—See *cursede*.

corteis, *adj.*; *courteous* 95. 157; cortas 26. 5, curtayse 82. 3, curteis 113. 1, curtese 115. 15.

cortesi, *sb.*; *courtesy* 115. 39; cortesye 95. 161, curtesi 96. 13.

cosyn, *sb.*; *relative* 109. 14.

counsayl, *sb.*; (1) *counsel* 26. 25; counseil 93. 65; cownsel 81. 27. (2) *council* 103. 58.

counselour, *sb.*; *counsellor* 93. 64.

counseyle, *vb.*; *counsel* (*pr.* 1 *s.*)

114. 58; *pr.* 3 *s.* counseileþ 11. 21.

counte, *vb.*; *count, reckon* (*imp.*) 100. 43.

countures, *sb.*; *counters* 100. 38.

cours, *sb.*, *course* 95. 17.

cout, *adj.* (OE cūþ); *known, famous* 72. 26.

coupe, *vb.*—See *can*.

couayte, *vb.*; *covet* 83. 2; coueyte 102. 81.

couaytyng, *sb.*; *coveting, desire* 84. 23.

couenaunt, *sb.*; *covenant* 96. 83.

couer, *vb.*; *cover* (*with clothes*) 27. 34.

couetous, *adj.*; *covetous* 109. 74.

coueytise, *sb.*; *avarice* 6. 58; couetyse 87. 8.

craft, *sb.*; *craft, art, professional skill*, 106. 106; *pl.* craftes 112. 12.

craue, *vb.*; *beg* 95. 75.

creacions, *sb. pl.*; *created objects* 106. 35.

creatoure, *sb.*; *creator* 82. 27; creatowre 85. 1.

creature, *sb.*; *creature* 100. 3; creatur 100. 104.

crede, *sb.*; *creed* 105. 60.

credel, *sb.*; *cradle* 56. 14.

crepe, *vb.*; (1) *go, depart* 107. 47. (2) *enter pt.* 3 *s.* crepte 95. 43.

crie, *sb.*; *cry* 91. 31; cry 32. 21.

criȝe, *vb.*; *cry* 65. 11; cri 96. 10; *pr.* 1 *s.* crie 26. 30, cri 29. 2; *pr. pl.* crie 106. 58; *pr. p.* cryand 82. 11; *pt.* 3 *s.* criȝede 107. 5, cried 91. 26.

Crist, *Christ* 101. 105.

cristendom, *sb.*; *Christianity* 114. 4; cristendame 95. 101.

cristenynge, *sb.*; *christening* 114. 9.

cristesmasse, *sb.*; *Christmas* 11. 32.

cristne, *adj.*; *Christian* 100. 3.

crois, *sb.*; *cross* 34. 18; croys 34.

2, croyz 13. 21, crosce 79. 10,
crosse 40. 1, cros 30. 110.
crok, *sb.*; *artifice, guile* 16. 57.
croke, *vb.*; *grow bent* 101.98; *pp.*
croked 121. 170.
crommed, *pp.*; *crammed* 95.
113.
crostes, *sp. pl.*; *crusts* 121. 219.
croun, *sb.*—See *crune*.
crouned, *pp.*—See *corounen*.
crounynge, *sb.*; *crowning* 16.
26.
crucifiȝe, *vb.*; *crucify* 55. 11.
crune, *sb.*; *crown* 55. 26; croune
15. 31, croun 95. 45.
cry, *sb.*—See *crie*.
cryand, *pr. p.*—See *criȝe*.
cudde, *vb.*—See *kyþen*.
culle, *vb.*; *strike* 101. 146.
cum, *vb.*—See *come*.
cumbraunce, *sb.*; *difficulty,
temptation* 119. 63.
cumbred, *pp.*; *entangled* 113.
70.
cumfort, *vb.*—See *conforte*.
cumpaignye, *sb.*; *company* 118.
70; cumpayne 97. 12, cum-
paygnye 110. 62. See also
company.
cumplin, *sb.*; *compline* 55. 27.
See also *compli*.
cumpliȝed, *pp.* (OF complir);
fulfilled, accomplished 55. 29.
cunde, *adj.*—See *kinde, adj.* ·
cunreden, *sb.*; *kindred* 112. 44.
cursede, *ppl. adj.*; *cursed* 103.
87; corsed 120. 61.
curtayse, curteis,˙ curtese, *adj.*
—See *corteis*.
curtesi, *sb.*—See *cortesi*.
cusse, *sb.*; *kiss* 121. 97.
cuynde, *sb.* (OE cynd); *nature*
113. 50.

dale, *sb.*; *dale* 65. 13.
dame, *sb.*; *lady* 16. 13.
damnith, *pp.*—See *dampnen*.

dampnacioun, *sb.*; *damnation*
123. 6.
dampnen, *vb.*; *condemn*: *pt. pl.*
dampned 57. 66; *pp.* damp-
ned 59. 15, damnith 57. 52.
dar, *vb.*; *dare* (*pr.* 1 s.) 103. 37,
(*pr.* 3 s.) 95. 35; *pr. pl.* dor
104. 19; *pt.* 1 s. durst 115. 43,
durste 109. 5; *pt.* 3 s. dorste
108. 55.
dare, *vb.*; (1) ?*refrain, delay* 6.
86. (2) *be dismayed* 110. 93.
(3) *lie helplessly* 29. 42.
daunce, *vb.*; *dance*: *pr.* 2 s.
dauncest 126. 12.
daunger, *sb.*; *danger* 104. 43.
dauy, *prop. name*; *David* 32.
26; *gen.* Davidþes 14. 3.
dawen, *vb.* (OE dagian); *dawn*
11. 44.
dawes, *sb.*—See *day*.
dawyng, *sb.* (OE dagung);
dawn 84. 94.
day, *sb.*; *day* 7. 6; dai 30. 22,
dey 87. 12; *gen.* dayes 11. 20;
pl. daiȝes 56. 65, dayȝes 56.
69, dayse 82. 8, dawes 28. 32.
day, *vb.*—See *deyȝen*.
day, *pron.*—See *þai*.
debonere, *adj.*; *gentle, kindly*
16. 17.
decend, *vb.*; *descend*: ?*pr.* 3 s.
decent 112. 60.
deceyue, *vb.*; *deceive* 58. 44; *pt.*
3 s. deseyued 121. 90; *pp.*
125. 29.
declare, *vb.*; *declare* 113. 62.
ded, *adj.*; *dead* 7. 58, 10. 6;
dede 31. 33, deed 90. 30.
ded, *sb.*—See *deth*.
dede, *sb.*; *deed* 6. 104; deede 95.
100; *pl.* deden 104. 60, dedes
10. 21, dedis 30. 62, dedus 93.
32.
dedlych, *adj.*; *mortal* 14. 6;
dedli 131. 118, dedely 86. 17.
deeme, *vb.*—See *demen*.
deemyng, *sb.*; *judging* 109. 71.

de-faas, *vb.*; *deface* 96. 70.

de-fame, *vb.*; *defame, slander* 115. 49. See also *diffame*.

defaute, *sb.*; (1) *fault* 103. 90. (2) *lack, want* (defaut) 91. 119.

defende, *vb.*; *defend, guard* ?73. 2; defend 48. 116; *imp. pl.* defendeþ 110. 71.

defense, *sb.*; *defence* 101. 150; defence 101. 162.

defoule, *vb.*; *befoul* 110. 17; *pr.* 3 *s.* defouleþ 110. 74; *pt.* 3 *s.* defoulet 91. 70.

de-grade, *vb.*; *humble, abase* 101. 11.

del, *sb.*; *whit, bit* 125. 21.

dele, *vb.*; (1) *deal* (with) 101. 5. (2) *divide, part*; *pt.* 1 *s.* delede 15. 20.

delful, *adj.*; *lamentable, wretched* 100. 33. See also *doolful*.

delite, *sb.*; *delight* 91. 124; delyte 85. 14.

delitfullere, *adj. comp.*; *more delightful* 89. 7.

delve, *vb.*; *delve, dig*: *pt.* 3 *s.* delf 81. 1.

delyce, *sb.*; *pleasure* 95. 141.

demen, *vb.*; (1) *pass judgement on* 22. 15; deme 20. 22; *pr.* 2 *s.* demest 96. 75. (2) *sentence*: *pp.* demed 83. 33, dempt 131. 54. (3) *conclude*: deeme 109. 70.

deor, *sb.*; *animals, deer* 95. 3.

departed, *pp.*; (1) *separated* 91. 86. (2) *distributed, allotted* 99. 13.

depe, *adj.*; *deep* 1 B. 2. See also *dop*.

depe, *adv.*; *deeply* 91. 41.

dere, *adj.*; *dear, precious* 26. 14; deore 95. 29, deere 111. 58.

dere, *adv.*; *dearly* 3. 2; deore 100. 5, doere 14. 1, duere 8. 18.

dere, *vb.*; *injure* 56. 106; *pr.* 3 *s.* derieþ 27. 15, deries 27. 65.

derely, *adv.*; *sumptuously* 92. 15.

dereworthly, *adj.*; *precious* 79. 17.

derewourþe, *adj.*; *precious* 22. 23; doerewourþe 22. 19, derwarte 105. 62.

derf, *adj.*; *bold* 29. 49.

derfnes, *sb.*; *tribulation* 117. 52.

dering, *sb.* (OE derung); *injury, malevolence* 44. 20.

derk, *adj.*; *foul* 98. 27.

derling, *sb.*; *darling* 60. 4; derlyng 79. 17, derlynge 32. 47.

derne, *adj.*; *secret, hidden* 23. 32.

desewen, *vb.* (OE dwǣsian *be foolish*); *grow dim*: *pr.* 3 *s.* desewet 2 B. 5.

despite, *sb. humiliation, mockery* 91. 69; dispyt 98. 54.

desyre, *sb.*; *desire*; 83. 9.

desyre, *vb.*; *desire*: *pt.* 2 *s.* desyredest 95. 74.

deth, *sb.*; *death* 3. 4; dethe 93. 87, det 67. 20, detȝ 55. 25, ded 26. 31, dede 81. 16, (gen.) deþes 6. 91.

dette, *sb.*; *debt* 95. 81.

deued, *pp.*; *made deaf* 23. 38.

deuel, *sb.*; *devil* 69. 23; deuyl 91. 74; *pl.* deueles 131. 47.

deuise, *sb.* (OF devis); *opinion, thought* 96. 36; deuys 111. 71.

deuocion, *sb.*; (1) *devotion* 91. 3. (2) *prayers* 119. 3.

deuoutli, *adv.*; *devoutly* 101. 6.

dey, *sb.*—See *day*.

deyȝen, *vb.*; *die* 65. 16; deyȝe 14. 9, deȝen 23. 2, deye 9. 10, deie 26. 4, die 134. 39, dye 101. 158; *pr.* 1 *s.* dy 77. 4; *pr.* 2 *s.* dyese 101. 140; *pr.* 3 *s.* deyȝet 67. 28, dyeþ 106. 49, dys 101. 87; *pr. subj.* day 95. 188; *imp.* day 34. 15 (see Note); *pt.* 2 *s.* deyedes 52. 2; *pt.* 3 *s.* diȝede 100. 52, dyed

100. 105; *pt. pl.* deyt 105.
43.

deying, *sb.*; *dying* 53. 5; deiynge
91. 89, deynge 91. 149.

deyne, *vb.*; *deign* 34. 5; digne
119. 12.

deynte, *sb.* (OF deinté); *fond-*
ness, pleasure 101. 5; deyn-
tee 121. 135.

diffade, *vb.*; *fade, perish* 101. 8.

diffame, *vb.*; *defame, slander*
120. 40. See also *defame*.

digne, *vb.*—See *deyne*.

dignyte, *sb.*; *high office* 114. 8.

dihten, *vb.*; *prepare, appoint*:
inf. dyȝth 120. 107; *pr.* 3 *s.*
diȝtes 27. 16; *imp.* diht 119.
34; *pt.* 3 *s.* dighte 131. 26,
dythte 23. 9; *pp.* diht 95. 29,
dight 45. 2, ydyht 6. 103,
ydiȝt 27. 49, i-dith 63. 3,
idyȝt 38. 9.

dim, *adj.*; *dim, obscure* 28. 27;
dym 98. 27.

dinge, *vb.*; *beat, strike*; *pr.* 3 *s.*
dinges 27. 89.

dintes, *sb. pl.*; *blows* 30. 57;
dyntes 79. 7. See also *dunt*.

diol, *sb.* (OF doel); *sorrow* 27. 2.

diolely, *adv.*; *dolefully* 27. 16.

dipt, *sb.* (ON dýpt); *depth* 112.
60.

disceiueable, *adj.*; *deceitfull* 134.
7.

discryue, *vb.*; *describe* 91. 60.

disese, *sb.*; *distress* 103. 7; dis-
seise 128. 8.

dismayed, *pp.*; *dismayed* 118.
62.

dispaire, *vb.*; *lose hope, despair*
47. 25.

dispise, *vb.*; *despise* 134. 32;
dispyce 132. 12; dispys 101.
143.

display, *vb.*; (1) *display*; dys-
play 120. 93; *pp.* displayed
118. 64. (2) *unfurl* dysplaid
48. 83.

disport, *sb.*; *entertainment* 97.
15.

dispyt, *sb.*—See *despite*.

disseuere, *vb.*; *part* 132. 91.

distres, *sb.*; *distress* 100. 52;
dystresse 120. 80.

distruyȝe, *vb.*; *destroy* 57. 55;
pp. distruiet 102. 71.

ditte, *vb.*; *shut* 118. 55; 117. 23.

diuinite, *sb.*; *theology* 106. 90.

dole, *sb.*; *one's portion of wealth*
116. 15.

dolefully, *adv.*; *pitifully* 79. 17.

doloure, *sb.*; *grief, mourning*
100. 89.

dome, *sb.*; *judgement* 30. 47;
doom 109. 54; *pl.* domus 93.
88.

domes-dai, *sb.*; *the day of judge-*
ment 29. 77; domes-day 98.
9, domes-daye 84. 35,
doomes-day 95. 30.

domes-mon, *sb.*; *judge* 16. 15.

don, *vb.*; (1) *do* 11. 9, doo 94. 8;
pr. 2 *s.* doist 90. 31, dostu
(= dost þou) 69 heading,
dose 47. 9; *pr.* 3 *s.* aot 70. 8,
doiþ 134. 4, dos 27. 52, dose
84. 57; *pr. pl.* don 56. 12; *pt.*
1 *s.* dede 58. 23, doede 15.
33; *pt.* 2 *s.* didest 89. 26,
dedest 72. 28; *pt.* 3 *s.* dide
100. 86, dede 57. 55, dude 10.
51; *pt. pl.* dude 98. 44, duden
95. 99; *pp.* do 15. 1, ido 28.
28, ydo 87. 3, y-don 6. 104.
(2) *put*: *pr.* 1 *s.* 102. 2; *imp.*
do 30. 112; *pt.* 3 *s.* dude 10.
51; *pp.* don 26. 18, done 77.
23, i-don 3. 7. (3) *make* 3. 15;
pt. 1 *s.* dede 121. 166.

doolful, *adj.*; *sorrowful* 94. 9.
See also *delful*.

dop, *adj.*; *deep* 1 A. 2. See also
depe.

dore, *sb.*; *door* 68. 1.

dote, *vb.*; *be weak-minded* 100.
79 (*pr. subj.*).

douhti, *adj.*; *doughty* 25. 4.

douhtynesse, *sb.*; *doughtiness* 25. 19.

doun, *adv.*; *down* 106. 56. See also *dun.*

dounward, *adv.*; ?*droopingly* 64. 6.

doute, *sb.*; *fear* 131. 47.

downe, *sb.*; *hill* 121. 181.

drau, *vb.*; *draw* 30. 72; *pr.* 1 *s.* draue 26. 31; *pr.* 3 *s.* draweþ 101. 17; *imp.* drauh 102. 35; *pt.* 1 *s.* drouȝ 96. 11; *pt.* 3 *s.* drou 66. 8, drowgh 121. 129; *pp.* drawen 91. 22, y-drawe 25. 23.

drede, *sb.*; *doubt* 26. 9.

drede, *vb.*; *fear* 16. 55; *pr.* 3 *s.* dredes 103. 35; *pr. pl.* dreden 120. 62; *imp.* dred 66. 13; *pt. pl.* dredde 100. 93, dradde 95. 130.

dredful, *adj.*; *fearsome* 6. 86.

dredinge, *vbl. sb.*; *dread* 12. 1.

dredles, *adj.*; *sure, without doubt* 102. 2.

dreem, *sb.*; *music, melody* 7. 16.

dregh, *adj.* (ON drjúgr); *long, tedious* 84. 12.

drerely, *adv.*; *sorrowfully* 79. 7.

dreri, *adj.*; *sorrowful* 8. 11.

dresse, *vb.*; *prepare* 120. 83, (*imp.*) 116. 15.

dreynte, *pt.* 3 *s.* (OE drencan); *drowned* 15. 21. Cf. *adreynt.*

driȝe, *adj.*; *dry* 65. 12; dreye 32. 28, druyȝe 106. 22.

driȝen, *vb.*; *suffer, endure* 65. 10; drye 129. 3; *pr. pl.* dreye 27. 2; *pt.* 1 *s.* drey 70. 7; *pt.* 2 *s.* (*wk.*) dreed 79. 7.

drihten, *sb.*; *Lord* 119. 34.

drink, *vb.*; (1) *drink* (*pr.* 1 *s.*) 62. 4; *pr.* 2 *s.* drincst 15. 28; *pt.* 1 *s.* dronk 15. 27.

driue, *vb.*; *drive*: *pt.* 3 *s.* drof 121. 156; *pp.* dreuen 39. 10, i-driue 123. 27.

2025.9

dronkenes, *sb.*; *drunkenness* 95. 140.

dropes, *sb. pl.*; *drops* 123. 7.

droppen, *vb.*; *drip*: *pr.* 3 *s.* droppet 64. 5.

droupe, *vb.*; *droop, sink down* 113. 22; *pr.* 3 *s.* drowepet 2 B. 6.

drury, *sb.*; *sweetheart* 32. 23.

duere, *adj.*—See *dere.*

duk, *sb.*; *dyke* 105. 62; duyk 114. 18, duke 134. 16.

dull, *sb.*; ?*palm of the hand*; *pl.* dulles 79. 7. Cf. NED doll *sb.²*

dun, *adv.*; *down* 28. 28. See also *doun.*

dunt, *sb.*; *stroke, blow* 23. 32. See also *dintes.*

dure, *vb.*; *hold out, endure* 108. 63.

duresse, *sb.*; *state of being oppressed* 118. 14.

durk, *vb.*; *lie in the dark, lurk* 29. 42.

dute, *vb.*; *fear* 29. 79.

duwe, *adj.*; *incumbent on* 95. 124.

dwellen, *vb.*; *dwell* 75. 28; duelle 9. 15; *pr.* 1 *s.* dwel 83. 21; *pr.* 2 *s.* dwelles ¯78. 9; *pr. p.* dwellyng 119. 3; *pt.* 3 *s.* dwelled 98. 45.

dwelling (duellingge), *sb.*; *dwelling* 68. 22.

dwyne, *vb.*; *languish, waste away* 83. 20.

dyche, *sb.*; *moat* 121. 194.

dyse, *sb.*; *dice* 95. 140.

dysseased, *pp.*; *distressed* 132. 52.

dyuelyn, *prop. name*; *Dublin* 10. 34.

eche, *adj.*; *each* 131. 80; euch 14. 6, oeuch 23. 7. See also *vch.*

X

edy, *adj.* (OE ēadig); *blessed* 17. 2.

eft, *adv.*; *afterwards* 23. 14.

efter, *prep.*; *after* 30. 1.

eggement, *sb.*; *incitement* 115. 12.

egginge, *sb.*; *instigation* 131. 38.

egle, *sb.*; *eagle* 121. 68.

ei, *sb.*; *eye* 30. 65; *pl.* eien 29. 68, eyen 23. 38, ene 83. 41. See also *eȝe* and *eyȝe.*

eke, *adv.*; *also* 7. 7; ek 16. 11.

elde, *sb.*; *old age* 6. 46; eld 29. 44.

elde, *vb.*; *grow old* 101. 98.

elde, *adj.*; *old* 11. 22. See also *old.*

eldren, *sb. pl.*; *elders* 28. 4; eldres 101. 46.

elle, *sb.* = *helle, q.v.*

elles, *adv.*; *else* 23. 27; ellis 135. 34.

eloquence, *sb.*; *eloquence* 134. 19.

emcristone, *sb. pl.*; *fellow-christians* 123. 11.

emperys, *sb.*; *empress* 111. 66.

empyre, *sb.*; *empire, kingdom* 87. 39.

enbrase, *vb.*; *embrace* 81. 34.

encenȝ, *sb.*; *incense* 11. 41.

enchesoun, *sb.*; *cause, occasion* 48. 75; *reason* enchesun 101. 26.

encrece, *vb.*; *increase* 106. 128; encres 119. 67.

ende, *sb.*; *end* 20. 9, 22. 4; eende 54. 3.

ende, *vb.*; *end*; *pr.* 3 s. endet 65. 30, endt 49. 4; *pp.* endid 90. 36.

ende-day, *sb.*; *ending-day, end* 12. 14.

ender-day, *sb.*; *recent day* 8. 10.

endlesse, *adj.*; *endless* 84. 90; hendles 49. 12, endelis 5. 5.

endouwe, *vb.*; *endow pt. pl.* endouwed 108. 53.

endure, *vb.*; *endure* 100. 74; endour 108. 45.

endyng, *sb.*; (1) *ending*; hendyng 49. 6, endinge 24. 7, endingge 55. 34. (2) *life's end* 7. 56.

ene, *sb. pl.*—See *ei.*

ene, *adv.* (OE æne); *once* 13. 8.

enemy, *sb.*; *enemy*; enymy 101. 153; *pl.* enemies 72. 33, enmys 84. 92.

engyn, *sb.*; *contrivance, craft* 7. 28.

enhaunce, *vb.*; *elevate* 134. 34.

enke, *sb.*; *ink* 16. 24.

en-nuye, *vb.*; *refl. become weary of* 101. 167.

enoint, *pp.*; *anointed* 55. 29. See also *anoynt.*

enqueste, *sb.*; *inquest* 91. 25.

ensaumple, *sb.*; *instance* 101. 155.

enseure, *vb.*; *assure* 101. 42.

enspyre, *vb.*; *inspire* 85. 9; enspire 100. 81.

entencioun, *sb.*; *intention, purpose* 106. 57.

entent, *sb.*; *will, desire, intent* 84. 22.

entere, *adv.*; *entirely* 109. 62.

enterliche, *adv.*; *entirely* 109. 91; enterly 109. 3.

entysement, *sb.*; *enticement* 110. 50.

enuye, *sb.*; *envy* 87. 5; enuyȝe 55. 12; enuy 107. 51.

envyous, *adj.*; *envious* 109. 79.

eny, *adj.* (OE ænig); *any* 10. 32; ey 21. 3, eni 26. 9. See also *ani.*

eorþe, *sb.*; *earth* 20. 18; erþe 26. 37, erth 77. 30, herþe 34. 26, herde 55. 22, oerþe 21. 17.

eorþe-quake, *sb.*; *earthquake* 113. 58.

eorþli, *adj.*; *earthly* 95. 69; eorþly 108. 6, erþly 132. 83, erthlich 12. 3.

er, *vb.* (*pr. pl.*)—See *ben.*

er, *conj.*; *before* 3. 13; *or* 48. 56.

erbe, *sb.*; *herb* 121. 157; *pl.*
  erbes 10. 33.
erber, *sb.*; *garden* 26. 29.
ere, *sb.*; *ear* 55. 9; *pl.* eren 23.
  38.
erer, *adv.*; *previously* 34. 26.
erliche, *adv.*; *early* 104. 12; her-
  liche 124. 28. See also *arli.*
ern, *vb.*; *procure* (*imp.*) 17. 12.
ern, *vb. pt.*—See *irnen.*
ernde, *sb.* (OE ǽrende); *peti-
  tion* 131. 76.
erndyng, *sb.*; *intercession* 7. 43.
erne-morwe, *sb.* (cf. OE (on)
  ærne mergen); *daybreak* 37.
  1.
errours, *sb. pl.*; *errors* 118. 62.
ert, *vb. pr.* 2 *s.*—See *ben.*
ert, *sb.*—See *herte.*
erþe, *sb.*—See *eorþe.*
erþly, *adj.*—See *eorþli.*
es, 3 *pers. pron. acc. pl.* them
  3. 12.
es, *vb. pr.* 2 *and* 3 *s.*—See *ben.*
eschewe, *vb.*; (1) *avoid* eschuwe
  95. 122, escheuwe 102. 42.
  (2) *shun* 120. 8.
ese, *sb.*; *ease* 103. 1.
est, *adj.*; *east* 28. 33; hest 105.
  28.
ester, *sb.*; *Easter* 11. 44; estre
  91. 153.
et, *pron.*—See *it* and *hit.*
ete, *vb.*; *eat* 121. 220; *pt.* 3 *s.* at
  125. 41; ete 28. 36.
euch, *adj.*—See *eche.*
eue, *prop. name*; *Eve* 28. 36;
  heue 41. 8; *gen.* eues 17. 8.
euel, *adj. and sb.*; *evil* 6. 46; *pl.*
  eueles 6. 25. See also *yuel.*
euele, *adv.*; *evilly* 87. 16; heuel
  68. 7. See also *yuele.*
euene, *sb.*; *evening* 126. 31.
evene, *sb.*; *heaven* 49. 8, 88. 19.
  See also *heuene.*
euene, *adj.*; (1) *equal* 58. 51.
  (2) *just* 95. 89.
euene, *adv.*; (1) *justly* 117. 81
  (euen). (2) *directly* 100. 95.

even-sang, *sb.*; *evensong* 79. 22;
  euesong 55. 23; *gen.* euen-
  sanges 30. 108.
euer, *adv.*; (1) *at any time* 6. 33.
  (2) *always* 6. 76; euere 26.
  28, 87. 19, eure 49. 9, heuer
  39. 8.
euer-vch, *adj.*; *every* 101. 39;
  eurich 131. 34, euereche 88.
  20, euerech 131. 7, eueri 100.
  64.
euerich-on, *pron.*; *every one*
  100. 43; euerychon 90. 39,
  euerechon 32. 29.
euermore, *adv.*; *evermore* 13.
  28; euermo 67. 36, eueremo
  75. 30, euermare 83. 48.
execucion, *sb.*; *execution* 95. 38.
ey, *adj.*—See *eny.*
eȝe, *sb.*; *eye* 7. 20; iȝe 134. 24,
  yȝe 89. 39; *pl.* eȝen 87. 11.
  See also *ei* and *eyȝe.*
eȝe-lid, *sb.*; *eye-lid* 109. 49.
eyȝe, *sb.*; *eye* 69, heading; eiȝe
  95. 62; *pl.* eyȝen 121. 86. See
  also *ei* and *eȝe.*
eyr, *sb.*; *air* 106. 39.
eysil, *sb.*; *vinegar* 55. 18; eysyl
  15. 16.

fa, *sb.*; *foe* 27. 14; *pl.* fas 27. 7,
  faes 48. 101. See also *fo.*
faas, *sb.*—See *face.*
fabel, *sb.*; *falsehood* 113. 55; *pl.*
  fables 103. 68.
face, *sb.*; *face* 30. 2; faas 99. 22.
fade, *vb.*; *fade, pass away* 101.
  43; *pr.* 3 *s.* fadeþ 104. 1.
fader, *sb.*; *father* 29. 1; fadur
  93. 1, fadyr 87. 22, uader 12.
  14; *gen. s.* fadris 59. 9, uader
  24. 16, uadres 21. 2, uaderes
  21. 5.
fail, *vb.*; *fail* 48. 86; *pr.* 3 *s.*

fayles 82. 16; *pr. subj.* faylle 105. 65; *imp.* fayle 51. 8.

fayle, *sb.*; fail 101. 157.

faine, *vb.*; *rejoice (pr. subj.)* 45. 24.

fair, *adj.*; *fair* I A. 2; feir 7. 54, faire I B. 2, feyre 2 B. 5, fayr 26. 20, vayr 13. 13; *comp.* fayrer 81. 14; *supl.* fayrest 26. 10.

faire, *adv.*; *fairly, pleasantly* 58. 20; vayre 25. 3; feyre 6. 44.

fairen, *vb.*; *appear fair, bloom*; *pr.* 3 *s.* fayret 49. 3.

fairhede, *sb.*; *beauty* 86. 28; fairehede 83. 45, fayrehede 81. 31.

falas, *sb.*; *fallacy, sophism* 81. 27.

falewen, *vb.*; *fade, grow pale* 10. 58; *pr.* I *s.* falewe 6. 90; *pr.* 3 *s.* faleweþ 9. 12, faluet 2 B. 5, falwyt 49. 3.

fallen, *vb.*; (1) *fall* 6. 102; falle 26. 32; fal 31. 28, ffall 29. 21. (2) *happen (to be)* 109. 68; *pr.* 3 *s.* fallet 56. 63, falles 77. 10, fals 86. 11; *pr. subj.* fall 29. 22; *imp.* fal 51. 21; *pt. pl.* fel 31. 32; *pp.* fallen 29. 60, falle 67. 21, fal 101. 99, i-falle 53. 4, yfalle 6. 39.

fals, *adj.*; *false* 27. 10.

falsed, *sb.*; *falseness* 113. 53.

falsedam, *sb.*; *dishonesty* 39. 6.

falsen, *vb.*; *betray, prove false to*; falsym (= fals hym) 105. 61.

falsschip, *sb.*; *deceitfulness* 27. 18.

fame, *sb.*; *slander* 115. 58.

fanchyt, *vb. pt.*—See *vanys.*

fande, *vb.*; *try, endeavour* 86. 3. See also *fonde.*

fanding, *sb.*; *temptation* 30. 31; fandyng 85. 27. See also *fonding.*

fang, *vb.*—See *finge.*

fantam, *sb.*; *illusion* 43. 1; fantum 101. 28.

fantasy, *sb.*; *illusion* 101. 30; fantasye 106. 24; *pl.* fantasyse 101. 21.

fare, *sb.*; *experience* 106. 109.

fare, *vb.*; (1) *journey, go* 23. 30. (2) *vanish* uare 23. 18; *pp.* faren 6. 32. (3) *turn out pr.* 3 *s.* fares 116. 28. (4) *take place pr.* 3 *s.* fareþ 100. 30. (5) *be concerned with* 43. 1.

fasoun, *sb.*; *nature* 95. 42.

fast, faste, *adj.*; *firm, fast* 6. 30.

fast, faste, *adv.*; *firmly, vigorously, quickly* 74. 6; *insistently* 27. 8, 6. 29.

fastned, *pp.*; *fastened* 125. 52.

fastynge, *sb.*; *fasting* 91. 115.

fat, *adj.*; *fat* 106. 41.

fawen, *adj.*—See *fayn.*

fawte, *sb.*; *fault* 115. 69.

fawyt, *vb. pr.* 3 *s.*—See *falewen.*

fay, *sb.*; *faith* 93. 19.

fayn, (1) *adj.*; *eager, glad* 6. 7; fane 41. 7, fawen 56. 94. (2) *adv. gladly* 97. 61; fawen 56. 59.

feble, *adj.*; *ailing* 27. 38.

fecchen, *vb.*; *fetch* 68. 18. See also *fett.*

fede, *vb.*; *feed* 48. 30; *pr. pl.* feede 110. 87; *pt.* I *s.* vedde 15. 15; *pt.* 3 *s.* fedde 66. 4; *pp.* fed 10. 22.

fedres, *sb.*—See *feþeres.*

feh, *sb.* (OE feoh); *property* 6. 32; fee 116. 29.

feir, *adj.*; *fair* 7. 54; feyr 11. 8, feire 104. 4, feyre 2 B. 5. See also *fair.*

feird, *num. adj.*—See *ferþ.*

feiri, *sb.*; *enchantment, illusion* 101. 28.

feiþ, *sb.*; *faith* 95. 137. See also *fay.*

feiþful, *adj.*; *faithful* 104. 2.

fel, *sb.* (OE fell); (1) *skin* 26.
39. (2) *physical form* felle 98.
19.

felau, *sb.*; *comrade, companion*
30. 105; *pl.* felawes 74. 3.

felauschip, *sb.*; *companionship*
99. 34.

felde, *vb.*—See *folde*.

felde, *sb.*; *field* 79. 21; feelde 109.
33.

fele, *vb.*; *feel, experience* 82. 15;
feel 109. 3; *pr.* 3 *s.* feleþ 10.
37; *pr. subj.* fele 100. 45; *pp.*
feelid 89. 7.

fele, *adj.*; *many, various* 27. 7;
feole 110. 94.

fell, *adj.* (OF fel); *fierce, cruel*
30. 55; fel 91. 14, felle 55. 3.

felle, *vb.* (OE fellan); *put down,*
destroy 93. 54; fell 84. 47, fel
135. 13; *pr.* 3 *s.* felles 27.
51.

felun, *adj.*; *malicious, cruel* 30.
22.

feluni, *sb.*; *villany, wickedness*
30. 113.

fende, *sb.*; *fiend, enemy* 26. 8;
fend 10. 20, feende 91. 11,
veonde 18. 9; *gen. s.* fendes
26. 55; *pl.* fendes 27. 100,
feindes 31. 52, uendus 37. 4.

fende, *vb.*; *defend* (*pr. subj.*)
110. 4.

fender, *sb.*; *defender* 79. 21.

fen-fore, *sb.* (OE fen, furh); *a*
trench in the earth (*grave*) 27.
91.

fer, *adv.*; *far* 86. 11; ferr 36. 8,
verre 12. 5.

fere, *sb.*; *companion, peer* 30.
105; uere 16. 1; *pl.* feris 39.
1, feeres 118. 51, fere 6. 59;
in fere *together* 120. 69.

fere, *sb.*; *fear* 104. 20.

fere, *adj.* (OE fēre); *in good health*
27. 38, 106. 8.

ferful, *adj.*; (1) *full of fear* 93.
56. (2) *dread* 101. 93.

ferli, *adj.*; *marvellous* 57. 74;
ferly 41. 30.

ferm, *adj.*; *immovable* 113.
50.

fers, *adj.*; *fierce* 96. 77.

fersliche, *adv.*; *fiercely* 95. 33.

ferste, *supl. adj.*; *first* 124. 30.

fert, *ppl. adj.*; *afraid* 96. 69.

ferþ, *num. adj.*; *fourth* 27. 14;
ferthe 121. 69, feird 31. 36,
furþe 11. 43.

fest, *vb.*; *fasten, fix firmly* 83. 14;
pp. fest 77. 7, feste 84. 1.

fest, *vb.*; *feast, regale* (*pt.* 3 *s.*) 44.
26.

feste, *sb.*; *feast* 12. 10; feest 91.
115.

festene, *vb.*; *fix firmly* 83. 7; *pr.*
p. festenand 44. 16.

fet, *sb.* (OE fet); *vessel, cup*
32. 5.

feþeres, *sb.*; *feathers* 117. 10;
fetheres 121. 228, fedres
121. 7.

fett, *vb.* (OE fetian); *fetch* 27.
91; *imp.* fott 29. 60; *pp.* fot
27. 73. See also *fecchen*.

feture, *sb.*; *shape, feature* 95.
42; *pl.* fetewrs 121. 84.

fewe, *adj.*; *few* 104. 2.

fewte, *sb.*; *fealty* 54. 5; feute
108. 60.

feyne, *vb.* (OF feindre); ?*dis-
semble* 103. 8.

feynt, *adj.*; *faint, feeble* 104. 8;
feynte 103. 20.

feyntysenes, *sb.*; *feebleness* 112.
53.

fif, *card. num.*—See *fiue*.

fifte, *ord. num.*; *fifth* 11. 49;
fijft 31. 41.

fiht, fyht, *sb.*; *fight* 20. 3; fyght
85. 25, fith 66. 18, viȝt 36. 6,
vyht 25. 1.

fiht, *vb.*; *fight* 118. 40; fith 63. 1,
fyght 48. 89; *pr. pl.* fiȝtes 27.
8; *pt.* 2 *s.* faȝt 35. 24, *pt.* 3 *s.*
faght 48. 61.

fikel, *adj.*; *treacherous, deceitful* 101. 30; fykel 20. 23.

file, *vb.*; *defile* 30. 3; *pp.* fyled 48. 28, fuylede 116. 67.

filisofre, *sb.*; *philosopher* 134. 20.

fill, *vb.*; *fill* 29. 36; *imp.* fylle 83. 15; *pt.* 2 *s.* fild 44. 26. See also *fulle.*

filþ, *sb.*; *filth* 27. 97, fylth 84. 37; *pl.* fulþes 116. 67.

finden, *vb.*; (1) *find* 56. 79; fynde 48. 31, vinde 2 B. 12; *pr.* 1 *s.* finde 16. 20; *pr.* 2 *s.* findest 4. 8; *pt.* 1 *s.* fond 72. 11; *pt. pl.* fand 31. 42; *pp.* fonden 79. 21, founden 102. 76. (2) *provide (with)* (*pt. pl.*) founden 6. 44.

fine, *vb.*; *cease* 30. 24.

finge, *vb.* (ON fengja); *take, accept pt.* 3 *s.* fang 48. 53.

finger, *sb.*; *finger* 44. 10; vinger 18. 5, fynger 6. 21.

fire, *sb.*—See *fyre.*

fisch, *sb.*; *fish* 95. 70; *pl.* fisses 28. 7.

fist, *sb.*; *fist* 109. 15.

fit, *sb.* (OE fitt); *ordeal, painful experience* 101. 93.

fithting, *sb.*; *fighting* 63. 4.

fiue, *num. adj.*; *five* 26. 19; fyue 10. 46, fif 1 A. 4, vif 4. 10.

flatere, *vb.*; *flatter* 103. 8.

flaterynge, *sb.*; *flattery* 103. 30.

flawme, *sb.*; *flame* 84. 14.

fle, *vb.* (OE flēon); (1) *intr. flee*, 31. 55; flee 91. 77; *pr.* 1 *s.* fle 64. 4; *pp.* fled 68. 8. (2) *tr. escape, forsake* 84. 36; *pr.* 1 *s.* flo 49. 13.

fiee, *vb.* (OE flēogan); *fly* 121. 10; *pr. p.* fleoyng 95. 70; *pt.* 3 *s.* fleiȝ 95. 18.

flecche, *vb.* (OF flechir); *waver* 95. 137.

fleme, *vb.*; *banish* 97. 47; *pp.* flemed 104. 50.

flesch, *sb.*; *flesh* 48. 102; ffless 36. 1, fles 3. 6, fleysh 10. 7, fleish 10. 22, flecsch 26. 39, flexs 30. 74, vlesȝe 18. 6, vlesh 24. 5.

fleishely, *adj.*; *fleshly* 91. 120.

flight, *sb.*; *flight (of a bird)* 81. 6, fliht 106. 3.

flitte, *vb.* (ON flytja); *change, shift*; flutte 95. 177; *pr.* 3 *s.* flittetȝ 73. 8.

flitte, *vb.* (OE flītan); *quarrel, wrangle* 118. 53.

flod, *sb.*; (1) *stream of blood* 3. 8. (2) *flood* 121. 216.

flour, *sb.*; *flower* 6. 90; flur 31. 49, flore 40. 3, flowre 84. 57; *pl.* floures (*blooming charms*) 10. 58.

flourdelys, *sb.*; *fleur-de-lis* 112. 8.

flutte, *vb.*—See *flitte.*

fo, *sb.*; *foe* 12. 1; vo 28. 19, foo 91. 24, *gen.* fohes 20. 23; *pl.* fon 72. 25, fose 79. 21. See also *fa.*

fode, *sb.*; *food* 7. 29; foode 89. 23.

fode, *sb.*; *child, offspring* 57. 74; fude 48. 23.

fol, *adj.*; *foolish* 6. 7.

fol, *adv.*; *full, very* 6. 69; uol 16. 33. See also *ful.*

fold, *sb.* (OE folde); *earth* 101. 50.

folde, *vb.* (OE fealdan); (1) *bend* 6. 21; felde 6. 40. (2) *clasp* 95. 177. (3) *wrap, enfold* 75. 15. (4) *collapse* 95. 137.

folie, *sb.*; *folly* 8. 12; folye 87. 17, foli 93. 94, folly 104. 18; *pl.* folies 6. 7, folyes 98. 20, folys 118. 64.

folk, *sb.*; *people, folk* 72. 1; folke 41. 29; *pl.* folkes 6. 60. See also *volk.*

folwe, *vb.*; *follow* 104. 12; *pr.* 2 *s.* folwest 91. 78, foluest 35. 19; *pr. pl.* foleweþ 6. 48; *pt.* 3 *s.* folewed 35. 25; *pt. pl.* foleweden 12. 4; *pp.* folewed 10. 23.

fomen, *sb.*; *foemen* 93. 54.

fonde, *vb.* (OE fandian); (1) *experience* 7. 23. (2) *endeavour imp.* 115. 8. (3) *tempt, entice; pt. pl.* 34. 14.

fonde, *vb.* (OE fundian); *go* 99. 34. See *founden*.

fonding, *sb.*; *temptation* 27. 7; *pl.* fondinges 27. 99.

fonge, *vb.*; *seize, catch* 93. 83; *pr.* 3 *s.* fonges 116. 29; *pt.* 2 *s.* vonge 17. 5.

fonne, *vb.*; *make a fool of*: *pt. pl.* fonned 121. 111.

font, *sb.*; *baptismal font* 27. 97.

fool, *sb.*; *fool* 101. 81; *pl.* fooles 109. 85.

foot-mon, *sb.*; *foot-soldier* 116. 18.

for, *prep.*; (1) *on behalf of* 3. 5, 88. 22. (2) *because of* uor 13. 4. (3) *in order* fer 7. 22.

for, *conj.*; (1) *because* 8. 7; vor 15. 4. (2) *in order that* 48. 77.

for-beoden, *vb.*; *forbid*: *pt.* 2 *s.* forbed 95. 82; *pp.* forboden 59. 14.

for-bere, *vb.*; (1) *miss, be deprived of* 75. 23. (2) *pp. weighed down* forborne 79. 12.

for-bette, *pp.*; *beaten excessively* 83. 41.

for-bled, *pp.*; *bled to excess* 127. 26.

forcere, *sb.* (OF forc(i)er); *coffer* 109. 110.

fordon, *vb.*; *undo, destroy* 108. 36; *pp.* fordon 110. 35, uordon 12. 9.

for-dred, *pp.*; *terrified* 10. 21.

fore, *prep.*; *for* 43. 3.

for-euer, *adv.*; *forever* 132. 89.

forfare, *vb.* (OE forfaran); (1) *perish, die* 95. 65. (2) *destroy* 97. 31.

forge, *vb.* (OF forger); *fabricate, contrive* 120. 47.

forgete, *vb.*; *forget* 84. 79; *pr.* 1 *s.* forȝete 96. 44; *imp.* forget 78. 10; *pt.* 1 *s.* uorȝet 25. 15; *pp.* for-gote 100. 77.

for-ȝiue, *vb.*; *forgive* 99. 46; *imp.* forȝef 68. 14, forgyf 80. 11; *pt.* 1 *s.* for-ȝaf 95. 51; *pt.* 3 *s.* forgaue 132. 23.

forgon, *vb.*; *forego, forsake* 10. 7.

forhed, *sb.*; *forehead* 121. 85.

for-lete, *vb.*; *forsake* 47. 36 (*pr. subj.*).

for-loren, *pp.*; (1) *lost* 54. 1. (2) *ruined* forlore 11. 30, uorlore 13. 18.

fors, *sb.*; *importance*; make no ~ of *be unconcerned about* 116. 52.

for-sak, *vb.*; *forsake* 30. 11; *pr.* 3 *s.* for-saket 73. 3; *pt.* 1 *s.* for-soc 87. 20; *pt.* 3 *s.* for-sok 113. 35, for-soke 47. 32.

for-smite, *pp.*; *utterly broken by blows* 76. 13.

for-soth, *adv.*; *assuredly* 91. 102; forsoþe 98. 21.

for-swere, *vb.*; (1) *swear profanely by* 95. 153. (2) *pp. perjured* for-sworen 93. 29.

for-syth, *sb.*; *foresight, providence* 41. 19.

fort, *adj.*; (*the*) *strong* (*man*) 39. 11.

forte (= for to); *in order to* 7. 8.

forth, *adv.*; *forth* 13. 1.

forþfare, *vb.*; *perish, die* 6. 90; *pp.* 100. 17.

for-þi, *conj.*; *therefore* 78. 4.

forþ-mide, *adv.*; *straightway* 100. 95.

fortune, *sb.*; *fortune* 42. 1.

for-whi, *adv.*; *why* 96. 15.

fostren, *vb.*; *foster*: *pr. pl.* fos-treþ 110. 87.

fot, *sb.*; *foot* 4. 7; fote (*dat.*) 6. 102, fute 46. 12, foot 95. 10; *pl.* uet 4. 5, fete 2 B. 9, feet 64. 11.

fot, fott, *vb.*—See *fett*.

foul, *sb.*; *bird* 98. 3; *gen.* foules 106. 3; *pl.* foules 28. 7, fouls 81. 6.

foul, *adj.*; *foul* 102. 76; fowl 53. 7, foule 91. 100.

foule, *adv.*; *foully, ill* 97. 46.

fouled, *pp.*; *corrupted* 27. 9.

founden, *vb.* (OE fundian); (1) *go, depart* 93. 74; *pr.* 1 *s.* founde 93. 16. (2) *begin, proceed*; *pr.* 1 *s.* fund 29. 39.

four, *card. num.*; *four* 27. 110; fowre 121. 41.

fourme, *sb.*; *form* 7. 59.

fourmen, *vb.*; *create*; *pt.* 3 *s.* fourmed 107. 34.

four-sum, *adj.*; *four together* 27. 100.

fourti, *card. num.*; *forty* 72. 13; uourty 15. 8.

fourti, *ord. num.*; *fortieth* 56. 73.

fous, *adj.* (OE fūs); *ready, eager* 6. 81.

fowled, *pp.*; *trampled, trodden* 81. 22.

fra, *prep.*; *from* 27: 97. See also *fro*.

fraist, *vb.* (ON freista); *tempt, assail*: *pr. pl.* fraistes 31. 52.

fram, *prep.*; *from* 4. 7; uram 33. 5. See also *from*.

frame, *vb.*; *devise* 120. 47.

frayne, *vb.*; *inquire* 115. 30.

fre, *adj.*; (1) *free* 10. 44. (2) *noble* 11. 7.

freelte, *sb.*; *frailty* 132. 14.

freike, *sb.*; *man* 116. 17.

frele, *adj.*; *frail* 95. 137, 48. 102.

frely, *adv. liberally* 102. 18.

frende, *sb.*; *friend* 27. 10; *pl.*

frendes 27. 112, froendes 23. 45.

frendles, *adj.*; *friendless* 104. 33.

frendschipe, *sb.*; *friendship* 97. 7; frenschipe 104. 1, frenchipe 72. 11.

freoli, *adj.* (OE frēolīc); *noble, fair* 112. 9; freoly 99. 22; *supl.* freolokest 112. 114.

frere, *sb.*; *friar* 103. 49.

fresch, *adj.*; *lusty* 101. 49; freisch 134. 4.

fresche, *?sb.* (?MDu. vrese); *dangers, miseries* 27. 99.

frith, *sb.*; *woodland* 112. 113.

fro, *prep.*; *from* 4. 7.

from, *prep.*; *from* 7. 28; vrom 12. 5. See also *fram*.

frouȝ, *adj.*; *fickle, untrustworthy* 27. 42.

frouering, *sb.*; *comfort* 131. 98.

fruit, *sb.*; *fruit* 31. 49.

fryk, *adj.* (OF frique); *lusty* 117. 65.

fude, *sb.*—See *fode*.

fuir, *sb.*—See *fyre*.

ful, *adj.*; (1) *full, complete* uul 18. 12. (2) *avowed* 28. 19.

ful, *adv.*; *full, very* 6. 41. See also *fol*, *adv.*

fulfille, *vb.*; *fulfil* 101. 114; *pt.* 3 *s.* fulfillede 57. 61; *pp.* ful-fild 110. 31 (filled full), ful-filt 62. 7, fulfilth 72. 4, folfild 112. 79, folfuld 119. 29, y-voluuld 13. 9.

fulle, *sb.*; *fill* 93. 28.

fulle, *vb.*; (1) *fill*: vulle 12. 11.; *imp.* vul 18. 2; *pp.* y-fuld 34. 21. (2) *fulfil* 34. 33. See also *fill*.

fulle-flet, *sb. person always in the way* 6. 16.

fullich, *adv.*; *altogether* 104. 1.

fulsum, *adj.*; *bountiful* 71. 6.

furst, *adj. supl.*; *first* 11. 25; furste 104. 15.

furþyre, *adv.*; *further* 105. 9.

fy, *interj.*; *fie!* 104. 8.

fye, *vb.* (cf. defíen); *digest, feed upon* 100. 65.

fyle, *adj.* (OF vil×OE fūl); *worthless, evil* 6. 60.

fyled, *pp.*; *defiled* 48. 28; y-uuled 25. 13.

fyn, *sb.*; *end* fyne 8. 27.

fyn, *adj.*; *fine, excellent* 10. 35; *supl.* fynest 92. 7.

fyre, *sb.*; *fire* 83. 11; fire 44. 7, fuir 100. 30, vur 18. 4.

ga, *vb.*; *go* 48. 77; *pr.* 2 *s.* gas 27. 109; *pr.* 3 *s.* gase 46. 4, 81. 21; *pr. pl.* ga 31. 63; *pp.* gan 27. 29. See also gon.

gabbe, *sb.*; *jesting, mockery* 6. 57; *pl.* gabbes 6. 73.

gabben, *vb.*; *mock, deceive* 103. 33; gabbe 111. 52.

gabbynges, *sb. pl.*; *mockings, slanders* 102. 53.

gadere, *vb.*; *gather, assemble* 56. 97; *pp.* gaderd 27. 81.

gai, *adj.*; *gay* 126. 22; gay 101. 118; *supl.* gayest 101. 16.

gain, *vb.*; *gain, profit*; *pr.* 3 *s.* gains 30. 113.

galle, *sb.*; *gall* 15. 28; ȝalle 131. 109.

game, *sb.* (OE gamen); *game, sport* 120. 45; gome 7. 52; *pl.* games 98. 42, gammes 29. 72.

gamen, *sb.* (same as preceding word) 67. 19; *pl.* gamens 30. 15, gomenes 6. 43.

gang, *vb.* (OE gangan); *go* (*pr. pl.*) 30. 101.

gar, *vb.*—See ger.

garlond, *sb.*; *garland* 125. 15.

gast, *sb.*; *spirit* 41. 9; gaste 44. 1. See also gost.

gastly, *adj.*; *spiritual* 48. 101.

gastly, *adv.*; *spiritually* 47. 29.

gat, *sb.* (ON gata); *way, road* 27. 19; gate 45. 22.

gate, *sb.* (OE geat).—See ȝate.

geld, *vb.*—See ȝelde.

gelde, *adj.*; *barren, profitless* 6. 43.

generacions, *sb. pl.*; *generations* 106. 26.

gent, *adj.*; *gentle, courteous* 10. 45.

gentri, *sb.*; (1) *courtesy* 115. 36; gentrie 95. 183. (2) *inherited rank* 110. 100.

gentyl, *adj.*; *gentle* 95. 161.

ger, *vb.* (ON gera); *make, cause* (*pr.* 1 *s.*) 31. 55; *pr. subj.* gar 84. 26; *imp.* gar 83. 14; *pt.* 2 *s.* gert 44. 4; *pt.* 3 *s.* 112. 23.

gersum, *sb.*; *treasure* 29. 69.

gesse, *vb.*; *guess, suppose* (*pr.* 1 *s.*) 113. 18.

gest, *sb.*; *guest* 106. 23; geste 81. 34, gist 28. 31.

geten, *vb.*; *get, acquire* 103. 74; gete 96. 60, gett 46. 18; *pr.* 2 *s.* getes 81. 27; *pr. subj.* gete 115. 38; *imp.* get 115. 10; *pt.* 1 *s.* gat 121. 141; *pp.* geten 27. 29, gete 121. 207; geten (*begotten*) 65. 15.

getyng, *sb.*; *getting, gains* 102. 59.

geynest, *adj. supl.* (ON gegn); *most direct* 112. 59.

gift, *sb.*; *gift* 31. 29; gifte 44. 9, ȝyft 18. 3; *pl.* giftes 27. 71, ȝiftes 95. 90.

gilt, *sb.*—See gult.

ginnen, *vb.*; *begin, do* (auxil.): *pr.* 3 *s.* gynneþ 6. 37; *imp.* gyn 15. 3; *pt.* 1 *s.* gon 10. 14; *pt.* 3 *s.* gan 47. 30, gon 11. 44; *pt. pl.* gunnen 55. 11, gunne 95. 3, gonne 34. 15, gan 83. 34.

gist, *sb.*—See gest.

glace, *vb.* (OF glacer); *glance off, slip* 102. 54.

glad, *adj.*; *glad* 37. 3; glade 38.
12; *supl.* gladdyst 92. 19.
gladen, *vb.*; *gladden*: *pr.* 3 *s.*
gladieþ 7. 52, gladdes 84. 49;
pr. pl. gladeþ 104. 3; *pp.*
y-gladed 32. 33.
gladly, *adv.*; *gladly* 116. 59.
gladsum, *adj.*; *gladsome* 41.
17.
gladuol, *adj.*; *joyous* 23. 11;
gladful 26. 13.
glas, *sb.*; *glass* 31. 22.
glasen, *adj.*; *glazed* 118. 38.
gle, *sb.*; *glee* 7. 52.
gleem, *sb.* (OE glǣm); *bright-
ness, gleam* 7. 13; glem 100.
28.
glemon, *sb.*; *gleeman, minstrel*
6. 53.
glent, *vb.*; *glance, move quickly*
102. 54; *pr. p.* glentand 100.
28.
glew, *sb.*; *joy, bliss* 84. 44.
glide, *vb.*; *glide* 58. 18; glyde 95.
3; *pr.* 3 *s.* glit 106. 23.
glorie, *sb.*; *glory* 126. 14.
glose, *sb.*; *gloss, interpretation*
103. 15.
glose, *vb.*; *gloze, flatter, deceive*
111. 52.
glosers, *sb. pl.*; *flatterers* 104. 3.
glosyngus, *sb. pl.*; *flatteries* 120.
87.
glotonie, *sb.*; *gluttony* 6. 53;
glotonye 87. 6; glotenye 95.
139.
glotoun, *sb.*; *glutton* 123. 18.
gloue, *sb.*; *glove* 23. 31.
gloued, *pp.*; *gloved* 126. 7.
gnat, *sb.*; *gnat* 106. 39.
god, *sb.*; *God* 6. 50; godd 31. 65;
gen. godes 6. 75, godis 41. 9;
goddis 34. 1, godus 37. 5, god
83. 1.
god, *adj.*; *good* 8. 2; good 94. 15,
gode 7. 30, goode 89. 24,
goud 26. 26, gud 46. 1.
god, *adj.* as *sb.*; *benefit* 3. 10;

gode 45. 12; *pl.* (*goods*) godes
6. 42.
godhede, *sb.*; *divinity* 48. 80;
goddhed 31. 32.
godliche, godli, *adj.* and *adv.*;
goodly 56. 25, 128. 6; good-
lich 104. 10, goodly 118. 33.
gold, *sb.*; *gold* 10. 39.
gome, *sb.* (OE guma); *man* 106.
23.
gome, gomenes, *sb.*—See *game,
gamen.*
gon, *vb.*; (1) *go* 71. 5; goo 91.
58; *pr.* 2 *s.* gos 115. 65; *pr.*
3 *s.* geþ 9. 5, gooþ 127. 7;
pp. gon 26. 40. (2) *pass away*:
pr. 3 *s.* geth 100. 28. (3)
walk: *pp.* ygwo 87. 14. (4)
be current, acceptable: *pr. pl.*
ges 27. 71. See also *ga.*
gost, *sb.*; *spirit* 12. 14; *pl.* gostes
13. 26, goostes 110. 18. See
also *gast.*
gostlych, *adj.*; *spiritual* 18. 4;
gosteli 44. 8. See also *gastly.*
gostly, *adv.*; *spiritually* 91. 2.
See also *gastly.*
goute, *sb.*; *gout* 6. 24.
gouernaunce, *sb.*; *control* 119.
61.
gouerne, *vb.*; *govern, control* (*pr.
subj.*) 97. 6; *pr.* 2 *s.* gouernest
104. 10.
gouernour, *sb.*; *ruler* 108. 42.
gra, *adj.*; *gray* 29. 57.
grace, *sb.*; *grace* 26. 13.
graiþe, *vb.*; *prepare* 45. 22 (MS
graȝe); *pp.* grayd 27. 47.
See also *greiþen.*
graiply, *adj.*; *promptly* 112. 23.
See also *greiþli.*
gras, *sb.*; *grace* 105. 20; graas
96. 22.
gras, *sb.*; *grass* 97. 5.
graȝe.—See *graiþe.*
graunte, *vb.*; *grant* (*imp.*) 7. 58;
grant 93. 90; *pp.* grant-hit
124. 71.

graunt-merci, *sb.*; *much thanks* 97. 60.

graue, *sb.*; *grave* 27. 47.

graue, *vb.*; *bury*: *pr.* 3 *s.* graueþ 9. 11.

grede, *vb.*; *cry aloud, proclaim* 34. 15; *pt.* 2 *s.* greddist 72. 16; *pt.* 3 *s.* gradde 34. 24; *pt. pl.* gradden 14. 2; *pp.* grad 88. 11.

gref, *sb.*; *grief* 118. 28; greef 101. 173; greue 96. 35.

greggen, *vb.*; *magnify* (*pr. pl.*) 110. 29.

grein, *sb.*; *grain, seed* 9. 11.

greiþen, *vb.* (ON greiða); *affect*: *pp.* ygreyþed 6. 24.

greipest, *adj. supl.*; *readiest* 112. 111.

greiþli, *adv.*; *fittingly* 112. 25.

grene, *adj.*; *green, possessing vitality* 9. 11.

grene, *sb.*; *green sward* 121. 5.

grene, *vb.*; *grow green*: *pr.* 3 *s.* grenys 135. 6.

gret, *adj.*; *great* 16. 3; grete 84. 87, greet 90. 33; *supl.* grest 106. 20.

grete, *sb.* (OE grēot); *earth, soil, mould* 23. 20; groeth 23. 43.

grete, *vb.*; *weep* 65. 19; *pt.* 3 *s.* grette 84. 87.

grete, *vb.*; *greet* 7.19; (*pr.* 1 *s.*) 13. 22; *pt.* 3 *s.* gret 41. 33, grette 56. 25; *pp.* gret 105. 20.

gretinge, *sb.*; *greeting* 131. 114; gretinge 56. 24, gretyn 41. 5.

greuaunce, *sb.*; *sorrow* 112. 111.

greue, *vb.*; *grieve*: *pr.* 3 *s.* greueþ 100. 55, greuet 75. 9, greues 77. 12; *pr. pl.* greues 48. 101; *pp.* greuyd 94. 19, i-greuet 107. 9.

grill, *adj.*; *harsh, cruel* 30. 15.

grille, *vb.*; *shudder, tremble* 112. 111.

grimly, *adj.*; *harsh, cruel* 110. 18.

gripe, *vb.*; *take possession of* 116. 26.

grise, *sb.* (OF gris); *gray fur* 29. 64.

grith, *sb.*; *protection, security* 29. 58; gryth 18. 9, gryht 17. 7.

grom, *sb.*; *boy* 65. 7.

grome, *sb.* (OE grama); *anger* 25. 11.

grope, *vb.*; (1) *search, investigate* 100. 99. (2) *be aware of* 109. 3.

ground, *sb.*; *ground, foundation* 96. 22; (*dat.*) grounde 6. 97, gronde 93. 87.

grounde, *vb.*; *establish*: *pt.* 1 *s.* grownded 121. 186.

grount, *sb.* 108. 67: *obscure.*

growen, *vb.*; *grow*: *pr.* 3 *s.* grouweþ 106. 22; *pt.* 3 *s.* greuȝ 112. 10.

gryse, *vb.*; *feel terror* 113. 19.

grysely, *adj.*; *grisly, terrible* 46. 15.

grysliche, *adv.*; *terribly* 25. 2.

gult, *sb.*; *guilt* 16. 34; gylt 48. 70, gilt 65. 26, gilth 62. 5; *pl.* gultes 7. 34, giltes 131. 13.

gulty, *adj.*; *guilty* 17. 9; gylty 91. 134.

gy, *vb.* (OFr guier); *refl. conduct one's life* 101. 35.

gyf, *conj.*—See *ȝif.*

gyle, *sb.*; *guile* 6. 57.

gylty, *adj.*—See *gulty.*

gynne, *sb.*; *snare* 121. 97.

gynnyng, *sb.*; *beginning* 21. 3.

gyse, *sb.*; *style, fashion* 101. 16.

gywes, *sb. pl.*; *Jews* 14. 7; giwes 34. 15. See also *iewes.*

ȝare, *vb.* (OE gearwian); *prepare* 65. 18.

ȝare, *adj.* (OE gearu); *ready* 23. 9, 97. 28.

ʒarken, vb. (OE gearcian); prepare 110. 88; imp. ʒarke 17. 22; pp. iʒarkid 28. 2, ʒarked 97. 28.

ʒate, sb. (OE geat); gate 17. 4; ʒat 19. 3, yate 41. 4, gate 32. 51; pl. ʒates 112. 61.

ʒe, 2 pers. pron. nom. pl.; ye 13. 11.

ʒede, vb. pt. (OE ēode); went 72. 10.

ʒelde, vb.; grant, requite 89. 27; yheld 48. 93; pr. 2 s. yeldUs 41. 22; pt. 3 s. ʒeldeth 25. 21; imp. ʒelde 81. 26, geld 49. 19; pp. iʒolde 38. 6.

ʒeldyng, sb.; payment 25. 15.

ʒelle, vb.; yell (pr. pl.) 118. 72.

ʒeme, sb.; heed 100. 99.

ʒeme, vb.; care for, guard (pr. subj.) 20. 24.

ʒepte, vb. pt. 69. 15; ?error for ʒerte 'cried out' (OE georran) or wepte (with inflectional rhyme).

ʒer, sb.; year 21. 14; pl. ʒer 15. 8, ʒere 77. 19, yere 132. 70.

ʒerd, sb. (OE gerd, gyrd); rod, sceptre 32. 17; ʒerde 72. 29.

ʒerne, adv.; eagerly, earnestly 8. 21; ʒeorne 107. 5, ʒoerne 23. 22.

ʒerne, vb.; yearn for 89. 37; pt. pl. ʒerned 112. 84; pp. ʒeorned 111. 89, y-ʒyrned 6. 95.

ʒhernyng, sb.; object of desire 83. 11.

ʒete, adv.; yet 27. 14; hyet 49. 21, ʒit 91. 6, ʒyth 105. 41, yiet 5. 5, yit 91. 12.

ʒeue, vb.; give 126. 39; gyf 77. 28; pr. 2 s. ʒyfst 15. 32, ʒiuest 35. 29; pr. pl. ʒeuen 67. 23; pr. subj. ʒiue 97. 50; imp. ʒef 8. 2, ʒeue 7. 7, ʒyf 17. 21, gif 44. 18, giue 44. 28; pt. 1 s. ʒaf 15. 9, gaf 3. 6; pt. 2 s. ʒaf 89. 22, gaf 29. 29, ʒeue 16. 31, ʒef 72. 20, ʒeue 55. 20, ʒoue 38. 4; pt. 3 s. ʒaf 105. 70, ʒahf 88. 22; pt. pl. ʒauen 127. 10; pt. subj. ʒef 71. 7; pp. y-ʒeue 34. 31, ʒiue 96. 65, ʒoue 90. 25.

ʒeyne, vb. (OE -gegnian); avail 95. 90.

ʒif, conj.; if 26. 49; ʒyf 23. 15, ʒyve 115. 35, hyf 2 B. 2, gyf 84. 85, ʒef 11. 23.

ʒok, sb.; yoke 114. 38.

ʒokkyn, pr.p. (Cf. MDu. jocken, jeuken to itch and NED yuke v.); with prurient desire 6. 95.

ʒolewe, adj.; yellow 125. 47.

ʒolis-day, sb.; Yule-day, Christmas 56. 147.

ʒong, sb. (OE geong); path, journey 27. 77.

ʒong, adj. (OE geong); young 23. 28; ʒyng 121. 107, ying 57. 79; pl. ʒonge 97. 58, ʒynge 11. 22.

ʒonge, vb. (cf. ONth. geonga); pr. 3 s. ʒongeþ 25. 4.

ʒore, adv.; yore, long since 6. 69.

ʒornful, adj.; sorrowful 34. 34.

ʒou, 2 pers. pron., dat., acc. pl.; you 95. 169, ʒow 124. 40, ou 98. 23, ow 97. 2.

ʒour, poss. pron. 2 pers.; your 95. 103; ʒowre 121. 211.

ʒowthe, sb.; youth 121. 18.

ʒus, adv.; yes 109. 20.

ʒuster-day, sb.; yesterday 101. 12.

ʒwrh = þurh.

ha, interj.; ah! 13. 13.

habbe, vb.—See hauen.

hailsand, pr. p.; saluting 45. 5.

hald, sb.; refuge 29. 35.

halde, vb.; hold 84. 52; imp. hald 46. 1; pr. p. haldand 41. 3. See also holden.

halely, adv.; wholly 48. 15.

halewen, vb.; hallow 12. 9; pp. haleghed 44. 25.

haligast, *sb.*; *Holy Ghost* 29. 1.
hall, *sb.*; *hall* 29. 18; halle 6. 36.
hallas, *interj.*—See *allas*.
halle, *adj.*—See *al*.
halt, *adj.* (OF halt); *of high
rank* 6. 84.
haltinde, *pr. p.*; *halting, limping*
6. 36.
haluen-dele, *sb.*; *half* 110. 118.
haly, *adj.*; *holy* 41. 22. See also
holi.
ham, 3 *pers. pron. dat., acc. pl.*;
them 32. 29; ham silf 28. 9.
See also *hem*.
ham, *vb. pr.* 1 *s.*—See *ben*.
hameres, *sb. pl.*; *hammers* 91. 45.
hand, *sb.*; *hand* 30. 28; *pl.*
handis 135. 11, handyn 94. 6.
See also *hond*.
handled, *sb.* (OE andwlīta);
face 1 A. 2.
hange, *vb.*; *hang* (*tr.* and *intr.*)
67. 18; *pr.* 3 *s.* hanget 2 B. 1,
hangis 40. 7; *pr. p.* hangende
56. 122; *pp.* hanged 79. 9,
i-hanged 55. 16. See also
honge and *hyng*.
hanne, *adv.* (*after* þanne *thence*,
whanne *whence*); *hence* 32. 18.
hap, *sb.* (ON happ); (1) *good
fortune, grace* 103. 46; hape
44. 3. (2) *chance* (*pl.*) happis
105. 3.
hapen, *vb.*; *chance* (*pr.* 3 *s.*)
hapnes 118. 49.
har, *poss. pron.* 3 *pl.*; *their* 91.
31. See also *here, heore*.
har, *adj.*—See *hard*.
hard, *adj.*; *hard* 29. 12; harde 3.
11, har 31. 60; *comp.* hardere
3. 4.
harlotrye, *sb.*; *ribaldry* 95. 133;
profligacy harlotrie 95. 163.
harm, *sb.*; (1) *evil, injury pl.*
102. 70. (2) *a pity* 103. 70.
has, *adv.*—See *as*.
hast, *vb.*; *hasten* (*pr. subj.*) 93.
5.

haste, *sb.*; *haste* 17. 19; aste 41.
11.
hasti, *adj.*; *hasty* 118. 65; hastif
131. 4.
hat, *sb.* (OE hāt); *promise* 27.
18. See also *hote*.
hate, *vb.*; *hate* 104. 15; *pr.* 1 *s.*
83. 10; *pr.* 2 *s.* hatest 109.
42; *pr. subj.* hate 84. 37; *pp.*
i-hated 133. 8.
hate, *adj.* (? = hatel); *hateful*
84. 31.
hatter, *adj. comp.*; *hotter* 84. 13.
hauen, *vb.*; *have* 11. 47; habbe
7. 46, haf 30. 98; *pr.* 1 *s.* haue
4. 4, ychabbe 6. 91, ha 7. 34,
haf 94. 19, hase 77. 16; *pr.*
2 *s.* hauest 13. 17, hast 38. 6,
hest 32. 33; *pr.* 3 *s.* haueþ 6.
13, hauet 12. 9, haues 39. 10,
haueht 19. 6, haþ 6. 78, hatʒ
56. 43, hathe 93. 60, hat 62.
2, haht 6. 100, heþ 32. 45, ad
35. 14; *pr. pl.* habbeþ 96. 14,
han 90. 12, as 39. 11; *pr.
subj.* habben 6. 106, haue 10.
52, hauen 11. 57; *imp.* hab
28. 15, haue 3. 1, haf 81. 9,
hafe 83. 47; *pl.* haueþ 97.
57; *pt.* 1 *s.* hadde 72. 8,
hedde 95. 55; *pt.* 2 *s.* haddest
22. 6, hedest 20. 5; *pt.* 3 *s.*
hedde 95. 181; *pt. pl.* adde
35. 4, *pt. pl. subj.* hed 112.
122, hadden 57. 51.
hauek, *sb.*; *hawk* 95. 14; *pl.*
haukes 95. 7.
hauing, *sb.*; *property* 53. 3.
hauporn, *sb.*; *hawthorn* 95. 179.
hay, *adv.*—See *ay*.
haye, *sb.*; *hay* 84. 33.
he, 3 *pers. pron. nom. s.*; *he* 2
B. 1.
he, *adj.*—See *heh*.
hecgh, *sb.*; *hedge* 109. 22.
hed, *sb.*—See *heued*.
hede, *sb.*; *heed* 95. 147; hyed 48.
26, hete 105. 63.

hede, *vb.* (OE hēdan); *care for* 110. 89.

hee, 3 *pers. pron. pl.*—See *hi.*

heh, *adj., sb.*; (1) *adj. high* 6. 30; hei 30. 16, hey 1 A. 3, heye 26. 44, heȝe 6. 1, hegh 82. 37, heih 113. 77, heiȝe 34. 28, heyȝe 13. 25, hyȝe 92. 24, hi 53. 4, hy 122. 31, hye 120. 79; *comp.* heyere 38. 2; *supl.* heiest 44. 3, hext 106. 79, heste 6. 20. (2) *sb. on high*: on he 85. 11, an heiȝ 106. 92, in hey 121. 68.

heilsum, *adj.*; *healthful* 72. 17.

heire, *sb.*; *heir* 117. 87.

heith, *vb.* (OE hātan); *was called* 121. 77.

hel, *sb.*—See *hil* and *hell.*

helde, *vb. intr.*; (1) *sink* 6. 37. (2) *incline pr. p.* heldand 84. 28.

hele, *sb.* (OE hǣl); *salvation* 21. 9.

hele, *vb.*; *conceal (pr. subj.)* 110. 46.

helen, *vb.*; *heal* 25. 6; *imp.* hele 30. 79.

hell, *sb.*; *hell* 31. 60; hel 31. 5, helle 9. 14.

helle-fuir, *sb.*; *hell-fire* 95. 104.

helm, *sb.*; *helmet* 125. 15.

help, *sb.*; *assistance* 7. 48; helpe 31. 45.

helpe, *vb.*; *help* 16. 22; *pr.* 3 *s.* helpeþ 11. 21, helpth 23. 17; *pr. pl.* helpeþ 6. 92; *imp.* help 6. 93; *pt.* 3 *s.* halp 112. 118.

helpyng, *vbl. sb.*; *succour* 111. 18.

helpynge, *adj.*; *helping* 25. 16.

helpe, *sb.*; *health* 131. 29.

hem, 3 *pers. pron. dat. acc. pl.*; *them* 6. 57; heom 114. 28, hoem 13. 27. See also *ham.*

hende, (1) *adj.*; *gracious* 26. 5; *comely* hendi 2 B. 6. (2) *sb.*

(gracious one) heende 112. 65.

hendles, *adj.*—See *endlesse.*

hendyng, *sb.*—See *endyng.*

henne, *adv.*; *hence* 43. 2; hoenne 23. 1, hoennes 23. 30, hennes 100. 75.

hent, *vb.*; *seize, snatch* 102. 70; *(pr. subj.)* 98. 6; *(pt.* 3 *s.)* 112. 63; *pp.* hent 84. 24, hente 95. 9.

heo, 3 *pers. pron. fem. nom. s.*; *she* 11. 9.

heo, 3 *pers. pron. nom. pl.*; *they* 11. 57; hoe 14. 9.

heore, *poss. pron. pl.*; *their* 101. 126; heor 98. 11, hor 101. 119, hoere 13. 28. See also *here.*

her, *sb.*; *hair* 58. 17.

her, *adv.*; *here* 9. 15; here 16. 44, heer 95. 89, heere 119. 30.

her-afturward, *adv.*; *after this* 112. 95.

herborwe, *sb.*; *shelter, lodging* 95. 55.

herde, *sb.*—See *eorþe.*

here, *sb.* (OE hǣre); *hair-shirt* 23. 20.

here, *poss. pron. pl.*; *their* 12. 4; her 27. 11. See also *heore.*

here, *vb.*; *hear* 7. 16; heere 89. 3; *pr. pl.* hereth 21. 20; *pr. subj.* here 7. 42, her 26. 3; *imp.* her 20. 4, here 6. 1, hyre 91. 142; *pt.* 3 *s.* herde 58. 19; *pt. pl.* herden 56. 54; *pp.* herd 84. 24, yhered 87. 11.

hering, *sb.*; *hearing* 121. 70.

herewed, *pp.*; *despoiled* 112. 65.

heritage, *sb.*; *heritage* 59. 11; herytage 48. 24.

herken, *vb.*; *hearken* 95. 22; herkne 99. 35.

herliche, *adv.*—See *erliche.*

her-of, *adv.*; *hereof* 101. 65.

herte, *sb.*; *heart* 6. 49; hert 44. 2, ert 29. 68, harte 76. 24,

huerte 6. 37, hurte 4. 9; *gen.*
hertis 121. 31; *pl.* heortes
18. 2.

herteliche, *adv.*; *sincerely* 67.
33; hertely 91. 18, hertly 106.
11.

herþe, *sb.*—See *eorþe*.

hertly, *adj.*; *sincere* 87. 24.

heryen, *vb.*; *praise* 6. 100; *pr.*
1 *s.* herie 125. 34; *pr.* 3 *s.*
heryʒeth 14. 5; *pr. pl.* heryʒe
13. 26; *pp.* heried 10. 46.

heryinge, *sb.*; *praise* 17. 25,
herying 20. 25, heriʒyng 14.
1, heriing 14. 13.

hest, *sb.*—See *est.*

heste, *sb.*; *commandment, bid-
ding* 6. 75; hest 98. 7.

hete, *sb.*; *heat* 77. 21.

hete, *vb.*; *assure, promise (pr.* 1 *s.*)
81. 19; *pt.* 3 *s.* hyght 81. 5.

heth, *sb.*; *heath* 100. 30.

heþen, *adv.*; *hence* 27. 37;
hethen 84. 17, heþene 102.
102.

heue, *prop. name.*—See *eue.*

heued, *sb.*; *head* 2 A. 6; heuede
32. 40, hiued 4. 6, hed 76. 10.

heued-hount, *sb.*; *chief hunts-
man* 6. 85.

heuel, *adv.*—See *euele.*

heuen, *vb.*; *raise, lift (pr. subj.)*
27. 11; *pt. pl.* heued 79. 15.

heuene, *sb.*; *heaven* 6. 107;
heouene 7. 60, heuyn 91. 19,
hewen 41. 4.

heueneriche, *sb.*; *kingdom of
heaven* 17. 4; hoeuene-ryche
22. 11, heuenryke 84. 15,
heuen-rike 29. 71.

heuenlich, *adj.*; *heavenly* 131.
120.

heuer, *adv.*—See *euer.*

heuy, *adj.*; *heavy* 113. 69.

hewe, *sb.*; *hue, colour* 103. 66;
hew 84. 69.

heyl, *interj.*; *hail!* 26. 1; heil
26. 5, heyle 85. 1.

heynesse, *sb.*; *high rank* 23. 16.

hi, *adj.*—See *heh.*

hi, 3 *pers. pron. pl.*; *they* 28. 9;
hie 49. 22, hiʒ 122. 26, hue 6.
45, hy 34. 14, hee 106. 27.

hiddous, *adj.*; *fearsome* 91. 31.

hidusly, *adv.*; *horribly* 79. 15.

hider-to, *adv.*; *hitherto* 87. 4.

hidre, *adv.*; *hither* 56. 87; hydyr
133. 3.

hiʒe, *vb.*; (1) *hasten,* hie 99. 35;
pr. 2 *s.* hiʒest 100. 64; *imp.*
hye 10. 48; *pt. pl.* hyde 95.
7. (2) *drive pp.* hyed 79. 9.

hiʒtes, *sb. pl.*; *promises* 27. 12.

hiht, *sb.* (OE hyht); *joy, delight*
116. 12.

hil, *sb.*; *hill* 72. 35; hel 32. 55.

hille, *vb.*; *cover, protect* 121. 218;
hule 117. 61.

him, 3 *pers. pron.*; *him* 2 A. 7;
hym 16. 16, ym 41. 26, im
50. 2.

him-silf, *pron.*; *himself* 28. 28;
him-seluen 46. 2.

hi-maked, hi-neiled, *pp.*—See
maken, nailen.

hirdes, *sb. pl.*; *shepherds* 11. 36.

hire, 3 *pers. pron. gen., dat., acc.
s.*; *her* 10. 15.

hire, *poss. pron. fem. s.*; *her* 10.
30; hyr 10. 46, hyre 11. 40,
here 121. 234.

hirmon, *sb.* (OE hīredmon); *re-
tainer* 6. 84.

his, *poss. pron.*; *his* 1 A. 2; hiis
2 B. 7, hys 1 A. 1.

hi-spred, *pp.*—See *sprede.*

hit, *pers. pron.*; *it* 3. 5; hitte 91,
heading, hyt 25. 5. See
also *it.*

hi-pitz, *vb.*—See *y-wite.*

hitt, *pp.* (ON hitta); *fulfilled,
verified* 81. 25.

hi-uinde, *vb.* (OE ge-findan);
find 2 A. 10.

ho, *interr. pron.*; *who* 99. 39.
See also *who.*

ho, *sb.; cessation, limit* 99. 36.
hode, *sb.; hood* 116. 28; hoode
121. 80.
hokes, *sb. pl.; hooks* 118. 67.
hol, *adj.; hale, healthy* 97. 4.
holde, *sb.; keeping, hold* 112. 34.
holden, *vb.; hold, uphold* 102.
34; holde 118. 74, helde 35.
28; *pr.* 1 *s.* holde 75. 6; *pr.
pl.* hold 27. 12; *imp.* holt 118.
55; *pt.* 1 *s.* huld 6. 75; *pt.*
2 *s.* heold 112. 33; *pt.* 3 *s.*
heold 95. 16; *pp.* holden 114.
12, holdyn 94. 16, holde 95.
133, yholde 6. 20. See also
halde.
hole, *sb.; hole, aperture* 38. 7.
holi, *adj.; holy* 34. 7; holy 11.
59, 112. 14.
holich, *adv.; wholly* 121. 198;
hollych 108. 42, holly 111.
15.
holilich, *adv.; holily* 131. 26.
hom, *adv.; homeward* 121. 150;
hoom 92. 29.
homage, *sb.; homage* 54. 6.
hon, *vb.; remain, linger* 29. 12.
hond, *sb.; hand* 22. 13; honde
2 B. 9, honnd 88. 1; *pl.* hon-
den 4. 5, hende 27. 11,
hondes 26. 32, hondis 59. 23,
hondys 124. 70. See also
hand.
hondewerk, *sb.; handiwork* 14.
6; hondy-werk 8. 20.
hondre, *num. adj.—*See *hund-
reth.*
hondren, *sb.—*See *vnderne.*
honge, *vb., tr.* and *intr.; hang:
pr.* 2 *s.* hongest 15. 34, honges
64. 3; *pr.* 3 *s.* hongeþ 113. 79;
imp. honge 91. 27; *pt.* 2 *s.*
heng 72. 15, henge 72. 35,
hynge 89. 12; *pt.* 3 *s.* henge
91. 135, hongid 34. 20; *pp.*
hongid 115. 52, honget 91.
56, y-honge 32. 48. See also
hange and *hyng.*

honour, *sb.; honour* 20. 14.
honowre, *vb.; honour* 82. 25;
pr. 3 *s.* honoures 10. 60; *pr.
pl.* onuren 55. 5; *pr. subj.*
honoure 114. 57.
hoome, *sb.; home* 90. 29.
hope, *sb.; hope* 13. 21.
hope, *vb.; believe, hope* (*pr.* 1 *s.*) 7.
46, hoppe 49. 24, hop 91.
149.
hor, *poss. pron.—*See *heore.*
hor, *adj.; hoar, gray* 58. 17; hore
121. 111.
hord, *sb.; hoard, treasure* 27. 86.
hore, *adj.—*See *hor.*
hore, *vb.; grow gray* 6. 93.
hore, *sb.—*See *ore.*
horn, *sb.; horn* 99. 35.
horre, *sb.* (MDu. horren *horn;
corner*)*; corner* 28. 27.
horse, *sb.; horse* 6. 30; hors 106.
129.
hos, hose, *pron.; who-ever* 103.
12, 100. 79.
hosprynge, *sb.—*See *of-spring.*
hote, *sb.* (OE hāt)*; promise* 44.
11.
hou, *adv.; how* 3. 2; hu 2 B. 3,
u 4. 2; how 46. 11.
hounde, *sb.; hound* 101. 74.
houre, *poss. pron.—*See *our.*
houre, *sb.; hour* 84. 58; hour 101.
39, our 93. 62; *pl.* houres
117. 67.
hous, *sb.; house* 6. 84.
housbonde, *sb.; husband* 91. 98.
housele, *sb.; the Eucharist* 87.
37; hosel 95. 188, hosul 114.
55.
houseled, *pp.; having received
the Eucharist* 124. 70.
hu, *adv.—*See *hou.*
hue, 3 *pers. pron.—*See *hi.*
huge, *adj.; huge* 106. 124.
humbel, *adj.; humble* 107. 27.
hundreth, *num. adj.; hundred*
132. 70; hondre 88. 22; *pl.*
hundredus 116. 11.

hunger, *sb.*; *hunger* 65. 15; hungyr 77. 21.

hungred, *pp.*; *famished* 95. 53.

hunte, *vb.*; *hunt* 108. 71.

hurld, *pp.*; *thrust, shoved* 79. 4.

hurned, *vb. pr. pl.*—See *irnen.*

hurte, *sb.*—See *herte.*

hy, 3 *pers. pron.*—See *hi.*

hyde, *vb.*; *hide, protect* 116. 39; huyde 117. 62; *pr. subj.* hyde 86. 8; *pp.* hud 23. 31.

hydyr, *adv.*—See *hidre.*

hyet, *adv.*—See *ȝete.*

hyf, *conj.*—See *ȝif.*

hyght, *sb.*; *height* 79. 15.

hyȝe, *adj.*—See *heh.*

hyne, *sb. pl.*; *servants* 22. 22.

hyng, *vb.* (ON hengja); *hang* 47. 5; *pr.* 1 *s.* hyng 47. 1; *pr. p.* hyngand 46. 3; *pt.* 1 *s.* hynged 77. 14; *pp.* hynged 46. 11. See also *hange* and *honge.*

hyr, *pers. pron.*—See *hire.*

hyre, *sb.*; *reward* 83. 12; huire 100. 83.

hyt, *pers. pron.*—See *hit.*

i, 1 *pers. pron.*; *I* 3. 2; y 6. 8. See also *ich.*

ich, 1 *pers. pron.*; *I* 4. 2. See also *i.*

iche, *adj.*; *same* 26. 47.

ichot = ich wot (8. 22).

ichou = ich ou (11. 5).

idel, *adj.* (*sb.*); *vain* 102. 25.

idelyche, *adv.*; *fruitlessly* 106. 34.

idoghte, *pp.* (OE gedugan); *thriven* 131. 72.

if, *conj.*; *if* 28. 13. See also *ȝif.*

i-fere, *adv.*; *together* 56. 74.

ifrede, *vb.* (OE gefrēdan); *know, experience* (*pr. subj.*) 131. 78.

il, *adj.*; *evil* 30. 31; ill 78. 5, ille 115. 19. Cf. *yll*, adv.

2025.9

iliche, *adv.*; *equally* 117. 76.

ilike, *adj.*; *alike, equal* 84. 14; illyke 39. 8.

ilk, *adj.* (OE ylc); *every* 83. 26.

ilk, *adj.* (OE ilca); *same* 30. 6; ilke 41. 5, ylke 23, heading.

in = i ne (58. 36).

in, *sb.*; *abode* 71. 5.

in, *prep.*; *in* 1 B. 4; ine 32. 59.

inbrace, *vb.*; *embrace* 118. 35.

incarnacion, *sb.*; *incarnation* 106. 52.

in-deyne, *sb.*; *offence* 118. 51.

inliche, *adj.*; *deep, heartfelt* 90. 37; inly 111. 83.

inmong, *prep.*; *among* 40. 1.

inne, *adv.*; *in, within* 26. 33; ynne 120. 101.

innocent, *sb.*; *innocent* 103. 82; *pl.* Innocens 57. 55.

inouh, *adv.*; *very* 95. 173.

i-nouwe, *adj.*; *many* 104. 11; *much* ynow 121. 189.

in-oynt, *pp.* *anointed* 34. 33. See also *enoint.*

intil, *prep.*; *into* 30. 31; in-till 83. 4.

in-to, *prep.*; *into* 10. 26.

in-wiþ, *prep.*; *within* 6. 38.

in-yiet, *vb.*; *infuse* 44. 14.

i-propheciȝed, *pp.*; *prophesied* 55. 30.

ire, *sb.*; *ire, anger* 83. 10.

iren, *sb.*; *iron* 91. 34.

irnen, *vb.*; *run, flow*: *pr.* 3 *s.* urnth 4. 6; *pr. pl.* hurned 2 B. 10; *pt.* 3 *s.* ern 3. 8, orn 7. 39; *pt. pl.* hurne 1 B. 4.

is, *sb.*; *ice* 134. 5.

is, *poss. pron.*; *his* 6. 76. See also *his.*

i-same, *adv.*; *together, united* 60. 8. See also *ysome.*

i-se, *vb.* (OE gesēon); *behold* 75. 2; y-se 13. 11; *pr. subj.* y-soe 17. 23; *pt.* 3 *s.* iseȝ 32. 28.

ischoue, *pp.*; *shoved, forced out* 131. 31.

Y

isse, *vb.* (OF issir); *issue, proceed* (*pr. subj.*) 44. 9.

i-styld, *pp.* (OE stillan); *quieted* 32. 65.

it, *pers. pron.*; *it* 26. 2; itte 50. 2, et 56. 48. See also *hit*.

it, *poss. pron.*; *its* 90. 44.

itent, *pp.* (OF tenter); *stretched* 90. 8.

itiht, *pp.* (OE tyhtan); *drawn, stretched* 2 B. 6.

iuels, *sb. pl.*; *evils* 45. 11. See also *euel* and *yuel*.

i-weene, *?sb.*; *hope(s)* 108. 2.

i-went, *?sb.* (*cf.* OE gewend, gewind); *mazes, depth* 117. 11.

iwis, *adv.*; *indeed, certainly* 91. 20; i-wys 48. 13, i-wysse 77. 29. See also *ywys*.

iewes, *prop. name*; *Jews* 125. 47; iewyis 83. 39, Iuus 30. 3.

ioie, *sb.*; *joy* 9. 5; ioi 30. 87, ioye 8. 27, ioyȝe 55. 26; *pl.* ioies 10. 46, iois 50. 4.

ioly, *adj.*; *lively* 101. 75.

iolyfte, *sb.*; *pleasure, gaiety* 10. 54; iolyte 101. 95.

ioyful, *adj.*; *joyful* 26. 9.

ioyne, *vb.*; *join, follow*: *pr. pl.* ioyneþ 106. 26; *pp.* ioynt 82. 39.

ioyng, *sb.*; *joy* 83. 30.

iuge, *sb.*; *judge* 82. 45.

iugement, *sb.*; *judgement* 30. 35; iuggement 120. 82.

iugen, *vb.*; *judge*: *pt. pl.* iugged 112. 46; *pp.* iugged 110. 21.

iugise, *sb.* (OF jugise); *pronouncement of judgement* 82. 44, 112. 46.

iuned, *pp.* (OF joign-, *stem of* joindre); *imposed* 114. 60.

iurneis, *sb. pl.* (OF jornee); *journeys* 28. 32.

iustise, *sb.*; *justice, judge* 29. 77.

kacche, *vb.*—See *cacchen* and *kecchen*.

kalle, *vb.*—See *calle*.

kam, *vb.*—See *comen*.

kan, *vb.*; *can, be able* (*pr.* 1 *s.*) 48. 104; kanne 84. 11; *pr. subj.* kan 84. 90; *pt.* 1 *s.* koude 56. 59. See also *can*.

kare, *sb.*; *distress* 23. 12; kar 28. 11. See also *care*.

kast, *vb.* (ON kasta); *cast, throw* (*pt.* 1 *s.*) 121. 6; *pp.* kasten 83. 46. See also *kest* and *cast*.

katel, *sb.*—See *catel*.

kecchen, *vb.*; (1) *obtain* 68. 17. (2) *receive pr. subj.* kacche 120. 73. (3) *drive pr. pl.* kechin 57. 71. See also *cacchen*.

kele, *vb.*; *cool* 84. 26.

kende, *adj.*—See *kinde*.

kene, *adj.*; *keen, violent* 69. 7.

kenne, *vb.*; (1) *know* 100. 66. (2) *cause to know, teach* (*pr.* 1 *s.*) 81. 17; *imp.* ken 30. 10; *pt.* 3 *s.* kenned 112. 12.

kenned, *pp.* (OE cennan); *begotten, born* 131. 61.

kepe, *sb.*; *heed* 77. 1.

kepe, *vb.*; *keep, guard, care* 56.14; *pr.* 2 *s.* kepes 117. 68; *imp.* kep 75. 18; *pt.* 2 *s.* keptest 65. 28; *pr. pl.* kepten 14. 9; *pp.* kept 126. 8, kepit 115. 22.

kessing, *sb.*; *kissing* 121. 95; kessenge 87. 13.

kest, *vb.* (ON kasta); *ordain, prepare* 112. 83. See also *cast* and *kast*.

keuere, *vb.* (OF covrer); *recover, restore* 108. 43; *pr. pl.* 110. .90.

keyes, *sb. pl.*; *keys* 6. 58.

kiht, *pp.* (?OE cīgan); *?summoned* 97. 42.

kin, *sb.* (OE cyn); (1) *kin, family* 28. 28; kyn 48. 17, kynne 102. 31, kunne 14. 3, kenne

57. 22. (2) *kind, race,* kinne
95. 43.

kinde, *sb.* (OE cynd); *kind,
nature* 45. 9; kynde 48. 29,
kynd 41. 30, kuynde 95. 19,
kunde 17. 16, kende 32. 24,
kyend 84. 44; *pl. created
species* kuyndes 106. 103.

kinde, *adj.* (OE gecynde); (1)
natural kuynde 100. 85. (2)
well-disposed 65. 27, kende
67. 25. (3) *benevolent* cunde
16. 28.

king, *sb.*; *king* 7. 1; kyng 7. 21,
kynge 11. 12, keyng 82. 33;
(*gen.*) kynges 13. 1, kingges
72. 29, keynges 84. 8; *pl.*
kynges 11. 39.

kirt, *sb.* (*cf.* ON kyrt *a.,* *adv.*;
kyrð *sb.*); *peace, tranquillity*
27. 21.

kist, *sb.* (OE cist); *chest* 27. 76.

kist, *pp.*—See *kysse.*

kiþ, *sb.* (OE cyðð); *kith, kindred*
100. 23; kyth 81. 36, kith 71.
7.

knackes, *sb. pl.*; *tricks* 104. 53.

knaue, *sb.*; *servant* 102. 89.

kne, *sb.*; *knee* 28. 14; *pl.* knoen
20. 16.

knele, *vb.*; *kneel* 120. 31, knel
96. 1; *pr. p.* knelyng 119.
46.

knelynges, *sb. pl.*; *kneelings* 92.
16.

kniht, *sb.*; *knight* 108. 9; knith
55. 21, knyht 25. 4, knyt 34.
25, knyght 84. 66.

knihthod, *sb.*; *the knightly class*
95. 157.

knitte, *vb.*; *knit, join* 118. 50;
imp. knyt 86. 13; *pp.* knitte
117. 21, knyt 120. 69, knette
105. 21, y-knett 27. 75.

knott, *sb.*; *knot* 27. 75.

knotted, *ppl. adj.*; *knotted* 30.
56.

knotty, *adj.*; *knotty* 91. 62.

knoulechen, *vb.*; *acknowledge*:
pr. pl. knoulecheth 20. 19.

knoulechinge, *sb.*; *knowledge,
understanding* 18. 11.

knowen, *vb.*; *know, recognize*
100. 3; knowe 91. 75, knawe
124. 68, knaw 47. 11; *pr. pl.*
knowen 95. 173; *pt. pl.*
kneuȝ 95. 14, kneuh 103. 43;
pt. subj. knewe 95. 129, knew
84. 71; *pp.* knowen 72. 34,
i-knowe 120. 75.

knyf, *sb.*; *knife* 121. 168.

kot, *pp.*; *cut* 56. 67.

kunde, *sb.*—See *kinde.*

kunredes, *sb. pl.*; *kindreds,
races* 106. 25.

kuyndely, *adv.*; *fittingly* 102.
104.

kyndel, *vb.*; *kindle* (*imp.*) 44.
13.

kyndeli, *adj.* (OE cyndelic); *ac-
cording to nature* 53. 1.

kyndenes, *sb.*; (1) *generosity* 48.
74. (2) *natural affection*
kyndnes 48. 17.

kynedom, *sb.*; *rule, monarchy*
15. 31; kyndom 34. 7.

kysse, *vb.*; *kiss* (*pr. 1 s.*) 132.
71; *pp.* kist 67. 12.

kyþen, *vb.*; *make known, show*
(*pr. 2 s.*) kuiþest 118. 76; *imp.*
kid 31. 47; *pt. 3 s.* cudde 12.
10, kedde 90. 20; *pp.* kud
107. 26, i-kud 101. 19, y-kud
13. 13.

laboure, *sb.*; *labour* 100. 91.

lac, *sb.*; *lack* 103. 47.

lache, *vb.* (OE læccan); *take,
seize* 27. 68; *pp.* lauht 97. 33.

lacyd, *pp.*; *laced* 84. 79.

ladi, *sb.*—See *leuedy.*

lak, *vb.*; *blame, criticize* 109. 97.

lake, *sb.*; *lake, pool* 67. 29.

lakken, *vb.*; *lack*: *pt. pl.* lakkyd
121. 219.

lame, *sb.*; *loam, earth* 27. 48.

lame, *adj.*; *lame* 95. 97.

lan, *sb.*; *loan* 27. 30.

land, *sb.*; *land* 31. 27; lande 39.
10. See also *londe*.

lang, *adj.* and *adv.*—See *longe*.

langen, *vb.*; (1) *belong*: *pr.* 3 *s.*
lange 35. 30. (2) *long, yearn*;
pr. 3 *s.* langes 48. 48; *pr. p.*
langand 84. 91.

langour, *sb.*; *languor* 96. 53.

languysshyng, *pr. p.*; *languish-
ing* 132. 90.

langyng, *sb.*; *longing, yearning*
48. 2.

lant, *pp.*—See *lene*.

lappe, *sb.* (OE læppa); *(folded)
piece of garment* 75. 16.

lare, *sb.*; *teaching* 47. 36. See
also *lore*.

lasse, *adv.*; *less* 6. 22; las 102.
77.

lasse, *adj.*; *less* 91. 93; lesse 84.
92, las 119. 23.

laste, *vb.*; *continue, endure* 6.
51; lesten 61. 10, last 124.
47; *pr.* 3 *s.* laste 126. 40,
lastes 83. 24, lesteth 91. 103;
pr. p. lastand 48. 32; *pt.* 3 *s.*
last 113. 36; *pp.* last 121.
192.

laste, *adj.* (as *sb.*); *last* 65. 30.

lastes, *sb. pl.*; *vices, faults* 6.
8.

lastyng, *ppl. adj.*; *enduring*
20. 2.

late, *adv.*; *late* 17. 3.

laten, *vb.*—See *leten*.

lathly, *adv.*; *hatefully* 79. 4.

lattest, *adj. supl.*; *latest* 61. 6.

latymer, *sb.*; *interpreter* 6. 61.

lau3whe, *vb.*; *laugh* 99. 3; *pt.*
3 *s.* lou3 27. 27.

laumpe, *sb.*; *lamp* 97. 44.

launde, *sb.*; *grassy plot* 95. 2.

lauendere, *sb.*; *laundress, con-
cubine* 6. 56.

lauerd, *sb.*—See *louerd*.

lawe, *adj.* and *adv.*—See *lowe*.

lawe, *sb.*; *law, religion, faith* 13.
10; law 39. 12; *pl.* lawes 56.
99.

laweful, *adj.*; *conforming to the
moral law* 102. 98.

lay, 11. 33: obscure. See Note.

lay, *sb.*; *lay, song* 121. 27.

lay, *vb.* (OF laier); *release* 116.
44.

lay, *vb.* (OE lecgan).—See *leye*.

leche, *sb.*; *leech, physician* 10.
35.

lecherie, *sb.*; *lechery* 6. 56;
lecherye 87. 6, leccherye 121.
94.

lechour, *sb.*; *lecherous man* 109.
65; lecchour 127. 16.

lede, *sb.*; *lead* 86. 11; led 113.
69.

leden, *vb.*; *lead* 108. 20; lede 81.
4; *pr.* 2 *s.* ledest 15. 5; *pr.*
3 *s.* lede 135. 17; *pr. pl.* lede
84. 63; *imp.* led 7. 60, lede
85. 28; *pt.* 1 *s.* ledde 72. 9,
ladde 15. 4; *pt.* 3 *s.* ledde 66.
5, led 48. 58; *pt. pl.* ledden
55. 4; *pp.* led 10. 24, lad 6.
69, i-lad 55. 7, y-lad 13. 1.

leder, *sb.*; *leader* 44. 19.

leding, *sb.*; *guidance* 56. 70.

leef, *sb.*; *leaf* 101. 13; *pl.* leues
9. 2.

lees, *adj.* (OE lēas); *vain, false*
6. 52.

lef (OE lēfan); *permit (imp.)* 6.
68.

lef, *adj.*; *dear* 26. 14; leef 114.
43, lefe 85. 17, leue 97. 62,
leof 101. 175, luef 6. 41, lyf
110. 106; *comp.* leuer 27. 85;
supl. leuest 34. 9, leouest
109. 97.

lele, *adj.*; *loyal, faithful* 31. 20.

leli, *sb.*; *lily* 31. 12; lylie 10. 1.

lely, *adv.*; *faithfully* 48. 94;
lelly 112. 97.

leman, *sb.*; *beloved* 52. 1; lem-
man 78. 1.

lemen, *vb.*; *shine, gleam*; *pt.* 3 *s.* lemede 57. 42.

lende, *vb.*; *arrive, remain, reside* 104. 22; leende 96. 82; *pr.* 3 *s.* lendes 84. 44; *pr. pl.* lende 110. 116; *pp.* lent 83. 25, lente 95. 2.

lene, *vb.*; (1) *lend*: *pp.* lent 27. 30; (*on interest*) *pp.* lened 27. 82. (2) *grant*: *inf.* len 86. 20; *pr. subj.* lene 6. 105; *pp.* lant 102. 12.

lengore, *adv. comp.*; *longer* 6. 51; lengor 107. 57.

lent, *sb.*; *Lent* 117. 52.

lentun-dayes, *sb.*; *Lenten season* 111. 33.

leod, *sb.*; *people, race, nation* 102. 1; leode 108. 12.

leodene, *sb. pl.* (OE lēoden); *language* 18. 6.

leon, *sb.*; *lion* 101. 77; *pl.* lyouns 95. 4.

leonen, *vb.*; *lean, rest, recline*: *pt.* 3 *s.* leoned 96. 18.

leosen, *vb.*; (1) *lose* 101. 44; *pr.* 3 *s.* leost 101. 40; *pr. subj.* loese 23. 8; *pt.* 1 *s.* les 59. 11; *pt.* 3 *s.* les 55. 22; *pp.* y-lore 32. 12. (2) *destroy, bring to perdition* 120. 38; *pp.* loren 93. 31, lorn 57. 3.

leoþe-wok, *adj.* (OE leoþuwāc); *yielding, weak* 18. 8.

lere, *sb.* (OE hlēor); *cheek, face* 91. 40; luer 2 B. 5.

lere, *vb.*; (1) *teach*: *pr.* 3 *s.* lereþ 6. 77; *imp.* lere 30. 96; *pt.* 3 *s.* lered 48. 34. (2) *learn* 102. 4; *pr.* 3 *s.* leris 39. 5; *imp.* ler 75. 1.

lerne, *vb.*; *learn* 103. 8; *imp.* lern 104. 34; *pl.* lerneþ 103. 95.

les, *sb.*; *leash* 27. 69.

les, *adj.* as *sb.*; *falsehood* 6. 73; lese 30. 19.

lese, *vb.*; *release*: *imp.* lees 41. 11, lese 45. 19.

lesne, *vb.*; *loosen, release* (*imp.*) 19. 11.

lesse, *vb.*; *lessen, diminish* 86. 23.

lessun, *sb.*; *lesson* 102. 97.

lest, *conj.*; *lest* 49. 20.

lest, *adj. supl.*; *least* 61. 6; leste (*sb.*) 6. 23; leeste 95. 125.

leste, *adv. supl.*; *least* 135. 5.

lesten, *vb.*—See *laste.*

lesyng, *sb.*; *falsehood* 48. 4; *pl.* lesynges 103. 32; lesyngus 120. 33.

leten, *vb.* (OE lǣtan); (1) *forsake, abandon* 6. 68; lete 7. 18; *pr.* 1 *s.* lete 64. 4. (2) *omit, forbear, neglect* 27. 67; lete 6. 77. (3) *let go* (*of*), *desist* (*from*) lete 27. 84; *pr.* 3 *s.* lettes 116. 46. (4) *shed* *pt.* 2 *s.* lete 122. 11; *pp.* i-leten 4. 4. (5) *permit, allow*; laten 60. 6; *pr.* 3 *s.* let 101. 110; *imp.* let 7. 51, lat 41. 23; *pt.* 1 *s.* let 3. 3; *pp.* y-let 6. 90. (6) *leave* *pp.* 65. 22. (7) *auxil.*: *imp.* let 111. 97; late 132. 91.

lette, *vb.*; *hinder* 80. 6.

letting, *sb.*; *impediment, delay* 27. 53; lettyng 109. 27; *pl.* lettynges 109. 25.

lettorne, *sb.*; *lectern* 96. 18.

leue, *vb.*; *grant*: 3 *pr. subj.* leue 11. 53.

leue, *vb.* (OE gelēfan); *believe* 18. 12; *pr.* 1 *s.* leeue 109. 17; *pr.* 3 *s.* leeueþ 100. 79; *pr. pl.* leueth 22. 16, leeueþ 106. 75; *imp.* leef 113. 55, leue 56. 44; *pp.* y-leued 6. 23.

leue, *vb.* (OE lǣfan); (1) *cease, leave off* 31. 8; *subj. pl.* 106. 97. (2) *leave*: *pp.* leued 23. 44.

leue, *sb.*; *departure* 55. 19.

leuedy, *sb.*; *lady* 10. 5; leuedi 42. 1, lewedy 41. 17, lefdi 26.

12, ledy 10. 17, ladi 26. 13,
ladye 92. 1; *pl.* ladyes 108. 11.
lewede, *adj.*; *ignorant* 120. 92.
lewte, *sb.*; *fidelity, loyalty* 39. 3;
leute 96. 82.
ley, *vb.*—See *ligge*.
leye, *vb.* (OE lecgan); *lay, place,
wager* 111. 67; lay 101. 130;
imp. ley 75. 17, lei 100. 41;
pt. 1 *s.* leyde 121. 5; *pt.* 3 *s.*
leyde 66. 9, layd 48. 60; *pt.
pl.* leide 34. 30; *pp.* leide 93.
27, leyd 90. 19, layd 27. 46,
laid 30. 128.
lib, *vb.* (OE libban); *live* 28. 3.
See also *liuen*.
lich, *adj.*; *like* 95. 42; lych 49.
1. See also *lik*.
lickham, *sb.*; *body* 27. 46.
lif, *sb.*; *life* 6. 52; lyf 6. 67, lijf
31. 10, lef 32. 41; *gen. s.* lyue
10. 43; *dat. s.* lyue 87. 4.
lifte, *vb.*; *lift* (*pr.* 1 *s.*) 107. 19;
pr. 3 *s.* lyftes 84. 15; *pr. p.*
lyftand 86. 9; *pp.* lyft 84. 9.
ligge, *vb.* (OE licgan); *lie*; ley
109. 49; *pr.* 1 *s.* lygge 10. 25;
list 75. 8, lyst 49. 14; *pr.* 3 *s.*
lith 58. 45, lys 101. 91, lyes
82. 27, lyse 82. 40, ligges 27.
60; *pr. pl.* liggen 113. 69,
ligge 110. 53, ligges 31. 62;
pr. subj. ly 97. 39; *pt.* 1 *and*
3 *s.* lay 55. 26; *pt.* 2 *s.* lay
31. 11; *pp.* leyne 95. 93, layn
6. 8.
light, *adj.*; (1) *light* (levis) 118.
38, lyght 84. 49. (2) *nimble*
99. 10; *adv. lightly* 113. 5.
lithte, *adv.*; *easily* 56. 129.
light, *vb.* (OE lihtan); *lighten*
84. 70.
lighte, *vb.*; *alight, descend* 131.
28; *imp.* liht 7. 27; *pr. p.*
lyghtand 79. 22; *pt.* 2 *s.*
lyhtest 93. 40; *pt.* 3 *s.* lithtede
57. 17, liȝte 96. 29.
liht, *sb.*—See *lyht*.

lihtly, *adv.*; *easily* 100. 21.
lik, *adj.*; *like* 74. 4; lyke 84. 16.
See also *lich*.
like, *vb.* (impers.); *please*: *pr.*
3 *s.* likyt 129. 2, likes 82. 19;
pr. subj. like 9. 10; *pr. p.*
lykand 48. 9; *pt.* 3 *s.* lyked
96. 3; *pt. subj.* lyked 48. 16.
likne, *vb.*; *liken* 101. 131; *pr.*
1 *s.* 111. 55, lyken 84. 6; ?*pr.
p.* lyckend 84. 33.
liknes, *sb.*; *likeness* 100. 50.
likyng, *sb.*; *liking, affection* 82.
40; lykyng 48. 8; *pl.* lykinges
116. 51.
lim, *sb.*; *limb* 98. 25; *pl.* limes
13. 16, lymes 121. 170.
lime, *sb.*; *mortar* 29. 66.
linage, *sb.*; *lineage* 109. 68.
lisse, *sb.*; *solace, joy* 7. 2.
lysse, *vb.*; *solace* 49. 7.
liste, *vb.*; (1) *be pleasing*, (with
refl. dat.) *be pleased*; *pr.* 3 *s.*
list 27. 68, lyst 84. 77, lust
95. 160; *pr. subj.* lest 115. 6;
pt. 3 *s.* lest 121. 220. (2)
desire; *pr.* 3 *s.* listet 65. 8;
pr. subj. luste 103. 1.
lite, *vb.* (ON hlíta); (1) *put trust
in*: *pr.* 3 *s.* lites 27. 28. (2)
count on 27. 53.
litel, *adj., adv.*; *little* 5. 4; lytel
32. 79, lutel 6. 22, luitel 95.
81, luytel 95. 138, litil 115.
5.
lipe, *adj.*; *supple* 90. 8.
liþing, *sb.* (OE liðung); *relief*
131. 50.
liuen, *vb.*; *live* 60. 6; liue 30. 50,
lyuen 34. 5, leuen 124. 56,
leue 122. 10; *pr.* 2 *s.* leuyst
105. 26; *pr.* 3 *s.* leueth 25.
14; *pr. p.* lyuand 86. 29.
See also *lib*.
lodes-mon, *sb.*; *leader, guide* 18.
10.
lofer, *sb.*—See *lufer*.
loffe, *sb.*; *loaf* 121. 219.

lofsum, *adj.*—See *lufsum.*
logged, *pp.*; *lodged* 100. 82.
loken, *pp.*—See *louke.*
loken, *vb.*; (1) *look* 76. 7: *pr.* 3 *s.*
loke 61. 1: *imp.* lok 51. 12,
loke 2 A. 1, luke 46. 14, *(pl.)*
loket 4. 1. (2) *look for*: *pt.* 1 *s.*
loked 25. 16.
lokes, *sb. pl.*; *locks* 27. 59.
loking, *sb.*; *aspect, expression*
58. 5.
lokkes, *sb. pl.*; *locks (of hair)*
68. 4.
lomb, *sb.*; *lamb* 12. 7.
londe, *sb.*; *land* 7. 21; *pl.* londis
64. 4. See also *land.*
longe, *adj.* and *adv.*; *long* 3. 12,
9. 15; lang 30. 56.
longen, *vb.*; (1) *belong*: *pr.* 3 *s.*
longeþ 131. 104. (2) *long,*
yearn: *pr.* 3 *s.* longeþ 35. 12.
See also *langen.*
longing, *sb.*; (1) *longing* 7. 55;
longging 56. 2, longyng 100.
91. (2) *object of desire* long-
ynge 24. 2.
Longis, *prop. name*; *Longinus*
55. 21.
loose, *vb.*; *loose, set free* 99. 31;
lose 135. 12.
lopen, *pp.*; *leaped, escaped* 27.
69.
lor = lord.
lord, *sb.*; *lord* 6. 67; lorde 82.
33, lor 111. 72; *gen.* lordes
2 A. 8. See also *louerd.*
lordling, *sb.*; *prince* 25. 1.
lordshype, *sb.*; *position of power*
23. 16; lordschip 134. 37.
lore, *sb.*; (1) *teaching* 6. 73. (2)
doctrine, code 49. 26. See also
lare.
lorein, *sb.*; *strap (in a horse's
trappings)* 29. 62.
loren, *pp.*—See *leosen.*
los, *sb.*; *praise* 18. 14.
lose, *vb.*; *lose* 39. 12; *pp.* lost
78. 2.

lot(i)en, *vb.*; *lie hidden*; *pt.* 3 *sg.*
lotede 34. 28.
lotes, *sb. pl.* (ON lát); *manners,
behaviour* 6. 68.
loþ, *adj.*; (1) *loath, reluctant* 27.
84. (2) *hateful, loathsome*:
loþe 10. 19, loht 6. 41, loth
91. 120.
loud, *adj.*, *adv.*; *loud* 72. 16;
loude 102. 51, lude 30. 29.
louʒ, *vb. pt.*—See *lauʒwhe.*
louinge, *pr. p.* (ON loga *vb.*);
flaming, burning 18. 12.
louke, *vb.* (OE lúcan); *lock (pr.
subj.)* 109. 110; *pp.* loken
68. 2.
lounesse, *sb.*; *humility* 57. 18.
loure, *vb.*; *crouch, skulk (pr.
subj.)* 116. 43.
loute, *vb.* (OE lútan); *bow, make
obeisance* 120. 31; *reuerence*
lowte 105. 79.
loue, *sb.*; *love* 7. 2; lowe 76. 18.
See also *lufe.*
loue-bonde, *sb. pl.*; *fetters of
love* 7. 24.
loued, *pp.* (OE lofian); *honoured,
praised* 29. 5.
loue-teeris, *sb. pl.*; *tears of love*
89. 32.
loueli, *adj.*; (1) *full of love* 58. 5.
(2) *beautiful* loueliche 90. 7.
loue-likyng, *sb.*; *loving desire*
111. 5.
louengge, *vbl. sb.*; *affection* 68.
21.
louerd, *sb.* (OE hlaford); *lord*
2 B. 1; lauerd 29. 5, louird
34. 22. See also *lord.*
louere, *sb.*; *lover* 89. 8. See also
lufer.
louesum, *adj.*; *lovable* 96. 29.
louely, *adv.*; *lovingly* 91. 15.
louien, *vb.* (OE lufian); *love* 7.
8; louen 67. 25, loue 26. 43,
luue 30. 26; *pr.* 1 *s.* loue 11.
13; *pr.* 3 *s.* loueþ 102. 98,
louet 54. 4; *pr. pl.* louen 57.

39; *imp.* loue 75. 5; *pt.* 3 *s.*
louid 129. 5; *pp.* loued 6. 22.
louyng, *sb; praise, worship* 44.
29.
lowe, *vb.* ; *make an obeisance*
105. 79.
lowe, *adj.* ; *low* 91. 113; lawe
94. 7; *comp.* lowere 129. 2;
supl. lowest 121. 154.
lowe, *adv.* ; *low* 34. 30; low 83.
42, lawe 27. 48.
loweliche, *adv.* ; *meekly* 57. 21;
loueliche 57. 63.
lude, *adv.*—See *loud.*
luf, *vb.* (OE lufian) ; *love* 48. 94;
pr. 2 *s.* lufes 47. 8; *imp.* lufe
77. 25; *pr. p.* lufand 86. 35;
pt. 3 *s.* lufed 84. 76.
lufe, *sb.* ; *love* 77. 4; luf 47. 2.
lufe-langyng, *sb.* ; *love-longing*
83. 29; louelongynge 11.
16.
lufer, *sb.* ; *lover* 85. 15; *pl.* lofers
84. 50. See also *louere.*
lufly, *adj.* ; *loving* 48. 96; *adv.*
lovingly 79. 22.
lufsum, *adj.* ; *lovable* 83. 42;
lofsum 111. 60.
luite, *adv.* ; *little* 101. 44.
lullen, *vb.* ; *lull, soothe* 56. 15;
pr. subj. lulle 56. 19.
lurke, *vb.* : *lurk* (*pr. subj.*) 116.
43.
lust, *vb.* ; *listen* (*imp.*) 21. 7; lest
32. 3.
lust, *sb.* ; *desire* 10. 7, 13. 22.
luste, *vb.*—See *liste.*
lustines, *vb.* ; *vigour, robustness*
95. 162.
luþer, *adj.* ; *evil, wicked* 6. 52;
luthere 6. 8, luþure 112. 62.
luuelili, *adv.* ; *lovingly* 30. 96.
lyare, *sb.* ; *liar* 6. 61.
lyflode, *sb.* ; *mode of living* 23,
heading.
ly3e, *vb.* (OE lēogan) ; *lie* 113. 9.
ly3es, *sb. pl.* ; *lies* 101. 141.
lyht, *sb.* ; *light* 6. 105; ly3t 26.

47, ly3th 12. 5, liht 44. 13,
li3t 115. 43, lithte 55. 22, lyt
58. 14.
ly3th, *adj.* ; *bright* 120. 105.
lyhtnesse, *sb.* ; *brightness, cheer*
11. 34.
lynes, *sb. pl.* ; *lines, cords* (*for*
snaring birds) 101. 130.
lynge, *vb.* (OE lengan) ; *linger,*
remain 96. 4; lyng 95. 58.
lyowen, *pp.* (ONth. *liwen,
*liowen, WS ligen) ; *lent* 27.
82.
lyþe, *sb.* ; *solace, comfort* 44. 23.
lyþe, *vb.* (ON hlýða) ; *listen*
(*imp.*) 11. 5.

ma, *adj. comp.* ; *more* 27. 102.
See also *mo.*
mad, *adj.* ; (1) *mad, demented*
27. 95; madde 105. 4. (2)
angry, furious 37. 4.
maden, *sb.*—See *mayden.*
mageste, *sb.* ; *majesty* 83. 1.
Magote, *prop. name* 29. 53.
make, *sb.* ; (1) *companion, mate*
67. 17. (2) *equal* 29. 55.
maken, *vb.* ; *make* 56. 104; *pr.*
1 *s.* make 16. 36, mak 29. 6;
pr. 3 *s.* makeþ 6. 14, makiþ
90. 1, maket 68. 11, makit
42. 2, makes 48. 102, mak
49. 6, mas 81. 32, mase 84.
15, maas 96. 38; *pr. pl.*
makeþ 6. 9; *imp.* make 7. 16,
mak 35. 10; *pr. p.* makyng
119. 19; *pt.* 2 *s.* madest 6. 2,
madyst 94. 17; *pt.* 3 *s.* made
12. 11, maade 96. 19, mad
41. 19; *pp.* mad 65. 3, maad
90. 34, i-mad 38. 7, y-maked
13. 19, imakid 28. 8, hi-
maked 2 A. 4.
maker, *sb.* ; *maker* 44. 1.
mald, *prop. name* ; *Maud* 29. 54.
malys, *sb.* ; *malice* 118. 4.
man, *sb.* ; *man* 2 A. 1; manne

84. 12; *gen. s.* mannis 56. 35,
mannys 91. 104; *pl.* men 11.
38; *gen. pl.* manne 49. 27,
mennys 91. 144. See also
mon.

manas, *vb.*; *menace, threaten*
(*pr. subj.*) 101. 145; *pp.*
manast 101. 158.

manere, *sb.*; *manner* 68. 12.

man-hed, *sb.*; (1) *mankind* 30.
125. (2) *human nature*, man-
hede 48. 78.

mani, *adj.*; *many* 26. 38. See
also *mony.*

mankindde, *sb.*; *mankind* 58.
11.

mankinne, *sb.* (OE mancynn);
mankind 3. 14; mankenne
65. 16, manken 69. 5.

manlich, *adj.*; *human* 131. 23.

marchauns, *sb. pl.*; *merchants*
108. 13.

mare, *adj. comp.*; *more* 27. 22.
See also *more.*

mariage, *sb.*; *marriage* 88. 11.

mariori, *prop. name*; *Margery*
29. 53.

mariot, *prop. name*; *Margot* 29.
54.

maris, *prop. name pl.*; *Maries*
30. 129.

markes, *sb. pl.*; *marks, scars* 16.
50.

marred, *pp.*—See *merre.*

masse, *sb.*; *Mass* 114. 23.

mast, *adv. supl.*; *most* 29. 2;
maste 82. 1, mest 6. 66.

mat, *sb.*; *?mat* 106. 43.

mateere, *sb.*; (1) *matter, reason*
109. 6; *pl.* *topics, problems*
maters 106. 69.

matines, *sb.*; *matins* 55. 1;
matynes 114. 21.

may, *vb.*; *can*: *pr.* 1 *s.* 6. 21;
mei 6. 28, mow 91. 3, mov
61. 8; *pr.* 2 *s.* maist 91. 6,
maiȝt 95. 62, mist 2 B. 2,
mit 2 A. 10, myth 16. 33,

mauth 65. 5, may 31. 58; *pr.*
3 *s.* mai 3. 4, may 7. 49, mey
6. 40; *pr. pl.* mowen 13. 11,
mawen 11. 43, mowe 8. 26,
mow 96. 83, moun 58. 63, mai
30. 50; *pr. subj.* mowe 62. 3;
pt. 1 *s.* mytte 124. 14; *pt. pl.*
mithten 57. 30; *pt. subj.*
miht 56. 107, myȝt 91. 75,
mitht 72. 3, myȝite 134. 38.

may, *sb.*; *maid* 11. 3.

may, *sb.*; *May* 84. 57.

mayde, *sb.*; *maid* 17. 17; *gen.*
maydes 22. 7.

mayden, *sb.*; *maiden* 11. 48;
maden 41. 3, 9; (*gen.*) may-
denes 20. 11, mayden 83. 5;
? pl. maiden 10. 50.

mayden-hede, *sb.*; *virginity* 26.
46; maydened 56. 51.

mayn, *sb.*; *strength, virtue* 81.
32; maine 45. 6. See also
meyn.

mayster, *sb.*; *master* 95. 149.

maystre, *vb.*; *prevail, overcome*
83. 43.

maystrie, *sb.*; *mastery, domin-
ion* 100. 35; maistrie 106. 94.

maystrise, *sb.* (OF maistrise);
power, dominion 101. 18.

me, 1 *pers. pron. dat. acc.*; (1)
me 3. 1; mee 92. 6. (2)
myself 3. 3.

me, *indef. pron.*; *one* 6. 16.

mede, *sb.*; *mead* 10. 32.

mede, *sb.*; *meed, reward* 6. 107;
meede 95. 118; *pl.* medes 25.
15.

medicine, *sb.*; *medicine* 10. 30;
medicyne 85. 1.

medle, *vb.*; (1) *mix, mingle*: *imp.*
medel 100. 35; *pp.* medlid
67. 23. (2) *be concerned with*
(*subj.*) 106. 94; *pr.* 3 *s.* med-
leþ 108. 34.

meete, *adj.*; *fit, suitable* 111. 16.

meetyng, *sb.*; *meeting* 112. 28.

mei, *vb.*—See *may.*

meire, *sb.*; *mayor* 117. 82.

mek, *adj.*; *meek* 26. 17; **meoke**
17. 20, **moeke** 20. 4, **meke**
59. 3; *superlative* **mekest** 84.
74.

meken, *vb.*; *humble*: *pr. pl.*
moeketh 14. 8; *pp.* **meked**
41. 10.

meknesse, *sb.*; *meekness* 35. 23;
mekenes 79. 19.

mele, *sb.* (OE mǣl); *meal, re-
past* 101. 179.

mele, *vb.* (OE mǣlan); *tell·* 112.
35.

melodi, *sb.*; *melody* 86. 32;
melody 84. 67.

melt, *vb.*; *waste away, die*; *pr.*
3 *s.* **melteþ** 106. 42.

memor, *sb.*; *remembrance* 83.
17.

menbres, *sb. pl.*; *members (of
the body)* 95. 154.

mende, *vb.*; *amend* 107. 60;
mend 30. 62; *pr. subj.* **mende**
44. 15.

mene, *adj.* (OE gemǣne);
humble, of low degree 104. 61.

mene, *vb.*; (1) *mean, signify, in-
tend* 119. 9; *pr.* 1 *s.* 100. 103;
pr. 3 *s.* **meneþ** 96. 15; *pt.* 3 *s.*
mente 95. 11; *pp.* **ment** 90.
5. (2) *remember* 30. 111
(*impers.*); **meen** 101. 121.

menen, *vb.*; (1) *lament* 109. 7;
imp. 27. 105. (2) *pity*: *to
mene* 6. 66. (3) *utter sadly*
10. 14, 26. 3.

menge, *vb.*; *mix, mingle*: *pr.* 3 *s.*
mengeþ 35. 9; *pp.* **menged**
123. 39, **meynt** 118. 4,
(*drenched*) y-**meind** 25. 7.

menske, *sb.*; *honour* 17. 26.

menske, *vb.*; *honour, give dignity*
116. 32.

merci, *sb.*; (1) *mercy* 6. 70;
mercy 16. 53. (2) *thanks*
107. 8.

merite, *sb.*; *merit* 56. 89.

merkes, *sb. pl.*; *marks, limits*
81. 30.

merlyon, *sb.*; *merlin, falcon*
95. 9.

merre, *vb.*; *hinder, injure, mar*:
pr. 3 *s.* **merres** 27. 102; *pp.*
marred 6. 11.

merueilous, *adj.*; *marvellous*
134. 15.

merueyle, *vb.*; *marvel*: *pr.* 3 *s.*
merueyles 101. 97.

merueyles, *sb. pl.*; *extraordinary
events* 113. 15.

mes, *sb.* (OF mes); *dish of food*
32. 6.

mest, *adv. supl.*—See *mast*.

mesured, *pp.*; *restrained, dis-
ciplined* 118. 21.

mete, *sb.*; *food* 6. 44.

meten, *vb.*; *meet* 6. 65; **mete** 29.
47, **meete** 112. 103; *pp.* **met**
112. 28.

meþ, *sb.* (OE mǣþ); *moderation*
100. 35.

methchef, *sb.*—See *mischef*.

meue, *vb.*; (1) *move, remove* 97.
22. (2) *agitate, discuss* 106.
69; *pr. pl.* **meueþ** 106.
74.

meuyng, *sb.*; *motion, quaking*
113. 49.

meyn, *sb.*; *strength* 6. 11. See
also *mayn*.

meyne, *sb.* (OF mesnie); *re-
tinue, company* ?102. 36;
menȝhe 79. 23.

meyntenaunce, *sb.*; *support*
108. 66.

meyntene, *vb.*; *uphold, support*
(*pr. subj.*) 108. 24; *pp.* **meyn-
tened** 108. 32.

mi, min, *poss. pron.*; *my, mine*
3. 6, 3. heading; **mine** 3. 11,
my 6. 11, **myn** 6. 13.

miche, *adj.*; *much* 134. 39;
great **myche** 91. 53. See also
muche.

mid, *prep.*; *with* 2 A. 4; **myd** 12.

13; myd ywisse *assuredly* 7. 3.

middai, *sb.*; *midday* 55. 15.

middelert, *sb.* (OE middan-eard × middel-); *earth* 6. 2.

mid-night, *sb.*; *midnight* 30. 1.

midwenter, *sb.*; *midwinter* 56. 50.

might, *sb.*; *power* 30. 23; myght 48. 93, miht 45. 3, myht 7. 7, myhte 12. 10, my3te 26. 17, my3th 94. 26, myth 41. 17, myt 34. 5, mytte 34. 28; *pl.* myhtes 20. 15, mi3thes 93. 3.

mikel, mykel, michel, michil, mychel, *adj.* and *adv.*; *much* 4. 2, 30. 20, 40. 2, 56. 29, 91. 76. See also *muchel.*

milce, *sb.*; *mercy* 131. 10. See also *mylse.*

milde, *adj.*; *mild* 3. 9; mild 30. 70, mylde 32. 1.

mildeliche, *adv.*; *mildly* 55. 24; myldely 89. 40.

mil3ful, *adj.*; *merciful* 131. 85.

milk, *sb.*; *milk* 111. 13; melke 32. 66.

milsfolnesse, *sb.*; *mercifulness* 13. 24; mylsfolnesse 25. 20.

min, *adj.*; *less* 27. 22; minne 116. 7, mynne 120. 99.

mining, *verbal sb.*; *remembrance* 30. 98.

minne, *vb.* (ON minna); (1) *have in mind, remember*; (*pr. subj.*) 95. 41. (2) *tell, specify* 96. 26.

mirie, *adj.* and *adv.*; *merry, joyous* 57. 29; miri 81. 32, murye 37. 2, myry 91. 107; *supl.* muriest 101. 1, murieste 112. 28, murgest 101. 179.

mirour, *sb.*; *mirror* 101. 59; Myrour 79. 26, myrrour 121. 90.

mirre, *sb.*; *myrrh* 56. 72; mir 31. 30, myrre 11. 41.

mirthe, *sb.*; *rejoicing, joy* 56. 54; merþe 102. 100, myrth 84. 44; *pl. pleasures* merþes 95. 160. See also *murþe.*

mis, *sb.*; *wrong-doing* 27. 105; mys 48. 117; *pl.* misses 116. 7.

mis, *adv.*; *amiss* 109. 70.

mischef, *sb.*; *adversity, misfortune* 96. 49; methchef 65. 8; *pl.* mischeues 82. 4.

misdede, *sb. pl.*; *misdeeds* 122. 42; mysdede 91. 140.

misdon, *vb.*; *do wrong* 58. 43; *pr. pl.* 97. 53; *pp.* misdoo 121. 75.

misesli, *adv.*; *uncomfortably* 58. 47.

mis-lyuing, *sb.*; *evil living* 95. 34.

mis-plawe, *sb.*; *sinful sport* 102. 87.

misse, *vb.*; (1) *be cut off from* 7. 4. (2) *fail* (*pr. subj.*) 11. 58. (3) *fail to attain* mysse 79. 26, mis 98. 38. (4) *lack* mysshe 91. 150.

mistred, *vb. pt.*; *?shewed, revealed* 30. 37.

mo, *adj.*; *more* 6. 25; moo 121. 113. See also *ma.*

mock, *sb.*; (lit. *muck*) *riches, property* 27. 95; mok 100. 80.

mod, *sb.*; *mood, mind, inclination* 3. 9; mode 26. 17, mood 93. 56.

moder, *sb.*; *mother* 3. 12; modir 45. 13, modyr 91. 55; *gen. s.* moder 28. 14, modris 64. 7, moderes 91. 57; *pl.* modres 56. 12.

moderhede, *sb.*; *motherhood* 41. 13.

moekynge, *sb.*; *obeisance* 14. 11.

molde, *sb.* (OE molda); *crown of the head* 2 B. 11.

mon, *auxil. vb.* (ON monu); *shall* 50. 7, 81. 26, 81. 33.

mon, *vb.* (OE munan); (1) *have in mind* 29. 17. (2) *remind* (*pr. subj.*) mone 131. 62.

mon, *sb.*; *lamentation, complaint* 56. 115; mone 26. 3, moon 95. 23.

mon, *sb.*; *man* 6. 3; *gen. s.* monnes 100. 39, monnus 120. 85; *gen. pl.* monne 6. 66. See also *man*.

mone, *sb.*; *moon* 6. 2.

monhod, *sb.*; *human existence* 95. 146.

monkunde, *sb.*; *mankind* 19. 2.

monkunne, *sb.* (OE mon-cynn); *mankind* 13. 3; man-kinne 3. 14, monkun 20. 7, monkyn 11. 30.

mony, *adj.*; *many* 96. 6; monye 6. 25, moni 9. 8. See also *mani*.

more, *adj.* and *adv. comp.*; *more* 6. 92; mor 72. 3; *supl.* moste 101. 81. See also *mare*.

morewenyng, *sb.*; *morning* 8. 10; morwenynge 96. 2.

mortualite, *sb.*; *mortality, mortal nature* 106. 93.

morwe, *sb.*; *morrow, morn* 95. 20.

most, *sb.*; *must, juice of grapes* 25. 8.

moste, *aux. vb.* (properly pt. of *mot*); *pr. must* 96. 34; most 75. 24, muste 62. 6, must 65. 15, mostou (= most þou) 28. 2.

mot, *aux. vb.* (OE mōtan); (1) *may* 91. 61; mote 7. 12, mute 52. 6; *pl.* moten 34. 5, mote 108. 22. (2) *must* (1 and 3 *s.*) mot 16. 43, 23. 30; (2 *s.*) mote 100. 75.

mote, *sb.*; *mote* 109. 50.

mouht, *sb.* (OE mohðe); *moth* 106. 42.

mourne, *vb.*; *mourn* 28. 3; moorne 89. 36; *pr.* 1 *s.*

mourne 9. 3; *pr. p.* murn-ingge 56. 78.

mournyng, *sb.* and *adj.*; *grief* 8. 11; mornyng 89. 32, murning 59. 19.

mouth, *sb.*; *mouth* 67. 12; mouhþ 17. 6, mowth 81. 32, muth 69. 3, mough 45. 6; *pl.* mouþes 95. 5.

mouwe, *sb.*; *grimace* 104. 23; *pl.* mowes 104. 53.

muche, *adj., adv.*; *much* 95. 31; *great* moche 26. 46. See also *miche*.

muchel, *adj.* and *adv.*; *much* 15. 33; *great* muchele 8. 16. See also *mikel*.

multiplie, *vb.*; *increase* 121. 184.

munde, *sb.*; *mind, memory* 16. 29; mund 28. 15, muynde 95. 13, meynde 34. 34, mende 68. 20, mynde 79. 26; haue in ~ *be bent on* 19. 6; *remember* 21. 10.

munne, *vb.*; *think* 6. 3.

muntyng, *vbl. sb.* (OE myntan); *thinking, estimation* 98. 52.

murþe, *sb.*; *mirth, joy* 95. 23; *pl.* murþes 6. 3.

musyng, *pr. p.*; *musing* 132. 2.

mylse, *sb.*; *mercy* 7. 35. See also *milce*.

mylsful, *adj.*; *merciful* 14. 12.

mynge, *vb.* (OE gemynegian); *mention, relate* 11. 24; *pr.* 1 *s.* munge 95. 169.

myre, *sb.*; *mire* 100. 80.

myrknes, *sb.*; *darkness, murkiness* 84. 64.

mys, *sb. pl.*; *mice* 108. 71.

mysulf, *pron.*; *myself* 25. 9.

na, *adj.*; *no* 7. 36; *conj. nor* 29. 50.

nacions, *sb. pl.*; *nations* 106. 30.

nafti, *adj.* (= naghti); *wicked, vicious* 110. 91.

nagt, *sb.*; *nought, nothing* 5. 2;

adv. not na3t 35. 28. See also
nouht.

naill, *sb.; nail* 91. 7; nayll 91.
34; *pl.* nailes 2 A. 7, nayles
16. 27, nalys 40. 5, naylis 90.
12.

nailen, *vb.; nail* 3. 3; *pp.* nailed
4. 5, nayled 26. 23, hi-neiled
2 A. 2, y-nailed 34. 19.

naked, *adj.; naked* 43. 2; nacked
2 B. 7, nakede 1 A. 1.

name, *sb.; name* 26. 2; nam 29.
8. See also *nome.*

namore, namare, nama, *adv.;
no more* 6. 70, 26. 51, 29. 20.

nan, *pron., adj.; none* 27. 101;
nane 48. 9. See also *non.*

narewe, *adv.; ?with legs close
together* 126. 12.

nas = ne was 16. 6.

nat, *adv.; not* 91. 133.

naþ = ne haþ 101. 55.

nathyng, *sb.* and *adv.; nothing*
80. 6.

nay, *adv.; no* 93. 23.

ne, *adv.; not* 2 B. 12; *conj. nor*
29. 56; ny 102. 52.

neb, *sb.* (OE nebb); *face* 1 B. 2.

nebshaft, *sb.; face, countenance;
gen. s.* nebshaftes 24. 21.

nede, *sb.; need, necessity* 26. 12;
noede 16. 32.

nede, *vb.;* (1) *constrain* 24. 25;
pr. subj. 24. 17. (2) *need, re-
quire; pr.* 3 *s.* neodeþ 102.
44.

nede, *adv.; necessarily* 16. 43.

nedes, *adv.; inevitably* 27. 90;
nedis 28. 2.

negh, *vb.; draw nigh* 86. 31; *pr.*
3 *s.* neyhit 64. 10; *pr. pl.*
nei3e 108. 23.

neih, *adv.; nigh* 108. 23; nei3
109. 29, nee 84. 11; *comp.*
neer 96. 11, nere 115. 27;
supl. nest 7. 48.

nei3ebore, *sb.; neighbour* 27. 90;
gen. s. nei3ebores 101. 148.

nelle, *vb.* (negative of *wille*); *be
reluctant, be unwilling; pr.* 1 *s.*
nel 125. 21, nul 6. 70, nyl 121.
35; *pr.* 2 *s.* nult 8. 20; *pr.* 3 *s.*
nelle 131. 52, nol 115. 44.

neore = ne weore 112. 51;
nere 9. 7.

ner, *adv.*—See *neuer.*

nere, *adj.* and *adv.; near* 26. 15;
neere 109. 14.

nert = ne ert. 28. 31.

nest, *sb.; nest* 67. 13.

neuene, *vb.; name, mention* 26.
2; *pr.* 1 *s.* neuen 30. 58.

neuer, *adv.; never* 16. 6; neuere
26. 4, ner 9. 7.

newe, *adj.; new* 57. 48; neowe
21. 23, neu 29. 38.

newe, *vb.; become new, renew;
pr.* 3 *s.* noeweth 21. 14.

night, *sb.; night* 30. 22; niht
101. 17, nith 56. 1, nyght 81.
36, ny3t 26. 48, nyht 7. 6,
nyth 58. 60; *gen.* nyhtes 11.
20.

nimen, *vb.; take, seize; pr. subj.*
nym 98. 31; *pt.* 3 *s.* nom 17.
16, nam 11. 51; *pt.* 2 *s.* nome
14. 11; *pp.* i-nome 34. 27,
in-nome 36. 5.

nis = ne is 10. 35; nys 8. 23.

niþe, *sb.; malice, hatred* 6.
59.

no, *conj.; nor* 27. 57.

nobleye, *sb.;* (1) *splendour* 24.
14. (2) *great eminence* noble-
lay 48. 54.

noiþer, *conj.; neither* 27. 57;
nouþer 102. 58.

no-kenes, *adj.; of no kind* 112.
123.

nome, *sb.; name* 17. 8. See also
name.

nomliche, *adv.; especially* 21.
21.

non, *pron., adj.; none* 3. 4;
none 26. 4, noon 87. 21,
noone 90. 30. See also *nan.*

none, *sb.*; *the ninth hour* 30. 88.
norissched, *pp.*; *brought up,
reared* 103. 83.
north, *adj.*; *north* 36. 4.
nou, *adv.*; *now* 6. 11; nu 29. 58,
now 26. 28, nov 49. 21, nowe
132. 89.
nouht, *sb., adj., adv.*; *nought,
nothing, not* 49. 17, noht 6.
75, nouth 12. 3, nou3t 110.
91, nou3th 122. 22, nowth
39. 13, nout 6. 15.
nouþe, *adv.*; *now* 13. 22.
no-wiht, *adv.*; *not at all* 113. 7.
noyes, *sb. pl.*; *afflictions* 81. 3.
noyse, *sb.*; *sound* 96. 11.
nuy3ed, *pp.* (OF nuire); *vexed,
injured* 102. 13.
ny, *conj.*—See *ne.*
nys = ne ys (8. 23).
nys, *adj.*; *foolish* 118. 11; *pl.* nyse
118. 71.
nysete, *sb.*; *folly* 121. 50.
nyten, *vb.* (negative of *witen*);
be ignorant: *pr.* 1 *s.* not 6. 26;
pr. 2 *s.* nost 23. 33; *pr.* 3 *s.*
not 23. 3.

o, *interj*; *O! oh!* 90. 5.
o, *adj.*; *one* 17. 26; oo 91. 125.
o, *indef. art.*; *a, an* 8. 10.
o, *prep.*; *on, in, with, of* 1 A. 4,
10. 12, 17. 26, 30. 91.
o, *adv.*; *ever, always* 99. 4; oo
126. 40.
ocasion, *sb.*; *?cause, reason* 106.
50.
ocupacions, *sb. pl.*; *control of
affairs* 106. 32.
ocupye, *vb.*; *occupy, engage* (*pr.
pl.*) 106. 34.
oerþe, *sb.*—See *eorþe.*
oeuch, *adj.*—See *eche.*
of, *prep.*; *of* 2 B. 2; *with* 1 A. 1;
from 3. 8; *for* off 93. 65.
offycer, *sb.*; *official* 96. 73.
offys, *sb* ; *office* 103. 35.

oforn, *prep.*; *before* 72. 10.
ofringe, *sb.*; *offering* 14. 12;
offrynge 32. 34, offringge 57.
46.
of-seche, *vb.*; *visit, descend into*:
imp. of-sech 18. 1.
of-spring, *sb.*; *descendants* 112.
66; hosprynge 132. 76.
ofte, *adv.*; *often* 7. 19; oft 48.
41.
oftesiþe, *adv.*; *oftentimes* 96. 23.
ogayne, *adv.*; *again* 48. 56.
o3ene, *adj.*—See *owen.*
old, *adj.*; *old* 23. 28; olde 13.
10; ald 30. 44, alde 84. 49.
See also *elde.*
olod, *pp.* (*cf.* ON lóga af, Icel.
aflóga); *dissipated* 81. 22.
olpy, *adj.* (OE ān-līpig); *single,
only* 21. 2.
omang, *prep.*; *among* 30. 103.
on, *prep.*; (1) *on* 2 B. 6; one 3.
1; *in* 1 A. 4.
on, *adj.*; *one* 14. 5; one 8. 13.
on, *adj.*; *alone* 25. 9; oon 90. 24,
one 16. 42.
onde, *sb.*; *envy* 6. 59.
onder, *prep.*; *under* 32. 69.
onder-fonge, *vb.*—See *ounder-
uon.*
ones, *adv.*; *once* 95. 68; onis 70.
9, onus 120. 27.
oniment, *sb.*—See *oynement.*
onliche, *adj. and adv.*; *alone* 13.
21; *only* onlich 121. 113;
peerless onely 41. 9.
onsle3e, *adj.*; *unwise* 131. 83.
onswere, *sb.*; *answer* 95. 59.
onswere, *vb.*; *answer* 101. 103;
imp. 15. 3. See also *ansuere.*
onuren, *vb.*—See *honowre.*
on-wemmed, *pp.*; *undefiled* 32.
75.
onworþlie, *adv.*; *unworthily* 131.
90.
ony *adj.*—See *ani.*
oost, *sb.*; *abode* 121. 155.
op, *adv.*; *up* 19. 5.

op-bere, *vb.*; *bear up, sustain*: *pt.* 2 *s.* 13. 16.

openly, *adv.*; *clearly* 120. 14.

opne, *vb.*; *open*: *pr.* 1 *s.* 68. 16; *pt.* 2 *s.* openedest 22. 11.

opon, *prep.*—See *upon*.

op-steye, *vb.*; *pt.* 2 *s.* ascended 24. 15.

opyne, *adj.*; *open* 126. 18.

or, *conj.*; *or* 27. 63; ore 10. 26.

or, *adv.*—See *er*.

ordeyne, *vb.*; *ordain* (*pr. subj.*) 103. 4, (*imp.*) 116. 30; *pr.* 3 *s.* ordans 86. 16; *pt.* 3 *s.* ordeyned 95. 27; *pp.* 132. 87.

ordre, *sb.*; *social class* 114. 29; *pl.* ordres 114. 17.

ore, *sb.*; *grace, favour* 7. 35; hore 124. 25.

orisons, *sb. pl.*; *prayers* 114. 26.

orn, *vb. pt.*—See *irnen*.

o-sunder, *adv.*; *asunder* 72. 21.

oþer, *conj.*; *or* 10. 39; ouþer . . . or (*either . . . or*) 95. 97.

oþer, *adj.*; (1) *second* 11. 31. (2) *other* 6. 47; oþir 29. 69, oþur 95. 160.

opes, *sb. pl.*—See *owth*.

ou, *pers. pron.*—See *ȝou* and *þu*.

ouȝt, *sb.*; *aught* 95. 98; outh 120. 47, aght 81. 19.

ounder-uon, *vb.*; *receive* 23. 26; *imp.* onder-fonge 32. 6. See also *vnderfonge*.

oune, *adj.*—See *owen*.

ounneþe, *adv.*; *scarcely* 23. 11.

our, *sb.*—See *houre*.

our, *poss. pron.*; *our* 12. 9; oure (*pl.*) 10. 36, houre 34. 3, ower 41. 14, owre 41. 15, howre 41. 28, vr 29. 35, vre 6. 101, vrre 41. 16.

ous, 1 *pers. pron. dat. acc. pl.*—See *vs*.

out, *adv.*; *out* 7. 39; owt 82. 10, oute 120. 27, vt 3. 8.

outh, *sb.*—See *ouȝt*.

outh, *adv.*; *aught, at all* 67. 25.

outlawed, *pp.*; *proscribed, banished* 132. 49.

outrage, *sb.*; *wantonness* 109. 69.

outrayede, *pp.*; *put down, humiliated* 118. 65.

out-take, *vb.*; *except* (*pr.* 1 *s.*) 114. 15.

ouer, *prep.*; *over, above* 21. 4.

ouerbide, *pp.*; *outlived* 100. 92.

ouer-cloþe, *sb.*; *upper coat* 39. 12.

ouer-come, *vb.*; *overcome*: *pr.* 3 *s.* ouercoms 84. 68; *pt.* 2 *s.* ouercome 22. 9; *pt.* 3 *s.* ouercom 98. 30.

ouer-pas, *vb.*; *come to an end* 96. 54; *pp.* ouer-past 113. 37.

ow, *pers. pron.*—See *ȝou*.

oway, *adv.*—See *away*.

owe, *vb.* (OE āgan); *owe, ought* (*pr.* 1 *s.*) 54. 5; *pr.* 3 *s.* aw (*impers.*) 77. 25; *pr. pl.* owen 131. 45; *pt.* 1 *s.* ouȝte (*owed*) 95. 81; *pt.* 3 *s.* auhte 16. 12. aght (*impers.*) 48. 44.

owen, *adj.*; *own* 56. 124; oune 12. 12, ouwe 14. 6, owe 25. 19, oȝene 32. 23, owne 120. 81, awen 82. 28.

owth, *sb.*; *oath* 39. 11; *pl.* oþes 102. 30.

ox, *sb.*; *ox* 75. 11.

oyl, *adv.* (OF oil); *yea, yes* 118. 74, 120. 85.

oynement, *sb.*; *ointment* 18. 4; oniment 55. 29.

paas, pace, *vb.*—See *passen*.

pacient, *adj.*; *patient* 102. 14.

page, *sb.*; *page, groom* 108. 63.

paine, *sb.*; *pain, suffering* 45. 7; payne 77. 11; *pl.* payns 46. 8. See also *peyn*.

pais, *sb.*—See *pes*.

pak, *sb.*; *pack* 23. 4.

pal, *sb.* (Lat. pallium); *fine cloth* 117. 66; pall 105. 46.

pale, *adj.*; *pale* 84. 10.

palefrey, *sb.*; *palfrey* 51. 13.

paleys, *sb.*; *palace* 96. 86.

palmere, *sb.*; *palmer* 119. 18.

pane, *sb.*; *raiment* 29. 63.

pappe, *sb.*; *female breast* 75. 17; *pl.* pappis 41. 20.

pardoun, *sb.*; *pardon* 119. 44.

parfyt, *adj.*; *perfect* 101. 164. See also *perfyte*.

parisch-prest, *sb.*; *parish priest* 117. 54.

parliment, *sb.*; *parliament* 103. 58.

parti, *vb.*; (1) *part, depart*; parte 116. 33; *pr.* 3 *s.* parteþ 101. 87; *pr. subj.* parte 103. 78; *pt.* 1 *s.* partid 72. 21. (2) *distribute* 27. 86.

partiȝe, *sb.*; *part, portion* 56. 103; party 121. 204.

partyng, *sb.*; *parting* 84. 31.

pas, *sb.* (OF pas); (1) *way* 27. 110. (2) *pace* pase 46. 5.

pasce, *pp.* (OF passé); *passed* 105. 33.

passen, *vb.*; (1) *pass (away)* 120. 54; passe 81. 33, pas 101. 149, paas 96. 86, pace 115. 11; *pr. pl.* pasen 74. 1, passeþ 106. 27; *pt. pl.* past 113. 44. (2) *surpass* 115. 20; *pr.* 3 *s.* passeþ 95. 12.

pay, *sb.*; (1) *reward* 120. 95. (2) *pleasure, liking* 56. 60; paye 92. 30, pai 119. 5.

payȝe, *vb.*; (1) *pay* 56. 123; *pt.* 3 *s.* payd 48. 69. (2) *please*: *pr.* 3 *s.* payes 84. 29; *imp.* pay 102. 39; *pt.* 3 *s.* paiȝede 56. 46; *pp.* payet 104. 71, payd 118. 60.

pays, *sb.*—See *pes*.

peined, *pp.*; *tormented* 65. 26.

pelur, *sb.* (OF pelure); *fur* 91. 118.

penaunce, *sb.*; *penitence* 10. 41.

penaunt, *sb.*; *penitent* 116. 20.

penyles, *adj.*; *penniless* 104. 35.

peple, *sb.*; *people* 103. 50; pepul 112. 38; puple 56. 103.

percen, *vb.*; *pierce* 91. 111; perche 48. 72, perse 56. 118; *imp.* perce 68. 21; *pp.* perched 48. 67, perset 118. 31, persid 127. 22.

pere, *sb.*; *peer, equal* 105. 28; peere 106. 9; *pl.* peris 39. 3.

pereles, *adj.*; *peerless* 79. 25; peerles 111. 68.

pereles, *sb. pl.*; *perils* 103. 50.

perfyte, *adj.*; *perfect* 80. 10. See also *parfyt*.

perilous, *adj.*; *perilous* 121. 179.

persones, *sb. pl.*; *persons* 17. 26.

pes, *sb.*; *peace* 27. 70; pees 92. 12, peis 88. 13, peys 88. 11, pais 44. 18, pays 32. 15.

pese, *sb.*; *pea* 103. 3.

pestilens, *sb.*; *pestilence* 113. 58.

pete, *sb.*; *pity* 48. 72. See also *pite*.

petefully, *adv.*; *pitifully* 48. 64.

peyn, *sb.*; (1) *pain, suffering* 99. 17; peyne 102. 14, peine 70. 10; *pl.* peines 3. 11, peynes 125. 66. (2) *care, pains*, peyne 103. 6.

peynte, *vb.*; *touch up, embellish* (*pr. pl.*) 103. 16; *pp.* peynted 103. 65.

peyre, *sb.*; *disadvantage* 117. 84.

picche, *vb.*; (1) *place*: *pt.* 3 *s.* pitthe 57. 23 (*refl.*); *pp.* ipith 55. 27. (2) *drive home*: *pt.* 3 *s.* pithte 55. 21.

pike, *vb.*; *rob, plunder* 39. 6; pyke 101. 178.

pilgrim, *sb.*; *pilgrim* 28. 25; pylegrym 36. 8; *pl.* pilgrimes 119. 19.

pinacles, *sb. pl.*; *pinnacles* 113. 47.

pinchyn, *vb.*; *oppress* 39. 6.

pine, *sb.*; *suffering* 4. 2; pyne 8. 24, pyn 11. 29; *pl.* pines 30. 100.

piningge, *sb.*; *suffering* 34. 18; peynyng 132. 19.

pistel, *sb.*; *epistle* 100. 1.

pit, *sb.*; *pit* 69. 6; pitte 117. 20.

pite, *sb.*; *pity* 57. 6; piete 10. 52, pyte 80. 12, pytee 121. 13. See also *pete*.

place, *sb.*; *place* 26. 56; plas 96. 6, plase 108. 23.

plai, *sb.*; *play* 29. 11; play 11. 2. See also *plawe*.

planys, *vb.*—See *pleyne*.

plas, *sb.*—See *place*.

plastre, *sb.*; *plaster, poultice* 10. 41.

plates, *sb. pl.*; *plates (of armour)* 125. 17.

plawe, *sb.*; *play* 27. 36. See also *plai*.

plede, *vb.*; *plead* 120. 91.

plein, *sb.*; *plain, meadow* 49. 2.

plente, *sb.*; *plenty* 27. 35.

plesaunce, *sb.*; (1) *pleasure* 96. 54. (2) *favour* 119. 60.

plese, *vb.*; *please* 95. 111; *imp.* 102. 39; *pt.* 3 *s.* plesed 107. 75.

pley3e, *vb.*; *play* 67. 19; *pr. subj.* play 118. 71.

pley3yng, *vbl. sb.*; *playing* 10. 12.

pleyne, *vb.*; *lament, complain*: *pr.* 1 *s.* 132. 19; *pr. pl.* planys 39. 17.

pleynt, *sb.*; *complaint* 103. 23.

plowe-fere, *sb.*; *play-fellow* 6. 55.

plyt, *sb.*; *condition* 112. 93.

pompe, *sb.*; *ostentation* 116. 19.

poo, *sb.*; *peacock* 99. 18.

pore, *adj.*—See *puire*.

pore, *adj.*; *poor* 28. 20; poure 43.

2, pouer 27. 35, pover 121. 14, pouere 53. 3, pure 79. 25.

poreli, *adv.*; *in poverty* 58. 45.

porful, *adj.*; *poor* 75. 8.

pot, *sb.*; *the abyss of hell* 27. 74.

pounde, *sb.*; *pound*; (1) (*money*) 101. 83. (2) (*weight*) 106. 128.

pourpre, *sb.*; *purple robe* 13. 14; purpur 134. 18, purpure 105. 46. See also *purpel*.

pouert, pouerte, *sb.*; *poverty* 48. 55, 57. 23.

powder, *sb.*; *powder, dust* 81. 33; poudir 134. 33.

powere, *sb.*; *power* 48. 46; pouwer 103. 6, pouwere 120. 64, poueere 109. 102, puwer 57. 64.

powste, *sb.* (OF pousté); *power, authority* 105. 73; pouste 114. 6.

poynte, *sb.*; *quality, virtue* 82. 37; *pl.* ?*considerations* 101. 177.

poysi, *sb.*; *poesy, poetry* 101. 73; poyse 121. 65.

praunce, *vb.*; *ride in showy style* 121. 125.

pray, *vb.*; (1) *pray* 132. 67; prai 119. 4; *pr.* 1 *s.* praye 26. 54, praie 124. 32, pray 48. 5. (2) *ask* 132. 67. See also *preien*.

prayse, *vb.*; *praise* (*pr.* 1 *s.*) 82. 2; *pp.* praysed 81. 13. See also *preise*.

prechour, *sb.*; *preacher* 103. 57.

precious, *adj.*; *sumptuous* 121. 142.

pref, *sb.*; *proof* 101. 171.

preien, *vb.*; *pray* 131. 46; preye 119. 78, prey 112. 128; *pr.* 1 *s.* preie 26. 3, prei 97. 4, preye 7. 42; *pr. subj.* preye 11. 55, prei 57. 77; *imp.* prey 93. 51, preye 10. 17. See also *pray*.

preiere, *sb.*; *prayer* 45. 14;

prayere 91. 129; *pl.* preye-ȝerys 94. 11.

preise, *vb.*; *praise* 110. 118; *pr. subj.* 110. 59; *pp.* preised 112. 6. See also *prayse*.

prenet, *pp.*; *transfixed* 104. 70.

preost, *sb.*; *priest* 96. 33; preest 114. 47, prest 114. 43; *pl.* preostes 114. 5.

preparacions, *sb. pl.*; *preparations* 106. 28.

pres, *sb.*; (1) *press*: leye in ~ *lay aside* 113. 20. (2) *throng*: puiten in ~ (*refl.*) *come forward* 118. 39.

prese, *vb.*; *undertake* 95. 35.

presens, *sb.*; *presence* 91. 150.

present, *sb.*; *presence*: in ~ *present* 110. 57.

present, *sb.*; *gift* 90. 1.

presente, *vb.*; *present, offer* 11. 40.

preson, *sb.*; *prison, captivity* 79. 6; presoun 105. 57. See also *prison*.

prest, *adj.* and *adv.*; *prompt, promptly* 19. 4, 23. 26.

preue, *vb.*; *prove, justify* 97. 30; *pp.* preued 107. 90. See also *proue*.

preye, *sb.*; *prey* 13. 20; pray 101. 178.

price, *sb.*—See *pris*.

pride, *sb.*; *pride* 29. 63; pryde 83. 10, pruide 95. 150, prude 6. 55.

prikken, *vb.*; *prick, pierce, impale* (*pr. pl.*) 76. 10; *pr.* 3 *s.* prykketh 132. 51; *imp.* prek 60. 4; *pt. pl.* prikede 2 A. 6; *pp.* prikked 86. 22.

prikung, *vbl. sb.*; *pricking* 4. 6.

prime, *sb.*; *the first hour* 30. 36.

prince, *sb.*; *prince* 57. 23; prynce 48. 46; *pl.* princes 15. 22, princis 134. 23.

principally, *adv.*; *chiefly* 121. 94.

pris, *sb.*; (1) *worth* 40. 2, 111. 68. (2) *valuables* 29. 65. (3) *esteem* 81. 13. (4) ?*reward* 85. 13.

prison, *sb.*; (1) *captivity* 95. 58. (2) *prisoner* (*pl.*) prisones 125. 66.

priueli, *adv.*; *unobtrusively* 96. 12; priuely 118. 75; *secretly* pryuely 78. 7.

priueti, *sb.*; *secret purpose* 106. 86.

profer, *vb.*; *proffer* 104. 42; profre 104. 45.

profyt, *sb.*; *benefit, advantage* 101. 102; profite 115. 23.

proke, *vb.*; *thrust, prod*: *pr.* 3 *s.* prokes 27. 58.

proper, *adj.*; *strictly applicable* 112. 109; propre 112. 93.

prophete, *sb.*; *prophet* 13. 10; *pl.* prophetis 57. 19.

prosperite, *sb.*; *prosperity* 108. 20.

proud, *adj.*; *proud* 127. 4; proude (*pl.*) 101. 115, prud 69. 7.

proude, *vb.*; *behave proudly*: *pr.* 3 *s.* proudeþ 99. 18.

proue, *vb.*; *prove* 23. 32; *pr.* 3 *s.* proueþ 112. 109; *pr. pl.* prouen 65. 14; *pp.* proued 112. 6. See also *preue*.

pryncypal, *adj.*; *principal* 121. 74.

puire, *adj.*; *mere, in itself* 112. 109; *sheer* pore 48. 72.

pulled, *pp.*; *dragged* 79. 6.

pur, *prep.* (AN pur); *for* 125. 76.

purchase, *vb.*; *purchase* 95. 117; *pt.* 1 *s.* purchaced 121. 191.

pure, *adj.*—See *pore*.

purpel, *sb.*; *purple raiment* 117. 66. See also *pourpre*.

purperpall, *sb.*; *robe of fine*

purple 29. 63; purpil-palle 34. 16.

purpos, *sb.*; *meaning*; to þis ~ to this effect 101. 103.

purueyed, *pp.*; *provided* 101. 151.

putten, *vb.*; *put* 57. 27; putte 119. 60, puiten 118. 39; *pr. subj.* pute 23. 5; *imp.* put 17. 11; *pp.* powt 105. 45.

pyne, *vb.*; *torture* 83. 39; *pp.* pyned 77. 23, pynde 128. 10.

quake, *vb.*; *quake, shiver* 91. 35; qwake 84. 61; *pr. pl.* quaken 75. 3; *pt.* 3 *s.* quakede 55. 22, qwok 113. 33.

quam, *rel. pron.*; *whom* 94. 21; qwom 94. 31.

quantite, *sb.*; *portion* 101. 40.

quare, *adv.*; *where* 73. 6; quer 31. 5.

quarel, *sb.*; *controversy, suit (at law)* 120. 101; *pl.* quereles 120. 66.

quat, *pron.*; *what* 67. 14.

qued, *sb.*; *Evil One* 26. 32; quede 124. 51.

quede, *adj.*; *wicked* 120. 87.

qwell, *vb.*; *kill* 84. 92.

queme, *vb.*; *please* 112. 131; *pr. subj.* 14. 12.

quen, *conj.*; *when* 30. 119.

quenche, *vb.*; *dispel, destroy*: *pr.* 3 *s.* quencheth 23. 36; *pt.* 1 *s.* quenched 95. 61.

quene, *sb.*; *queen* 7. 43; qwen 111. 6.

quer, *adv.*—See *quare.*

qwer, *sb.*; *choir* 96. 9.

queristres, *sb. pl.*; *choristers* 96. 9.

quert, *sb.*; *peace, health* 44. 3; qwert 83. 18, qwart 84. 15.

questus, *sb. pl.*; *judicial inquiries* 120. 65.

queynte, *adj.*; *cunning, crafty*; make it ~ *behave deceitfully* 103. 14.

queyntise, *sb.*; *underhand ways* 103. 51.

qui, *adv.*; *why* 59, heading.

quic, *adj.*; *living* 44. 7; quik 95. 176.

quicked, *vb. pt.* 2 *s.*; *quickened* 30. 95.

quile, *sb.*; *while, time* 30. 6. See also *while.*

quite, *adj.*; *white* 31. 12.

quite, *vb.*; *deliver, set free (imp.)* 17. 19.

rage, *vb.*; *play, sport* 109. 66.

rape, *vb.* (ON *hrapa*); *refl. hasten (imp.)* 29. 37; *pt.* 3 *s.* rap 29. 31 (*refl.*).

rath, *adv.*; *soon* 29. 23.

raþer, *adv.* (*comp. of* rath); (1) *sooner* raþere 58. 41. (2) *earlier, previously* 19. 8. (3) (?*adj.*) *preferably* 134. 9.

raumping, *pr. p.*; *rearing up* 95. 4.

raunsoun, *sb.*; *ransom* 13. 18; raunsoune 48. 69, ransoun 56. 123.

raue, *vb.*; *be deluded (pr. subj.)* 106. 65.

rauysch, *vb.*; *draw forcibly (into)*: *pr.* 3 *s.* rauysches 84. 16.

rayse, *vb.*; *raise* 82. 4; *pp.* raysed 41. 18.

real, *adj.*; *royal* 121. 155; rial 82. 31.

realte, *sb.*; *sumptuous splendour* 101. 88.

reche, *vb.* (OE *rǣcan*); (1) *stretch, extend*: *pp.* rauȝt 95. 64. (2) *bestow on, grant*: *pp.* raght 81. 19. (3) *acquire* 103. 54.

rechelesly, *adv.*; *negligently* 107. 38.

reclis, *sb.* (OE rēcels); *incense* 31. 30.

record, *sb.*; *testimony* 108. 51.

red, *adj.*; *red* 1 A. 1; rede 31. 31.

rede, *sb.*; *counsel, purpose* 30. 97; reed 7. 57.

rede, *vb.*; (1) *advise, recommend*: red 105. 23; *pr.* 1 *s.* rede 8. 25. (2) *utter (in the act of reading)* 114. 7; *pr. pl.* 26. 11; *pt.* 1 *s.* 105. 7. (3) *utter* 6. 14.

redi, *adj.*; *ready* 27. 110; redy 121. 168; redye 101. 162.

redres, *vb.*; *redress (pr. subj.)* 100. 56.

redresse, *sb.*; *redress* 118. 16.

redyly, *adv.*; *readily* 91. 136.

regne, *vb.*; *reign, rule* 101. 138; *pr.* 2 *s.* regnest 87. 40; *pr.* 3 *s.* regnis 39. 19; *pr. p.* regnyng 98. 50.

reherce, *vb.*; *rehearse, relate* 95. 40.

rein, *sb.*; *rain* 49. 4; reyn 106. 18.

rek, *vb.* (OE reccan); *reck, care* 81. 24; *pr. pl.* recchen 103. 63; *pr. subj.* recche 89. 42; *imp.* rek 86. 8; *pt.* 3 *s.* rouȝte 36. 4, routh 67. 26.

rekken, *vb.* (OE gerecenian); *reckon, calculate* 81. 26; *pr. pl.* riken 110. 30.

relese, *sb.*; *release* 111. 31.

releue, *vb.*; *relieve* 97. 38; releeue 103. 39.

remedi, *sb.*; *remedy* 101. 111; remedye 120. 23.

remenaunt, *sb.*; *remainder* 111. 81.

rend, *vb.*; *pt.* rente 51. 24; rent 51. 1; *pp.* rent 57. 76, reṅd 23. 14, i-rent 120. 94.

renne, *vb.*; (1) *course swiftly* 99. 10. (2) *flow, stream* 77. 5; *pr. p.* rennynge 91. 46; *pt.* 3 *s.* ranne 84. 9; *pt. pl.* runnen 26. 19, runne 89. 18, ronne 13. 8, ran 1 A. 4. (3) *live* 47. 14; ?103. 89 (*pp.*).

rent, *sb.*; *rent, payment* 120. 70.

repele, *vb.*; (1) *cancel* 101. 177. (2) *abandon (pr. subj.)* 110. 70.

repentaunce, *sb.*; *repentance* 93. 91; repentaunse 124. 53.

repente, *vb.*; *repent (imp.)* 117. 63.

repreue, *vb.*; *reprove* 97. 46; repraue 104. 29.

rer, *vb.* (OE rǣran); *raise, lift (imp.)* 19. 5.

res, *sb.* (OE rǣs); *rush, hurry* 29. 31.

resayue, *vb.*; *receive* 47. 17; *pr.* 3 *s.* reseyueþ 114. 37. See also *receyue*.

receyue, *vb.*; *receive (imp.)* 93. 61. See also *resayue*.

rescores, *sb.*; *rescue* 120. 23.

reseruet, *pp.*; *set apart* 109. 102.

reson, *sb.*; *statement, speech, utterance* 57. 20; resoun 95. 40, resun 117. 14.

reson, *vb.*; *regard, consider* 118. 52.

respiȝt, *sb.*; *respite, delay* 95. 187.

respounde, *sb.*; *answer* 101. 81.

rest, *sb.*; (1) *peace* 7. 46. (2) *tranquillity* 118. 10. (3) *abode* 15. 10.

reste, *vb.*; (1) *remain, dwell* 118. 78; *pr. pl.* resteþ 32. 58; *pt.* 3 *s.* restede 32. 59, rest 67. 11. (2) *cease (pr. subj.)* 110. 80.

restore, *vb.*; *restore* 105. 11.

restreyne, *vb.*; *restrain* 103. 11.

reuli, *adv.*; *pitifully* 57. 76.

reuthful, *adj.*; *pitiful* 91. 54.

reuthly, *adj.*; *sorrowful* 91. 39.

reue, *vb.*; *take away, rob, despoil* 101. 176; rew 105. 38; *pr.* 3 *s.* reueth 12. 3, reues 84.

83; *imp.* reue 83. 3; *pp.* raft
97. 35, reued 23. 40.

reuele, *vb.*; *revel* 101. 15.

rewe, *vb.* (OE hrēowan); *rue,
grieve, pity* 103. 68; reve 26.
52, reu 29. 37; *pr.* 3 *s.*
reoweþ 7. 33, reues 29. 40;
pr. subj. rewe 95. 131; *imp.*
reu 64. 1; *pt.* 3 *s.* rewed 47.
33.

rewfull, *adj.*; *pitiful* 48. 68.

reufuliche, *adv.*; *pitifully* 64. 3.

rewth, *sb.*—See *rupe.*

rial, *adj.*—See *real.*

ribaudi, *sb.*; *ribaldry, obscenity*
115. 37; ribaudye 95. 159.

rich, *adj.*; *rich* 28. 20; riche 31.
31, richӡ 50. 1, ryche 92. 14;
supl. richest 114. 20.

richand, *pr. p.* (tr. Lat. ditans);
endowing 44. 12.

riche, *sb.*; *kingdom* 98. 50; rike
39. 4.

richesse, *sb.*; *wealth* 91. 116;
rychesse 23. 17, ryches 86.
8; *pl.* richesses 97. 35.

ride, *vb.*; (1) *ride* ryde 121.
150; *pt.* 1 *s.* rod 11. 1. (2) *be
suspended* 51. 11.

rif, *adj.*; (1) *widely current* 57.
20. (2) *inclined, disposed* ryf
102. 61.

rig, *sb.* (OE hrycg); *back* 4. 3;
reg 2 A. 5, ryg 79. 14.

riӡt, *sb.*; *right* 35. 9; riht 95.
131, ryӡt 90. 35, riӡth 122.
24, ryӡth 120. 102, rithte
39. 4.

riӡt, *adj.*; *right* 89. 34; right 29.
67, ryght 48. 95, ryht 20. 2,
ryth 22. 12, rith 41. 20, rytte
32. 20.

riӡt, *adv.*; *rightly, directly* 108.
10; right 31. 63, ryght 85. 26,
riht 93. 53, ryӡt 92. 2, rith
56. 30, ryӡte 32. 53, ryth 23.
15, rithte 57. 44.

riht, *vb.* (OE rihtan); (1) *guide,*

govern (*imp.*) 93. 99; *correct,
amend* (*pp.*) y-ryӡt 32. 11.

rihtfulnes, *sb.*; *justice* 100. 57;
rithfolnesse 13. 23.

rihtwyse, *adj.*; *righteous* 95.
39; righwis 44. 11.

rihtwysli, *adv.*; *righteously* 107.
70.

riken, *vb.*—See *rekken.*

ripede, *vb. pt.*; *ripened* 131. 101.

rise, *vb.*; *rise, arise* 30. 13; ris
101. 89, ryse 91. 151, rys 112.
70; *pt.* 2 *s.* ras 30. 7; *pt.* 3 *s.*
ras 31. 37, rase 83. 45, rayse
48. 80.

risingge, *sb.*; *rising, resurrection*
56. 142; rysyng 19. 6.

riue, *vb.*; *tear, split, cleave* 29.
57.

ro, *sb.* (OE rā); *roe, deer* 6. 27.

ro, *sb.* (ON ró); *rest, quiet* 29.
50.

robbe, *vb.*; *rob* 120. 37.

robe, *sb.*; *robe* 16. 18.

rode, *sb.*; *cross* 1 A. 3; rod 3. 7,
rood 109. 81, roode 89. 12.

roed, *sb.* (OE hrēod); *reed* 15.
30.

rogget, *adj.*; *rough* 91. 44.

rokking, *pr. p.*; *rocking* 56. 4.

ron, *sb.*; *song* 21. 20.

ronere, *sb.* (on ME ron *vb.*,
< ME ro *sb.*); *comforter, con-
soler* 44. 30.

ronk, *adj.*; *rank, haughty* 133. 7.

ronsake, *vb.*; *probe, examine*
103. 40.

ropis, *sb. pl.*; *ropes* 125. 63;
ropus 123. 14.

rose, *sb.*; *rose* 10. 1.

rote, *sb.*; *root* 7. 10; roote 91.
111.

rote, *vb.*; *root* (*imp.*) 83. 17; *pp.*
52. 6, rooted 95. 159.

rote, *vb.*; *rot* 81. 20; rooten 106.
125; *pp.* rote 106. 127.

roting, *sb.*; *putrescence* 53. 7.

rounde, *adj.*; *round* 106. 124.

route, *sb.*; *company* 25. 17; rowte 121. 8.
rud, *sb.*; *complexion* 121. 81.
rule, *vb.*; (1) *rule* 105. 74. (2) *control*: *imp.* 115. 10. (3) *refl. order one's life* 99. 42; *pr. subj.* 96. 67.
russche, *vb.*; (1) *shatter, force*: *pt.* 3 s. russchede 112. 61. (2) *hurry, rush*: *pr. pl.* rosscheþ 106. 17.
ruþe, *sb.*; (1) *pity, compassion* 20. 5; rouþe 118. 19. (2) *occasion for sorrow* rwthe 39. 18, rewth 48. 68. (3) *pl. lamentations* rouþes 6. 14.
ryally, *adv.*; *in royal fashion* 92. 14; ryaly 105. 26.
rys, *sb.*; *thicket* 40. 4.

sa, *adv.*; *so* 29. 56.
sacratarie, *sb.*; (Lat. secretarium); *private place, sanctum* 103. 29. See Note.
sad, *adj.*; (1) *firm, stable* 109. 82. (2) *sad* sadde 105. 2.
sade, *vb.*; *become serious* 101. 4.
sadli, *adv.*; *seriously* 58. 14; sadliche 116. 3, sadly 47. 16.
safe, *vb.*—See sauen.
sai, *vb.*—See seyn.
sailled, *vb. pt.*; *sailed* 121. 183.
sak, *sb.*; *sack* 23. 5.
sake, *sb.*; *guilt* 29. 73.
sakeles, *adv.*; *without just cause* 104. 30.
salt, *adj.*; *salt* 121. 183; *pl.* salte 7. 20.
salue, *sb.*; *salve, ointment* 79. 13; *pl.* 103. 44.
salue, *vb.*; *heal with salve* 48. 40.
same, *adj.*; *same* 47. 35.
samen, *adv.*; *together* 112. 101.
sammned, *pp.*; *assembled* 27. 55.
sandes, *sb. pl.*—See sonde.
sannest, *adv. supl.* (MDu. saen *suddenly, quickly*); *suddenly* 104. 68; *most quickly* 101. 128.

sant, *sb.*; *saint* 31. 14; *pl.* santes 29. 46. See also *sontes*.
sare, *sb.*; *wound* 48. 40.
sare, *adj.*; *in pain* 27. 23.
sare, *adv.*; *sorrowfully* 9. 3.
sari, *adj.*; *sad* 30. 126.
saryful, *adj.*; *sorrowful* 79. 13.
sauȝten, *vb.*; *reconcile* 102. 38; *pp.* sahte 6. 5.
saul, *sb.*; *soul* 31. 10; saule 26. 56, sawle 82. 43, sawule 83. 6; *pl.* sauls 83. 44, sawls 84. 61.
saumples, *sb.*; *examples* 103. 80.
sauter, *sb.*; *psalter* 120. 14.
saue, *conj.*; *except* 106. 53.
sauely, *adv.*; *securely* 116. 4.
sauen, *vb.*; *save* 57. 60; sauue 22. 5, saue 91. 78, safe 83. 44; *imp.* saue 26. 28; *pt.* 2 s. sauuedest 20. 7; *pt.* 3 s. saued 86. 23; *pp.* saue 106. 61, ysaued 32. 41.
sa).ereþ, *vb. pr.* 3 s.; *gives savour to* 119. 52.
sauiour, *sb.*; *Saviour* 114. 24; saueowre 85. 2, saueour 112. 132.
sauour, *sb.*; (1) *fragrance* 10. 2. (2) *pleasure* sauor 117. 69.
sawe, *sb.*; *utterance, speech* 13. 9; *pl.* sawes 6. 10.
say, *vb.*—See seyn.
scam, *sb.*—See schame.
sceu, *vb.*; *show* (*imp.*) 30. 40.
sch-. See under *sh-*.
science, *sb.*; *knowledge* 107. 85.
sclaundre, *sb.*; *slander* 120. 100.
sclaundre, *vb.*; *slander* 120. 98.
sclepie, *adj.*; *sleepy* 5. 3.
scloe, *adj.*—See *slow*.
scop, *vb. pt.*—See schape.
score, *sb.*; *score, twenty* 110 40.

scorne, *sb.*; (1) *mockery, derision* 91. 69; schorn 34. 16, skoren 55. 12. (2) *(public) contempt* skorn 116. 46. (3) *pl. jeers* scornys 91. 123.

scourgest, *vb. pr.* 2. *s.*; *scourge* 15. 26.

scrift, *sb.*; *absolution* 30. 43; srift 87. 37. See also *schrift.*

scrope, *vb.* (?ON skrópar *pl. hypocrisy*); *?dissemble* 116. 45. See Note.

scrud, *sb.*—See *schroud.*

scurge, *sb.*; *scourge, whip* 2 A. 5; scourge 123. 14; *pl.* skurges 30. 56, scourges 76. 21.

scwre, *vb.* (NED scour v.¹); *pass rapidly*; *pr.* 3 *s.* scwret 49. 4.

sece, *vb.*; *cease, leave off* 107. 78. See also *cese.*

seche, *vb.*; (1) *seek* 11. 2; *imp.* seche 100. 8; *pr.* 2 *s.* sohtest 8. 21; *pt.* 3 *s.* souȝte 96. 7; *pt. pl.* souhten 12. 5; *pp.* souȝt 95. 107, south 66. 14. (2) *try to discover* 100. 42. (3) *attack* 110. 51. (4) *consult* 106. 70. (5) *search, scrutinize* 44. 2; *pt.* 1 *s.* souhte 25. 17. (6) *investigate pp.* souht 16. 40. (7) *intr. have recourse* seke 117. 16.

secte, *sb.*; *sect* 106. 61.

see, *sb.*; *sea* 15. 20; se 21. 17.

see, *sb.*; *seat* 56. 38.

seed, *sb.*; *seed* 112. 13.

segge, *sb.*; *man, person* 112. 13.

seinte, *adj.*; *holy* 26. 5; seynte 26. 49.

seintes, *sb. pl.*; *saints* 96. 87. See also *sant, sent,* and *sontes.*

sek, *adj.*; *sick* 10. 47. See also *sike.*

seketur, *sb.*; *executor* 116. 37; *pl.* secutowrs 81. 23.

seknes, *sb.*; *sickness* 95. 66; seknesse 101. 76, seeknesse 100. 32.

selcowȝe, *adv.*; *exceedingly* 51. 18.

seli, *adj.*; *blessed, innocent* 29. 46; sely 17. 4.

selle, *vb.*—See *sulle.*

seluer, *sb.*; *silver* 113. 43; soeluer 23. 18.

semblant, *sb.*; *appearance, image* 58. 6; semblaunt 111. 62, sembland 48. 21.

seme, *vb.* (OE sēman); (1) *fit, suit*: *pr.* 1 *s.* semy (= sem y) 6. 15. (2) *seem, appear*: *pr.* 3 *s.* semeþ 115. 52, seemeþ 109. 9; *pr. pl.* semen 103. 21; *pt.* 3 *s.* sempte 58. 15.

semly, *adj.*; *goodly* 6. 10; semlich 25. 3, semeli 112. 18.

sen, *conj.*—See *seþþen.*

sen, *vb.* (OE sēon); *see* 72. 23; sene 11. 54, seone 100. 101, seo 95. 26, se 7. 50; *pr.* 2 *s.* sees 86. 2, sest 102. 44; *pr.* 3 *s.* seet 69. 13; *pr. pl.* seeþ 124. 80; *pr. subj.* se 44. 22; *pr. p.* seand 45. 23; *pt.* 1 *s.* seh 6. 33, seiȝ 96. 5, sayh 36. 1, sau 56. 3, say 56. 145; *pt.* 2 *s.* seie 26. 34, seye 26. 23, seȝe 95. 57, syȝe 92. 21, sauȝ 93. 44; *pt.* 3 *s.* seh 7. 40; *pp.* seene 118. 41, seie 11. 35, i-sen 101. 123.

send, *vb.*; *send* 91. 110; sen 105. 29; *pr.* 3 *s.* sent 101. 104; *imp.* sent 93. 36; *pt.* 1 *s.* sente 72. 13; *pt.* 2 *s.* sentist 72. 19; *pt.* 3 *s.* sende 26. 6, sente 131. 95, sent 112. 99; *pp.* y-send 18. 3.

senfol, *adj.*; *sinful* 87. 12; senful 38. 8; *pl.* senfolle 32. 78. See also *sunfol.*

senfolliche, *adv.*; *sinfully* 87. 15.

sen3ede, *vb. pt.*—See *sunge.*

senne, *sb.*; *sin* 26. 16; zenne 33.
5; *pl.* sennes 26. 4. See also
sinne.

sent, *adj.*; *saint* 32. 67.

sepperdis, *sb. pl.*; *shepherds* 56.
53.

sere, ˉ*vb.* (MDu. seren *or* ON
særa); *injure, wound* 106. 73.

serewe, *sb.*; *sorrow* 6. 33; serwe
93. 35; *pl.* serewes 10. 36.
See also *sorow.*

sereweþ.—See *sorewe.*

sergant, *sb.*; ?*man* 58. 13.

sertes, *adv.*—See *certes.*

serteynly, *adv.*; *certainly* 56.
145; serteynliche 110. 8.

seruaunt, *sb.*; *servant* 102. 60;
pl. seruandes 79. 3.

seruen, *vb.*; *serve* 10. 42; serue
86. 1; *pr.* 3 *s.* serueþ 101. 79,
serues 30. 104.

serueþ, *vb. pr.* 3 *s.*; *deserves* 104.
46.

seruise, *sb.*; *service* 44. 8;
seruyse 87. 7.

sese, *vb.*; *put in possession (pr.
1 s.)* 112. 75. See also *cese.*

se-stoerre, *sb.*; *star of the sea*
17. 1.

sesun, *sb.*; *season* 117. 86.

sete, *adj.*; (1) *settled in mind,
content* 10. 40, 101. 4. (2)
fitting, profitable 114. 51.

sete, *sb*ₜ; *seat* 29. 46.

seþþen, *conj., adv.*; (1) *from the
time when* 27. 97, seth 124.
9. (2) *because* sen 47. 3,
soethþe 16. 19. (3) *after-
wards* seþþe 7. 60, seıþen 65.
21. See also *siþen.*

sett, *vb.*; (1) *set, place: pr.* 1 *s.*
85. 10; *imp.* sete 7. 10; *pr. p.*
settand 41. 7; *pt.* 3 *s.* sett 48.
21; *pp.* set 6. 15, i-set 26. 39,
yset 121. 197. (2) *establish:
imp.* sette 17. 7; *pp.* 29. 26.
(3) *fix: imp.* 48. 7. (4) *ac-*

count 113. 5. (5) *phrase* ~
sawes *express oneself* 112. 29.

settel, *sb.*; *seat* 84. 9.

seuene, *num. adj.*; *seven* 18. 5.

sewe, *vb.*; (1) *follow, pursue:
pr.* 3 *s.* siweþ 6. 29; *pr. pl.*
suwe 95. 126. (2) *petition,
make suit to, imp.* sewe 132.
31.

seyn, *vb.* (OE secgan); *say* 6.
10; seyne 95. 92, seye 49. 26,
seie 96. 34, sey 56. 75, sigge
99. 3, say 82. 21, sai 31. 56;
pr. 1 *s.* sugge 6. 83, sey3e 57.
60, sei 99. 16; *pr.* 2 *s.* seist
115. 62; *pr.* 3 *s.* seyth 120.
13, seiþ 9. 8, seit 55. 28, seys
27. 1, says 46. 2; *pr. pl.* sei
96. 24, seyen 104. 19; *imp.*
sey 72. 2, say 16. 14; *ger.*
seyng 120. 97; *pt.* 3 *s.* seyde
92. 2, seide 11. 27, sayde 13.
11; *pt. pl.* seiden 55، 9; *pp.*
said 31. 56, sayd 41. 6, saide
44. 5.

schaded, *pp.*; *shaded* 121. 3.

schadewe, *sb.*; *shadow* 101. 123.

schame, *sb.*; *shame* 60. 6; shame
91. 31, scam 29. 7, shome
17. 7.

schamfully, *adv.*; *shamefully*
84. 66; samfully 56. 121.

schap, *sb.*; *shape, form* 101.
60.

schape, *vb.*; (1) *create; pt.* 2 *s.*
scop 29. 29. (2) *contrive* 111.
77. (3) *refl. resolve, aim* 107.
76.

scharp, *adj.*; *sharp* 53. 5; sharpe
13. 6, sarp 55. 21, sarpe 56.
117.

scharpe, *adv.*; *sharply* 95. 46.

scharply, *adv.*; *sharply* 121. 215.

sche, *fem. pers. pron.*; *she* 58. 4;
che 42. 2. See also *sho.*

sched, *sb.*; *parting of the hair,
top of the head* 113. 68.

schede, *vb.*; *shed* 107. 12; *pt.* 1 *s.*

sched 46. 6; *pt.* 2 *s.* sheddest
7. 32; *pp.* sched 67. 21.

schef, *sb.* (OE sceaft); *creature*
28. 8.

scheld, *sb.*; *shield* 79. 23; schelde
93. 68, seld 63. 2.

schende, *vb.*; (1) *put to shame*
54. 4. (2) *ruin, destroy (pr.
subj.)* 48. 118, y-schent 34.
4. (3) *discomfit pp.* schent
69. 23.

schende, *sb.*; *disgrace, ignominy*
104. 30.

schendful, *adj.*; *ignominious*
131. 5.

schene, *adj.*; *bright, resplendent*
121. 7; shene 7. 41, scene 29.
62.

shennesse, *sb.* (OE gescend-
nyss); *humiliation* 25. 23.

schep, *sb.*; *ship* 121. 67.

schete, *vb.*; (1) *vanish*: *pr.* 3 *s.*
schet 101. 128. (2) *discharge*:
pt. pl. schot 79. 8.

schete, *sb.*; *sheet* 81. 36.

sheued, *pp.* 23. 41. See Note.

schewe, *vb.*; *show* 113. 2; schaw
47. 10; *pr.* 1 *s.* schewe 76. 18;
pr. 3 *s.* scheweþ 101. 92; *imp.*
sheu 13. 24, sceu 30. 40, shou
17. 13, show 45. 13, sew 41.
13; *pt.* 2 *s.* shewedest 12. 13;
pt. pl. sheuden 12. 6; *pp.*
schewed 120. 10, schewid 90.
33.

schines, *sb. pl.*; *shins* 34. 13.

sho, *fem. pers. pron.*; *she* 91. 58.

shonedest, *vb. pt.* 2 *s.*; *shun-
nedst* 22. 8.

schorn, *pp.*; *pierced* 116. 62.

short, *adj.*; *short* 91. 127.

schorte, *vb.*; *grow brief* 101. 63.

schortliche, *adv.*; *briefly* 110.
119.

schower, *sb.*; *time of stress* 121.
182; *pl.* shoures 10. 56.

schrift, *sb.*; *absolution* 114. 51.
See also *scrift.*

schriue, *vb.*; *absolve (pr. subj.)*
98. 43.

schroud, *sb.*; *garment, clothing*
25. 7; scrud 29. 62.

schrude, *vb.*; *clothe*: *pt.* 1 *s.*
shrudde 15. 15; *pp.* y-shrud
13. 14.

schulder, *sb.*; *shoulder* 34. 18;
sulder 55. 14.

schulen, *aux. vb.*; *shall*: *pr.* 1
and 3 *s.* schal 32. 18, shal 3.
15, ssal 28. 16, sall 77. 28, sal
56. 10; *pr.* 2 *s.* shalt 20. 22,
salt 28. 33, ssalt 28. 13, salth
65. 20, saltu (= salt þu)
2 B. 12; *pr. pl.* shullen 91. 8,
shulen 10. 29, schulle 88. 1,
shule 9. 10, shulle 91. 17,
sulen 65. 18, solen 56. 74,
schul 27. 96, shul 43. 2, schal
26. 40, sal 29. 47; *pt.* 1 and
3 *s.* shulde 15. 12, scholde 26.
7, sulde 56. 35, suld 56. 22,
schuld 94. 8; *pt.* 2 *s.* shuldest
14. 9; *pt. pl.* shulden 7. 19,
shold 91. 112.

shuppere, *sb.*; *creator* 18. 1.

schylde, *vb.*; *shield, protect, for-
bid* 84. 76; *pr. subj.* 84. 91;
imp. shild 9. 14, schild 98.
39, shyld 17. 7, sceild 29. 7,
schilde 93. 37, childe 115. 4,
ssylde 33. 5, schuld 26. 8.

schyne, *vb.*; *shine* 121. 178; *pr.*
3 *s.* schineþ 131. 36, schines
31. 22, schynes 85. 6; *pt.* 3 *s.*
schon 34. 26.

schynyng, *vbl. sb.*; *radiance* 83.
24.

shyr, *adj.*; *clear* 12. 11.

side, *sb.*; *side* 1 B. 1; syde 1 A.
1; *pl.* sides 6. 78, sydes 48.
65.

sigge, *vb.*—See *seyn.*

sighe, *vb.*; *sigh* sygh 84. 69,
sich 28. 3; *pr.* 1 *s.* sike 9. 3;
pr. 2 *s.* sikest 69. 1; *pr.* 3 *s.*
sighes 31. 6; *imp.* sygh 84.

69; *pr. p.* syghand 84. 85;
pt. 1 *s.* sykyt 105. 2.

syghyng, *vbl. sb.*; *sighing* 83. 21.

siȝt, *sb.*; *sight* 35. 8; siht 107.
85, sicte 2 B. 5, sight 29. 68,
syht 6. 106, syȝth 120. 100,
syght 79. 8, sith 56. 3, sithte
56. 145, sythe 124. 39.

sike, *adj.*; *sick* 131. 29. See also
sek.

siker, *adj.*; *sure* 27. 1; syker 17.
22, seker 45. 22.

syker, *adv.*; *undeniably* 6. 72.

sikerli, *adv.*; *undoubtedly* 58. 7.

sikernes, *sb.*; *certainty* 116. 41.

simple, *adj.*; *simple, plain* 56.
101; sympil 91. 92.

singgen, *vb.*; *sing* 56. 16; singge
50. 7, sengge 56. 8, synge 114.
7; *pr.* 1 *s.* synge 11. 18; *pr.*
2 *s.* singest 69. 4; *pr. pl.*
syngeth 14. 10, singes 31. 61;
pr. p. singging 121. 39; *pt. pl.*
songen 57. 34, song 112.
101.

sinke, *vb.*; *sink*: *pr.* 3 *s.* synkes
86: 11; *pr. pl.* synkeþ 106.
56; *pr. subj.* sinke 123. 17.

sinne, *sb.*; *sin* 3. 13; synne 10.
22, sunne 6. 6, sin 29. 73, syn
82. 38; *pl.* sinnes 26. 52,
sunnes 6. 74, syns 46. 16. See
also *senne.*

synner, *sb.*; *sinner* 132. 31.

site, *sb.* (AN site); *position* 27.
55.

site, *sb.* (ON *sýt); *sorrow, care*
31. 57; *pl.* sites 27. 24.

siþe, *sb. pl.*; *times* 97. 3.

siþen, *adv.* and *conj.*; *since* 30.
4; sythen 47. 30, sin 101. 121.
See also *seþþen.*

sitte, *vb.*; (1) *sit* 96. 87; sytt 84.
64; *pr.* 1 *s.* sytt 83. 29; *pr.*
2 *s.* sittest 14. 10, sittes 30.
86, sist 22. 13; *pr.* 3 *s.* sit 106.
79, syt 49. 28; *pr. pl.* sete 30.
101; *pr. p.* sitting 121. 8; *pt.*

3 *s.* sat 58. 13. (2) *afflict,
distress*: *pr.* 3 *s.* sitteþ 99. 27.
(3) *lodge*: sitt my hert ful
nere *move me deeply* 85. 24.

sittyngli, *adv.*; *fittingly, appro-
priately* 112. 29.

skath, *sb.*; *harm, injury* 29. 22;
skaþe 116. 46.

skek, *vb.*; *raid, plunder* 81. 24.

skelk, *vb.* (?ON skelkja); *?mock*
81. 24. See Note.

skelpe, *vb.* (?ON skelpa *wry
face*); *?pull faces* 116. 45.
See Note.

sker, *adj.*; *clear, unspotted* 21.
16.

skile, *sb.*; *reason* 101. 109; skille
112. 109, skyll 48. 19, skylle
83. 14; *pl.* skiles 117. 15.

skilfuli, *adv.*; *reasonably* 58. 21.

skyn, *sb.*; *skin* 71. 3.

skorn, *sb.*—See *scorne.*

skreue, *vb.* (OF descrivre); *de-
scribe* 109. 91.

skrynkeþ, *vb. pr.* 3 *s.*; *withers*
10. 1.

skurges, *sb. pl.*—See *scurge.*

slake, *slacken, abate* 48. 112;
sleke 69. 17; *pr.* 3 *s.* slakes
95. 104.

slame, *sb.* (cf. NED slem, slam
sb.[3]); *slime* 81. 3.

slauer, *sb.*; *slaver, spittle* 79. 8.

sle, *vb.*; *slay* 95. 37; slee 115.
59, slo 93. 70; *pr.* 3 *s.* sleþ
100. 32; *imp.* sle 102. 49; *pt.*
1 and 3 *s.* slou 66. 7, shlou 15.
19; *pp.* slawen 11. 45, slawe
90. 13, slowe 100. 34, slayne
83. 45.

sleightes, *sb. pl.*; *tricks, devices*
121. 185.

slep, *sb.*; *sleep* 6. 62; slepe
56. 6.

slepe, *vb.*; *sleep* 81. 36; *pr. pl.*
95. 164; *imp.* slep 65. 29.

sleuthe, *sb.*; *sloth* 6. 62; slouþe
95. 163.

sley3e, *adj.*; *wise, prudent* 106.
53; sle 84. 10, slih 118. 76.

slide, *vb.*; *slip*: *pr.* 3 *s.* slidiþ
134. 3; *pp.* i-slyde 100. 88.

sliper, *adj.*; *?small, slight* 109.
71.

sloken, *vb.*; *extinguish* 84. 6.

slo, *vb.*; *slay* 93. 70.

slow, *adj.*; *slow* 124. 17; scloe 5.
3, slawe 27. 40.

slyme, *sb.*; *slime* 79. 8.

smal, *adj.*; (1) *small* 63. 8. (2)
slender, shapely 10. 45.

smarte, *adj.*; *severe, painful* 123.
37; smerte 65. 10.

smartliche, *adv.*; *quickly* 131.
79.

smert, *vb.*; *cause pain* 86. 12.

smulle, *vb.*; *smell*: *pr. pl.* smul-
leþ 10. 33; *pr. p.* smellyng
121. 4.

smyte, *vb.*; *smite* 23. 33; *pr.* 3 *s.*
smyteþ 135. 32; *pt.* 2 *s.*
smettest 72. 24; *pt. pl.* smiten
55. 9; *pp.* ismyte 121. 73.

smytyng, *vbl. sb.*; *smiting* 86. 12.

snare, *sb.*; *snare* 113. 70.

snelle, *adj.*; *quick, active* 27. 40.

snou3, *sb.*; *snow* 106. 18.

so, *adv.*; *so* 2 B. 4; soo 92. 33.
See also *swo*, *sa*, and *swa*.

sob, *vb.*; *sob* 84. 69.

socour, *sb.*; *succour* 108. 47;
socoure 82. 29, sokowre 85. 3.

socoure, *vb.*; *succour* (*imp.*) 114.
63; socur 112. 5.

soden, *adj.*; *sudden* 124. 54.

sodeynli, *adv.*; *suddenly* 97. 42;
sodeynly 101. 33.

soft, *adj.*; *soft* 30. 5; softe 91.
52.

softe, *adv.*; *softly* 65. 29.

soget, *sb.*; *subject* 112. 31.

soil, *sb.*; *soil, earth* 112. 13.

solas, *sb.*; *joy, delight* 11. 14;
solace 82. 24.

somer, *sb.*; *summer* 10. 3.

sonde, *sb.*; *sending, gift* 107. 30;
pl. sondes 56. 136; *?creatures*
sandes 29. 28.

sone, *adv.*; *soon* 6. 5; son 29. 9.

sone, *sb.*; *son* 10. 17; sun 29. 1,
gen. sones 16. 39.

song, *sb.*; *song* 8. 4; sang 31. 61.

sontes, *sb. pl.*; *saints* 6. 106.

sor, *sb.*; *pain, suffering* 10. 37;
sore 32. 10.

sore, *adj.*; *sore, painful* 51. 18;
sor 49. 21, sare 27. 23.

sore, *adv.*; *grievously* 6. 72;
sorrowfully sare 9. 3.

sorewe, *vb.*; *grieve* 134. 36; *pr.*
3 *s. impers.* sereweþ 6. 96.

sorfol, *adj.*; *sorrowful* 31. 3;
sorwuel 37. 4, sorwful 41. 21.

sorfuliche, *adv.*; *sorrowfully* 68.
11.

sor3e, *sb.*—See *sorow*.

sori, *adj.*; *sorry* 107. 78; *sorrow-
ful* sari 30. 126, sory 62. 1.

sorow, *sb.*; *sorrow* 28. 3; sorewe
23. 12, sorwe 35. 3, sor3e 87.
30, soru 30. 130, sorue 2 A.
10; *pl.* sorowis 105. 21. See
also *serewe*.

sorowyng, *vbl. sb.*; *sorrowing*
85. 1.

soþ, *adj.*; *true, sooth* 8. 22.

soþe, *sb.*; *truth* 27. 1; *pl.* soþes
118. 1.

sothfast, *adj.*; *true* 12. 5.

sothfastnesse, *sb.*; *truthfulness*
120. 78.

sothly, *adv.*; *truly* 121. 36.

sotilte, *sb.*; *clever device* 103.
93.

souken, *vb.*; *suck* 38. 4; *pt.* 2 *s.*
sokyd 132. 54; *pt.* 3 *s.* soked
41. 20, sek 111. 13.

soule, *sb.*; *soul* 7. 51, (*gen.*) 7.
29; *pl.* soulis 90. 22, sowlys
94. 30. See also *saul*.

soun, *sb.* (OF soun); *sound,
speech* 106. 59.

sound, *adj.*; *sound, healthy* 10.
40; sounde 101. 76.

sounde, *adv.*; *accurately, in full*
100. 42.

south, *adv.*; *south* 7. 47; souȝ
36. 3.

souereyn, *sb.*; *sovereign, ruler*
100. 78.

souereynly, *adv.*; *supremely*
111. 22.

sowe, *vb.*; *sow*: *pt.* 3 *s.* seuȝ 112.
13; *pp.* i-sowe 100. 58.

spaier, *sb.*; *slit in a garment*: *pl.*
spaiers 126. 18.

spare, *vb.*; (1) *spare* 94. 32. (2)
save, hoard (*pr. subj.*) 106.
113. (3) *be sparing with* 110.
95.

sparely, *adv.*; *sparingly* 27. 83.

spas, *sb.*; *time, opportunity* 96.
14; *space* 93. 91.

speche, *sb.*; *speech* 21. 4; *pl.*
speches 91. 9.

speciali, *adv.*; *specially* 78. 4.

spede, *vb.*; (1) *succeed, prosper*
16. 12; *pp. sped* 68. 7. (2)
further, assist 102. 103; *imp.*
sped 13. 23, 91. 142.

speke, *vb.*; *speak* 84. 77, (*pr.*
1 *s.*) 25. 5; *imp.* spek 16. 42;
pt. 2 *s.* spake 91. 15, speke
69. 16; *pr. pl.* spoken 57. 65.

spel, *sb.*; *speech, discourse* 17. 5.

spele, *vb.*; *talk, discourse* 106.
76; *pt.* 3 *s.* spellede 32. 56.

spende, *vb.*; *spend* (*pr. subj.*)
106. 113; *pp.* spened 27. 83,
spend 111. 37.

spendyng, *vbl. sb.*; *wealth to
spend* 99. 33.

spere, *sb.*; *spear* 13. 6.

spere, *sb.* (OF espeire); *hope* 31.
59.

spere-wnde, *sb.*; *spear-wound*
2 B. 4.

spete, *vb.*; *spit* 34. 14.

spille, *vb.*; (1) *ruin, destroy, shed*
(*blood*) 107. 53; spill 29. 33;
spil 91. 144; *pt.* 3 *s.* spilt 49.
22; *pp.* spilth 62. 6, spylt 83.

35, i-spilt 110. 27. (2) · *be
ruined, destroyed*: spille 26.
54, spyll 48. 39.

spinne, *vb.*; *spin* 110. 99; *pt.*
3 *s.* span 81. 1.

spir, *vb.*; *ask, inquire* (*imp.*)
81. 1.

spise, *vb.*; *despise* 103. 55.

spittyng, *vbl. sb.*; *spitting* 85. 22.

spot, *sb.*; *speck* 109. 50.

spottel, *sb.*; *spittle* 91. 70.

spouse, *sb.*; *spouse* 20. 12; spuse
68. 1.

sprede, *vb.*; (1) *intr. spread* 120.
28. (2) *tr. stretch out pt.* 2 *s.*
spred 30. 71; *pt.* 3 *s.* spradde
93. 80; *pp.* hi-spred 1 B. 3.
(3) *cover* 85. 22. (4) *unfold*
112. 56.

springe, *vb.*; *spring, spread* 7.
12; sprynge 120. 28, spring
45. 27; *pr.* 3 *s.* springis 121.
230; *pr. p.* spryngynde 32.
28; *pp.* sprongen 112. 48.

sprynge, *sb.*; *dayspring, sun-
rise* 84. 94.

sprynge-wel, *sb.*; *spring of
water* 130. 1.

spye, *vb.*; *ascertain, discover*
101. 160.

stab, *vb.*; *thrust* 79. 16.

stable, *adj.*; *stable* 93. 19;
stabele 113. 50.

stabylte, *sb.*; *stability* 83. 4.

stabyl, *vb.*; *make stable* 84. 27;
establish: *pp.* stabuld 29. 27.

staf, *sb.*; *staff* 6. 34.

staleworþe, *adj.*; *stalwart* 36. 6;
inflexible stalworth 84. 48.

stall, *sb.*; *place, stall* 105. 78;
stalle 6. 35.

stallyng, *vbl. sb.*; *benefit, service*
86. 26. See *stedde vb.*, and cf.
stand (*in*) *stall*, NED *stall
sb.²* 2 *b.*

stande, *vb.*; (1) *stand*; stonde
135. 28; *pr.* 1 *s.* stond 68. 2;
pr. 3 *s.* stant 68. 10; *imp.*

stand 46. 9, stonde 93. 73;
pt. 1 *s.* stod 95. 21; *pt.* 2 *s.*
stod 31. 16, stode 30. 121;
pt. 3 *s.* stod 7. 40, stode 79.
16; *pt. pl.* stoden 57. 41, stod
112. 85. (2) *be* 100. 9, 113. 66,
120. 89 (see *stede sb.*, *stude*).

stanged, *vb. pt.* (ON stanga);
pierced 79. 11.

stare, *vb.*; *stare* 101. 53; *pt. pl.*
stareden 57. 41.

stark, *adj.*; (1) *rigid* 10. 4;
starke (*pl.*) 1 B. 3. (2) *im-
perious* 10. 4.

stat, *sb.*; *state, condition* 118.
15; state 81. 18.

stedde, *vb.*; (1) *impers. to avail*:
~ *in stallyng* 86. 26 (*be of
help*). (2) *establish firmly* 86.
33.

stede, *sb.*; *steed* 6. 34; *pl.* steden
6. 35.

stede, *sb.*; (1) *place* 78. 9; *pl.* ste-
den 1 B. 4. (2) *benefit, service*:
stande in ~ *avail* 100. 90,
113. 66.

stedfast, *adj.*; *steadfast* 49. 19;
stœddefast 40. 1, stydefast
105. 59, stodefast 124. 73.

stedfastliche, *adv.*; *steadfastly*
67. 34.

steere, *adj.*; *strong, sturdy* 112.
49.

steere, *vb.*; *restrain, govern* 109.
86; *pr.* 3 *s.* sterys 39. 7.

steeres-men, *sb. pl.*; *helmsmen*
112. 50.

steken, *pp.*; ?*stuck fast* 93. 4.

stekked, *pp.* (OE stician);
?*fixed in position* 79. 16.

stel, *sb.*; *steel* 32. 51; stele 82.
13, steel 111. 70.

stele, *vb.*; (1) *tr. steal* (*imp.*) 102.
57. (2) *intr. creep upon one
secretly* 101. 170.

stele, *vb.* (OE stælan); *inflict,
wreak* 113. 10.

steples, *sb. pl.*; *steeples* 113. 47.

steppes, *sb. pl.*; *steps* 79. 11.

ster, *sb.* (OE steorra); *star* 11.
35; stere 56. 70, sterre 12. 4,
steer 112. 49; *pl.* sterres 20. 1,
sterre 32. 70.

sterne, *sb.* (ON stjarna); *star*
45. 1; *pl.* sternys 41. 18.

sterne, *adj.*; *stern* 59. 2.

sterre-lyth, *sb.*; *star-light* 12. 5.

stert, *vb. pt.*; *started* 91. 50.

steuen, *sb.*; *voice* 30. 75; steuene
26. 3.

steuen, *sb.*; *appointed time*: at
vnset ~ *by chance* 117. 83.

steye, *vb.*; *ascend* 26. 35; *pr.
subj.* sty3e 106. 55; *pt.* 2 *s.*
stei 30. 94, stei3 89. 21.

stei3ynge, *vbl. sb.*; *ascension*
112. 85.

stif, *adj.*; *strong, valiant* 101.
53; styf 120. 35.

stifli, *adv.*; *sturdily* 125. 10;
resolutely styflyche 25. 4.

stikede, *vb. pp.*; *stuck* 2 A. 7.

stille, *adv.*; *quietly* 102. 51;
loude ne ~ *in all conditions.*

stilleness, *sb.*; *secrecy* 102. 58.

stilly, *adj.*; *silent, secret* 106. 78.

stinge, *vb.*; *stab, pierce*: *pr.* 2 *s.*
styngest 15. 17; *pt.* 3 *s.* stong
125. 13; *pp.* stoonge 125. 57,
y-stonge 13. 6.

stinke, *vb.*; *stink*: *pr.* 3 *s.*
stynkeþ 120. 100; *pr. p.*
stinkande 53. 7.

stinte, *vb.*—See *stunte.*

stiuiet, *vb. pr. pl.* (OE stīfian);
become rigid 2 B. 8.

stok, *sb.*; (1) (*tree-*)*trunk* 13. 15.
(2) *block* 112. 68.

stokes, *vb. pr.* 3 *s.*; *holds back,
desists* 27. 57.

stomble, *vb.*; *stumble* 35. 28; *pr.
pl.* stumble 106. 73.

ston, *sb.*; *stone* 15. 27; stane 29.
66.

stoney, *vb.*; *be stupefied, con-
founded* 95. 87.

stoppe, *vb.*; *hinder, obstruct* 120. 32; *pr.* 3 *s.* stoppeþ 109. 45, *pr. pl.* stoppen 120. 66.

stor, *sb.*; *incense* 12. 6.

stor, *sb.*; *possessions* 23. 5.

storis, *sb. pl.*; *stories, histories* 112. 102.

stounde, *sb.*; *hour, time* 6. 94; stonde 93. 81; *pl.* stundes 3, heading.

stour, *sb.* (OF estour); *battle* 101. 37.

stour, *adj.*; *haughty* 10. 4.

stout, *adj.*; *strong* 91. 45.

strande, *sb.*; (1) *river* 83. 40. (2) *current of blood*: *pl.* strondes 123. 25. (3) *shore, country*, stronde 58. 2.

stray, *vb.*; *roam, wander* 112. 50.

stre, *sb.*; *straw* 115. 57.

streit, *adv.*; *tightly, closely* 90. 8; streite 126. 7, straytly 79. 18. Cf. *strete*, *sb.*

streme, *sb.*; *stream* 83. 40; *pl.* stremes 1 A. 4, stremys 89. 18.

strengþe, *sb.*; *strength* 18. 8; strenkeþe 134. 14, streinþe 7. 7.

strengthen, *vb.*; *strengthen*: *pr.* 3 *s.* strenghes 85. 6, strongeþ 131. 98.

strengthy, *adj.*; *full of strength* 81. 15.

strete, *sb.*; *strait, place of confinement or difficulty* 85. 6. Cf. *streit*, adv.

streyned, *pp.*; *stretched forcibly* 79. 18.

strif, *sb.*; *violence* 102. 58.

striue, *vb.*; *strive, contend* 27. 78; stryf 83. 43, strywe 105. 68.

strokes, *sb. pl.*; *strokes, blows* 91. 45.

strong, *adj.*; *strong* 23. 29; *severe* stronge (*pl.*) 3. 11; strang 31. 62.

strong, *adv.*; *relentlessly* 110. 51.

strynd, *sb.*; *race, offspring* 48. 27.

stude, *sb.*; (1) *place* 8. 6; *pl.* studes 1 A. 4. (2) *advantage, profit* 120. 89. See also *stede*.

studefast, *adj.*; *steadfast* 101. 172; studfast 93. 3. See also *stedfast*.

studi, *adj.*; *steady, fixed* 112. 49.

studie, *vb.*; *study* 102. 3; *pt.* 1 *s.* studied 117. 13.

stunchg, *sb.*; *sting* 22. 10.

stunte, *vb.*; *stop* 101. 53; *pr.* 3 *s.* stintes 27. 57; *pr. pl.* stunteþ 106. 131, stunte 95. 151; *imp.* stynt 46. 5, stunt 6. 94, stunte 100. 44, (*pl.*) stunteþ 110. 79, stynteth 91, heading; *pt.* 2 *s.* stint 31. 16; *pt.* 3 *s.* stynt 91. 47.

stype, *adj.*; *stout, strong* 6. 35.

such, *adj.*; *such* 6. 46. See also *swich*.

suffise, *vb.*; *suffice* 118. 15; suffyse 101. 136.

suffraunce, *sb.*; *patience, endurance* 96. 60.

suffren, *vb.*; *suffer* 59. 22; suffyre 91. 106; *pr.* 3 *s.* suffret 59. 6; *pt.* 3 *s.* sufferd 85. 2, soffrede 100. 53; *pt.* 2 *s.* suffredis 52. 8, suffredest 55. 33.

suite, *sb.*; *company, retinue* 31. 50.

sulle, *vb.*; *sell* 102. 61; selle 108. 14; *pr.* 2 *s.* sullest 15. 22; *pr. subj.* sell 84. 46; *pp.* sold 88. 19, solde 95. 135, salde 77. 22.

sum, *adj.*; *some* 28. 9; som 25. 16, summe 103. 17.

sumdel, *adv.*; *to some extent* 103. 41.

sum-wat, *sb.*; *something* 56. 20.

sunfol, *adj.*; *sinful* 20. 6; sinful

26. 26; (*pl.*) sunfole 13. 24;
synfol 124. 5. See also *senfol*.

sunge, *vb.*; *sin* 102. 83, (*imp.*)
102. 73; *pt.* 1 *s.* senȝede 87.
19; *pp.* y-senȝed 87. 10.

sunne, *sb.*; *sun* 55. 22; sune 26.
44, sonne 7. 14.

sunne, *sb.*—See *sinne*.

suppose, *vb.*; *suppose* 103. 17,
(*pr. subj.*) 120. 42.

suppryse, *vb.*; *overcome, go be-*
yond 82. 38.

sure, *adj.*; *sure* 120, 106.

surquidri, *sb.*; *presumption* 107.
54.

suster, *sb.*; *sister* 16. 7; syster
132. 93.

sute, *sb.*; *suit, petition* 69. 18.

suwe, *vb.*—See *sewe*.

swa, *adv.*; *so* 27. 15. See also
swo, sa, so.

swart, *adj.*; *dark* 34. 26.

swelt, *vb.*; *die* 27. 85.

swer, *adj.*; *sluggish, slow* 27. 39.

swerde, *sb.*; *sword* 56. 117;
swerd 125. 12.

swere, *vb.*; (1) *swear* 114. 35;
pp. sworen 39. 11, sworne 86.
24. (2) *pledge oneself* 57. 56.

suerue, *vb.*; *wander, depart* 56.
82.

suete, *vb.*; *sweat* 65. 20, (*pr.*
1 *s.*) 76. 1.

suete, *adj.*; *sweet* 2 B. 10; swete
26. 21; *comp.* sweter 40. 7;
supl. suetest 11. 4, swettyst
92. 4. See also *swote*.

swetly, *adv.*; *sweetly* 91. 23.

swetnes, *sb.*; *sweetness* 48. 1.

suetyth, *vb. pr.* 3 *s.*; *sweetens*
49. 11.

suich, *adj.*; *such* 55. 25; swych
90. 20, swech 34. 29. See
also *such* and *swilk*.

swilk, *adj.*; *such* 47. 3; swylk 40.
3, swyl 32. 71.

swiþe, *adv.*; *exceedingly, quickly,*
strongly 3. 12; suith 31. 47.

swo, *adv.*; *so* 6. 50; zuo 33. 4.
See also *swa, so, sa*.

swolle, *pp.*; *swollen* 95. 164.

swote, *adj.*; *sweet* 7. 11; *supl.*
swotyst 92. 4. See also *swete*.

swyft, *adj.*; *prompt* 124. 16.

swyke, *vb.* (OE swīcan); (1)
leave off, desist (*pr.* 1 *s.*) 6. 28.
(2) *deceive* 116. 38.

swyn, *sb.*; *swine* 95. 164.

swyng, *vb.*; *scourge* 83. 34; *pp.*
suongen 31. 38, i-suunge 2 A.
5, y-swonge 13. 5.

sylk, *sb.*; *silk* 91. 118; selk 96.
17.

symonye, *sb.*; *simony* 95. 135;
symony 107. 54.

syns, *sb. pl.*; *sinews* 77. 8.

syre, *sb.*; *lord* 87. 40.

t', ta = *to* (with infin.) *q.v.*

tabernacle, *sb.*; *niche in a wall*
132. 1.

taken, *vb.*; (1) *take* 71. 5, 30. 74;
pr. 1 *s.* take 16. 25; *pr.* 3 *s.*
tas 112. 59; *imp.* tak 56. 129,
tac 100. 38; *pt.* 1 *s.* tok 95. 8;
pt. 2 *s.* toke 21. 12; *pt.* 3 *s.*
toke 48. 37; *pt. pl.* tok 113.
43; *pp.* tan 26. 37. (2) *seize*
93. 87; *pt. pl.* token 55. 3;
pp. i-take 55. 1. (3) *attack*
27. 6. (4) *accept* 17. 14; *pr.*
p. takand 45. 5. (5) *receive*
11. 11; ? *pp.* tane 84. 53.

tale, *sb.*; *story* 93. 56; *pl.* tales
58. 24.

tam, *adj.*; *tame* 29. 28; tame
121. 171.

tarie, *vb.*; *occupy, beguile* 103.
31.

tarijng, *vbl. sb.*; *tarrying* 116. 8.

taste, *vb.*; (1) *experience* 134. 40.
(2) *test*: *imp.* tast 100. 27.

tat = *þat*.

tayled, *pp.*; *entailed* 132. 94.

te, *vb.* (OE tēon); *take one's way*
7. 51.

te = *to* 109. 7.

techen, *vb.*; *teach, show* 57. 50;
pr. 1 *s.* teche 127. 6; *pr.* 3 *s.*
techeþ 16. 54; *imp.* teche 31.
2; tech 91. 96; *pr. p.* tech-
ingge 56. 80; *pt.* 3. *s.* tauȝte
112. 64, tauȝt 95. 183.

telle, *vb.*; (1) *tell, relate* 11. 5;
pr. 1 *s.* telle 93. 56, tel 84. 11;
imp. tel 63. 7; *pt.* 3 *s.* tald 41.
32; *pp.* told 120. 27, talde 84.
50. (2) *regard, reckon*: *pp.*
ytolde 6. 22, i-tolde 110. 39,
y-told 23. 29, i-told 28. 32.

tem, *sb.*; *offspring* 15. 19.

tempest, *sb.*; *tumult* 120. 5.

temptacion, *sb.*; *temptation* 119.
42.

tempted, *pp.*; *tempted* 56. 93;
tempt 101. 134.

ten, *num. adj.*; *ten* 86. 17; tene
23. 35.

tend, *vb.*; *kindle* (*imp.*) 18. 7.

tender, *adj.*; *tender* 85. 19.

tenderly, *adv.*; *tenderly* 84. 87.

tene, *sb.*; *suffering, vexation,
affliction*; teene 119. 41,
toene 23. 12, teone 116. 72;
pl. tenes 27. 6.

tenede, *pp.*; *afflicted, injured*
116. 53; toened 15. 2, tenet
104. 6.

tent, *sb.*; *attention, heed* 27. 61;
tente 95. 8.

tere, *sb.*; *tear* (*lacrima*) 30. 65;
ter 69, *heading*; *pl.* teres 7.
20, teerys 94. 9, terres 2 B. 2.

teren, *vb.*; *rend, lacerate* 95.
152; *pp.* tore 23. 14, toren
98. 25.

terme, *sb.*; *term, time* 81. 30.

teynte, *pp.*; ?*attainted, con-
victed* 103. 18.

þa, *dem. pron. fem. acc. s.*; *that*
26. 47.

þa, *dem. pron. nom. acc. pl.*;
those 50. 4; þaa 30. 22. See
also *þo*.

þa, *adv.*—See *þo*.

þah, *conj.* (OE þēah); *though* 9.
10; þaȝ 32. 5, þeiȝ 100. 18,
þei 27. 11, þey 120. 31, þogh
91. 5, þouȝ 103. 70, þou 57.
73, þof 84. 12.

þai, 3 *pers. pron. nom. pl.*; *they*
27. 11; þei 55. 18, þey 91. 19,
day 124. 15.

þaim, 3 *pers. pron. dat. acc.
pl.*; *them* 31. 53; þem 39. 7.

þair, *poss. pron.* 3 *pers. pl.*;
their 29. 46; þaire 79. 7, þar
44. 20.

þan, *adv.* (OE þænne); *then* 57.
11; thanne 121. 204; þoenne
14. 12, þenne 95. 91, þen 120.
28.

þane, *dem. pron. masc. acc. s.*
(OE þone); *that* 32. 9, 32. 69.

þar, *adv.*; (1) *there* 30. 121; þare
23. 24, þore 58. 26. (2) *where*:
þar 2 B. 1, þare 29. 46. See
also *þer*.

þare-fore, *adv.*; *therefore* 7. 19;
þarfore 48. 94.

þare-to, *adv.*; *in addition* 77.
28.

þarf, *vb. pr.* 3 *s.*; *need* 16. 55;
þar 119. 57.

þar-in, *adv.*; *therein* 82. 48. See
also *þer-yn*.

þat, *conj.*; *that, in order that* 6.
5; þet 36. 3.

þat, *rel. pron.*; *that, which* 2 B. 6;
þet 33. 2.

þat, *dem. pron.*; *that* 2 B. 10, tat
39. 18.

þe, *def. art.*; *the* 1 A. 4; *dat. sg.*
þen 23. 2; þe 44. 29. See also
þo.

þe, 2 *pers. pron. dat. acc. s.*;
thee 3. 2; þee 89. 1.

þe, *rel. pron.*; *which* 4. 10.

þe, *vb.* (OE þēon); *prosper* 28.
13.

þede, *sb.* (OE þēod); *people,
race*: *pl.* 26. 10.

þef, *sb.*; *thief* 76. 2; þefe 85. 18,
þeef 114. 45; *pl.* þeues 34.
20.

þen, *conj.*; *than* 6. 93; þan 27.
86, þanne 121. 213.

þenche, *vb.* (OE þęncan); *think*
35. 11; þenken 106. 31,
þynke 91. 4, thinc 30. 27;
pr. 1 *s.* þenke 55. 32, þinge
39. 13; *pr.* 3 *s.* þencþ 23. 15;
pr. pl. þinke 110. 78, þenkeþ
120. 67; *pr. subj.* þenche 23.
7; *imp.* þenc 3. 2, thenk 51.
4, þench 10. 56, þynk 105.
14, þenke 93. 78; *pl.* þynk-
eth 91. heading, þenkeþ 98.
55; *pt.* 1 *s.* þohte 8. 12,
thought 121. 143; *pt.* 3 *s.*
þouth 3. 12, þouthte 56. 7;
pp. y-thouʒt 124. 10.

þer, *adv.*; (1) *there* 2 A. 10; þere
98. 30. (2) *where* 6. 15. See
also þar.

þer-bi, *adv.*; *thereby* 101. 115.

þer-bysyde, *adv.*; *beside it* 130.
3.

þeruore, *adv.*; *therefore* 20. 7.
See also þarfore.

þer-fro, *adv.*; *from it* 44. 20.

þer-on, *adv.*; *in it* 21. 18.

þertille, *adv.*; *for it* 112. 108.

þer-wile, *adv.*; *during the time*
26. 16.

þerwiþ, *adv.*; *with them* 127. 32.

þer-yn, *adv.*; *therein* 7. 27; þer-
in 26. 56. See also þar-in.

þese, *dem. pron. pl.*; *these* 76.
23; þees 135. 36, þies 81. 11,
þeos 95. 85, þeose 113. 59,
þise 44. 24, þis 9. 2, þys 135.
30.

þewes, *sb. pl.*; *qualities* 131. 17.

þi, *poss. pron.* 2 *pers.*; *thy* 2 A.
8; þin 4. 9, 7. 26, þine 3. 1.

þider, *adv.*; *thither* 10. 48.

þilke, *dem. pron.*—See þylke.

þing, *sb.*; (1) *thing*; *pl.* þinges
93. 98, þynges 92. 13. (2)

2025.9

creature 8. 13, þynge 32. 43;
gen. pl. þinge 11. 4.

þir, *dem. pron. pl.*; *these* 29. 72.

thirst, *sb.*; *thirst* 77. 21; furst
95. 54.

þis, *dem. pron. s.*; *this* 6. 87; þys
14. 12, þysse (*dat.*) 34. 23;
pl. þise 44. 24, þis 27. 13.

þo, *def. art.*; *the* 2 A. 2; *pl.*
2 A. 7.

þo, *dem. pron. pl.*; *those* 95. 155;
þoo 92. 22, thoo 121. 115.

þo, *adv.*; *then* 34. 30; ?þa 79.
11.

þolien, *vb.*; *suffer, endure* 24.
10; þolen 64. 7; *imp.* þole
(*allow, permit*) 5. 4; *pt.* 1 *s.*
þolede 3. 14, þoled 3. 9; *pt.*
2 *s.* þoledist 89. 13, þoledest
125. 54.

tholmodnes, *sb.*; *patience* 30. 20.

þonk, *sb.*; *thanks*; to þonk
graciously 14. 11.

þonke, *vb.*; *thank* 96. 25; *pr.* 1 *s.*
þank 105. 8; *pr. pl.* þonke
96. 23; *imp.* þonk 96. 63; *pt.*
1 *s.* þankid 58. 57; *pt.* 3 *s.*
þankyt 105. 48; *pp.* þankyt
105. 80.

þore, *adv.*—See þar.

þorn, *sb.*; *thorn* 15. 32; *pl.*
þornes 2 A. 6.

þoro, 11. 33: obscure. See
Note.

þorou-out, *prep., adv.*; *through-
out* 21. 7; þroʒt-out 105. 74.

þorw-geþ, *vb. pr.* 3 *s.*; *passes
through* 38. 8.

þos, *dem. pron. pl.*; *those* 28. 7;
þeose 119. 76.

þouht, *sb.*; *thought* 16. 41;
þouth 56. 29, thowth 39. 14,
thouʒt 94. 20, þout 3. 1,
þoute 14. 2, þoht 9. 4, þoʒt
91. 2, thoght 29. 26; *pl.*
þouhtes 18. 1.

þousand, *num. adj.*; *thousand*
101. 83; þousend 97. 3.

þra, *adj.*; *stubborn, persistent*
27. 13.

þral, *adj.* and *sb.*; *thrall* 10. 44;
thrall 48. 57.

þraldom, *sb.*; *bondage* 57. 78.

þrast, *pp.* (OE þræstan); *forced,
shoved* 161. 69; i-þrest 120. 7.
See also *þrusten*.

þrat, *pp.*; *threatened* 120. 49.

þreo, *card. num.*; *three* 17. 26;
þre 27. 13, þree 92. 17, tre
44. 24.

þrete, *sb.*: *threat* 101. 148.

þrid, *ord. num.*; *third* 31. 26;
þridde 11. 37.

thrin, *adj.*; *three different* 31. 27.

þristet, *vb. pr.* 3 *s.*; *thirsts* 67.
22.

þritti, *num. adj.*; *thirty* 101. 42;
þretti 56. 81.

þriue, *vb.*; *thrive* 64. 11; þryue
92. 23.

throly, *adv.*; *fiercely* 112. 43.

throng, *pp.*; *bruised* 112. 43.

þrotes, *sb. pl.*; *throats* 44. 12.

þrowe, *sb.*; *space of time* 65. 1;
þrawe 124. 67.

þrowe, *pp.*; *thrown* 97. 36.

þrunchg, *sb.* (OE geþring); *in-
sistence* 22. 12.

þrusten *pp.* (ON þrýsta); *jostled*
112. 43. See also *þrast.*

þryftes, *sb. pl.*; *gains, profits* 6.
9.

þu, 2 *pers. pron. nom. s.*; *thou*
2 A. 9; þou 6. 1, þov 26. 54,
þo 2 B. 2, þow 86. 3, tou 45.
13, tow 27. 112; þat ou,
þatow (21. 15, 27. 94) =
þat þou.

þunne, *adj.*; *thin, meagre* 6. 9.

þurh, *prep.*; (1) *right through*
ȝwrh 51. 14. (2) *through the
agency of* thurght 45. 6. (3) *by
means of* þurch 2 A. 9, 10. 30;
thoru 30. 75, þorw 41. 22,
thurgh 85. 28. (4) *as a result
of* þorou 12. 12, þorw 26. 55,

þroȝ 28. 30, torw 41. 19,
þorgh 131. 3. (5) *because of*
þrouȝ 115. 62. (6) *by* þourh
7. 43.

þurhsoht, *pp.*; (1) *penetrated* 6.
78. (2) *examined* þorw-souȝt
100. 7.

þursdaye, *sb.*; *Thursday* 92. 27.

þus, *adv.*; *thus* 27. 17.

þylke, *dem. pron.*; *that, that
same* 16. 38; þylk 17. 5, thilke
121. 143, þulke 34. 10.

þynk, *vb.* (OE þyncan); *seem,
appear*: *pr.* 3 *s.* þinkeþ 90. 6,
þunkeþ 6. 49, thynk 84. 10,
79. 12; *pt.* 3 *s.* þouthe 56. 3,
thought 121. 235.

thyrl, *vb.*; *pierce* (*imp.*) 83. 6;
pt. 2 *s.* þorledest 24. 12; *pt.*
3 *s.* þerlede 34. 25; *pp.*
þerled 10. 10, þorled 126. 9.

tidingge, *sb.*; *tidings* 57. 48.

tiȝe, *vb.* (OE getīgan); *tie, bind*:
pt. 3 *s.* tiȝed 112. 68.

til, *conj.*; *until* 72. 30; till 121.
153.

til, *prep.*; *to* 27. 54; tyl 14. 4,
tylle 83. 16.

tirne, *vb.*; *roll* (*something*)
about; *pr.* 3 *s.* tirneþ 27. 43.

tite, *adv.*; *quickly* 27. 54; tyd
112. 92; *supl.* tytes 104. 68.

titte, *vb.*; *pull*: *pr.* 3 *s.* tittes 27.
54.

tixt, *sb.*; *text* 103. 15.

to, *prep.*; *to* 2 A. 1; te 109. 7;
t' 20. 10, 24. 11; ta 6. 82, 24.
18, 29. 58.

to, *conj.*; *until* 81. 7.

to, *adv.*; *too* 30. 41.

to, *num. adj.*—See *two.*

to, *sb.*; *toe* 2 B. 11; too 121. 106;
pl. ton 32. 69.

to-breke, *vb.*; *break in pieces* 84.
78.

to-brest, *vb.*; *burst asunder* (*pr.
pl.*) 77. 8; *pt. pl.* to-barst
113. 45.

to-cominge, *sb.*; *advent* 12. 2.

to-day, *sb.*; *to-day* 12. 13.

todes, *sb. pl.*; *toads* 95. 57.

to-drawe, *pp.*; *pulled asunder* 90. 11; to-draw 126. 17.

to-gedre, *adv.*; *together* 117. 21; to-gedere 112. 70, to-gedure 123. 39.

to-gnawe, *pp.*; *gnawed in pieces* 90. 12.

token, *sb.*; *token* 112. 8; tokne 13. 2; *pl.* toknes 16. 53.

toknyng, *vbl. sb.*; *symbol* 113. 51.

to-morn, *sb.*; *to-morrow* 116. 8.

tonge, *sb.*; *tongue* 18. 6.

top, *sb.*; *top*: top to to *head to foot* 95. 152.

to-quils, *conj.*; *whilst* 30. 102.

to-rend, *vb.*; *tear in pieces*: 3 *s.* 112 61; *pl.* to-rente 95. 6; *pp.* to-rent 90. 7.

tort, *sb.*; *wrong* 39. 11.

to-scrywe, *pp.*; *shriven* 105. 71.

to-seo, *vb.*; *behold* (*imp.*) 112. 31.

to-sprad, *pp.*; *spread out, displayed* 13. 2.

tote, *vb.* (OE tōtian); *look, observe* (*imp.*) 100. 27.

toþer, *adj.*; þe ~ (= þet oþer) *the second* 31. 21.

to-torn, *pp.*; *lacerated* 112. 45; to-toren 67. 5.

touȝ, *adj.* and *adv.*; *tough* 27. 43 (*roughly*); makeþ touh *makes difficulties* 103. 14.

to-uore, *prep., adv.*: *before* 16. 45; to-uoren 21. 3, to-fore 97. 51.

trace, *sb.* (OF trais); *track, steps* 30. 42.

trace, *vb.*; *explore* (*pr. pl.*) 106. 95.

traitour, *sb.*; *traitor* 91. 11; traytour 91. 10.

trayturly, *adv.*; *treacherously* 79. 1.

trauail, *sb.*; *labour* 48. 88;

trauel 77. 20, trauayle 101. 139.

trauaille, *vb.*; (1) *toil*: *pt.* 1 *s.* 121. 78. (2) *suffer trials* trauel 81. 6.

trayst, *adj.*; *trusty* 84. 41.

trayst, *vb.*—See *truste*.

tre, *num. adj.*—See *preo*.

tre, *sb.*; *tree, cross* 3. 3; tree 91. 62, treo 106. 122, troe 13. 13.

treacle, *sb.*; *salve* 101. 111.

tremlede, *vb. pt.* 3 *s.*; *trembled* 55. 22.

trend, *vb.*; *turn* (*something*) *about* (*imp.*) 2 A. 8.

tresor, *sb.*; *treasure* 10. 39; tresowr 121. 184, tresowre 79. 1.

tresory, *sb.*; *receptacle for money or valuables* 78. 8.

tresoun, *sb.*; *treason* 95. 88.

trespas, *sb.*; (1) *wrongs* 98. 51. (2) *sin* trespace 111. 31.

trete, *vb.*; *set forth, discuss* 101. 155.

treuþe, *sb.*; (1) *truth* 108. 8, truþe 132. 85, trowth 48. 115. (2) *fidelity* trwthe 39. 17, trout 29. 67.

trewe, *adj.*; *true* 6. 4; trwe 130. 5; *supl.* treuest 29. 3.

trewly, *adv.*; *truly* 48. 106; treuly 56. 13, trewely 108. 26.

trey, *sb.* (OE trega); *affliction, grief* 112. 42; tray 118. 3.

trinite, *sb.*; *Trinity* 13. 25.

troddares, *sb. pl.*; *treaders* 25. 8.

(y)-trodded, *pp.*; *trodden* 25. 9.

trone, *sb.*; *throne* 6. 4.

trouble, *sb.*; *trouble* 120. 5.

trouþe, *sb.*; *troth* 109. 20.

trowe, *vb.*; *believe* 120. 77; *pr.* 1 *s.* tru 29. 15, trouwe 100. 79; *pr. pl.* trowe 44. 24, trous 31. 65; *imp.* trowe 27. 106.

truage, *sb.*; *tribute, toll* 54. 6.

trun, *sb.* (OE truma); *troop, multitude* 30. 103.

trusse, *vb.*; *pack up* (*pr. subj.*) 23. 4.

trust, *sb.*; *trust* 13. 21; trost 94. 21.

truste, *vb.*; *trust* 23. 24; trist 27. 72; *pr.* 1 *s.* troste 58. 37, trayst 48. 38; *pr.* 3 *s.* trust 103. 91; *pr. subj.* trist 109. 13, triste 42. 4, traiste 84. 68; *imp.* tristou (= trist þou) 28. 19.

trusti, *adj.*; *trusty* 6. 4.

trustly, *adv.*; *confidently* 27. 106.

trye, *adj.* (OF trié); *choice, excellent* 101. 164.

tunder, *sb.*; *tinder* 27. 52.

ture, *sb.*; *tower* 50. 1; toure 82. 31, towr 121. 196.

turmented, *pp.*; *tormented* 104. 6; i-turmente 99. 30.

turnen, *vb.*; *turn* 70. 9; turne 111. 43; *pr.* 2 *s.* turnst 17. 8; *pr.* 3 *s.* turnet 42. 4, tornyþ 105. 30, turneȝ 42. 3, turnes 84. 94, tornes 84. 44, tournes 84. 3; *pr. pl.* tornen 95. 134; *imp.* turn 4. 8, torn 102. 46; *pr. p.* turnand 45. 8, tornand 41. 8; *pt.* 3 *s.* turnde 12. 12; *pp.* tornd 101. 24.

twa, *num. adj.*; *two* 48. 73; tua 30. 77. See also *two, tweye.*

tuelue, *num. adj.*; *twelve* 56. 69; tuel 32. 70.

twenti, *num. adj.*; *twenty* 96. 43.

tweye, *num. adj.*; *two* 34. 20; tweyȝe 55. 16, tweyne 103. 9.

two, *num. adj.*; *two* 95. 146; twoo 94. 6, to 56. 113.

twynklyng, *vbl. sb.*; *twinkling* 100. 63; twinkeling 134. 24.

twynne, *vb.*; *part, be separated* 86. 19; *pr. pl.* 95. 146; *pr. subj.* twyn 84. 19.

tyde, *sb.*; *tide, time* 10. 3.

tyde, *vb.*; *befall* 95. 109.

tyȝt, *pp.*; ?*resolved* 94. 28.

tyme, *sb.*; *time* 10. 23; tym 90. 43, (*gen.*) times 24. 7; *pl.* tymes 96. 43.

tymliche, *adv.*; *betimes* 23. 5.

tyne, *vb.* (ON týna); (1) *lose* 84. 52. (2) *destroy*: tynt *pp.* 116. 64.

u, *adv.*—See *hou.*

vch, uche, *adj.*; *each* 6. 19. See also *eche.*

vmbe-while, *adv.*; *from time to time, at intervals* 6. 64; vnbe-while 6. 63.

vmbesette, *pp.*; *encompassed* 83. 42.

vn-bouȝt, *pp.*; *unpaid for, free of cost* 117. 66.

vnboxumnes, *sb.*; *disobedience* 107. 29.

vnbuxs, *adj.*; *disobedient* 30. 41.

vn-bynd, *vb.*; *unbind* (*imp.*) 17. 9; vnbynt 109. 99.

vncele, *sb.* (OE unsǽl); *unhappiness* 102. 21.

vncertein, *adj.*; *uncertain* 134. 2.

vnclustri, *vb.*; *unbar, unfasten* (*pr. subj.*) 27. 59.

vncouþe, *adj.*; (1) *unknown* 36. 8, vncowth 121. 134, vnkut 65. 3. (2) *strange* 28. 6. (3) *marvellous* 41. 5.

vnder, *prep.* and *adv.*; *under* 6. 39, 27. 33; under on 14. 5 *together.*

vn-dere, *adj.*; *hated, dreaded* 135. 19.

vnderfonge, *vb.*; *take, receive* 7. 59; (*imp.*) 75. 29; *pt.* 2 *s.* vnderfenge 131. 19; *pt.* 3 *s.* underfeng 34. 29; *pp.* under-uon 15. 13. See also *ounder-uon.*

vnderne, *sb.*; *third hour of the day* (*ca.* 9 *a.m.*) 55. 11; vndrin 30. 52, hondren 34. 15.

vnderstonde, *vb.*; *understand* 7. 22; *pr.* 1 *s.* vndyrstonde 92. 8.

vndo, *vb.*; *undo, open* 29. 49; (*imp.*) 7. 27; (*pp.*) *undone, ruined* 49. 27.

vnicorn, *sb.*; *unicorn* 32. 63.

vnknowe, *pp.*; *unknown* 65. 3.

vnknowyng, *pr. p.*; *not knowing* 121. 232.

vnkut, *pp.*—See *vncoupe.*

vnkynde, *adj.*; (1) *unkind* 77. 1. (2) *unnatural* vnkuynde 95. 123.

vnkyndely, *adv.*; *unkindly* 47. 9.

vnlaced, *vb. pt.*; *unlaced* 79. 23.

vnlawis, *sb. pl.*; ?*law-breakers* 39. 8.

vnles, *vb.*; *unloose* (*imp.*) 45. 9.

vnleueful, *adj.*; *unlawful* 102. 74.

vnleuefully, *adv.*; *unlawfully* 102. 82.

vnlust, *sb.*; *sluggard* 127. 25.

vnlustily, *adv.*; *slothfully* 95. 145.

unmy3t, *sb.*; *weakness* 125. 25; vnmigh 44. 15.

vnredi, *adj.*; *unprepared* 29. 76.

vn-redines, *sb.*; *imprudence, folly* 110. 70.

vnrest, *sb.*; *trouble* 121. 166.

vnrith, *sb.*; *injustice, injury* 58. 11.

vnsau3te, *adj.*; *at loggerheads* 102. 37.

vn-set, *adj.*; *unappointed* 117. 83. See *steuen.*

vn-sete, *adj.*; *unfitting, unprofitable* 6. 74.

vnskilfully, *adv.*; *unreasonably* 102. 90; vnskilfuly 111. 24.

vntil, *prep.*; *unto* 30. 40.

vnto, *prep.*; *unto* 30. 132, 45. 10.

vntrewe, *adj.*; *untrue* 76. 20.

vnwarned, *adj.*; *without warning* 101. 170.

vn-witti, *adj.*; *witless* 110. 13.

vnwunne, *sb.*; *unhappiness* 6. 13.

vn-wyse, *adj.*; *unwise* 110. 16; unwise 125. 40.

vn-wysliche, *adv.*; *unwisely* 110. 14.

vpon, *prep.* and *adv.* 7. 31; opon 1 B. 3, up-hon 1 A. 3, up-one 4. 3; op-on 32. 26.

vpryght, *adv.*; *at full length* 79. 18.

vpsedoun, *adv.*; *up-side-down* 106. 103.

vp-soght, *pp.*; *sought out* 82. 14.

vp-sty3e, *vb.*; *ascend* 92. 28; *pt.* 2 *s.* op-steye 24. 15.

vr, *pers. pron.* 1 *pers. pl.*—See *our.*

vres, *sb. pl.*; *offices of the canonical hours* 114. 21. See also *houre.*

urnth, *vb. pr.* 3 *s.*—See *irnen.*

vs, 1 *pers. pron. dat., acc. pl.*; us 7. 60; ous 6. 83.

vsen, *vb.*; *use, practise* 108. 16; *pr.* 3 *s.* vseþ 109. 78.

vt, *adv.*—See *out.*

uader, *sb.*—See *fader.*

vanite, *sb.*; *folly* 101. 90; vanyte 94. 24.

vanys, *vb.*; *vanish* 112. 94; *pt.* 3 *s.* fanchyt 105. 44; *pp.* wanischid 134. 24.

uare, *vb.*—See *fare.*

vayns, *sb. pl.*; *veins* 77. 8.

vayr, *adj.*—See *fair.*

ve, 1 *pers. pron. pl.*—See *we.*

vedde, *vb. pt.*—See *fede.*

veir, *sb.* (OF vair); *fur* 29. 64.

uengaunce, *sb.*; *vengeance* 93. 95; vengeaunce 95. 155, vengauns 113. 82.

venget, *pp.*; *avenged* 118. 30.

veonde, *sb.*—See *fende.*

verdites, *sb. pl.*; *verdicts* 120. 68.
uere, *sb.*—See *fere.*
uerray, *adj.*; *true* 93. 91; verrey
113. 51.
verrayment, *adv.*; *truly* 93. 40;
verament 117. 55.
verre, *adv.*—See *fer.*
uertu, *sb.*; *virtue* 118. 6; *pl.* ver-
tues 95. 134.
vertuous, *adj.*; *virtuous* 109. 77.
vessel, *sb.*; *vessel* (vas) 100. 4.
vestement, *sb.*; (*clerical*) *vest-*
ment 121. 138.
uet, *sb. pl.*—See *fot.*
ueyne, *adj.*; *vain*; veyne 132.
67, vein 134. 1, weyne 56.
132.
ueyne-glorie, *sb.*; *vainglory* 126.
20.
vice, *sb.*; *vice, faults* 95. 134;
vys 118. 6, vyce 132. 10.
vicyous, *adj.*; *vicious* 109. 76.
victori, *sb.*; *victory* 101. 79.
vif, *num. adj.*—See *fiue.*
viȝt, vyht, *sb.*—See *fiht.*
vilany, *sb.*; (1) *vicious words* 115.
34. (2) *viciousness* uelanye
122. 17, vileinie 131. 96.
vild, *vb. pt.*; *reviled* 30. 23.
vinde, *vb.*—See *finden.*
virgyne, *sb.*; *virgin* 10. 28.
visage, *sb.*; *face, countenance*
76. 11.
vise, *vb.* (OF viser); *devise* 101.
14.
visyte, *vb.*; *visit* 95. 68; *imp.*
visite 91. 89.
vipote, *prep.*—See *wiþoute.*
vlesh, *sb.*—See *flesch.*
vo, *sb.*—See *fo* and *wo.*
voche, *vb.*; *to warrant*; *pt.* 2 *s.*
vochedest saue *bestowed* 95.
77.
vokete, *sb.*; *intercessor* 132. 10.
volk, *sb.*; *folk, people* 14. 7. .See
also *folk.*
vollouth, *sb.* (OE fulluht); *bap-*
tism 12. 9.

vonge, *vb. pt.* 2 *s.*—See *fonge.*
vor, *conj.*—See *for.*
uorȝet, *vb. pr.* 1 *s.*—See *forgete.*
uor-spekere, *sb.*; *advocate* 18.
3.
voyde, *vb.*; *set aside, annul* 132.
10.
voys, *sb.*; *voice* 55. 5.
uram, vrom, *prep.*—See *fram,*
from.
vuel, *sb.*—See *yuel.*
uul, *adj.*—See *ful.*
vur, *sb.*—See *fyre.*
uurst, *adv. supl.*; *first* 13. 5.
vyl, *adj.*; *vile* 87. 5.

wa, *sb.*; *woe* 29. 51. See also *wo.*
wage, *sb.*; *reward* 109. 71.
wage, *vb.*; *pledge* 108. 61.
wageringe, *pr. p.*; *wandering*
134. 9.
wailaway, *interj.*; *alas!* 50. 7;
welawo 126. 36, wolawo 89.
20.
waite, *vb.*; *watch, take care* 116.
2; *imp.* wayte 102. 62.
wake, *vb.*; (1) *summon up* 27.
63. (2) *become active* 117. 38,
be diligent 116. 1. (3) *keep*
vigil, remain awake 91. 125;
pr. 1 *s.* 76. 6; *pt. pl.* wak-
keden 56. 53.
waken, *vb.*; *stir up*; *pr.* 3 *s.*
wakeneþ 9. 1; *pt.* 3 *s.*
wakened 95. 150.
walke, *vb.*; (1) *go*; *pr. p.* walk-
ynge 117. 2; *pt.* 1 *s.* walked
82. 6. (2) *be abroad* 121. 59.
walle, *sb.*; *wall*; wall 105. 6,
wal 101. 123; *pl.* walle 6. 38.
walle, *vb.*; *be strongly moved* 67.
24.
wam, *sb.*—See *wem.*
wan, *adv.*—See *when.*
wan, *sb.*—See *wone.*
wan, *adj.*; *pale, wan* 76. 11;
wanne 84. 10, won 126. 6.

wande, *vb.* (OE wandian); *hesitate, fear* 83. 39; *imp.* wonde 112. 77.

wandren, *vb.*; *wander*: *pr.* 2 *s.* wandrest 28. 26; *pr. p.* wandrand 27. 4, wandryng 105. 1; *pt.* 1 *s.* wandrede 107. 1.

wandreth, *sb.* (ON vandræði); *misery, distress* 84. 19; wondreþ 116. 58.

wane, *sb.*—See **won**.

wane, *vb.*; *wane, diminish* 83. 8; *pr.* 3 *s.* wanet 49. 2; *pr. pl.* wanieþ 106. 129.

wanyyng, *vbl. sb.*; *waning* 49. 10.

wanhope, *sb.*; *despair* 107. 50.

wanischid, *pp.*—See **vanys**.

war, *adj.*; *watchful, vigilant* 27. 50; ware 101. 55.

warantise, *sb.*; *sure means of safety* 30. 118.

warde, *vb.*; *guard, defend* (*imp.*) 110. 114; *pp.* i-warded 121. 194.

ware, *sb.*; *?goods, merchandise* 23. 15.

warie, *vb.*; *curse* 103. 25.

warison, *sb.*; *a fortune, great wealth* 109. 90.

warkes, *sb. pl.*—See **werk**.

warli, *adv.* (OE wærlīce); *prudently, wisely* 51. 8.

warne, *vb.*; *warn* (*pr.* 1 *s.*) 98. 5; *pr.* 3 *s.* warneþ 101. 173.

warnyng, *vbl. sb.*; *warning* 113. 8; *pl.* warnynges 101. 55.

was, *sb.* (cf. MDu wase *torch*); *torch* (*of straw, etc.*) 81. 33.

wassʒen, *vb.*; *wash* 13. 7; was 30. 65; *pt.* 3 *s.* wesche 27. 97, wesched 48. 27; *pp.* y-wasʒe 12. 8.

wast, *sb.*; *useless expenditure*; in wast *to no purpose* 104. 36.

wast, *vb.*; *waste* 100. 31.

water, *sb.*; *water* 12. 11.

wawe, *sb.*; *misery* 27. 44.

waxen, *vb.* (OE weaxan); *grow, become*: *pr.* 2 *s.* wexist 105. 34; *pr.* 3 *s.* waxit 76. 11, wext 49. 2; *pr. pl.* waxeþ 6. 43; *pr. subj.* wex 105. 17; *pr. p.* waxand 83. 20; *pt.* 2 *s.* wexe 55. 17; *pt.* 3 *s.* wax 105. 42; *pt. pl.* woxen 89. 19, wox 113. 38; *pp.* waxen 95. 136.

way, *sb.*—See **wey**.

wayk, *adj.* (ON *weikr, > veikr); (1) *weak*; *supl.* weikest 118. 42. (2) *fragile* 118. 38.

wayle, *vb.*; *wail* 96. 51; waylle 105. 67.

waynoun, *sb.* (OF waignon *dog, scoundrel*); *good-for-nothing* 6. 17.

wayte, *vb.* (ON *weita, > veita); *inflict on*; ~ schame 104. 30.

wayte-glede, *sb.*; *one who sits gazing at the fire all day* 6. 17.

we, 1 *pers. pron. nom. pl.*; we 6. 106; ve 45. 12, woe 14. 8.

wed, *sb.* (OE wedd); *pledge* 48. 60; wedde 86. 34.

wede, *sb.*; *clothing, garment* 16. 31; *pl.* wedys 105. 47, weedes 112. 90.

ween, *sb.* (OE wēn); *doubt* 135. 3.

wei, *sb.*, (ON *wei, > vei); *sorrow* 119. 15.

wel, *adv.*; *well, very* 6. 81; wele 48. 44, wol 55. 8, weel 109. 1.

wel, *adj.*; *well* 7. 49; wyl 41. 1.

welde, *vb.*: *have power over, rule* 24. 18; weld 29. 43; *pr.* 3 *s.* weldeþ 26. 44, weldes 10. 53; *pr. subj.* weide 112. 115; *imp.* welde 83. 13.

wele, *sb.*; (1) *joy, happiness* 12. 13; woele 18. 13, wel 28. 21, welle 110. 12. (2) *glory* weole 20. 25.

welle, *sb.*; *fountain, spring* 18. 4; well 79. 5.

welþ, *sb.*; *wealth* 27. 31; *pl.*
blessings welþis 134. 2.

wem, *sb.*; *moral blemish, stain*
14. 4; wam 88. 6.

wemles, *adj.*; *spotless* 21. 11.

wenche, *sb.*; *wench, maid-ser-*
vant 102. 89.

wende, *vb.*; *tr.* (1) *turn imp.* 131.
85; puend 2 A. 8. (2) *reverse*
131. 93. (3) *change* 69. 22.
(4) *go* 96. 41; *pt.* 3 *pl.* wenden
12. 4. *Intr.*: (5) *turn aside*
57. 58; *pr.* 3 *s.* wenduþ 120.
86. (6) *pass, go* 23. 1, 28. 18;
pr. 2 *s.* wendes 27. 108; *pr.*
pl. wende 110. 114; *pt.* 1 *s.*
went 121. 79, *pt.* 2 *s.* wentyst
92. 32; *pt.* 3 *s.* wende 34. 23,
went 48. 81; *pp.* went 48. 51.
(7) *refl. betake oneself* 10.
12.

wene, *vb.* (OE wēnan); *expect,*
hope, believe; *pr.* 1 *s.* wene
93. 53, wen 30. 36; *pr.* 2 *s.*
wenys 135. 5; *pr. pl.* weene
101. 7; *pt.* 1 *s.* wende 111.
36.

wene, *vb.* (OE wenian); *enter-*
tain, cheer, please pr. pl. weneþ
6. 63.

weolewe, *vb.* (OE *welwian; *cf.*
wealwian); *fade, waste away*
(*pr.* 1 *s.*) 6. 79.

wep, *sb.*; *weeping* 49. 6.

wepe, *vb.*; *weep* 28. 2; *pr.* 2 *s.*
wepist 59. 12, wepistou 28.
1; *imp.* wep 2 B. 2; *pr. p.*
wepand 41. 23; *pt.* 2 *s.*
weptyst 94. 10; *pt. pl.* weped
79. 24.

weping, *vbl. sb.*; *weeping* 59.
16; wepynge 91. 67; *attrib.*
adj. 65. 13.

were, *sb.*; *doubt* 102. 2; weere
109. 54; *?danger, difficulty*
108. 45.

were, *vb.*; *guard, protect* (*imp.*)
31. 60.

weren, *vb.*; *wear* (*pr. subj.*) 114.
19; were 114. 39; *pt.* 1 *s.*
werede 6. 31.

werk, wirk, *vb.*—See *worchen*.

werk, *sb.*; (1) *deed* 16. 41; werck
30. 28, worke 94. 20; *pl.*
werkes 7. 30, werckes 30. 12.
(2) *activity*: *pl.* warkes 84.
84.

werne, *vb.*; *refuse* 131. 52.

werpe, *vb.* (OE weorpan);
weave, contrive: *pt.* 3 *s.* worp
28. 29. See Note.

werre, *vb.*; *make war* 32. 72.

werse, *adv. comp.*; *worse* 70.
8.

wery, *adj.*; *weary* 11. 39; werye
(*pl.*) 32. 58.

west, *adj.*; *west* 7. 47.

wet, *pp.*; *moistened* 6. 13.

wete, *adj.*; *wet* 7. 20.

wey, *sb.*; *way* 5. 6; weyȝe 57. 50,
way 12. 4, wai 29. 10, waie
124. 62; *pl.* weyes 93. 19,
waies 29. 45, ways 27. 3, wais
31. 2.

wey, *adv.*; *away* 106. 116.

weye, *sb.* (OE wǣge); *pair of*
scales, balance 13. 19.

weye, *vb.*; *weigh* 109. 106.

wey-wendyng, *sb.*; *departure*
106. 116.

wha, whas, wham.—See *who*.

whan, *adv.* (OE hwanan);
whence 28. 16.

what, *rel. pron.*; *what* 15. 1; wat
4. 4, wath 3. 14, whet 6. 26.

what, *conj.*; *until* 131. 92.

whele, *sb.*; *wheel* 28. 23; whel
42. 4.

when, *adv.*; *when* 6. 35; whan
123. 38, whane 90. 14,
whanne 35. 4, whon 93. 20,
whonne 95. 94, wen 11. 44,
wan 26. 10, wanne 32. 18.

where, *adv.*; *where* 23. 19, whar
13. 3, whare 23. 3, wer 49.
14, war 124. 38.

wher-euer, *adv.*; *wherever* 97. 5;
whare-euer 115. 76.

wherfore, *adv.*; *wherefore* 121.
51; werfore 56. 87.

wher-of, *adv.*; *for what, of what*
101. 79; whar-of 12. 1, wer-
offe 56. 22.

wher-so, *adv.*; *wherever* 10. 47.

wher-so-euer, *adv.*; *wheresoever*
110. 114.

wher-þorw, *adv.*; (1) *whereby*
117. 50. (2) *because of
which* wherthorgh 121. 19.

wher-to, *adv.*; (1) *to what* 121.
229. (2) *why* warto 105. 67,
worto 56. 127.

wheþer, *conj.*; *whether* 7. 47;
wher 99. 2.

whi, *adv.* and *pron.*; *why* 6. 50;
why 6. 86, wy 60. 1.

which, (1) *rel. pron.*; *which* 38.
8; whiche 121. 72, whuche
95. 8, wȝuche 95. 86. (2) *adj.*;
of what sort whuch 106. 37.

whider, *adv.*; *whither* 9. 15;
whoder 112. 58, 28. 24.

wider-ward, *adv.*; *whither-ward*
35. 20; whoderward 97. 26.

while, (1) *sb.*; *space of time* 6.
54 wyle 32. 3. (2) *conj.*;
while: whil 28. 4; wil 56. 64.
(3) *adv.*; *formerly, once*: whil
6. 18. See also *quile.*

whilen, *adv.*; *formerly* 10. 2;
whilum 44. 25.

whilk, *rel. pron.*; *which* 44. 5.

whils, *adv.*; *whilst* 81. 6; wiles
123. 30.

who, *interr.* and *rel. pron.*; *who*
16. 9; wo 55. 9, wha 48. 1;
gen. wos 49. 9, whas 20. 15;
dat. whom 22. 19, wham 14.
2, wam 2 A. 9, wan 32. 56.
See also *ho.*

whoder.—See *whider.*

who-so, *pron.*; *who-ever* 16. 10;
wha-sa 82. 15, whose 10. 7.
See also *hos, hose.*

whos-euere, *pron.*; *whosoever*
107. 69.

why, *adv.*—See *whi.*

whyt, *adj.*; *white* 10. 55; whyte
83. 37, wit 1 B. 1, wyth
1 A. 1.

wide, *adj.*; *wide* 1 A. 2; uide
1 B. 2, wyde 83. 38.

widewe, *sb. pl.*; *widows* 110. 63.

wif, *sb.*; *wife* 57. 79; wiif 29. 30,
wyf 11. 48; *pl.* wyue 10. 50.

wight, *sb.*; (1) *person* 31. 3;
wyht 17. 2, with 58. 9, wyȝth
120. 98; *pl.* wiȝtes 27. 4,
wyhtes 20. 16, wihtis 110.
13. (2) *thing* wit 2 B. 12.

wiȝt, *adj.*; *brave, valiant* 27. 50;
wiht 106. 7.

wiht-stonding, *vbl. sb.*; *resist-
ance* 51. 23.

wikkid, *adj.*; *wicked* 50. 6;
wykked 12. 1, wicked 48.
118.

wikkedliche, *adv.*; *wickedly* 72.
7.

wikidnis, *sb.*; *wickedness* 28.
25; wickednes 30. 112,
wyckenesse 24. 18.

wil, *sb.*; (1) *will* 49. 24; wyl 14.
11; (2) *pleasure* wille 6. 18.

wil, *adj.*; *erroneous* 27. 3.

wild, *sb.* (cf. MDu. wilde *wilder-
ness*); *?wilderness* 28. 12.

wilde, *adj.*; *wild* 6. 27; wild 29.
28, wylde 93. 45; *supl.* wild-
est 6. 38.

wildirnesse, *sb.*; *wilderness* 121.
156.

wile, *sb.*; *guile* 69. 9; *pl.
stratagems* wiles 101. 94.

wile, *vb.* (OE willan); *will* (*pr.*
1 *s.*) 59. 8; ichulle 6. 71, wol
93. 11, wole 11. 23; *pr.* 2 *s.*
wilt 62. 8, wolt 6. 86; *pr.* 3 *s.*
will 82. 15, wol 10. 7; *pr. pl.*
wolen 103. 57; *pt.* 1 and 3 *s.*
wold 45. 27, wald 30. 1; *pt.*
2 *s.* woldys 124. 86, woldestou

95. 54, wild 30. 73; *pt. pl.*
wald 83. 39.

wileþ, *vb. pr.* 3 *s.*; *beguiles* 27.
17.

wilful, *adj.*; *erroneous* 112. 52.

wylfully, *adv.*; *wilfully* 120. 18.

will, *adv.*; *astray* 82. 6.

wilne, *vb.*; *desire* 111. 27; wiln
56. 104; *pr. pl.* wilne 106. 85,
(*pr. subj.*) 102. 19.

wilnyng, *vbl. sb.*; *desire, wish*
112. 57.

winne, *vb.*; *gain, win* 109. 90;
wynne 11. 60, win 50. 2, wyn
48. 23; *pt.* 2 *s.* wan 27. 94;
pp. wonnen 66. 18, wonne
90. 10, y-wonne 32. 12.

wisse, *vb.*; *guide, direct*: *pr. subj.*
wys 48. 115, wise 124. 55;
imp. wiss 29. 10, wis 30. 14,
wisse 44. 12.

wit, *sb.*—See *wight* (2).

wite, *vb.* (OE witan) *know* 95.
32; wijt 29. 70; *pr.* 1 *s.* wat
27. 17, wate 31. 21, woth 53.
6; *pr.* 2 *s.* wost 23. 19, woost
134. 35, wast 29. 75, wot 100.
103, wat 27. 107, wate 81.
18; *pr. pl.* witiþ 90. 38, witen
90. 39; *pr. subj.* with 44. 21;
imp. wite 111. 61; *pt.* 1 *s.*
wist 27. 80; *pt.* 2 *s.* wustest
117. 27; *pt. pl.* wuste 101.
23, wust 119. 20, wyste 32.
30; *pp.* wist 101. 121.

wite, *vb.* (OE wītan); *guard, pre-
serve*: *pr. subj.* wyten 18. 10;
imp. wite 7. 28.

wite, *vb.* (OE wītan); *go, depart*:
pr. 3 *s.* wites 27. 32; wytes
86. 2.

wiþ, *prep.*; (1) *with* 6. 5; wyth
12. 5, wit 26. 53, wiht 49. 18,
wid 3. 9, wyht 14. 8. (2)
towards, against 57. 53. (3)
by 115. 13.

wiþ-drawe, *vb.*; *set aside* 118.
20; *imp.* wythdrawe 94. 23.

with-in, *adv.* and *prep.*; *within*
83. 13, 48. 21; wiþ-Inne 109.
92.

wiþoute, *prep.*; *without* 7. 6;
whit-outen 120. 23, wyt-
outen 34. 8, wythouten 12.
14, wyþoute 14. 4, with-oten
67. 17, viþote 26. 48.

withstonde, *vb.*; *withstand* 121.
151; withstand 81. 16.

witt, *sb.*; *wit, intelligence* 81. 25;
wijt 30. 61, with 124. 14; *pl.*
wyttes 18. 7, wittes 44. 13.

witterli, *adv.*; *assuredly* 103. 4;
witerly 117. 27.

witti, *adj.*; *wise, intelligent* 103.
53.

wityngly, *adv.*; *knowingly* 102.
67.

wlanke, *adj.*; *proud, fine* 95. 3.

wo, *sb.*; *woe* 2 B. 12; woo 91.
57, vo 105. 15.

wo-begone, *adj.*; *in great dis-
tress* 91. 48.

wode, *sb.*; *wood, forest* 11. 2.

wode, *adj.*; *savage, mad* 51. 2;
woode 110. 13, wood 100.
100.

wol, wole, *vb.*—See *wile*.

wolde, *sb.*; *wold* 56. 53.

wolde, *sb.* (OE -wald). (1) *pos-
session, keeping* 112. 36. (2)
domination 6. 18.

woliche, *adv.* (cf. OE wālīc);
woefully 51. 2.

wolues, *sb. pl.*; *wolves* 95. 5.

wombe, *sb.*; *womb* 22. 7.

womman, *sb.*—See *wymmon*.

won, *sb.*; (1) *hope, expedient* 25.
10; wane 84. 55. (2) *abun-
dance* 56. 119.

wonde, *vb.*—See *wande*.

wonder, *vb.*; *wonder* 72. 36; *pr.*
2 *s.* wondrest 58. 21; *pr.* 3 *s.*
wondreth 19. 9; *pt.* 3 *s.* won-
drede 32. 32.

wonder, *sb.*; *wonder, marvel* 16.
3; 27. 64.

wonder, *adv.*; *wonderfully* 96. 3;
wondur 113. 26.

wonderly, *adv.*; *wondrously* 100.
94.

wondreþ, *sb.*—See *wandreth.*

wone, *adj.* (OE gewuna); *ac-
customed* 56. 15.

wone, *sb.*; *custom* 21. 4.

wone, *sb.*; *dwelling-place, abode*
20.13; *pl.* wones 95. 78, wonys
135. 30.

wonges, *sb. pl.*; *cheeks* 6. 13;
wanges 27. 88.

wonyen, *vb.* (OE wunian);
dwell, remain 23. 3; wonye
23. 19, wone 65. 2, won 48.
120; *pr.* 2 *s.* wones 112. 106;
pr. pl. woneþ 11. 56; *pr. subj.*
20. 28; *pt.* 3 *s.* wonede 6. 54;
pp. (*accustomed*) woned 6.
10, wont 95. 158.

wonyng, *vbl. sb.*; *dwelling* 83.
32; woniing 56. 39.

wonyng-stede, *sb.*; *dwelling-
place* 90. 28.

worchen, *vb.*; (1) *make, create*
18. 2; *pt.* 3 *s.* wroȝt 28. 35,
wrouthte 66. 2; *pp.* wroht 6.
101, wrohte 10. 20, wroȝt 35.
1, whrout 22. 6, ywrouth 22.
18, ?ywrout 34. 22. (2) *do*
(*trans. and intr.*), *act* 118. 73,
worche 107. 71, wirk 48. 95;
pr. subj. wurchen 8. 25; *imp.*
wurch 112. 77, werk 51. 8;
pt. 1 *s.* wroht 6. 76; wrowth
121. 53, wrouthte 56. 132;
pt. 3 *s.* wroght 48. 35; *pt. pl.*
wroutten 57. 69; *pp.* wroght
31. 18, wrouȝt 89. 43.

worching, *vbl. sb.*; *working* 106.
68.

word, *sb.*; *word* 16. 41; wurd 94.
20, worde (*dat.*) 44. 12; *pl.*
wordes 5. 3, wordus 120.
81.

worke, *sb.*—See *werk.*

world, *sb.*; *world* 6. 101; wordl

20. 5, wordle 20. 22, werld
29. 25, warld 27. 43, word
112. 116, werd 55. 6; *gen.*
worldes 9. 5, wordles 13.
18, werlds 29. 65, werdis
71. 1.

worly, *adj.* (OE weorþlīc);
costly 6. 31. See also *worþli.*

worm, *sb.*; *worm* 121. 68: *pl.*
wormes 95. 114, wormes 100.
65.

worse, *adj. comp.*; *worse* 120.
26.

worshype, *sb.*; *honour, worship,
prestige* 14. 1; worshipe 14.
10, worschip 101. 3, wur-
schipe 45. 26, worschupe 95.
165, worchup 99. 25.

worshipe, *vb.*; *worship, honour:*
pr. 3 *s.* worþschipeþ 131. 44;
pr. subj. worchipe 58. 61;
pt. 3 *s.* worschuped 110.
61.

worshypinge, *vbl. sb.*; *worship-
ing* 17. 26; worsȝyping 14. 9,
wurcheping 45. 28.

worschipeliche, *adv.*; *reverently*
131. 100; worschupely 107.
86.

worste, *adj.* as *sb.*; *worst* 109.
87.

worth, *vb.*; *become be: pr.* 2 *s.*
worst 23. 21; *pr.* 3 *s.* worth
23. 20.

worþ, *adj.*; (1) *of value* 118. 37.
(2) *of merit* 20. 19.

worþi, *adj.*; (1) *worthy* 57. 15,
13. 15. (2) *honourable* 94. 1.
(3) *virtuous; supl.* 96. 30.

worþli, *adj.* (OE weorþlīc); *ex-
cellent, worthy* 108. 13, 111.
41.

wouȝ, *sb.* (OE wōh); *distress*
27. 26.

wounde, *sb.*; *wound* 6. 91;
wonde 93. 85, wnde 1 A. 2;
pl. woundes 26. 19, woundis
89. 14, wundys 94. 5, wondes

34. 2, wnden I B. 2, wndes 3.
heading.

wounde, *vb.*; *wound*: *pr.* 3 *s.*
woundet 73. 4, woundes 78.
6; *pp.* wounded 13. 5.

wowe, *sb.*; *wall* 97. 34.

wrake, *sb.* (OE wracu); *ven-
geance* 113. 60. See also
wreche.

wrang, *sb.*; *injustice* 56. 7; with
wrang *sinfully* 48. 51.

wrang, *adj.*; *false* 27. 87.

wrang, *adv.*; *(morally) astray* 31.
63.

wrangwysly, *adv.*; *unjustly* 79. 5.

wrappen, *vb.*; *wrap* (*pr. pl.*) 110.
85; *pp.* wrapped 132. 6.

wrathe, *vb.*; *provoke to anger*
(*pr. subj.*) 132. 13.

wraþþe, *sb.*—See *wreþe.*

wrecche, *sb.* (OE wrecca);
wretch 87. 2; wreche 85. 23,
wryche 48. 44; *pl.* wreches
37. 8, wrechis 57. 69.

wrecched, *adj.*; *wretched* 48. 53;
wreched 16. 34.

wrecchidhede, *sb.*; *wretchedness*
135. 27.

wrech, *adj.* (OE wrecca):
wretched 28. 10; wreche 34. 8,
wrecche 133. 1.

wreche, *sb.* (OE wrǣc); *ven-
geance* 16. 38. See also *wrake.*

wreke, *vb.*; *avenge, exact ven-
geance for* 81. 15, wrak 29.
56; *pp.* wreken 27. 79.

wrenches, *sb. pl.*; *tricks* 16. 57.

wrest, *pp.* (OE wrǣstan);
twisted, bent 115. 70.

wreþe, *sb.*; *wrath* 25. 11; wreth
84. 75, wraþþe 90. 6.

wreþen, *pp.* (OE wrīþan);
bound, encircled 67. 6.

wrien, *vb.* (OE wrigian); *turn,
twist*: *pr. pl.* wrieþ 6. 45.

writ, *sb.*; *writ, writing* 125. 49;
writh 55. 28.

write, *vb.*; *write* 91. 6; *imp.*

30. 100; *pt.* 3 *s.* wrot 16. 23;
pp. writen 100. 2, wryten 84.
2, wyrtyn 105. 6.

wro, *sb.*; *corner, obscure place*
99. 26.

**wroght, wrouht, wroutten, y-
wrouth,** *vb.*—See *worchen.*

wrong, *sb.*—See *wrang.*

wrongwys, *adj.*; *unjust* 112. 22.

wroth, *adj.*; *wroth* 75. 13; wroht
6. 45, wroþe 96. 51, wrooþ
127. 5.

wrouhte, *sb.*; *Creator, founder*
20. 1; whrouhte 24. 4.

wrye, *vb.* (OE wrēgan); *accuse*
120. 21; *pp.* wryed 79. 5.

wryng, *vb.*; (1) *wring* 84. 65;
(2) *force out*: *pr.* 2 *s.* wringest
27. 87.

wrynge, *sb.*; *wine-press* 25. 8.

wunne, *sb.*—See *wynne.*

wy, *sb.* (OE wiga); *man* 112.
87; *pl.* wyȝes 112. 90.

wymmon, *sb.* (OE wīfmon);
woman 10. 54; wymman 11.
25, wyman 4. 1, wommon 16.
1, womman 58. 25, wumman
38. 3; *pl.* wemen 41. 10,
wymman 32. 54, wymmen
93. 58; *gen. pl.* wimmen 110.
15.

wyn, *sb.*; *wine* 10. 32.

wynde, *sb.*; *wind* 101. 52; wiynd
134. 9; *pl.* wyndes 106. 17.

wynde, *vb.*; (1) *tr. turn* 79. 27.
(2) *wrap pp.* wounde 23. 20,
i-wonden 34. 16; (*in shroud*)
pp. wonden 30. 127.

wynde, 112. 116: obscure.

wyndyng-schete, *sb.*; *shroud* 81.
20.

wynge, *sb.*; *wing* 121. 42.

wynne, *sb.*; *joy, bliss* 17. 12;
wunne 6. 12, wyn 71. 1.

wynnyng, *vbl. sb.*; *profit, gain*
113. 75.

wynter, *sb.*; *winter* 9. 1; *pl.*
wenter 72. 13, wynter 101. 42.

wys, *sb.*; *certainty* 22. 16 (to wysse *for certain*).

wys, *adj.*; *wise* 101. 85; *comp.* wysore 101. 82; *supl.* wyseste 84. 2.

wyse, *sb.*; *wise, manner* 23. 22.

wysely, *adv.*; *wisely* 92. 35.

wysse, *adv.*; *assuredly* 92. 32.

wyssere, *sb.*; *guide, director* 13. 28.

wyssynge, *vbl. sb.*; *guidance* 32. 82.

wytnesse, *sb.*; *witness* 11. 36; wytnessinge 16. 25.

wyth, *adj.*—See *whyt*.

y, I *pers. pron.*—See *i*.

y-coyntised, *adj.*; *apparelled* 25. 3.

y-glened, *pp.*; *gleaned* 27. 81.

y3e, *sb.*—See *e3e*.

yhandled, *pp.*; *handled* 87. 14.

yit, yiet, *adv.*—See *3ete*.

y-kore, ycoren, *pp.*—See *chese*.

y-leued, *pp.*—See *leue*, vb.

ylle, *adv.*; *badly* 9. 10; yll 48. 101. Cf. *il*, adj.

ymone, *adv.* (OE gemāna × gemǣne); *together* 20. 17.

ynow, *adj.*—See *i-nouwe*.

y-pult, *pp.*; *driven, thrust* 16. 35.

y-raked, *pp.*; *covered over* 133. 6.

y-schet, *pp.*; *shut* 32. 52.

ysome, *adv.*; *together* 25. 12. See also *i-same*.

y-spekeþ, *vb. pr.* 3 *s.*; *speaks* 32. 60.

y-streith, *pp.* (OE streccan); *stretched* 1 A. 3; istreid 2 B. 8.

y-þurst, *pp.*; *having suffered thirst* 34. 21.

yuel, *sb.*; *evil* 115. 9; vuel 93. 11; *pl.* vuelus 93. 8. See also *euel*.

yuele, *adv.*; *badly* 131. 72.

ywys, *adv.*; *certainly, indeed* 9. 7; ywis 27. 64, ywisse 7. 3. See also *iwis, mid*.

y-wite, *vb.* (OE gewitan); *observe, take in*: *pr.* 2 *s.* hi-pitz 2 A. 3. See Note.

zenne, *sb.*—See *senne*.

zuo, *adv.*—See *swo*.

PRINTED IN GREAT BRITAIN
AT THE UNIVERSITY PRESS, OXFORD
BY VIVIAN RIDLER
PRINTER TO THE UNIVERSITY